Campaign Finance

Campaign Finance
The Problems and Consequences of Reform

Robert G. Boatright, editor

International Debate Education Association

New York, London & Amsterdam

Published by
International Debate Education Association
400 West 59th Street
New York, NY 10019

Library of Congress Cataloging-in-Publication Data

Campaign finance : the problems and consequences of reform / Robert G. Boatright, editor.
    p. cm.
  Summary: This anthology describes patterns in the financing of different types of campaigns in the US and in other democracies with particular attention to how campaign finance laws relats to democratic values.
  ISBN 978-1-61770-019-4
  1. Campaign funds--United States. 2. Campaign funds--Law and legislation--United States. 3. Campaign funds. 4. Campaign funds--Law and legislation.
I. Boatright, Robert G.
  JK1991.C3426 2011
  324.7'80973--dc23

                                              2011030467

Printed in the USA

 IDEBATE Press

Contents

Introduction

The past two decades have been a period of rapid change in the financing of American elections. In 1996, both parties raised large sums of so-called soft money from corporations and labor unions, and major interest groups also engaged in expensive "issue advocacy" campaigns designed to help candidates. In 2002, the Bipartisan Campaign Reform Act was passed, outlawing soft money and curtailing the ability of interest groups to spend money in elections. Two years later, George W. Bush raised $105 million in his primary campaign, becoming the first major-party nominee since the early 1970s to forgo public financing and its accompanying spending limits. Bush again declined public financing in 2004, as did Democratic nominee John Kerry. In 2008, Barack Obama declined public financing of his primary campaign and his general election campaign, raising more than eight times what Democratic nominee Al Gore had raised just eight years earlier. Shortly after that election, in its 2010 *Citizens United v. Federal Election Commission (FEC)* decision, the Supreme Court struck down the interest group restrictions of the Bipartisan Campaign Reform Act, and the Court also ruled that corporations and interest groups could spend unlimited amounts of money expressly calling for the election or defeat of candidates.

Many voters were undoubtedly aware of these changes, but there is little evidence that their votes were affected by their views about campaign finance. Campaign finance is a classic example of a "process" issue—an issue pertaining to the ways in which election campaigns are run. Voters tend to rank process issues low in their list of priorities. Survey results show that fewer than 40 percent of Americans say that they pay attention to campaign finance reform debates, and that they rank campaign finance low in importance (Moore 2001a, b). A poll conducted during the debate over the Bipartisan Campaign Reform Act indicated that two-thirds of Americans believed reform would have no noticeable effect on politics (Gallup Poll 2002). This does not mean, however, that voters do not have views about the appropriate role of money in politics. Americans have become more cynical about the responsiveness of government, and they often cite the role of money as a reason for their dim attitudes toward government.

The United States is not unique in its campaign finance history or in its citizenry's skepticism about politics. The German government was shaken in

1999 by scandals involving unreported contributions to the governing party (see Scarrow 2006). The Canadian campaign finance reforms of the early 2000s were a response to a scandal involving political advertising spending (Cross 2004). Influence peddling has been rife in Japanese politics for decades (see Cox and Thies 2000). Political financing scandals occurred in Italy, South Korea, and several other nations as well (Alexander 2001). And corruption is a frequent problem in the newer democracies of Eastern Europe. Meanwhile, several scholars (Dalton 2004, Nevitte 2002) have called attention to the "democratic deficit" in the world's democracies, in which growing education levels and a growing desire for a role in politics has accompanied a declining sense among citizens that political leaders are listening to them. The democratic deficit is not solely a function of campaign finance laws, but the role of money in campaigns is part of the problem. The democratic deficit research also reaches a depressing conclusion—even when countries have introduced reforms, these reforms have done little to stem the growing dissatisfaction of voters with politicians.

CAMPAIGN FINANCE LAWS ARE NOT NEUTRAL

One reason why reforms have done little to reconcile citizens to their leaders is that there is simply too much at stake in any change in a nation's campaign finance regime. Any campaign finance law has its winners and losers, and governing parties tend to implement campaign finance laws that will be to their benefit. In the wake of political scandals, campaign finance reform can appear to be a positive step by government, even where the components of the reform do little to change the system (see, e.g., La Raja 2008, 10; Boatright 2011). This may seem an obvious point—after all, any governing party will pursue policies that are to its advantage—but for many issues, parties will gain an advantage by pursuing policies that are popular among the general public. In the case of campaign finance laws, however, the issues are sufficiently complex that few citizens have strong preferences among different laws. To the outside observer, the concepts inherent in any debate over campaign finance—to name a few, the laws governing the size and sources of contributions, the role of outside groups, the role of public financing and the different public financing mechanisms, and the scope of disclosure requirements—can be sufficiently bewildering that citizens do not provide any clear guidance to politicians even if politicians wish to heed the public's wishes.

This collection of essays is apropos, then, for two reasons. First, it seeks to acquaint the reader with the core campaign financing mechanisms and concepts. What, for instance, is the trade-off inherent in limiting contributions to politicians? What is the appropriate amount of spending for outside groups? What role should public financing play in elections? And how much should we know about campaign contributors? Second, this book provides an exploration of campaign finance laws in several different countries. This comparative angle allows us to measure the success or failure of many different reform proposals. For instance, in many American reform debates, good-government advocates have called for public financing, yet, as we shall see, there are many different public financing mechanisms, and different nations have had varying degrees of success in implementing public financing. Different nations also must enact laws that address problems specific to their own governments or histories.

CORE CONCEPTS IN CAMPAIGN FINANCE

In the effort to regulate campaign finance, several mechanisms have been adopted in order to direct and monitor the flow of money to politicians. Although the electoral systems considered in this book differ, all provide a common set of restrictions on political expenditures:

Source Restrictions: Many nations permit only individuals to contribute money to candidates, parties, or political groups, while others permit contributions from corporations or other organized groups. While it is not complicated to place restrictions on direct contributions, campaign finance law can become substantially more complicated when it seeks to regulate the expenditures of organizations that function as conduits for money. Treatment of foreign contributions also varies—for instance, foreign contributions are illegal in the United States but legal in Australia (Mayer 2006). France and Israel prohibit corporate contributions. The United States is one of the few nations that prohibits both corporate and labor contributions; Australia has no similar prohibitions, nor does Germany (although Germany prohibits contributions from trade unions and business associations). Canada enacted a prohibition on corporate and labor contributions in 2003; prior to that time, these contributions made up a substantial percentage of party funding (Cross 2004). Great Britain allows some contributions from corporations, but it limits their size and limits them to companies headquartered in the United Kingdom.

Contribution Limits: Most of the nations considered here also place limits on the amounts of money contributed by those who are permitted to give money. There are three types of contribution limits of note here—limits on the aggregate expenditures of individuals or groups; limits on the contributions of individuals or groups to any one candidate, party, or political organization; and limits on what political candidates can spend on their own campaigns. In the

United States, individuals are limited in the first two regards, but there are no limits on candidates' contributions to their own campaigns. Registered political groups are limited in the second regard, but not the first. There is a wide range of contribution limits in other democratic nations. Australia has no contribution limits at all, while Canada prohibits group contributions and has enacted limits of less than $1,100 per person per year (as of 2009). Contribution limits are often dependent upon the existence of public financing; nations with public financing systems tend to have lower contribution limits.

Public Funding: Many nations considered here provide some form of public financing for candidates or parties, but the public financing provisions vary widely. The United States does not provide public funding for candidates, but it does provide a form of public financing for presidential candidates. In presidential primaries, candidates who accept an overall spending limit are given a one-to-one match for the first $250 of each individual contribution. Candidates must raise a threshold amount of money in small contributions in several states to qualify for these funds. Major-party presidential nominees are also given the option of receiving a flat grant for the general election if they forgo fundraising entirely during this period. These provisions are meant to be an inducement to limit spending and to reward candidates for soliciting small contributions, but candidates can decline public funds.

These are examples of floors and ceilings for public financing; the "floor" (the threshold amount needed to qualify for funds) is intended to ensure that funds are available only to serious candidates, and the "ceiling" (the limit set on total expenditures) is intended to even the playing field among candidates. The reasonableness of these floors and ceilings is important; if the floor is too low, frivolous candidates may receive funds, and if it is too high, some serious candidates are excluded. A ceiling set too high is effectively no ceiling at all, while if it is too low, candidates are encouraged to opt out and decline funds. It is also possible to have floors without ceilings—that is, to provide funds to parties or candidates without limiting their overall spending—or to limit spending without providing a floor (although here, public financing tends to be nonexistent).

We shall consider several different public financing systems in this book. Some nations provide full public financing, in which the parties and candidates forgo fundraising entirely, relying only on federal grants. Several American states provide full public financing, subject to a small number of qualifying contributions. More common, though, is partial public funding, where candidates or parties are given an initial block grant and subsequently permitted to raise private money subject to an overall limit, or are given matching funds in accordance with their private fundraising—again, subject to an overall limit. Campaigns may also be funded indirectly—for instance, by providing tax refunds to contributors (discussed below) or by providing free or discounted services, such as a television coverage or advertising time. France, Germany, and Canada all provide partial public financing that incorporates some of these elements.

Disclosure Requirements: The Internet has dramatically altered the ability of citizens to access campaign finance information. The ability of citizens to use this information, however, is affected by the disclosure laws of different countries. Information about contributions of $200 or more to presidential candidates, political parties, or groups is publicly available in the United States, as is contribution information in American state races. Other nations set the threshold at different levels. Australia set a threshold of $10,000 (in Australian dollars), regardless of the contribution source. Canada also has a threshold of $200 for contributions to candidates or parties. Germany requires disclosure of contributions of above 10,000 euros, while France requires disclosure for contributions of over 150 euros. There is some variation, however, in the information disclosed and the speed of disclosure. U.S. campaign contributors are required to provide the name of their employer; in several other nations, this information is not required. U.S. contributions must be reported according to a schedule set by the government, and most contribution data are available prior to the election. In German elections, large contributions (of over 50,000 euros) must be reported immediately, along with the names of the contributors, but the parties are not required to itemize smaller contributions.

Tax Treatment of Political Spending: There is also substantial variation in how different countries treat political contributions for tax purposes. Canada provides a substantial tax credit for individual contributions to political candidates or parties, thereby providing an indirect governmental subsidy. The Canadian tax credit is sufficiently large that a substantial percentage of political spending is refunded by the government to contributors. The United States provided a 50 percent tax credit for small contributions from 1971 to 1986. Five American states (Arizona, Arkansas, Ohio, Oregon, and Virginia) currently provide small tax credits for contributions (Boatright and Malbin 2005; Rosenberg 2002), and several European nations provide a shifting tax credit or deduction, with the percentage that is credited or deducted dependent on the size of the contribution—that is, donors can recoup a larger percentage of small contributions than of large contributions.

Other types of political spending also can be encouraged through the tax code. In the United States, many organizations that engage in politics are organized under section 501(c)(4) of the tax code; these groups are also tax exempt, but contributions to these groups are not tax deductible. Such organizations cannot make direct contributions to candidates, but they can discuss political issues in a manner that can influence elections. The Canadian tax credit applies to contributions to political parties, not outside political groups, thereby making donations to political groups less attractive to donors. Other nations that allow tax credits or deductions for political spending tend to limit the credit or deduction for contributions to candidates or parties, not to outside political groups.

Not all political money, in other words, is contributed directly to candidates or political parties. The United States imposes a prohibition on coordination between outside groups and the candidates or parties, but such prohibitions have been difficult to enforce. In the United States, citizens, corporations, or other organizations can contribute unlimited amounts of money for the purposes of issue advocacy, or the promotion of political issues that go beyond the simple endorsement of a particular candidate. Prior to the Supreme Court's 2010 *Citizens United v. FEC* decision, such organizations could not directly endorse candidates, but they are now able to do this as long as their primary reason for existence is not solely to help elect or defeat candidates.

Nonmonetary Contributions: It is notoriously difficult to regulate in-kind contributions to candidates or parties. In some instances, it is easy to place a cash value on such contributions; an individual who, for instance, provides yard signs to a candidate free of charge can be said to have made a contribution equivalent to the value of those signs. There is no clear way, however, to measure the cash value of volunteer work on behalf of a candidate. American law exempts volunteer labor from the campaign finance system but requires that some expenditures, such as advertising or the provision of public opinion data, be treated either as a contribution or an independent expenditure. When the Canadian government enacted a prohibition on contributions by labor unions to political parties, it prohibited only cash contributions; labor unions could still, for instance, pay the salaries of workers who took leave from their jobs to help a candidate or provided voter information to parties.

Space here does not permit a complete discussion of the various permutations of the above features of campaign finance law. There are, however, several excellent studies that categorize different national systems, such as Daniel Smilov's 2008 study "Dilemmas for a Democratic Society." It should be evident, however, that all of these features are related. For instance, nations that provide substantial public financing also tend to have strict limits on the size and sources of contributions. Nations that do not provide public funding often rely on more-comprehensive disclosure regimes in order to stave off allegations of corruption. Smilov distinguishes between libertarian and egalitarian models of campaign finance—that is, between models that treat political spending as a matter of individual freedom and models that concern themselves with ensuring an equal voice for different types of citizens or candidates. Furthermore, within each type, he distinguishes between strong party and weak party systems. In most nations, the strength or weakness of parties is a function of the nation's constitution, while libertarian and egalitarian tendencies are more a matter of national political culture. In analyzing the fit of these models to different countries, we must return to the notion that campaign finance laws are enacted with an eye toward the advantage of politicians. In strong party systems, we would expect campaign finance laws to advantage the parties over candidates and independent actors, and vice versa for weak party systems. Likewise, if there is a dominant ideology within the governing party, we would expect the system's libertarian or egalitarian inclinations to reflect such leanings.

NORMATIVE PERSPECTIVES ON CAMPAIGN FINANCE

As the above discussion shows, the precise mechanisms in any system involve decisions about what the "right" amount of individual contributions or federal subsidies should be. I have noted above that historically, governing parties have enacted campaign finance laws with an eye toward their own advantage. This does not mean, however, that we cannot evaluate campaign finance regulations with larger, normative goals in mind. These are goals that politicians employ—after all, even where there are nakedly partisan motives for the enactment of any new campaign finance law, politicians will still describe campaign finance laws with reference to democratic values. In "Regulating Campaign Finance in Canada," which appears in this anthology, Canadian political scientist Lisa Young evaluates her nation's 2003 campaign finance reform legislation in light of four goals: accountability of politicians, transparency of the political system, integrity (both of the system and of its participants), and equity among participants. In his 2009 commentary on American campaign finance, "Small Donors, Large Donors, and the Internet," Michael J. Malbin frames his analysis with three goals in mind: participation, competition, and engagement. Young's goals pertain to the nature of the government itself, while Malbin's concern the role of citizens in elections. There is much overlap between these goals, but they are worth considering at some length insofar as they encapsulate many of the debates featured in this book.

Integrity and Corruption: Young's explanation of integrity touches upon the relationship of democratic politicians to the citizens. We can question the integrity of politicians without necessarily arguing that said politicians are corrupt. Certainly no political actor would argue in favor of corruption, but there is disagreement about what corruption entails. If a politician promises favors to a large contributor, then we might allege that there has been a *quid pro quo* arrangement. Yet all politicians make promises to voters, and contributors generally have some return in mind. In "The Myth of Campaign Finance Reform," Bradley Smith argues that votes, not contributions, determine elections, there is little evidence that politicians flout the will of the voters in return for campaign contributions, and that it is easy to tar any politician with the brush of corruption if campaign promises are seen as signs of favor. For many Americans (although not Smith) it is the size of contributions that matters; if contributions are limited, no individual contributor will be able to exact favors from a candidate who requires thousands of contributions in order to campaign. This is the rationale of the U.S. Supreme Court's *Buckley v. Valeo* decision, in which the Court argued that individual contributions could be capped, but the overall sums candidates contributed to their own campaigns (candidates cannot corrupt themselves) and that candidates raised from all sources could not.

Accountability and Transparency: Most of the authors in this volume argue in favor of disclosure laws, on the grounds that they enable citizens to see where politicians' money is coming from and draw their own conclusions about the integrity of these politicians. In this view, campaign contributions can be a valuable means of discovering whose views a candidate represents. If the decision to contribute is viewed as an instance of political speech, it can be argued that candidates and their donors should be held accountable for this speech. It is not always easy, however, to draw inferences about the motivations of donors or candidates from campaign finance data. Furthermore, some have argued that disclosure can harm donors, insofar as they may be punished for contributions to candidates who, for instance, their employer does not support; and some have merely argued that anonymous speech should be protected as well. Many of those who have argued against many forms of regulation have fallen back on the argument that disclosure will prevent corruption, but others have contended that, just as voting is an anonymous activity, it is simply not the business of the public to monitor the decisions of campaign contributors about how to spend their money.

Equity, Competition, and Discourse: A goal of many advocates of public financing is equalizing the playing field between candidates. Yet if we are to argue for equality, we are implicitly arguing that all views about politics are equal, and in most political systems this is not so. Should, for instance, a candidate who takes an extreme, unpopular position be given money from the government for his campaign? Should a candidate who clearly has no chance of winning be given money for her campaign? In a system with any sort of public financing, it is the business of the government to determine which views, or which candidates, should be given financing. In the Canadian system, parties are given an annual allowance, which is calculated based upon their vote share in the previous election. This is a public financing system that can be said to reward popular views, but it might also be argued that it impedes outsiders from entering politics.

Taking a softer position, we might argue that campaign finance laws should ensure that there is competition in elections, or that campaigns feature discourse about responsible alternatives. In this view, floors and ceilings become more important. If all credible candidates have at least a sufficient amount of money to make their voices heard, and no candidate can spend so much money that his or her opponent is drowned out, we can expect some competition. In addition, it might be argued that an emphasis on discourse privileges the ability of outside groups to enter into the political process—the more information that is provided to the voter, the more likely it is that voters can make up their minds based on their knowledge about a wide array of political issues. This is a proposition that Michael Franz evaluates in his contribution to this book, "The Interest Group Response to Campaign Finance Reform."

Participation and Engagement: For Michael Malbin, the more citizens who contribute to politicians, even in token amounts, the more supportive citizens will be of the government and the more engaged they will be in learning about politics. Caps on contributions are one way to force politicians to raise more contributions. Matching funds for small contributions can also make small contributions more valuable. As the 2008 American presidential election showed, one benefit of Internet fundraising has been that the cost of soliciting repeat contributions and keeping in touch with contributors has declined; a citizen who initially contributes $10 to a candidate can receive updates on the campaign from the candidate and may ultimately be inspired to make further contributions. The small contributor, in other words, can now become part of the campaign team, just as has been the case for larger contributors.

The democratic deficit paradigm discussed above provides a convenient rubric under which to unify these various normative criteria. Presumably any campaign finance reform that increases citizens' confidence in elections and provides them with a feeling that they have a role in politics is a step toward reducing the size of this deficit. As noted above, this is a tall order—citizens' confidence in government and sense of efficacy is a function of more than the financing of campaigns, and there is little evidence that changes in campaign finance law have affected citizens' views on government in the countries considered here. It might be argued that this is because of the inevitable partisan dimension to campaign finance reform—just as parties will seek laws to their advantage, citizens may prefer reforms that they believe will work to the advantage of their favored party. In other words, liberal advocates of public financing may argue that in a publicly financed system, more liberal politicians will be elected. The experience of democracies that have tried public financing indicates that this is not necessarily the case.

These results, as well as the results of more-modest reforms, have led some to espouse the cynical "hydraulic theory" of money in politics—the notion that, whatever reforms are enacted, money will always find its way into the political system. As the articles here will show, this theory understates the importance of campaign finance laws. It may well be that some money will find its way into politics, and it is difficult to imagine a politics conducted entirely without a role for individual contributors. Campaign finance regulations can, however, provide a way to prevent the worst abuses in the political system, or at least make them sufficiently visible so that citizens can respond with their votes. Campaign finance laws frequently have unintended consequences; there are so many permutations of these laws, and technological and political changes constantly present new methods of political fundraising. These consequences call for frequent reevaluations of campaign finance law. It is my hope that the survey of the experience of different nations in regulating campaign spending can provide an understanding of the uncertainties involved in regulation of campaign finance and an understanding of how future elections well affect, and be affected by, changes in campaign financing practices and campaign finance law.

OUTLINE OF THE BOOK

This book begins with a consideration of competing perspectives on the proper role of money in campaigns and of the way in which American courts have considered this role. In "The Nine Lives of *Buckley v. Valeo*," constitutional scholar Richard Hasen discusses the coherence of the manner in which the U.S. Supreme Court has balanced the goal of free expression with the goal of limiting corruption. In "The Myth of Campaign Finance Reform," Bradley Smith, also an expert on constitutional law, argues that there is neither a constitutional mandate for regulating campaign spending nor empirical evidence that campaign finance regulation will be effective in achieving reformers' goals. The articles of Hasen and Smith are recent enough that they take note of the efforts by the Supreme Court under Chief Justice John Roberts to roll back existing campaign finance regulations and permit a greater role in American campaigns for spending by corporations and other groups whose activities were limited during much of the 1990s and 2000s.

Part 2 of this book provides a detailed look at the most important actors in federal campaign finance in the United States. In "Individual Contributors: A Fundraising Advantage for the Ideologically Extreme?" Bertram Johnson considers the incentives of individual donors to campaigns, asking whether individual donors are representatives of the population as a whole and whether candidates who rely on small, individual contributions are different from those who do not. Michael Franz considers the role of organized interests in American politics, with an emphasis on how groups' activities changed in response to the Bipartisan Campaign Reform Act. Franz pays particular attention to activities of groups that go beyond merely contributing to candidates, and to the areas of group spending that are relatively unregulated. In "Reform in an Age of Networked Campaigns," Anthony Corrado, Michael Malbin, Thomas Mann, and Norman Ornstein document changes in fundraising by presidential candidates over the past three election cycles; the authors argue that Barack Obama's fundraising success in 2008 raises the possibility that Internet fundraising can privilege small donors even in the absence of broader changes in campaign finance law, but they caution that many unique features of 2008 may be difficult to replicate. Finally, Marian Currinder's "Paying to Play: Fundraising in the U.S. House of Representatives," provides a history of the financing of congressional campaigns over the past decade. Currinder calls particular attention to the increasing role of the congressional leadership in directing members' money toward the party campaign committees and toward competitive campaigns. Currinder contends that fundraising and governing are far more closely linked today than they were in decades past.

If we are to entertain ideas about changing the role of money in campaigns, however, it is not sufficient to compare campaign spending across time within any one nation. What we can do, however, is compare campaign financing practices across different types of governments or political systems. Part 3 provides one such comparison, focusing on the American states. In "State Campaign Finance Regulations and Electoral Competition," Donald Gross, Robert Goidel, and Todd Shields look at the interactions between different components of campaign finance reform in the American states; and in "Campaign Finance Laws and Candidacy Decisions in State Legislative Elections," Keith Hamm and Robert Hogan assess the ways in which campaign finance laws in the states can encourage or discourage potential candidates.

Part 4 presents research on campaign financing practice across different types of governments. Collectively, these pieces show the range of campaign financing mechanisms available in Western democracies, and they point to problems in the success or enforcement of campaign finance laws. In "Regulating Campaign Finance in Canada: Strengths and Weaknesses," Lisa Young discusses the consequences of campaign finance reform measures enacted in Canada since 2003. Menachem Hofnung's "Unaccounted Competition: The Finance of Intra-Party Elections" uses the example of Israel to draw a contrast between general election campaigns, the financing of which tend to be highly regulated, and the relatively unregulated processes by which parties often choose their candidates. Eduardo Posada-Carbó provides a similar study of the relationship between corruption and the enactment of public financing laws in Colombia and other Latin American nations in his contribution, "Democracy, Parties, and Political Finance in Latin America." And in "Big Business and Political Finance in Australia: Ideological Bias and Profit-Seeking Pragmatism," Iain Mc-Menamin discusses the role of corporate contributions in the relatively unregulated Australian system.

This book does not pretend to provide a comprehensive overview of all democratic nations' campaign financing practices or of the various permutations of campaign finance regulation that are available. Rather, the intent here is to show the commonality of the problems facing democratic governments and to foster dialogue about the consequences of reform. Problems in the financing of elections are endemic to political systems with open and free elections. This collection is intended to show the nuanced ways in which money affects elections and in which regulation of the flow of money can also influence the conduct of elections. Hopefully, it also will provide the reader with some indication that the democratic deficit can be reduced, that knowledge of the role of money in politics can help an informed citizenry discuss the values we should seek to balance in debating campaign finance reform and the ways in which we can use these values to hold our politicians accountable.

Bibliography

Alexander, Herbert E. 2001. "Approaches to Campaign and Party Finance Issues in Various Countries." In *Foundations for Democracy: Approaches to Comparative Political Financing*, ed. Karl-Heinz Nassmacher. Baden-Baden: Nomos, pp.198–208.

Boatright, Robert G. 2011. *Interest Groups and Campaign Finance Reform in the United States and Canada.* Ann Arbor: University of Michigan Press.

Boatright, Robert G., and Michael J. Malbin. 2005. "Political Contribution Tax Credits and Citizen Participation." *American Politics Research* 33 (6): 787–817.

Cox, Gary W., and Michael Theis. 2000. "How Much Does Money Matter? 'Buying' Votes in Japan, 1967–1990." *Comparative Political Studies* 33: 37–57.

Cross, William P. 2004. *Political Parties: The Canadian Democratic Audit.* Vancouver, BC: University of British Columbia Press.

Dalton, Russell J. 2004. *Democratic Challenges, Democratic Choices: The Erosion of Political Support in Advanced Industrial Democracies.* New York: Oxford University Press.

Gallup Poll. 2002. Roper Center at the University of Connecticut, February 8–10.

La Raja, Raymond J. 2008. *Small Change: Money, Political Parties, and Campaign Finance Reform.* Ann Arbor: University of Michigan Press.

Malbin, Michael J. 2009. "Small Donors, Large Donors, and the Internet: The Case for Public Financing after Obama." Washington, DC: Campaign Finance Institute. Online, http://www.cfinst.org/president/pdf/PresidentialWorkingPaper_April09.pdf.

Mayer, Kenneth R. 2006. "Sunlight As the Best Disinfectant: Campaign Finance in Australia." Canberra: Democratic Audit of Australia, Australian National University.

Moore, David W. 2001a. "Public Dissatisfied with Campaign Finance Laws, Supports Limits on Contributions." Online, http://www.gallup.com/poll/releases/pr10803.asp.

———. 2001b. "Widespread Public Support for Campaign Finance Reform." Online, http://www.gallup.com/poll/releases/pr991022.asp.

Nevitte, Neil. 2002. "Introduction: Value Change and Reorientation in Citizen-State Relations." In *Value Change and Governance in Canada*, ed. Neil Nevitte. Toronto: University of Toronto Press, pp. 3–36.

Rosenberg, David. 2002. "Broadening the Base: The Case for a New Federal Tax Credit for Political Contributions." Washington, DC: American Enterprise Institute.

Scarrow, Susan E. 2006. "Beyond the Scandals? Party Funding and the 2005 German Elections." *German Politics* 15 (4): 376–392.

Smilov, Daniel. 2008. "Dilemmas for a Democratic Society: Comparative Regulation of Money and Politics." Budapest: Center for the Study of Imperfections in Democracy, Central European University.

Part 1:
Competing Perspectives on Campaign Finance Regulation

The publication of this book comes at a pivotal moment in the history of American campaign finance. Less than a decade after the passage of the Bipartisan Campaign Reform Act of 2002, the most consequential piece of campaign finance legislation since the 1970s, it is now apparent that the Supreme Court is poised to overturn many components of American campaign finance law. As both of the articles in this section make clear, there are no agreed-upon reasons for restricting campaign spending in the United States. For some, such as Richard Hasen, this lack of agreement indicates that reformers must work to reframe their arguments in order to develop a more compelling legal case. For others, such as Bradley Smith, this lack of agreement is an indication that there is no constitutional reason to limit campaign spending. The Supreme Court's involvement in campaign finance law has created an odd situation for both sides—neither the American left nor the right is satisfied with contemporary campaign finance law, in part because the Court's 1976 *Buckley v. Valeo* decision struck down some components of federal campaign finance law while upholding others. As a result, we have a set of laws that neither side would have sought to create had they been starting from scratch.

These two articles show, as well, that the legal questions at stake in the American campaign finance debate are quite different from the concerns of empirical researchers. As we shall see in coming chapters, many of those who study campaign finance concern themselves with matters of equity, fairness, inclusiveness, and competition. These are important concerns, but they are not the concerns of the Supreme Court. A crucial question here is whether the Court should defer to legislators in the crafting of campaign finance laws—legislators, after all, have firsthand experience with campaign spending and may have strong views about these concerns—or whether it should regard any decisions by legislators with suspicion, since legislators may merely be seeking their own advantage. These are matters that will continue to be of importance in the coming decade, during which the Court will likely continue to reconsider many of its earlier decisions on campaign finance.

Richard Hasen is one of the foremost defenders of campaign finance regulation. Although Hasen supports many of the restrictions embodied in contemporary American campaign finance law, he has long been a critic of the Supreme Court's reasoning in many of its campaign finance decisions. In his article here, Hasen presents a history of the Court's landmark *Buckley v. Valeo* decision of 1976 and of the jurisprudence that has followed. The crux of Hasen's argument, however, is in the third section of the article. Hasen makes it clear that he believes the *Buckley* decision lacks coherence—and, as a consequence, the decision has always been on somewhat shaky ground. Although the Court has never overturned *Buckley*, it has zigged and zagged in evaluating campaign finance laws in accordance with *Buckley's* emphasis on preventing corruption as the only permissible standard for limiting campaign activity. Hasen's argument indicates that the Court's recent *Citizens United v. Federal Election Commission* decision may be a turning point—liberals on the Court will need to articulate a stronger legal defense of regulating campaign spending, otherwise the Roberts Court may continue to overturn many components of the current regulatory system.

Bradley Smith is, along with the Cato Institute's John Samples, one of the foremost advocates of completely deregulating American campaign finance—that is, of abolishing limits on how much money individuals can give to campaigns, of removing prohibitions against business and labor contributions, and of removing restrictions on independent expenditures by groups and individuals. In his article here, as in his 2001 book *Unfree Speech*, Smith makes both a constitutional and a pragmatic argument for abolishing most contemporary campaign finance laws. Any limits on expenditures, Smith argues, will inherently privilege some groups while penalizing others; campaign finance law cannot help but limit the freedom of speech for some groups or individuals. Furthermore, Smith argues, there is little evidence that campaign contributions corrupt politicians. Money is no different from rhetorical skill, political experience, or other qualities that politicians have or seek. Smith's provocative arguments no doubt played a role in shaping the Supreme Court's *Citizens United* decision. Here, Smith argues that the Court's decision is essentially a ratification of arguments made in the *Federalist Papers* about the role of government in refereeing conflict between groups, and that it is a victory for free speech.

The Nine Lives of *Buckley v. Valeo*

by Richard L. Hasen*

"Don't bury me 'cause I'm not dead yet."

—*Elvis Costello*, Mystery Dance (*first recorded, 1976*)

INTRODUCTION

Buckley v. Valeo[1] has been the leading case governing the constitutionality of campaign finance laws in the United States since the Supreme Court decided it in 1976. But it is an unlikely candidate for influence and longevity. The decision upheld federal limits on campaign contributions but it struck down federal limits on campaign spending as violating the First Amendment. It was a compromise opinion written by a committee of Justices; three of the eight Justices deciding the case dissented from parts of its core holdings on contributions and expenditures. Over the years, there have been Court majorities ready to overturn parts of *Buckley*, though *Buckley* has remained good law because the Justices have not agreed on which parts to overturn and Justices in the Court's center have refused to overturn any of *Buckley*'s central tenets. The Court's later campaign finance cases have vacillated wildly in their treatment of the First Amendment issues—yet each of these cases has claimed fidelity to *Buckley*. More than one commentator, including this author, has declared the case on the verge of death.[2] Yet *Buckley* has survived.

This Chapter tells the story of *Buckley v. Valeo*, beginning with an examination of the legislation that prompted the litigation, the 1974 Amendments to the Federal Election Campaign Act (FECA). It situates the legislation and litigation in the context of the early 1970s, a time when there was increasing public distrust of politicians and social turmoil, driven especially by controversy over the Vietnam War, changes wrought by the civil rights and women's rights movements, and a series of political scandals culminating with Watergate and the resignation of President Richard Nixon.

The story of *Buckley v. Valeo*'s origins turns out to be two stories, both drawn from the themes of that era. One story is that of good government reformers, especially the group Common Cause, who adopted a legislation and litigation strategy aimed at rooting out corruption among politicians. The legislation strategy appealed to incumbents' desires to control campaign costs and not be on the wrong side of voter anger over Watergate. The litigation strategy forced courts to enforce widely-ignored campaign finance rules. The other story is that of skeptics of government power, including the American Civil Liberties Union, conservative United States Senator (and now D.C. Circuit judge) James Buckley and liberal United States Senator Eugene McCarthy. They mistrusted campaign finance regulation, which they saw as a form of incumbency protection and government censorship. They filed the *Buckley* litigation, challenging the core provisions of the FECA, to prevent what they viewed as government tyranny.

The Chapter then traces *Buckley* through the litigation process. The case followed an unusual procedure set forth in the FECA itself, providing for a hearing before the entire United States Court of Appeals for the D.C. Circuit, sitting *en banc*, followed by direct appeal to the United States Supreme Court. The *en banc* court upheld the contribution and spending limits on both anticorruption and political equality grounds. When the high stakes litigation shifted to the Supreme Court, the government filed two briefs in the case: one brief supported the constitutionality of parts of the law, and the other brief was an unprecedented *amicus curiae* brief not taking a position on the law's constitutionality. The Supreme Court too was divided on the law's constitutionality, and it produced a Solomonic unsigned opinion that left both sides in the litigation partly unsatisfied. Within the *Buckley* opinion one could see contradictory strands of both the Common Cause and ACLU visions of the appropriate relationship of money and politics under the United States Constitution.

The Chapter concludes with the unlikely story of how *Buckley* has survived as a precedent, and looks into the future of campaign finance jurisprudence. In the last decade, the current Supreme Court has moved from its period of greatest deference toward campaign finance legislation to its period of greatest skepticism. All the while, the Court has (at least formally) adhered to the *Buckley* precedent, perhaps more as a result of political compromise by Court centrists than coherent legal reasoning. However, change could be on the way. The Supreme Court's most recent significant campaign finance decision, *Citizens United v. Federal Election Commission*,[3] struck down spending limits imposed on corporations and labor unions. *Citizens United* overruled earlier cases upholding such limits; unsurprisingly, both the earlier cases and *Citizens United* relied upon *Buckley*. The Court in *Citizens United* indicated great skepticism about the constitutionality of all limits on campaign financing, putting new pressure on the Court to overrule that part of *Buckley* upholding contribution limitations. But do not count on *Buckley* being overruled; it may last longer than the readers of this chapter.

I. ANTI-CORRUPTION AND ANTI-TYRANNY: THE ORIGINS OF THE FECA AND THE *BUCKLEY* LITIGATION

Against Corruption: The Story of the FECA

Modern federal campaign finance law dates back to the early 20th century, when Congress in the Tillman Act barred corporations from making contributions to federal candidates.[4] Congress periodically changed and updated its laws, such as when it imposed tougher disclosure regulations on political committees in the 1920s following the Teapot Dome scandal.[5] Notably, in the 1940s, Congress extended to labor unions the bar on corporate contributions to candidates;[6] the new law also prevented both kinds of organizations from independently spending their entity's funds supporting or opposing candidates to federal office.[7] Labor unions responded by setting up separate segregated funds, or political action committees (PACs), to engage in such spending through political contributions from union members rather than from the union's own coffers.

Although a number federal campaign finance laws were on the books, through the first six decades of the twentieth century, they were rarely enforced.[8] Disclosure reports were often missing, incomplete, or wrong, and when filed they were difficult even for experts to inspect.[9] Enforcement was so lax that the Justice Department refused to prosecute 20 Nixon fundraising committees that had not filed a single report in the 1968 presidential campaign, or 107 congressional candidates who had violated disclosure rules, on grounds that "fair play" required adequate notice that violators of the law would actually be prosecuted.[10] From the 1920s until the 1970s, in the rare cases in which prosecutors went after those accused of corporate spending or disclosure violations, the prosecutions did not always lead to convictions.[11] The Supreme Court considered some First Amendment challenges to these laws over the years, but mostly avoided deciding the constitutional questions.[12]

Though Congress considered a variety of additional campaign finance laws in the 1950s and 1960s, including contribution limitations, spending limitations, improved disclosure, public financing, and the creation of an independent agency to enforce campaign finance laws,[13] Congress did not pass any significant legislation in the area until the 1970s,[14] when it passed the FECA of 1971 (which was actually signed into law in early 1972) and amendments to the FECA in 1974. What changed to allow for the passage of such legislation?

Great social upheavals beginning in the 1960s, including controversies over the Vietnam War and civil rights, contributed to a marked decline in public trust in the government.[15] In this environment, a coalition of "legislators, experts, philanthropists, foundations, and public interest groups" emerged who believed that the system of representative government could be improved through campaign finance reform.[16] In the 1970s the reform coalition found a more receptive message in Congress, in part because the increasing costs of campaigns[17] and the decline in the power of political parties[18] made some reforms in congressional self-interest. For this reason, reform proposals in the 1970s began as those aimed at dealing with campaign costs.[19] Thus, in 1970, Congress passed a bill that, among other things, provided discount air rates to candidates; President Nixon vetoed the law, claiming it was full of loopholes.[20]

In the early 1970s, Common Cause, a new group headed by John Gardner, a liberal Republican and former member of Democratic President Lyndon B. Johnson's cabinet, spearheaded reform efforts.[21] The group built on public distrust to create an interest group aimed at reforming the political system and rooting and political corruption.[22] It relied heavily upon direct mail aimed at "well-educated people in the upper reaches of the income distribution."[23] By 1972 it had nearly 250,000 members.[24]

Common Cause's strategy was a mixture of lobbying Congress for reform, litigating over enforcement of existing campaign finance laws,[25] and engaging the press in a sophisticated public relations strategy. The media covered stories of possible corruption with relish, drawing on the data mined by Common Cause and other groups.[26] Democrats walked a fine line between supporting the goals of Common Cause, which were popular with constituents, and placating organized labor, which was suspicious of proposed campaign finance legislation.[27]

The strategy worked, helped by the fact that Democrats became more interested in campaign finance reform as large donor money shifted from Democrats to Republicans following Nixon's 1968 election and as Democrats endured Democratic presidential nominee Hubert Humphrey's lackluster fundraising.[28] President Nixon signed the FECA in January 1972, strengthening disclosure requirements, expressly allowing for the creation of political action committees, repealing some ineffective contribution limitations, and forcing broadcasters to sell advertising to candidates at reduced rates.[29] One of its more controversial provisions limited federal candidate spending on media to $50,000 or less per election.[30] A related bill created a system for the public financing of presidential elections, but it was not to go into effect until the 1976 elections.[31]

After FECA passed, the reform community continued to push for greater regulation as allegations of improprieties involving the Nixon campaign came to light in the Watergate scandal. The group Public Citizen "filed a lawsuit claiming that the president accepted money from the milk co-ops in exchange for reversing a decision by the Department of Agriculture that had lowered milk prices."[32] Common Cause engaged in a concerted effort to gather and disseminate disclosure data mandated by the new law.[33] Common Cause also publicly pressured candidates to voluntarily reveal contributions received before the FECA disclosure provisions went into effect in April 1972. When Nixon finally relented in the face of public pressure and threatened litigation, the campaign's disclosures revealed million-dollar contributions from some individuals, as well as millions of dollars in illegal corporate contributions from corporations.[34]

Watergate revealed all kinds of abuses connected to the campaign finance system. Major corporations gave large sums to the Nixon campaign—the usual request was for $100,000[35]—despite the longstanding prohibition on corporate giving to federal candidates. American Airlines was the first corporation to plead guilty to funneling $55,000 in illegal corporate cash, laundered through a Lebanese bank, to the 1972 Nixon re-election effort.[36] Cash also arrived to the campaign in paper bags from millionaires. The secret cash allowed for all kinds of out-of-sight dirty tricks, such as breaking into offices of rivals, planting spies with opposition campaigns, and attempts at outright bribery of officials.[37]

Though Watergate brought unprecedented attention to illegal campaign activities of the Nixon reelection campaign, such activities were hardly so confined. An internal review of the activities of one major corporation, the Gulf Oil Company, revealed a pattern of the company making "domestic political contributions with corporate funds…The activity was generally clandestine and in disregard of federal, as well as a number of state, statutes."[38] The Ervin commission investigating Watergate found evidence of illegal campaign contributions to other candidates, including 1972 Democratic presidential nominee George McGovern.[39]

The Watergate scandal created momentum for further campaign finance reform: the public, for a time, became intensely interested in the issue, with "well over 25 percent of all mail [sent to members of Congress] in the post-Watergate period [] on campaign finance, far more than on any other issue."[40] Democrats saw it as "a defining issue in 1974."[41]

The 1974 FECA amendments were debated at the same time as the Watergate hearings, trials, and investigations.[42] Facing public pressure to tighten campaign finance laws, Republicans joined Democrats in Congress in agreeing to strict contribution and spending limits in federal campaigns, public financing for presidential campaigns, and the creation of an independent agency, the Federal Election Commission, to administer the laws. As Congress considered the

1974 Amendments, much of the disagreement in Congress concerned whether public financing should be extended to congressional campaigns or be limited to presidential campaigns.[43] The final version of the FECA amendments reaching the President contained public financing for only presidential campaigns. President Nixon had threatened to veto the bill if it contained any public financing provisions, but he resigned before the FECA passed. President Ford, fearing political consequences and a congressional override if he vetoed the bill, signed the bill despite his dislike for it.[44]

Against Tyranny: The Story of Litigation against the FECA

The story of the FECA just told is a story of crusaders against corruption teaming up with politicians acting in their self-interest and using a sophisticated legislation, litigation, and media strategy to pass far-reaching campaign finance legislation. It is a story of triumph of the forces of progressive reform against corruption. But it is not the only story to be told of the era.

The other story of the time views the FECA through the lens of skepticism about government power, skepticism also nourished by the Vietnam War and corruption scandals. To opponents of the FECA, the Common Cause folks were "goo goos"[45] who were duped by self-interested incumbent politicians to urge the passage of laws aimed at squelching political competition.[46] Upon the passage of the 1974 Amendments, Senator James Buckley, one of the principal opponents of the law, "labeled the bill an incumbent protection measure because of its low spending limits. 'To offer this bill in the name of reform is an act of cynicism,' he said."[47]

Joel Gora, one of the plaintiffs' lawyers in the *Buckley* litigation, explained the basis for the fear of tyranny that he and others saw in the FECA:

I first encountered campaign finance reform as a young ACLU lawyer… in 1972. Three old-time dissenters came to the ACLU offices in New York with an incredible story. In May of that year the group had run a two-page advertisement in the *New York Times* advocating the impeachment of President Richard Nixon for the bombing of Cambodia and praising those few hardy—and clearly identified—Members of Congress who had sponsored an Impeachment Resolution. The advertisement was turgid, wordy, legalistic and not very slick, but it embodied the essence of what the First Amendment stands for: the right of citizens to express their opinion about the conduct of their government, free from fear of sanctions or reprisals from the government. Nonetheless, before the ink on the advertisement was barely dry, the federal government had hauled the group into federal court.

How, we wondered, could this be possible? We were especially mystified since this was a time, the Spring of 1972, when *New York Times Company v. Sullivan* was protecting the most rigorous criticism of government officials against libel suits, *Brandenburg v. Ohio* was protecting advocacy of violent revolution against criminal punishment, and, just the year before, the Pentagon Papers case was protecting the press against prior restraint on political speech. What, in the face of these speech-protective rulings, could justify Congress to pass a law that was only slightly better than the Alien and Sedition Acts in terms of stifling citizen criticism of government?[48]

Gora soon learned that the basis for the 1972 lawsuit was the government's belief (or as Gora put it, the belief of the "Richard Nixon Justice Department") that the purpose of the advertisement was to influence the outcome of federal elections, and that the group therefore should be considered a political committee subject to disclosure requirements.[49] Moreover, the law required the group to certify that the ad, which the government believed was spent in support of George McGovern's bid against President Nixon's reelection, would not put the McGovern campaign over the $50,000 cap on media expenditures contained in the 1971 FECA.[50] The ACLU both defended the group running the advertisement from having to meet the disclosure requirements and it filed its own lawsuit seeking the right to sponsor advertisements critical of President Nixon's handling of certain issues during the election season without having to get the approval of any politician who might benefit from the advertisements. It won both lawsuits on First Amendment grounds.[51] The ACLU's opposition to campaign finance laws only intensified as Congress amended the FECA in 1974, which Gora referred to as "the mothership of government control of political funding and, therefore, political speech."[52]

Gora explained the ACLU's opposition to the 1974 FECA provision barring independent spending exceeding $1,000 supporting or opposing a federal candidate: "The new law…effectively silenced speakers in an unprecedented fashion. The ceiling was about equal to the cost of a one-quarter page advertisement in the *New York Times*…Spend a dime more to express your political opinion and go to jail."[53] As then-lawyer and law professor (now Second Circuit Judge) Ralph K. Winter put it, "[i]t was our view that if the government is able to control the resources needed for communication, then government can control that communication."[54]

Key opposition to the law also came from two Senators who depended upon seed money from wealthy contributors to launch insurgent campaigns. James Buckley was "a political newcomer who had won a Senate seat [as a third party candidate] from New York by being able to raise a significant amount of money from relatively few supporters; Senator Eugene McCarthy['s] 1968 Presidential campaign [in the Democratic presidential primary against Lyndon Johnson] was funded in a similar way and managed to bring down a sitting President over the issue of the war in Vietnam."[55]

II. The Story of the Buckley Litigation

The Case Begins

The *Buckley* plaintiffs were a group of "political underdogs and outsiders."[56] The coalition included Senators Buckley and McCarthy, "Stewart Mott, one of McCarthy's main backers; and an unusual assortment of groups like the Libertarian Party, the Mississippi Republican Party, the American Conservative Union, and the New York Civil Liberties Union."[57]

While the ACLU had been motivated primarily by a belief that campaign finance laws impinged on the right to criticize the government, many of the *Buckley* plaintiffs appeared more concerned with how such laws might benefit incumbents. "What united the various challengers was a belief that Congress' comprehensive regulations would make it more difficult for challengers to defeat incumbents, and for minor parties and independents to challenge the hegemony of the two major parties."[58] As Senator Buckley explained: "What we had in common was a concern that the restrictions imposed by the new law would squeeze independent voices out of the political process by making it even more difficult than it already was to raise effective challenges to the political status quo."[59] Though they were odd political bedfellows, the plaintiffs' lawyers believed that their unity against the FECA gave them "an even stronger bond."[60] Despite coming from the left and right side of the political spectrum, however, they "generally shared a libertarian ideological stance."[61]

Though Senator Buckley was out in front in the lawsuit, Francis R. Valeo, the first named defendant who was then Secretary of the Senate, was not. Valeo was sued only in his official capacity, and he had nothing to do with the defense of the lawsuit. As he recounted years later, he had such a hard time getting a ticket to the Supreme Court oral argument, despite being the first named defendant, that he had to call up Chief Justice Burger's office to get a seat.[62] It was the United States government (including the newly-created Federal Election Commission), not Secretary Valeo, who defended the constitutionality of the law. The reform groups intervened to defend the law as well, and eventually took the lead in doing so.

Lower Court Proceedings

Well before the *Buckley* lawsuit was filed, Senator Buckley had been thinking ahead. While the 1974 FECA Amendments were being debated, he proposed an amendment (later incorporated into the legislation) requiring a special procedure and expedited court review of any constitutional challenges to the legislation.[63] Under the unusual procedure, plaintiffs filed a lawsuit in a federal district court in Washington, D.C. The district court's job was to certify constitutional questions to an *en banc* panel of the United States Court of Appeals for the D.C. Circuit.[64] The *en banc* Court decided the constitutional issues, with its decision to be appealed to the Supreme Court. The statute further provided that each court was to expedite the litigation as quickly as possible. Senator Buckley explained on the Senate Floor that his amendment "merely provides for the expeditious review of the constitutional questions I have raised. I am sure we will all agree that if, in fact, there is a serious question as to the constitutionality of this legislation, it is in the interest of everyone to have the question determined by the Supreme Court at the earliest possible time."[65]

Not everybody was happy with the mandated procedures, however. Some thought the expedited procedures did not leave enough time for the development of facts, or any chance to see how the 1974 FECA Amendments as a whole would have worked in practice.[66] Because the procedure was new and some issues of jurisdiction uncertain, the case bounced among a federal district court, the *en banc* D.C. Circuit, and a three-judge panel before the courts settled on the correct procedure to follow.[67] The parties submitted proposed findings of fact and conclusions of law; there was not a full-blown developed trial on the evidence of how the FECA amendments might affect federal election campaigns.

Following certification of 28 constitutional (sub-)questions by the federal district court, the *en banc* D.C. Circuit court, made up of eight judges, heard extensive argument and issued a *per curiam* (unsigned) opinion upholding virtually all of the challenged provisions of the 1974 FECA Amendments. There were three separate opinions dissenting in part from the *per curiam* opinion.

The *per curiam* opinion noted the extraordinary nature of the case before it, declaring the court's task "awesome" in light of revelations about Watergate that the upcoming "time of bicentennial that sharpens our awareness of our heroic experiment in democracy."[68] The court stated that "[n]o one can doubt the compelling government interest in preserving the integrity of the system of elections through which citizens exercise the core right of a free democracy of selecting the officials who will make and execute the law under which we all live."[69] Although promoting political equality did not appear to figure prominently in the Common Cause legislative campaign for the 1974 FECA Amendments, or play a major role in the legislative debates, the *en banc* court's *per curiam* decision placed great weight on these equality interests (as well as anticorruption interests) in upholding the regulation against First Amendment challenge.[70] The "skyrocketing" costs of campaigns, by themselves, figured little in the court's analysis.

The *en banc* court, after recounting the history of campaign finance regulation from a reformist perspective, cited to findings about the current role of money in the federal political process and stated its belief that large campaign spending was undermining public trust in the electoral process.[71] It then held that the First Amendment did not require strict scrutiny of limitations on contributions and expenditures, and it endorsed the view that limitations on contributions and spending could be justified on grounds of promoting political equality: "By reducing in good measure disparity due to wealth, the Act tends to equalize both the relative ability of all voters to affect electoral outcomes, and the opportunity of all interested citizens to become candidates for elective federal office."[72]

The court upheld the contribution limits and the spending limits, arguably the most controversial parts of the law.[73] The court held that the provision limiting an individual from spending more than $1,000 relative to a clearly identifiable candidates "is a necessary and constitutional means of closing a loophole that would otherwise destroy the effectiveness" of the contribution limitations.[74] However, out of First Amendment concerns, the court wrote that it would read the clause limiting spending "relative to a clearly identified candidate" in a "restrictive" way.[75] The court also upheld the limits on a candidate spending her personal or family funds on federal elections above a statutory limit. It held that these limits "serve to merely relax the $1,000 per candidate contribution limit for a candidate and his immediate family."[76] The court concluded that the provision "establishes additional candidate options without raising barriers to more modestly circumstanced candidates and without substantially undermining movement toward equalized spending by very rich and very poor candidates."[77]

The court also upheld overall spending limits imposed on candidate, on grounds that a limit "reduces the incentive to circumvent direct contribution limits and bans."[78] The court added:

Plaintiffs suggest that Congress lacks the power to decide when a candidate for office has had "too much communication with the voters." They argue that if the public is to benefit from the full and robust debate of public issues and personalities, then the range of debate may not be limited. But given the power of money and its various uses, and abuses, in the context of campaigns, there is compelling interest in its regulation not withstanding incidental limitations on freedom of speech and political association.[79]

The court also generally upheld the law's disclosure requirements, while noting that the FEC might need to make an exception for disclosure of contributions or spending that could subject a person to harassment.[80] In a victory especially for the ACLU (which led on this issue since its earlier cases[81]), the court struck down one very broad disclosure provision, section 437a, which the court held required onerous and unconstitutional "reporting by groups whose only connection with the elective process arises from completely nonpartisan public discussion of issues of public importance."[82] The court also upheld the voluntary public financing provisions for presidential candidates.[83] Finally, the court rejected a number of challenges to how the Federal Election Commission was constituted, ruling some of the challenges unripe for decision.[84]

The court concluded by stating that

[t]he corrosive influence of money blights our democratic processes. We have not been sufficiently vigilant; we have failed to remind ourselves, as we move from the town halls to today's quadrennial Romaneseque political extravagances, that politics is neither an end in itself nor a means for subverting the will of the people. The excesses revealed by this record—the campaign spending, the use to which the money is put in some instances, the campaign funding, the *quid pro quo* for the contributions—support the legislative judgment that the situation not only must not be allowed to deteriorate further, but that the present situation cannot be tolerated by a government that professes to be a democracy.... Certainly [the new laws] should not be rejected because they might have some incidental, not clearly defined effect on First Amendment freedoms. To do so might be Aesopian in the sense of the dog losing his bone going after its deceptively larger reflection in the water.[85]

To the Supreme Court

Though things went well for the defenders of the law in the D.C. Circuit, the Supreme Court does not defer to lower courts on the meaning of the First Amendment, and so all of the legal questions were up for grabs on appeal. The plaintiffs quickly appealed the case to the Supreme Court, hoping for a better result.

Within the Ford Administration there was a great debate over the position the government was going to take in the Supreme Court. At one point, Solicitor General Bork threatened to file a brief opposing the constitutionality of key parts of the law.[86] Attorney General Edward Levi and Bork decided to take "a less drastic measure than opposing the statute:"[87] a "neutral" amicus brief. The Chair of the newly-formed FEC did not want the Justice Department to file such a brief, and President Ford himself had to mediate the dispute. Ford agreed to the filing of a neutral amicus brief on behalf of the Attorney General.[88] This government brief was filed in addition to a separate government brief supporting the law filed on behalf of the FEC.

The amicus brief, signed by Attorney General Edward Levi, Solicitor General Robert Bork, Deputy Solicitor General A. Raymond Randolph, Jr., and Assistant to the Solicitor General Frank Easterbook,[89] stated it was not taking a position on the constitutionality: "Because we intend this to be a true *amicus* brief, one that attempts to assist in analysis without pointing the way to particular conclusions, we shall do no more than analyze the case law and the statute."[90] However, its tone was one of marked skepticism to the core provisions of FECA. For example, after describing the rationales for spending limits on individuals relative to a clearly identified candidate, the brief asked: "is this justification [in preserving the integrity of the system of elections] so pressing that it permits substantial restrictions on the rights of political activity? Could it be redressed by some less restrictive means or, perhaps, is it an evil that we are compelled to suffer, without redress, lest the cure be worse than the disease?"[91]

Given the government's ambivalence about the legislation's constitutionality, lawyers for the reform groups led the defense. Lloyd Cutler and others from the Washington firm of Wilmer, Cutler & Pickering represented intervenors the Center for the Public Financing of Elections and the League of Women Voters.[92] Common Cause was represented by its own counsel, Kenneth Guido and Fred Wertheimer. Former Attorney General Archibald Cox argued as amicus curiae for Senators Kennedy and Scott. The California Fair Political Practices Commission, the Missouri Elections Commission, the New Jersey Election Law Enforcement Commission, and the New York Board of Elections filed an amicus brief arguing for the constitutionality of the expenditure provisions, noting that 37 states in recent years had adopted statutes limiting campaign expenditures,[93] as well as FECA's disclosure provisions. The Socialist Labor Party filed a brief arguing for an exemption to certain disclosure requirements for minor parties.

Though usual Supreme Court oral argument time is one hour (30 minutes per side), Court set an extraordinary day of oral arguments (featuring arguments by seven lawyers) to consider the constitutionality of the case.[94] There was urgency to the matter: not only did the statute providing for jurisdictions over appeal require that the matter be expedited; the Court felt pressure to decide the case before the 1976 presidential election season.

The Internal Debate at the Supreme Court

Two days after the day-long oral argument, the Justices of the Supreme Court met in a private conference to discuss their tentative views of the case.[95] The conference notes reveal that the Justices did not all have definite opinions about the constitutionality of the core contribution and spending provisions of the FECA.[96] At conference the Justices appeared to divide into two camps: Five justices—Chief Justice Burger and Justices Stewart, Potter, Rehnquist and Blackmun—appeared skeptical that the core provisions were constitutional. Three Justices—Brennan, Marshall and White—appeared more deferential to Congress's determination that the FECA was constitutional.[97] Thus, Justice Brennan remarked at conference that "self gov[ernmen]t is arguably furthered" by the limitations contained in the law, while Justice Rehnquist said that "those who say this Act *furthers* 1st A[mendment] values[] argue an absurdity."[98] Still, Justice Rehnquist, along with some of the other skeptical Justices appeared ready at the conference to uphold some of the contribution limitations.

Given the press of time and the complexity of the case, Chief Justice Burger assembled a "drafting team" of Justices to write on different aspects of the case. Justice Powell agreed to draft the disclosure provisions, Justice Brennan the public funding section, Justice Stewart the contribution and expenditure limitations section, and Justice Rehnquist the section on the FEC composition issue. He also asked Justice White to write on the FEC issue. The Chief Justice stated he had assigned each Justice to write in an area in which five or more Justices appeared to be in agreement.

Over the next few months, there was much give-and-take among the Justices on the various pieces of what would become the Court's opinion in *Buckley*.

At one point, Justice Brennan stated that he had changed his preconference view that the spending limits imposed on individuals were likely constitutional because he was concerned that the provision that the law applied only to spending "relative to a clearly identified candidate" was unconstitutionally vague. The Court's ultimate discussion of this issue put great weight on the vagueness problem.[99] Justice Brennan apparently had much more sympathy to the equality argument for the spending limits than appeared in the original opinion; he may have sacrificed expressing his views on this question in his desire for as much unanimity as possible when the Court announced its decision.[100]

Justice Brennan took the lead in trying to put the different parts of the opinion into a coherent whole, and the Court was able to get the opinion out by January 30, 1976. This pleased Justice Powell, who wrote to the other Justices that "[i]t is important to make that date if possible. The act directs us to 'expedite' this case. It sounds more 'expeditious' for the record to show we brought the case down in *January* rather than February!"[101]

The Supreme Court's Opinion

The Court's opinion itself was long, complex, and unsigned. It was a 143-page *per curiam* behemoth with 178 footnotes, followed by separate opinions (by five of the eight Justices on various issues, covering 83 pages) and appendices, for a total of 294 pages.[102] The Court decided a number of important legal issues in its opinion, including upholding the challenged disclosure provisions, upholding the constitutionality of the voluntary public financing system for presidential elections, and striking down the process for choosing members of the FEC.[103] Most of the attention courts and scholars have paid to the case, however, has focused on that part of the opinion generally upholding the contribution limitations and striking down the spending limitations.

Although recognizing that any law regulating campaign financing was subject to the "exacting scrutiny required by the First Amendment,"[104] the Court mandated divergent treatment of contributions and expenditures for two reasons. First, the Court held that campaign expenditures were core political speech, but a limit on the amount of campaign contributions only marginally restricted a contributor's ability to send a message of support for a candidate.[105] Thus, expenditures were entitled to greater constitutional protection than contributions. Second, the *Buckley* Court recognized only the interests in prevention of corruption and the appearance of corruption as justifying infringement on First Amendment rights.

The Court held that large contributions raise the problem of corruption "[t]o the extent that large contributions are given to secure a political *quid pro quo* from current and potential officeholders."[106] But truly independent expenditures do not raise the same danger of corruption because a *quid pro quo* is more difficult if politician and spender cannot communicate about the expenditure.[107]

With the corruption interest having failed to justify a limit upon independent expenditures, the Court considered the alternative argument that expenditure limits were justified by "the ancillary governmental interest in equalizing the relative ability of individuals and groups to influence the outcome of elections . . . ."[108] In one of the most famous (some would say notorious) sentences in *Buckley*, the Court rejected this equality rationale for campaign finance regulation, at least in the context of expenditure limits: "[T]he concept that government may restrict the speech of some elements of our society in order to enhance the relative voice of others is wholly foreign to the First Amendment."[109] The Court's view of whether political equality could trump First Amendment interests was the polar opposite of that expressed by a firm majority of the *en banc* D.C. Circuit.

Portions of *Buckley* certainly show some deference to legislative judgments. For example, the Court refused to consider whether the amount of the individual contribution limits (set at $1,000—just over $3,800 in 2010 dollars[110]) was too low.[111] The amount of contribution limitations would raise constitutional problems only when they prevented candidates and committees from "amassing the resources necessary for effective advocacy."[112] But the overall tenor and tone of *Buckley* was one of skepticism of legislative judgments about the need for campaign finance regulation.

Thus, the Court rejected expenditure limits not only because they interfered with free speech and association rights but also because, given the Court's narrowing interpretation of the FECA's reach only to cover advertisements containing express words of advocacy (such as "Vote for Smith"),[113] the limits could be circumvented easily, meaning that such limits would serve "no substantial societal interest."[114] Indeed, the Court even applied its narrowing construction to FECA's disclosure rules,[115] leaving many election-related campaign expenditures lacking any regulation whatsoever until 2002 when Congress passed the Bipartisan Campaign Reform Act (BCRA, commonly known as McCain-Feingold).[116]

Three Justices disagreed with the Court's split over the constitutionality of contributions and expenditures. Chief Justice Burger thought the contribution limitations were unconstitutional as well.[117] "For me contributions and expenditures are two sides of the same First Amendment coin."[118] Justice White would have sustained the spending limits. He wrote that the limit on independent spending "is essential to prevent transparent and widespread evasion of the contribution limits."[119] He also would have upheld the limit on spending of personal funds, which he said "helps to assure that only individuals with a modicum or support from others will be viable candidates."[120] He supported candidate spending limits on grounds that they would "ease the candidate's understandable obsession with fundraising, and so free him . . . . from the influence inevitably exerted by the endless job of raising increasingly large sums of money. I regret that the Court has returned them all to the treadmill." [121] Justice Marshall wrote of his support for the constitutionality of the limit on personal and family funds, noting that "the interest [in promoting equality that has been derided by the Court] is more precisely the interest in promoting the reality and appearance of equal access to the political arena."[122]

III. THE STORY OF BUCKLEY'S SURPRISING RESILIENCE

Criticizing Buckley

Buckley v. Valeo has been quite influential. It has been the Rosetta Stone of American campaign finance jurisprudence for more than a generation. It has been cited in over 2,500 cases, is in the title of 18 books, and is mentioned in 4,000 law review articles.[123] But perhaps unsurprisingly, the split decision in *Buckley* did not fully please everyone. Burt Neuborne, a former ACLU legal director who now believes in the constitutionality of more campaign finance regulation than the Court upheld in *Buckley*,[124] wrote that the opinion "resulted in the distortion of Congress' intent, imposed a regime on the nation that no Congress would ever have enacted, and, most importantly, has created a campaign finance system abhorred by virtually all political participants."[125]

Senator Buckley, the named challenger in *Buckley v. Valeo* who eventually became a judge on the same D.C. Circuit that heard his challenge, wrote that after *Buckley* and a more recent Supreme Court decision upholding the 2002 McCain-Feingold campaign finance law, "we are left with a package of federal campaign finance laws and regulations that have distorted virtually every aspect of the election process. The 1974 amendments were supposed to deemphasize the role of money in federal elections. Instead, by severely limiting the size of individual contributions, today's law has made the search for money a candidate's central preoccupation."[126]

These points echoed Chief Justice Burger's observation that the FECA Amendments after the Court finished them created a "piecemeal" package of legislation that Congress likely would not have approved.[127] The Chief would have scrapped the entire law on that basis, but the *Buckley* majority rejected that argument and severed the unconstitutional parts.

Even Francis Valeo, the Secretary of the Senate and nominal defendant in *Buckley*, was critical of the decision:

> I knew the minute that they took off the limitations on personal expenditures that you were setting up a Senate of millionaires, or people who could rely on other people's money for their support. There would be no other way to run for the Senate. I thought that was a disaster in terms of what it would do to the Senate, and it is. The Senate has become much too much a money place. But I'm not a lawyer and I don't know the refinements of the law that the justices were reasoning from. I was a little hard pressed to see how putting a limitation on how much you could spend was an infringement on your right of free speech. But that was one of the findings.[128]

Post-*Buckley* at the Supreme Court

Supreme Court Justices over the years also have expressed dissatisfaction with the *Buckley* ruling. For example in the early 2000s, it appeared that there were six Justices on the Court ready to overturn either the portion of *Buckley* allowing contribution limits or the portion barring individual spending limits.[129] The case survived because there was no majority to overrule it in the same way. Justices in the center of the Court have refused to move *Buckley* in either direction. Though a court majority has professed allegiance to the *Buckley* case through the years, the Court's decisions have swung rather widely, like a pendulum, between periods of deference to legislatively-enacted campaign finance laws and periods of intense skepticism.[130]

Consider, for example, the Court's post-*Buckley* treatment of corporate and union spending limits. The Court in *Buckley* itself did not consider whether the pre-FECA limits on spending by corporations or labor unions were constitutional.[131] In *First National Bank of Boston v. Bellotti*,[132] the Court followed *Buckley*'s lead, striking down spending limits applied to individuals and candidates with a ruling striking down limits on spending by corporations in ballot measure elections.[133] The Court took an expansive view of corporate free speech rights, but dropped an important footnote suggesting corporate spending limits in *can-*

didate elections might be permissible to prevent corruption of candidates,[134] a footnote in tension with *Buckley*'s statement that independent spending by individuals cannot corrupt candidates because of the absence of the possibility of a *quid pro quo*.[135]

The Court then held in the *Massachusetts Citizens for Life* case that nonprofit ideological corporations that do not take corporate or union money cannot be limited in spending their treasury funds in candidate elections,[136] but a few years later the Court in *Austin v. Michigan Chamber of Commerce* confirmed that for-profit corporations *could* be so limited.[137] The Court in *Austin* did not address whether corporate limits might be justified to prevent corruption of candidates (as the Court had suggested in *Bellotti*[138]), but held the law was justified to prevent a "different type of corruption:" "the corrosive and distorting effects of immense aggregations of wealth that are accumulated with the help of the corporate form and that have little or no correlation to the public's support for the corporation's political ideas."[139] Though the Court called this interest one in preventing "corruption," an interest recognized as a permissible basis for regulation in *Buckley*, it really represented an embrace of the equality rationale (at least as to corporations) that the Court had rejected in *Buckley*.[140]

The Court then appeared to backpedal even further from *Bellotti*. In *FEC v. Beaumont*[141] the Court held that even *MCFL* corporations could be barred from making *any* campaign contributions, adding that

> corporate contributions are furthest from the core of political expression, since corporations' First Amendment speech and association interests are derived largely from those of their members, and of the public in receiving information. A ban on direct corporate contributions leaves individual members of corporations free to make their own contributions, and deprives the public of little or no material information.[142]

Then, in *McConnell v. FEC*, the Court reaffirmed *Austin* and extended its holding to unions without explaining why unions, which amass wealth in a much more egalitarian way than corporations, presented the same "distortion" dangers of corporations recognized in *Austin*.[143] The *McConnell* Court said that corporations and unions could exercise their First Amendment rights through other means, such as raising money for a PAC that could then spend money on election-related activities and make contributions to candidates.[144]

Justice O'Connor, one of the Court centrists on campaign finance regulation, had changed her mind on the constitutionality of corporate spending limits in candidate elections three times on the Court.[145] In MCFL, she seemed to agree that for-profit corporate spending could be limited to PAC spending. In *Austin*, she sided with the dissenters in holding such limits unconstitutional. In *McConnell*, without explanation, she sided with the majority in reaffirming *Austin*. Once Justice O'Connor left and Justice Alito replaced her, the Court moved decidedly in a deregulatory direction.

The post-O'Connor Court first called *McConnell*'s holding about corporate and union spending limits into question in the *Wisconsin Right to Life* case, creating a broad "as applied" exemption for advertisements that reasonably could be construed as something other than support or opposition to a federal candidate. Then, in the Court's most recent case, *Citizens United v. Federal Election Commission*,[146] the Court overturned *Austin* and the relevant part of *McConnell*, holding that any limitations on corporate spending limitations violated the First Amendment.

Despite this vast vacillation, the Court has never overruled any part of *Buckley*, and each of these cases professed adherence to the teachings of *Buckley*. Indeed, until *Citizens United*, the Court had not overruled *any* of its campaign finance precedents. The language of the *Buckley* opinion itself was expansive enough to allow for all of these disparate results.

What explains *Buckley*'s staying power? Before the Supreme Court even decided *Buckley*, Professor Fleishman urged the Court toward compromise: "An overly broad pronouncement of unconstitutionality could make regulation of campaign finance impossible for years to come. The other extreme—rationalization of the legislation's shortcomings in the name of a public response to Watergate—is equally undesirable."[147] Compromise is a natural position for the Court in the face of two strong competing arguments: the Common Cause idea that money needs to be limited in politics to prevent corruption and preserve public confidence and the ACLU idea that government regulation of campaign money can squelch political expression and help incumbents.

Moreover, aside from compromise, the very expansiveness, vagueness, and internal inconsistencies of the *Buckley* precedent have allowed shifting Court majorities to change constitutional doctrine without having to expressly overrule the case. Professing adherence to *Buckley* while changing doctrine at the same time has the benefit of giving the appearance of a Court acting modestly and keeping the law consistent with precedent. In short, *Buckley* has not been a major impediment, at least thus far, to Justices interested in moving campaign finance jurisprudence in a particular direction.

The Supreme Court's new opinion in *Citizens United* will put renewed pressure to overrule *Buckley*'s upholding of campaign contribution limitations. In *Citizens United*, the Court stated it was not addressing the constitutionality of contribution limitations, including the ban, going back to the early twentieth century, on direct corporate contributions to candidates.[148] But the Court did offer a relatively stingy definition of "corruption," stating that "ingratiation and access" do not constitute corruption.[149] Following *Citizens United*, the D.C. Circuit (once again sitting *en banc*) struck down a federal $5,000 individual contribution limit on contributions to committees that make only independent expenditures, on grounds that larger individual contributions to such committees cannot corrupt.[150]

Whether the newly skeptical Supreme Court under the leadership of Chief Justice Roberts would be willing to overrule *Buckley* and allow unlimited contributions directly to candidates presents a much more difficult question. The *Citizens United* Court rejected, once again, equality arguments for campaign finance regulation.[151] But a Court majority may be more wary of recognizing a First Amendment right of individuals to give very large (multi-million dollar) contributions directly to federal candidates and officeholders.[152] To allow such contributions would require the Court to reject the core anticorruption purpose of contribution limitations.[153] If the Court faces such a question, the abuses brought to light from Watergate again will be raised in the Court in defense of contribution limits to candidates. At least some of the Justices on a deregulatory Court at that point may think twice before jettisoning the anticorruption portion of the *Buckley* case. In the meantime, the competing visions of the role in money in politics continue to divide the Court, and the country.

ENDNOTES

The author thanks Inna Zazulevskaya for research assistance, Lisa Schultz for library assistance, and Joel Gora, Michael Malbin, David Mason, Bob Mutch, Burt Neuborne, John Samples, Roy Schotland, and Fred Wertheimer, for useful comments and suggestions.

1. 424 U.S. 1 (1976).

2. Richard L. Hasen, Buckley *is Dead, Long Live* Buckley: *The New Campaign Finance Incoherence of* McConnell v. Federal Election Commission, 152 U. PA. L. REV. 31 (2004); Burt Neuborne, Buckley's *Analytical Flaws*, 6 J. L. & POL'Y 111, 117 (197–1998) ("*Buckley* is like a rotten tree. Give it a good hard push and, like a rotten tree, *Buckley* will keel over. The only question is in which direction.").

3. 130 U.S. 876 (2010).

4. See ROBERT E. MUTCH, CAMPAIGNS, CONGRESS AND THE COURTS ch. 1 (1988) and Adam Winkler, *Other People's Money: Corporations, Agency Costs, and Campaign Finance Law*, 92 GEORGETOWN L.J. (2004) for an overview on the origin of federal and state campaign contribution bans. See also Robert E. Mutch, *The First Federal Campaign Finance Bills*, 15 J. POLICY HIST. 30 (2002) for a look at proposed federal campaign finance bills in the 19th Century.

5. MUTCH, *supra* note 4, at 24. The Teapot Dome scandal involved large contributions given to the Republican Party by Harry F. Sinclair of Sinclair Oil Corporation. The corporation "had leased

Wyoming's Teapot Dome Oil reserve from the Interior Department. A Senate committee investigating these transactions, acting on rumors of a link between the Teapot Dome lease and developer's contributions to the Republican Party, discovered that Sinclair had indeed given sizeable sums to the GOP. … Although RNC officials denied any connection between the oil leases and the retiring of the 1920 party debt, their testimony …led Congress to require political committees to report financial activity for all years, even those in which no election is held." *Id.*

6. Congress did so for the duration of World War II in the Smith-Connally Act, in effect through the war, and then permanently in 1947 in the Taft-Hartley Act. MUTCH, *supra* note 4, at 152–53.

7. *Id.* at 155–57.

8. Julian Zelizer, *Seeds of Cynicism: The Struggle over Campaign Finance, 1956–1974*, 14 J. POLICY HIST. 73, 764 (2002) ("The Progressive Era reforms had a negligible effect. Candidates easily found loopholes to evade unenforced regulations.").

9. *See* MUTCH, *supra* note 4, at 25–26 (reporting that Louise Overacker, a political scientist, was led to a tiny washroom near a congressional office, where party committee reports were stored, unlabeled in dusty paper-covered bundles on a top shelf).

10. *Id.* at 28 (citation omitted).

11. Allison Hayward, *The Michigan Auto Dealers Prosecution: Exploring the Department of Justice's Mid-Century Posture Toward Campaign Finance Violations*, 9 ELECTION L.J. (forthcoming 2010); MUTCH, *supra* note 4, at 28.

12. *See* Mutch, *supra* note 4, at 158–65; DANIEL H. LOWENSTEIN, RICHARD L. HASEN, & DANIEL P. TOKAJI, ELECTION LAW—CASES AND MATERIALS 680 (4th ed. 2008).

13. MUTCH, *supra*, note 4, at 29–42; Zelizer, *supra* note 8, at 78–88; JULIAN E. ZELIZER, ON CAPITOL HILL: THE STRUGGLE TO REFORM CONGRESS AND ITS CONSEQUENCES, 1948–2000 51–52 (2004).

14. In 1966 Congress passed a bill providing for the public financing of presidential elections which it promptly repealed a year later. KURT HOHENSTEIN, COINING CORRUPTION: THE MAKING OF THE AMERICAN CAMPAIGN FINANCE SYSTEM 207 (2007).

15. *See* MUTCH, *supra* note 4, at 42–44 (citing ANDREW S. MCFARLAND, COMMON CAUSE: LOBBYING IN THE PUBLIC INTEREST (1984)).

16. Zelizer, *supra* note 8, at 74.

17. Zelizer, *supra* note 8, at 74.

18. *Id.* at 77.

19. *Id.* at 88.

20. *Id.* at 89.

21. ZELIZER, *supra* note 13, at 100.

22. Zelizer, *supra* note 8, at 90; ZELIZER, *supra* note 13, at 101–03.

23. MUTCH, *supra* note 4, at 44; *see also* ZELIZER, *supra* note 13, at 100.

24. MUTCH, *supra* note 4, at 44.

25. In one of the lawsuits, Common Cause sued the Democratic and Republican National Committees and the Conservative Party of New York in a class action lawsuit claiming that the parties were creating multiple committees for candidates and spending more on single candidates than allowed under existing law. Zelizer, *supra* note 8, at 91.

26. *See Id.* at 92; ZELIZER, *supra* note 13, at 104.

27. Zelizer, *supra* note 8, at 90. Labor had good reason to be concerned. As Congress debated the 1971 FECA bill, Republicans turned their attention to limiting the political activities of labor

unions. In 1968, a St. Louis union, the Pipefitters Local Union 562, had been prosecuted for violating the prohibition on labor contributions to federal candidates. The union claimed that it had a constitutional right to contribute the funds, because they came not from the union's general treasury funds but from segregated PAC funds. *See* MUTCH, *supra* note 4, at 160-63. A jury convicted the union, and the union's prosecution was upheld by the United States Court of Appeals for the Eighth Circuit. United States v. Pipefitters Local Union No. 562., 434 F.3d 1116 (8th Cir. 1970). The Supreme Court agreed to hear the case while Congress was debating the FECA. Some Republican members of Congress proposed including in the FECA limitations on union political activity, but Representative Hansen, fearful of losing labor's support for the FECA supported an amendment which allowed union political spending on communications with members, nonpartisan voter registration and get-out-the-vote activities, and contributions collected through a separate segregated fund. MUTCH, *supra* note 4, at 162–63. After the FECA passed with the Hansen amendment, the Supreme Court struck down the union's conviction, holding it had a constitutional right to spend money collected from members through a separate PAC. *Pipefitters Local Union No. 562 v. United States*, 407 U.S. 385 (1972).

28. Zelizer, *supra* note 8, at 92.

29. See generally 1971 CQ ALMANAC (Vol. XXVII) 675-96, *Campaign Spending; Major Reform Bill Neared Passage* for a detailed description of the legislative history of the FECA.

30. HOHENSTEIN, *supra* note 14, at 208.

31. Zelizer, *supra* note 8, at 94–95.

32. *Id.* at 95.

33. *See* MUTCH, *supra* note 4, at 45; Zelizer, *supra* note 8, at 95–96.

34. MUTCH, *supra* note 4, at 45–46.

35. HERBERT E. ALEXANDER, FINANCING THE 1972 ELECTION 514 (1976).

36. *Id.* at 514.

37. *Id.* at 54–62, 489–93.

38. JOHN J. MCCLOY, THE GREAT OIL SPILL: THE INSIDE REPORT: GULF OIL'S BRIBERY AND POLITICAL CHICANERY 31 (1976); *see also* Zelizer, *supra* note 8, at 79 (recounting ways in which corporations violated federal law during the 1950s and 1960s).

39. *Id.* at 97.

40. MUTCH, *supra* note 4, at 46. In addition to Common Cause, other groups involved in pushing for further legislation included the Center for the Public Financing of Elections. The group's director, Susan B. King "made the new group into a means through which a diverse coalition of existing organizations—church, labor, and professional groups which shared a common interest in addressing the question of the role of money in politics,' but which could not place that issue at the top of their agendas—joined in lobbying Congress on behalf of the new laws." *Id.* (citation omitted). *See also* Zelizer, *supra* note 8, at 91 (reporting that by 1974 there were eighteen groups lobbying Congress for campaign finance reform).

41. Zelizer, *supra* note 8, at 100. Fleishman concludes that "[b]ut for the embarrassing and widening wake of Watergate—the plethora of illegal corporate campaign contributions, the illegal sale of high office in return for contributions, among others—there would very likely have been no new campaign finance reforms in 1974…" Joel E. Fleishman, *The 1974 Federal Election Campaign Act Amendments: The Shortcomings of Good Intentions*, 1975 DUKE L.J. 851, 852 (1975).

42. *See* MUTCH, *supra* note 4, at 48–50. For a detailed description of the legislative history of the 1975 FECA Amendments, see 1974 CQ ALMANAC (VOL. XXX) 611–33, *Congress Clears Campaign Finance Reform*.

43. Zelizer, *supra* note 8, at 100–02. The Senate passed a public financing plan for the Senate, but

the House rejected such a system for itself, and the Senate plan was killed in conference. 1974 CQ ALMANAC, *supra* note 42, at 632.

44. *See* MUTCH, *supra* note 4, at 49; ZELIZER, *supra* note 13, at 123; JOHN SAMPLES, THE FALLACY OF CAMPAIGN FINANCE REFORM 219 (2006) (Ford "had little choice in the matter"); Christopher Lydon, *Campaign Reform Nears Court Test*, N.Y. TIMES, May 25, 1975, at 24 ("When President Food signed the campaign reform bill into law last October, he conceded that he had 'some reservations about it.'").

45. The term is used to describe naïve "good government" supporters. *See* David Brooks, *The Two Obamas*, N.Y. TIMES, June 6, 2008, http://www.nytimes.com/2008/06/20/opinion/20brooks.html ("All I know for sure is that this guy is no liberal goo-goo.").

46. Even two of the leading lawyers defending the FECA in the *Buckley* litigation recognized that "[t]he debate about campaign finance regulation is not conducted solely at lofty legal and political science levels. The issue is redolent of realpolitick. Incumbent officeholders consider the crucial effect of legislative changes on their relative strength vis-à-vis challengers. Democrats and Republicans consider how regulation might affect their relative party strength." Lloyd N. Cutler & Roger Witten, *Preface*, 9, in "Regulating Campaign Finance," 486 THE ANNALS OF THE AMERICAN ACADEMY OF POLITICAL AND SOCIAL SCIENCE (July 1986). In the same volume, Cutler suggested that after *Buckley* parties could voluntarily require their candidates to comply with spending limits. *See* Lloyd N. Cutler, *Can the Parties Regulate Campaign Financing?*, in *id.* At 115–20.

47. 1974 CQ ALMANAC, *supra* note 42, at 633. Samples later viewed Watergate as both a crisis for the nation and an "opportunity for advocates of campaign finance restrictions." SAMPLES, *supra* note 44, at 217.

48. Joel M. Gora, *Campaign Finance Reform: Still Searching Today for a Better Way*, 6 J. L. & POL'Y 137, 137–38 (1997–1998) (footnotes omitted).

49. *Id.* at 138.

50. *Id.* at 139. Gora further explained that the *Times* would not run the ad without the certification, and the McGovern campaign would not give the certification because to do so would count the spending against its own expenditure limit. *Id.*

51. ACLU v. Jennings, 366 F. Supp. 1041 (D.D.C. 1973), *vacated sub nom.*, Statts v. ACLU, 422 U.S. 1030 (1975); United States v. National Comm. for Impeachment, 469 F.2d 1135 (2d Cir. 1972).

52. Gora, *supra* note 48, at 141.

53. *Id.* at 142. Gora explained that the anti-Nixon ad which was the subject of the earlier lawsuit cost $18,000 in 1972, about $50,000 in 2003 dollars. Joel M. Gora, *The Legacy of* Buckley v. Valeo, 2 ELECTION L.J. 55, 56 (2003).

54. Ralph K. Winter, *The History and Theory of* Buckley v. Valeo, 6 J. L & POL'Y 93, 95 (1997–1998).

55. Gora, *supra* note 48, at 58.

56. James L. Buckley, *Bucks and* Buckley: *The Plaintiff Makes His Case*, NAT'L REV., Sept. 27, 1999, at 40.

57. Gora, *supra* note 48, at 58.

58. BURT NEUBORNE, CAMPAIGN FINANCE REFORM & THE CONSTITUTION: A CRITICAL LOOK AT BUCKLEY V. VALEO 10 (1998), http://brennan.3cdn.net/f124fc7ebf928fb019_hqm6bn3w0.pdf.

59. JAMES L. BUCKLEY, GLEANINGS FROM AN UNPLANNED LIFE: AN ANNOTATED ORAL HISTORY 149 (2006).

60. MUTCH, *supra* note 4, at 50 (quoting Joel Gora).

61. Winter, *supra* note 54, at 93.

62. Interview # 11 with Francis R. Valeo, Oct. 17, 1985, at 488-89, *available at*: http://www.senate.gov/artandhistory/history/resources/pdf/valeo_interview__11.pdf.

63. *See* ALEXANDER, *supra* note 35, at 594; *see* 2 U.S.C. § 437h (1974); *Bread Political Action Comm. v. FEC*, 455 U.S. 577 (1982) (discussing the scant legislative history of this provision).

64. The *en banc* panel included all the active judges in the Circuit.

65. 120 CONG. REC. 10562 (1974). See Michael E. Solimine, *Institutional Process, Agenda Setting, and the Development of Election Law on the Supreme Court*, 68 OHIO ST. L.J. 767 769–79 (2007) for more on the use of the expedited procedures in this context.

66. *See* NEUBORNE, *supra* note 58, at 8.

67. Appendix B of the D.C. Circuit's *en banc* opinion, *Buckley v. Valeo*, 519 F.2d 821 (D.C. Cir. 1975) gives the history of the litigation in excruciating detail. A separate three-judge court, comprised of circuit judges Bazelon and Robinson, and district court judge Corocran, considered and rejected a challenge to the Internal Revenue Code provisions establishing the public financing provisions applicable to the presidential election system. *Buckley v. Valeo*, 401 F. Supp. 1245 (D.D.C. 1975) (three-judge court).

68. *Buckley*, 519 F.2d at 835.

69. *Id.*

70. Two of the judges on the D.C. Circuit *en banc* court later defended the court's decision and criticized the Supreme Court's rejection of political equality to justify spending limits in some circumstances. J. Skelly Wright, Comment, *Politics and the Constitution: Is Money Speech?*, 85 YALE L.J. 1001 (1976); Harold Levanthal, *Courts and Political Thickets*, 77 COLUM. L. REV. 345, 373 (1977). *See also* J. Skelly Wright, *Money and the Pollution of Politics: Is the First Amendment an Obstacle to Political Equality?*, 82 COLUM. L. REV. 609, 633 (1982).

71. *See Buckley*, 519 F.2d at 835–39.

72. *Id.* at 841.

73. Judge Tamm, joined by Judge Wilkey, dissented on the constitutionality of some of the contribution and spending limits. *Id.* at 912, 914–18 (Tamm, J., concurring in part and dissenting in part). Judge Tamm also dissented on the constitutionality of the public financing provisions and the appointment provisions related to the Federal Election Commission. *Id.* at 918–21. Judge MacKinnon, in a separate decision, also dissented on issues related to the Federal Election Commission's composition and powers. *Id.* at 922 (MacKinnon, J., concurring in part and dissenting in part).

74. *Id.* at 853.

75. *Id.*

76. *Id.* at 854.

77. *Id.* at 855.

78. *Id.* at 859.

79. *Id.* at 860.

80. *Id.* at 868. Chief Judge Bazelon dissented on the question of the constitutionality of some of the disclosure requirements when applied to minor parties. *Id.* at 907 (Bazelon, C.J., concurring in part and dissenting in part).

81. *See supra* note 51 and accompanying text.

82. *Buckley*, 519 F.2d at 870. The government did not appeal from the court's decision on this provision.

83. *Id.* at 879–87.

84. *Id.* at 887–96.

85. *Id.* at 897–98.

86. Mutch, *supra* note 4, at 51.

87. *Id.*

88. *Id.*

89. This was an especially impressive group of lawyers. Bork, Randolph, and Easterbrook all went on to become U.S. Court of Appeals judges. Bork is no longer on the court. Randolph sits on the D.C. Circuit and Easterbrook on the Seventh Circuit.

90. Brief for the Attorney General as Appellee and for the United States as *Amicus Curiae* at 8, Buckley v. Valeo, Nos. 75–436, 75–437 (October 1975). For some reason, this brief is not available on Lexis or Westlaw.

91. *Id.* at 45. Judge Bork made it clear in his later writings that he personally was quite skeptical of the result in *Buckley.* Robert H. Bork, A Time to Speak: Selected Writings and Arguments 246 (2008) (had limits in *Buckley* been in effect in 1978 "they would have made impossible Eugene McCarthy's primary challenge that led Lyndon Johnson not to run for reelection."); Robert H. Bork, Coercing Virtue: The Worldwide Rule of Judges 58–61 (2003) ("The speech clause began to go soft with the 1976 decision in *Buckley v. Valeo*"); *id.* at 59 (The FECA and *Buckley* "shifted political power in America toward those with the leisure to engage in political activity....Many of these shifts in power were planned intentionally by these groups, and most of them favor the New Class's liberal agenda").

92. Mutch, *supra* note 4, at 50–51.

93. Brief Amici Curiae on Behalf of California Fair Political Practices Commission et al., *Buckley v. Valeo*, 1975 WL 184941, * 7; *see also id.* ("Amici believe that the expenditure limitations of the FECA are carefully drawn to serve the compelling governmental interest of minimizing disproportionate influence over politics and government enjoyed by those individuals and institutions able to pump large amounts of money into election campaigns. We believe that the expenditure limitations are constitutional and should be upheld.").

94. Audio of the oral argument, in two parts, is available for listening at http://www.oyez.org/cases/1970–1979/1975/1975_75_436. In addition to Cutler and Cox, the other oral advocates were Bruce Clagett, Ralph Spritzer, Daniel Friedman, Joel Gora, and Ralph Winter. Clagett and his co-counsel John Bolton published an analysis of the *Buckley* decision shortly after it was issued. *See* Bruce M. Clagett & John R. Bolton, Buckley v. Valeo: *Its Aftermath, and its Prospects: The Constitutionality of Government Restraints on Political Campaign Financing*, 29 Vand. L. Rev. 1327 (1976).

95. Unless otherwise noted, the discussion in this section follows Richard L. Hasen, *The Untold Drafting History of* Buckley v. Valeo, 2 Election L.J. 241 (2003).

96. There was less disagreement—and discussion—about the disclosure and public financing provisions of the Act. The Justices appeared uncertain on questions about the constitutionality of the formation of the Federal Election Commission. *Id.* at 244–45.

97. Justice Stevens, new to the Court, did not participate in the case.

98. Hasen, *supra* note 95, at 243.

99. This led to the emergence of *Buckley*'s famous Footnote 52 on the standards for which advertising will count as express advocacy. *See generally id.* at 247–48, 250–51 and Allison R. Hayward, *Drafting* Buckley v. Valeo: *The Court, Liberty and Politics*, Federalist Society for Law and Public Policies Studies, Apr. 4, 2004, http://www.fedsoc. org/publications/pubID.265/pub_detail.asp, on the drafting of the footnote.

100. *See* Hasen, *supra* note 95, at 247 n.15, 251.

101. *Id.* at 249.

102. NEUBORNE, *supra* note 58, at 12. Not to be outdone, when the Court decided a challenge to the Bipartisan Campaign Reform Act of 2002 (the "McCain-Feingold" campaign finance law), it issued an opinion that had the largest U.S. Reports page count (270, excluding the heading and syllabus) and second largest word count (89,694) in Supreme Court history. LOWENSTEIN, HASEN, & TOKAJI, *supra* note 12, at 794.

103. Congress later changed the rules for appointing members of the FEC to a system of presidential appointment with Senate confirmation, with no more than three members of the six-member FEC coming from the same political party. 2 U.S.C. § 437c (2008).

104. *Buckley*, 424 U.S. at 16.

105. *Id.* at 21.

106. *Id.* at 26–27.

107. *Id.* at 46–47.

108. *Id.* at 48.

109. *Id.* at 48–49. Seven of the eight Justices deciding the case concurred in this statement, though the drafting history reveals that at least two more of the Justices were ambivalent about the equality rationale. *See* HASEN, *supra* note 95, at 249–50.

110. Calculated using the "inflation calculator" at the Bureau of Labor Statistics website, http://data.bls.gov/cgi-bin/cpicalc.pl.

111. *See Buckley*, 424 U.S. at 30. The Court also upheld an aggregate annual $25,000 individual contribution limit to federal candidates, parties, and political committees. *Id.* at 38. *See also* California Medical Association v. Federal Election Commission, 453 U.S. 182 (1981) (upholding $5,000 limit on annual contributions by individuals and unincorporated associations to multicandidate political committees supporting federal candidates).

112. *Buckley*, 424 U.S. at 22.

113. *See id.* at 44 n.52. This is the famous Footnote 52.

114. *Id.* at 45.

115. *Id.* at 68.

116. *See* Richard L. Hasen, *The Surprisingly Easy Case for Disclosure of Contributions and Expenditures Funding Sham Issue Advocacy*, 3 ELECTION L.J. 251 (2004) (discussing disclosure provisions of BCRA).

117. *Buckley*, 424 U.S. at 235 (Burger, C.J., concurring in part and dissenting in part).

118. *Id.* at 241.

119. *Id.* at 262 (White, J., concurring in part and dissenting in part).

120. *Id.* at 266.

121. *Id.* at 265.

122. *Id.* at 287 (Marshall, J., concurring in part and dissenting in part).

123. Statistics based upon Lexis, Westlaw, and Worldcat searches conducted in March 2010.

124. On June 19, 1998, a group of former ACLU officials, including Neuborne, released a "Statement of Persons Who Have Served the American Civil Liberties Union in Leadership Positions Supporting the Constitutionality of Efforts to Enact Reasonable Campaign Finance Reform" opposing the ACLU's position in *Buckley*. The statement is available at http://www.brennancenter.org/page/-/d/aclu.pdf.

125. NEUBORNE, *supra* note 58, at 22.

126. BUCKLEY, *supra* note 59, at 150. Both of the Senator-plaintiffs in *Buckley* stated that large contributions bought nothing from them. Senator McCarthy wrote that "The

largest contributor to my 1968 campaign gave $500,000. For that I spent an hour and a half talking with him. I do not know how much time I would have spent with the same contributor had I been elected President, but I am sure that the amount of time would have been based on his professional knowledge and competence, rather than the size of his contribution." Eugene J. McCarthy, The Ultimate Tyranny: The Majority over the Majority 56 (1980). Senator Buckley wrote: "I received major unsolicited help from two individuals. The first made a contribution of more than $200,000; the second provided a $100,000 line of credit against which my campaign drew $55,000. The understanding was that it would have to be repaid only if I won. During my six years in office, I never heard from the second benefactor. The first, however, did call my office on one occasion to ask if it would be possible for his wife and grandson to have lunch in the Senate dining room. I plead guilty to having obliged him." Buckley, *supra* note 59, at 151.

127. *Buckley*, 424 U.S. at 245-55 (Burger, C.J., concurring in part and dissenting in part).

128. Interview # 11, *supra* note 62, at 489–90.

129. Lowenstein, Hasen & Tokaji, *supra* note 12, at 768 n.2. In one of the cases from that period, *Nixon v. Shrink Mo. Gov't PAC*, 528 U.S. 377 (2000), Justice Breyer, writing for himself and Justice Ginsburg, said that *Buckley's* statement rejecting the equality rationale for campaign finance regulations "cannot be taken literally." 528 U.S. at 401 (Breyer, J., concurring). Justice Stevens used his concurrence to "make one simple point. Money is property; it is not speech." *Id.* at 397 (Stevens, J., concurring). On the other side, Justice Thomas wrote in his dissent for himself and Justice Scalia in the case that "our decision in *Buckley* was in error, and I would overrule it. I would subject campaign contribution limitations to strict scrutiny, under which Missouri's contribution limits are patently unconstitutional." *Id.* at 410 (Thomas, J., dissenting). Justice Kennedy, expressing some reservations, pronounced himself in "substantial agreement" with Justice Thomas's dissent. *Id.* (Kennedy, J., dissenting).

130. *See generally* Hasen, *supra* note 2.

131. During the drafting of *Buckley* at the Supreme Court, Justice Powell repeatedly questioned whether the FECA provisions were going to give too much power to corporations and labor unions. *See* Hasen, *supra* note 95, at 246, 248, 249.

132. 435 U.S. 765 (1978).

133. *See Id.* at 767.

134. *See Id.* at 788 n.6.

135. *See also* Federal Election Commission v. Wisconsin Right to Life, 551 U.S. 449, 490 n.4 (2007) (Scalia J., concurring in part and concurring in the judgment) (commenting on *Bellotti* footnote, and stating that "[n]o one seriously believes that *independent* expenditures could possibly give rise to *quid-pro-quo* corruption without being subject to regulation as *coordinated* expenditures.").

136. *Federal Election Commission v. Massachusetts Citizens for Life*, 479 U.S. 238, 241 (1986).

137. *Austin v. Michigan Chamber of Commerce*, 494 U.S. 652, 655 (1990).

138. *See Bellotti*, 435 U.S. at 788 n.6.

139. *Austin*, 494 U.S. at 660.

140. *See* Richard L. Hasen, The Supreme Court and Election Law: Judging Equality from Baker v. Carr to Bush v. Gore 111–14 (2003); *see also* Citizens United v. Federal Election Commission, 130 S. Ct. 876, 922 (2010) (Roberts, C.J., concurring).

141. 539 U.S. 146 (2003).

142. *Id.* at 161 n.8 (citation omitted).

143. *McConnell*, 540 U.S. at 207–08.

144. *Id.* at 206; *see also* Richard L. Hasen, *Justice Souter: Campaign Finance Law's Emerging Egalitarian*, 1 ALBANY GOV'T L. REV. 169 (2008).

145. *See* LOWENSTEIN, HASEN & TOKAJI, *supra* note 12, at 852.

146. 130 S.Ct. 876 (2010).

147. Fleishman, *supra* note 41, at 853.

148. 130 S.Ct. at 909.

149. *Id.* at 910. This is in tension with *McConnell*'s broader definition of corruption. *See* Hasen, *supra* note 2, on that broader definition.

150. *Speechnow.org v. FEC*, 599 F.3d 686, 693–94 (D.C. Cir. 2010) (en banc).

151. 139 S.Ct. at 904-08.

152. It could be wary especially because of the negative public reaction to the decision in Citizens United. Dan Eggen, *Poll: Large Majority Opposes Supreme Court Decision on Campaign Financing*, WASH. POST, Feb. 17, 2010, http://www.washingtonpost.com/wpdyn/ content/ article/2010/02/17/AR2010021701151.html.

153. Somewhat ironically, following *Citizens United* the ACLU partially reversed course and endorsed the constitutionality of reasonable limits on campaign contributions to candidates. The reversal sparked a negative reaction from some ACLU leaders, including Joel Gora. *See* Floyd Abrams, Ira Glasser, & Joel Gora, *The ACLU Approves Limits on Speech*, WALL ST. J., Apr. 30, 2010, http://online.wsj.com/article/SB10001424052748704423504575521215282087 5486.html.

*Richard L. Hasen is the William H. Hannon Distinguished Professor of Law, Loyola Law School, Los Angeles. He is a coeditor of *Election Law Journal* and the author of the Election Law blog.

Richard L. Hasen. "The Nine Lives of *Buckley v. Valeo*." In *First Amendment Stories*, ed. Richard Garnett and Andrew Koppelman. Eagan, MN: Foundation Press, 2010.

Used by permission.

DISCUSSION QUESTIONS

1. Is the alleged incoherence of the *Buckley* decision necessarily a problem for advocates of campaign finance regulation?

2. Do large contributions necessarily constitute corruption? Do large independent expenditures?

3. Should the Supreme Court defer to legislators in matters of campaign finance?

4. Should groups have the same political speech rights as individuals?

The Myth of Campaign Finance Reform

by Bradley A. Smith*

March 24, 2009, may go down as a turning point in the history of the campaign-finance reform debate in America. On that day, in the course of oral argument before the Supreme Court in the case of *Citizens United v. Federal Election Commission*, United States deputy solicitor general Malcolm Stewart inadvertently revealed just how extreme our campaign-finance system has become.

The case addressed the question of whether federal campaign-finance law limits the right of the activist group Citizens United to distribute a hackneyed political documentary entitled *Hillary: The Movie*. The details involved an arcane provision of the law, and most observers expected a limited decision that would make little news and not much practical difference in how campaigns are run. But in the course of the argument, Justice Samuel Alito interrupted Stewart and inquired: "What's your answer to [the] point that there isn't any constitutional difference between the distribution of this movie on video [on] demand and providing access on the internet, providing DVDs, either through a commercial service or maybe in a public library, [or] providing the same thing in a book? Would the Constitution permit the restriction of all of those as well?" Stewart, an experienced litigator who had represented the government in campaign-finance cases at the Supreme Court before, responded that the provisions of McCain-Feingold could in fact be constitutionally applied to limit all those forms of speech. The law, he contended, would even require banning a book that made the same points as the Citizens United video.

There was an audible gasp in the courtroom. Then Justice Alito spoke, it seemed, for the entire audience: "That's pretty incredible." By the time Stewart's turn at the podium was over, he had told Justice Anthony Kennedy that the government could restrict the distribution of books through Amazon's digital book reader, Kindle; responded to Justice David Souter that the government could prevent a union from hiring a writer to author a political book; and conceded to Chief Justice John Roberts that a corporate publisher could be prohibited from publishing a 500-page book if it contained even one line of candidate advocacy.

In June, the Court issued a surprising order. Rather than deciding *Citizens United*, the justices asked the parties to reargue the case, specifically to consider whether or not the Court should overrule two prior decisions on which Stewart had relied: *Austin v. Michigan Chamber of Commerce*, a 1990 case upholding a Michigan statute that prohibited any corporate spending for or against a political candidate, and *McConnell v. Federal Election Commission*, the 2003 decision that upheld the constitutionality of the 2002 McCain-Feingold law. The *Citizens United* case was reargued on September 9, and a decision is pending. But however the Court rules, the debate over campaign-finance laws appears to have suffered a shock.

To anyone following the evolution of the campaign-finance reform movement, it should have been obvious that book-banning was a straightforward implication of the McCain-Feingold law (and the long line of statutes and cases that preceded it). The century-old effort to constrict the ways our elections are funded has, from the outset, put itself at odds with our constitutional tradition. It seeks to undermine not only the protections of political expression in the First Amendment, but also the limits on government in the Constitution itself—as well as the understanding of human nature, factions and interests, and political liberty that moved the document's framers.

By putting the point so bluntly before the Supreme Court, Malcolm Stewart may have inadvertently set off a series of events that could, in time, erode the claim to moral high ground upon which the campaign-finance reform movement has always relied. At the very least, his frankness invites us to consider the origins and consequences of that movement—and the implications of its efforts for some cherished American freedoms.

THE MISCHIEFS OF FACTION

Concerns about the political influence of the wealthy have never been far from the surface of American political life. The effort to restrict political spending—with the twin goals of preventing corruption and promoting political equality—began in earnest in the late 19th century. But in order to understand that movement and the intense debate it spawned, it is necessary to look back even further—to the founding of the American republic.

Figuring out how to keep special interests under control was a dilemma at the core of the Constitutional Convention. James Madison's most original contribution to political thought may well be his effort, in the Federalist Papers, to demonstrate how the new Constitution would ensure that private interests could not seize control of the government and use its power for their private benefit. Federalist No. 10 in particular addressed the tendency toward, and the dangers of, a government controlled by what Madison termed "factions."

In that essay, Madison recognized that there will always be individuals and interests seeking to use the government to their own ends. His entire approach to government, after all, was based on the notion, expressed in Federalist No. 51, that government is "but the greatest of all reflections on human nature"— and that by nature, men are not angels. Because partiality, the ultimate cause of faction, was "sown into the nature of man," Madison argued in No. 10, the causes of faction could not be controlled in a free republic—at least not without "destroying the liberty that is essential to its existence." This, he quickly added, would be a cure "worse than the disease." Madison's approach to the problem was therefore not to limit the emergence of factions, but to control their ill effects and, where possible, even to harness them for good.

To achieve this end, the Constitution relied on three primary devices. One was the separation of powers within the federal government. In three of the Federalist Papers—Nos. 47, 48, and 49—Madison elaborated at length on how the separation of powers would protect liberty and, by implication, prevent "factions" (what we would call special interests) from gaining control of the government. The other two devices, federalism and the idea of enumerated powers, were to work in tandem. The creation of separate spheres of action for the various state and federal governments—and the sheer size of the republic—would make it difficult for factions to gain control of the levers of power. "[T]he society itself will be broken into so many parts, interests, and classes of citizens," wrote Madison in Federalist No. 51, "that the rights of individuals, or of the minority, will be in little danger." Because the federal government would concern itself only with matters of "great and aggregate interests"—such as national defense, foreign policy, and regulation of commerce between the states—factions would be limited to minor squabbles of local concern, where they could do relatively little harm. The idea, then, was not to limit the freedom of factions, but to divide and limit the power of government itself so that factional interests could not dominate American politics. And the very fact of the multiplicity and diversity of factions would be a limit on the power of governing majorities.

Of course, a fourth bulwark was soon added: the Bill of Rights, and in particular the First Amendment. The First Amendment was in part a reflection of Lockean principles of natural rights. In Cato's Letters—which constitutional historian Clinton Rossiter has called "the most popular, quotable, esteemed source of political ideas in the colonial period"—John Trenchard and Thomas Gordon wrote that freedom of speech was "the right of every man." But the First

Amendment guarantees of free speech, assembly, and press were not seen purely as protections against government encroachment on natural rights. Rather, as political scientist John Samples notes, the founders believed that "the liberty to speak would force government officials to be open and accountable." During the crisis over the Alien and Sedition Acts in the early years of the new republic, Madison himself noted that the "right of freely examining public characters and measures, and of communication...is the only effectual guardian of every other right." As Samples argues, these founders realized that for "knowledge to inform politics and decision making, it must be publicly available. If the government suppresses freedom of speech, it prevents such knowledge from becoming public." Thus, freedom of speech was seen as both an individual liberty and a means of advancing the public interest.

Despite these protections, spending on political campaigns was often a source of concern in antebellum America, especially after the rapid expansion of the franchise and the rise of mass campaigns for the presidency and other offices. In 1832, the Bank of the United States spent approximately $42,000—the equivalent of about a million dollars today, in inflation-adjusted terms—to try to defeat Andrew Jackson, who was seeking to revoke the bank's charter. With the growth of industry in the aftermath of the Civil War, political spending began to rise rapidly—and corporations became an important source of campaign funding. It has been estimated that by the campaign of 1888, the national Republican Party and its state affiliates were receiving 40 to 50% of their campaign funds from corporations (which benefited from high tariffs supported by the GOP). Democrats, though usually poorer, had their own financial titans—such as banker August Belmont and later his son, August Belmont, Jr., who could be counted on for at least $100,000 (nearly $2 million in inflation-adjusted terms) in just about every campaign in the last half of the 19th century.

But even as money was becoming more important to campaigns, the Constitution's limits on government power (which, in the view of the framers, would also limit the power of factions to manipulate public policy) began to fall out of favor in some important quarters. Beginning in the late 19th century, the influential Progressive movement launched a sharp critique of the founders' notions of enumerated powers and limited government, and even federalism and the separation of powers. Progressive theorists such as Herbert Croly and Columbia University law professor Walter Hamilton railed against the constraints that the Constitution placed on government power. Hamilton argued that the Constitution was "outworn" and "hopelessly out of place." Croly argued for the need to "overthrow" the "monarchy of the Constitution." Eltweed Pomeroy—a New Jersey glue manufacturer who became prominent as an author and the leader of the National Direct Legislation League—argued that "representative government is a failure," and sought ways to bypass the checks and balances of the constitutional system. In short, the Progressives' goal was a more energetic, less restrained government, which they believed was necessary to meet the demands of a modern industrial society.

It was in this context of hostility to federalism, checks and balances, and limited government that the modern drive to restrict political speech emerged. It started not as an effort to protect our constitutional arrangements from factions that would overpower them, but rather an effort to overcome our constitutional limits on the power of government. It was also intended to overcome the loud, messy, unpredictable democratic process, so as to empower a more "elevated" vision of government.

At the 1894 New York state constitutional convention, the progressive Republican icon Elihu Root called for a prohibition on corporate political giving. "The idea," said Root, "is to prevent...the great railroad companies, the great insurance companies, the great telephone companies, the great aggregations of wealth from using their corporate funds, directly or indirectly, to send members of the legislature to these halls in order to vote for their protection and the advancement of their interests against those of the public." Root explained that he was concerned about "the giving of $50,000 or $100,000," amounts equal to roughly $1.2 or $2.4 million today. His effort ultimately failed to change the laws in New York—but it did effectively launch the modern movement to limit campaign contributions and speech.

THE PARTY OF SELF-INTEREST

At the same time that Root's speech gave rise to a movement, it also pointed to one of that movement's fundamental weaknesses. Legal historian Allison Hayward of George Mason University Law School argues that Root's real objective was less to secure passage of his proposal than to score partisan points against the Democrats (whose leaders were then being grilled for accepting bribes from the Sugar Trust). Thus, the movement was born less from noble ideals of good government than from ignoble motives of partisan gain.

This has remained a fundamental dilemma for the "reform" movement, as the century-old effort to restrict and regulate campaign spending has come to be known. If the problem is that venal legislators are betraying the public trust in exchange for campaign contributions, why would we expect them not to be equally motivated by base impulses when passing campaign-finance legislation?

Wouldn't the ability to control political speech empower the faction that wields it, rather than constraining the power of all factions? A review of the evidence suggests this concern is well founded.

After Republican William McKinley won the presidential election of 1896 with corporate support organized by the legendary political strategist Mark Hanna, the Democratic-controlled legislatures of Missouri, Tennessee, and Florida (three states that had voted for McKinley's opponent, William Jennings Bryan), as well as the legislature in Bryan's home state of Nebraska, passed bills prohibiting corporate spending and contributions in state races. Even if one accepts that the authors of these state bans were sincere in their belief that limiting the speech of McKinley and his allies was in the public interest, it is still easy to recognize the danger of regulators' mistaking their partisan advantage for the public good.

The first federal law in this arena, passed in 1907, was also a ban on corporate contributions to campaigns. The law was dubbed the Tillman Act, after its sponsor, South Carolina senator "Pitchfork Ben" Tillman. Tillman wrote and said little of his motives for sponsoring the ban on corporate contributions, but he hated President Theodore Roosevelt and appears to have wanted to embarrass the president (who had relied heavily on corporate funding in his 1904 election campaign). Tillman's racial politics also clearly contributed to his interest in controlling corporate spending: Many corporations opposed the racial segregation that was at the core of Tillman's political agenda. Corporations did not want to pay for two sets of rail cars, double up on restrooms and fountains, or build separate entrances for customers of different races. They also wanted to take advantage of inexpensive black labor, while Tillman sought to keep blacks out of the work force (except as indebted farm laborers).

Corporations supported Republicans, and Tillman—a Democrat, like most post-war Southern whites—often bragged of his role in perpetrating voter fraud and intimidation in the presidential election of 1876 in order to overthrow South Carolina's Republican reconstruction government. It is clear, then, that Tillman was no "good government" reformer; and far from being born of lofty ideals, federal campaign-finance regulations were, from their inception, tied to questionable efforts to gain partisan advantage.

Within a few years of the Tillman Act, in 1911, came "publication" laws requiring disclosure of campaign contributors and limits on campaign expenditures. These were followed by the Federal Corrupt Practices Act of 1925, aimed at tightening the Tillman Act's limits on corporate donations. In 1943, the Smith-Connally Act prohibited contributions to candidates by labor unions.

In 1947, Congress extended the ban on corporate and union contributions to cover "expenditures" made directly to vendors in behalf of campaigns, rather than contributed to candidates or parties.

While these laws influenced the way in which groups and individuals participated in politics, they did little to stem the overall flow of money into campaigns, due to weak enforcement mechanisms and various loopholes that could readily be exploited. The Federal Election Campaign Act, passed in 1972 and substantially amended in 1974, sought to address these problems by creating the most comprehensive set of regulations in history and an independent agency, the Federal Election Commission, to enforce the law.

The FECA maintained the ban on corporate and union contributions and expenditures, instituted a detailed system of reporting on contributions and expenditures, and placed limits on contributions and expenditures by individuals, including any expenditure "relative to" a federal candidate. Individual contributions to candidates were limited to $1,000 (a limit that has since been raised to $2,400), and contributions to Political Action Committees were capped at $5,000. PACs, in turn, were limited to contributing $5,000 to candidates. The law also limited total giving in an election cycle (no person may give more than $115,500 over two years to candidates and PACs combined), and placed a host of limits on the sizes of various other contributions.

The Supreme Court pulled back some of these limits in the 1976 case *Buckley v. Valeo*, holding that FECA's limits on expenditures made independently of a candidate violated the First Amendment. The decision further confined regulation so that it covered only expenditures that "expressly advocated" the election or defeat of a candidate, using specific words such as "vote for" or "vote against." This allowed for heavy spending on "issue ads" that might criticize or praise a candidate but stop short of expressly urging a vote one way or the other.

The 2002 McCain-Feingold law attempted to cut off this spending, which became known as "soft money." Among its many provisions, McCain-Feingold prohibited political parties from accepting any unregulated contributions, and prohibited corporate or union spending on any cable, broadcast, or satellite communication that mentioned a candidate within 30 days of a primary or 60 days of a general election. The law applied to non-profit membership corporations, such as the Sierra Club or the National Rifle Association, as well as to for-profit corporations. This is the law that Citizens United is alleged to have violated.

Even this account understates the complexity of the law. In an amicus brief filed in the Citizens United case, eight former FEC commissioners note that the FEC has now promulgated regulations for 33 specific types of political speech, and for 71 different types of "speakers." The statute and accompanying FEC regulations total more than 800 pages; the FEC has published more than 1,200 pages in the *Federal Register* explaining its decisions; and it has issued more than 1,700 advisory opinions since its creation in 1976.

Considered in detail, each step in the effort to limit campaign spending turns out to advantage the party that sought it. If its own numbers are insufficient to pass the legislation (as was the case with McCain-Feingold in 2002), then it seeks to broaden its base by adding incumbent-protection sweeteners to attract enough members of the opposing party to create a bipartisan majority. John Samples notes that McCain-Feingold drew most of its support from Democrats—who, he argues, saw long-term electoral disaster in the growing Republican fundraising edge, which was increasing after Republicans won the presidency in 2000. But to gain a legislative majority, the minority Democrats had to gain Republican votes; Samples finds that the Republicans who supported McCain-Feingold were, by and large, those most in danger of losing their seats. For them, the incumbent-benefit protections of the law made it irresistible.

Samples makes the Madisonian observation that "politicians use political power to further their own goals rather than the public interest....Campaign finance laws might be, in other words, a form of corruption." Noting that "scholars date the largest decline in congressional electoral competition from 1970" and that the Federal Election Campaign Act—the foundation of modern campaign-finance law—was passed in 1972, Samples points out that "the decline in electoral competition and the new era of campaign finance regulation are virtually conterminous."

This is no accident. Since the passage of the FECA, the average incumbent spending advantage over challengers in U.S. House races has soared from approximately 1.5-to-1 to nearly 4-to-1. Incumbents begin each cycle with higher name recognition and a database of past contributors, making it easier to raise more money through small contributions from more people. They also typically make the decision to run earlier than challengers do—since a challenger often waits to see if the incumbent will run before making his choice—so they have more time to raise small contributions. And because campaign-finance regulations essentially require that candidates fill their coffers in small increments, the law clearly advantages the incumbents who passed it.

The effect of campaign-finance regulations has therefore been to help the people who passed them and to strengthen special interests, rather than to cleanse American politics of the influence of self-interested factions. Even the well-meaning reformers, it appears, have failed at their stated goals.

A FAILURE IN PRACTICE

Campaign-finance reform has not managed either to promote political equality or prevent corruption. And data show that one reason campaign-finance regulations are of little value in attacking corruption is that contributions simply don't corrupt politicians. In a 2003 article in the *Journal of Economic Perspectives*, three MIT scholars—Stephen Ansolabehere, James Snyder, Jr., and John de Figueiredo—surveyed nearly 40 peer-reviewed studies published between 1976 and 2002. "[I]n three out of four instances," they found, "campaign contributions had no statistically significant effects on legislation or had the 'wrong' sign—suggesting that more contributions lead to less support." Given the difficulty of publishing "non-results" in academic journals, the authors suggested in another paper, "the true incidence of papers written showing campaign contributions influence votes is even smaller." Ansolabehere and his colleagues then performed their own detailed study, which also found that "legislators' votes depend almost entirely on their own beliefs and the preferences of their voters and their party," and that "contributions have no detectable effects on legislative behavior."

Truly corrupt legislators will, after all, be lured by the prospect of personal financial benefits, not merely holding office (since most legislators, at least at the congressional level, could make more money doing other things). Those on the recent who's-who list of corrupt politicians were all brought down by their love of money: Louisiana Democratic congressman William Jefferson was caught with $90,000 in bribe money stashed in his freezer; Ohio's Bob Ney enjoyed an all-expenses-paid golf outing in Scotland on the dime of disgraced lobbyist Jack Abramoff, and accepted thousands of dollars in gambling chips from a foreign businessman; California's Duke Cunningham solicited bribes and bought, among other things, a yacht; and Illinois governor Rod Blagojevich sought lucrative positions on corporate boards for himself and his wife. These politicians were corrupted by money and gifts given directly to them, not by funds provided to pay for pamphlets and ads.

Most legislators run for office because they have strong political beliefs, and they are surrounded most of their days by aides and constituents with similarly strong beliefs. On reflection, far from being counterintuitive, it seems only logical that legislators would not want to betray their political principles—or those of the electorate—for a campaign contribution. After all, votes—not dollars—are what ultimately get put into ballot boxes. And it would make little sense to anger one's constituents for a contribution that can only be used to try to win those constituents back.

By insisting that campaign contributions corrupt members of Congress and the legislative process despite the repeated failure of dozens of systematic studies to find any evidence of such corruption, reform advocates ask us to set aside important speech rights without proving the need for doing so. Their assumption that the sheer scope of campaign spending somehow proves that our system is corrupted simply has no basis in evidence—and fails entirely to keep political spending in perspective. Total political spending in the U.S. in 2008—for state, local, and federal races—amounted to approximately $4.5 billion. By comparison, the nation's largest single commercial advertiser, Proctor & Gamble, spent about $5 billion on advertising in the same year.

The second widely stated goal of "reform" is to promote political equality. Reformers argue that some people and organizations have more money to spend on political activity than others do, and that it is unfair to allow this discrepancy to give the wealthy a major advantage. But inequality is not unique to money: Some people have more time to devote to political activity, while others gain political influence because they have a special flair for organizing, speaking, or writing. It is not clear how political equality is enhanced when a Harvard law student can spend his summer volunteering on a campaign while a small-business owner must spend his working.

In the political arena, money is a means by which those who lack talents or other resources with direct political value are able to participate in politics beyond voting. It thus increases the number of people who are able to exert some form of political influence. Limitations on monetary contributions therefore elevate those with more free time—such as retirees and students—over those (like most working people) who have less time, but more money. Such regulation also favors people skilled in political advertising over those skilled in growing corn or building homes; it favors skilled writers over skilled plumbers; it favors those, such as athletes and entertainers, whose celebrity gives them a public megaphone over people like stockbrokers and investors, who lack a public platform for their views. And this is before we arrive at the influence of media and other elites. Under the rules established by the "reform" regime, editorial-page editors, columnists, and talk-show hosts may endorse candidates—but others may not pay to take out an ad of equal size or length to explicitly endorse their candidates.

Easing the restrictions on campaign contributions would not constrain any of these other forms of political support. Rather, allowing more contributions simply permits more people to participate in the system—thus diffusing influence, rather than concentrating it. Campaign-finance reform, then, actually *undermines* the effort to promote equal access to the political arena.

Campaign-finance reform hasn't succeeded in achieving various secondary goals often attributed to it, either. For example, the McCain-Feingold law included the "Stand by Your Ad" provision, which now requires candidates for federal office to state in each ad: "I'm So-and-So, and I approved this message." The idea was that forcing candidates to take direct responsibility for what they say would reduce negative advertising. Of course, it's worth questioning whether negative advertising *should* be reduced: As Bruce Felknor, the former head of the Fair Political Practices Committee, observed as far back as the 1970s, "without attention-grabbing, cogent, memorable negative campaigning almost no challenger can hope to win unless the incumbent has been found guilty of a heinous crime." But even leaving this question aside, the provision has failed miserably to curb negative campaigning. In 2008, for example, researchers at the University of Wisconsin found that more than 60% of Barack Obama's ads, and more than 70% of ads for John McCain—that great crusader for restoring integrity to our politics—were negative. Meanwhile, the required statement takes up almost 10% of every costly 30-second ad—reducing a candidate's ability to say anything of substance to voters.

Some also argue that reform will reduce the amount of time elected officials must spend fundraising, thus allowing them to devote more time to their official responsibilities. It turns out, though, that the campaign-finance regulations themselves are the primary reason for the extensive time spent fundraising. Raising large amounts of money in small contributions is much more time-consuming than raising fewer large contributions.

Given these circumstances, it is almost impossible to argue that campaign-finance reform has improved government. *Governing* magazine—in connection with the (pro-campaign finance reform) Pew Charitable Trusts—regularly ranks state governments on the quality of their management. In both of *Governing*'s last two studies, in 2005 and 2008, Utah and Virginia were ranked the best-governed states in the nation. Utah and Virginia also tied for first place in the first *Governing* survey, from 1999, and Utah ranked first in the second study in 2001. What do these two states have in common? Among other things, they appear on the short list of states that have no limits on campaign spending and contributions. Meanwhile, states such as Arizona and Maine—which have enacted full taxpayer financing of their state races—score unimpressive marks. In terms of management, *Governing* ranked Arizona in the middle of the pack, tied for 14th with 17 other states. Maine was ranked next to last—ahead of only New Hampshire. This alone does not prove an inverse relationship between campaign-finance laws and good governance, of course, but it does help to show the absence of a direct relationship. At the very least, campaign-finance restrictions do not seem to improve government.

As campaign-finance reform has failed to achieve its goals, it has also exacted serious costs. Studies have shown that political spending helps voters to learn about candidates, to locate them on the ideological spectrum, and to be better informed about issues and contests. Reducing the amount that may be spent, and constraining the ways it may be used, can thus hurt the quality of political discourse. More important, the laws involve serious restrictions on the exercise of fundamental rights.

RESTRICTING RIGHTS

For years, advocates of campaign-finance regulation have worked to establish a reputation as plucky underdogs: the nation's moral conscience, fighting the good fight against powerful special interests. They did this even as the leading reform groups spent some $200 million in the 1990s and early in this decade to pass the McCain-Feingold bill. In addition to liberal donors like the Pew Charitable Trusts, the Carnegie Foundation, and the Joyce Foundation, the groups' financial backers included several large corporations and firms, among them Bear Stearns, Philip Morris, and Enron. Yet somehow the reformers successfully branded their opponents as the purveyors and defenders of a corrupt system, bent on protecting it for personal gain. This gambit won the reformers some moral authority, which they wielded to great effect—making deep inroads with Congress, the press, and the public.

This is why the unexpected turn in the oral argument of the Citizens United case caused such a stir (and such concern among campaign-finance-reform advocates). Americans, like most free people, react with visceral disgust to the notion of banning books. It is seen as a fundamental violation of the freedom of speech and the open exchange of ideas. To equate campaign-finance reform with book-banning is to threaten the moral high ground of the case for campaign-finance limits. Ceding that high ground would be very costly for reformers, since their efforts have produced so little in the way of demonstrable results.

But there is simply no question that restricting the freedoms guaranteed in the Bill of Rights—no less than side-stepping the limits on government power established by the Constitution itself—is inseparable from the movement's goals. Restrictions on campaign contributions and spending affect core First Amendment freedoms of speech, press, and assembly. While the Supreme Court has quite correctly never held that "money is speech," it has recognized, equally correctly, that limiting political spending serves to limit speech (by restricting citizens' ability to deliver their political messages). In fact, only one of the 19 Supreme Court justices to serve in the past 30 years—John Paul Stevens—has ever argued that political campaign and expenditure limits should not be treated as First Amendment concerns. Those who doubt that basic constitutional rights are at stake should imagine how they would react if the Supreme Court were to interpret the free exercise clause as allowing the faithful to hold their religious beliefs, but not to spend money to rent a church hall, purchase hymnals, or engage in church missions. Presumably, the move would be seen as much more than a mere regulation of property.

These limits on expression do not affect only wealthy donors or prominent candidates. On the contrary: Groups without a broad base of support are the ones that rely most heavily on large donors to make their voices heard. Almost by definition, political minorities, newcomers, and outcasts will find it harder to reach enough people to raise the money they need through many small contributions. Their base of support is simply too narrow. One can analogize the process to that of raising capital in financial markets: If no investor could put more than $5,000 into a company, large-scale IPOs would become a thing of the past. Established companies might be able to raise large amounts of capital from tens of thousands of small investors, but capital-intensive start-ups would be doomed.

So it is with political entrepreneurs, who would get nowhere without large donors. In the 1990s, for example, large-scale spending by Ross Perot gave voice to millions of Americans who were concerned that the major parties were failing to address the national deficit. Perot's spending did not "drown out" ordinary citizens, but rather helped them to be heard. In 2004, early contributions from a few big donors to the Swift Boat Veterans for Truth allowed the group to get its message on the air at a time when the national media were ignoring it. Once the group's first ads were seen by the public, the organization was bombarded with hundreds of thousands of small donations—and of course millions more supported or were influenced by the group's message. Similarly, large contributions by George Soros to MoveOn.org gave the organization the ability to contact millions of Americans and develop one of the most phenomenal grassroots political machines in American history.

Not surprisingly, it is often upon the most authentically grassroots candidacies and campaigns that the burden of regulation weighs heaviest. For example, in 2006, a group of neighbors in the unincorporated community of Parker North, Colorado, joined together to fight annexation into the neighboring city of Parker. Because they printed yard signs, made copies of a flyer, and formed an e-mail discussion group, they were charged with operating as an unregistered political committee. Three years later, their case remains entangled in the courts. And when Mac Warren ran for Congress in Texas in 2000, he spent just $40,000 on his campaign—roughly half of it his own money. All of his campaign materials contained the name and address of his campaign committee. But two pieces of literature failed to contain the required notice that the literature was paid for by the committee—and for that omission, Warren's long-shot campaign was fined $1,000 by the Federal Election Commission.

Worse Than the Disease

As Madison understood, some people will always try to use government for their private aims. But with the Madisonian restraints on government rent-seeking largely discarded, campaign-finance regulation becomes a futile and misguided effort—one that, as Madison argued, is not only bound to fail, but also bound to make matters worse.

A classic example is the Tillman Act and its ban on corporate contributions. The law was easily evaded, it turns out, by having corporations make "expenditures" independently of campaigns, or by having executives make personal contributions reimbursed by their companies. And when the Tillman Act was extended to include unions in 1947, unions and corporations formed the first political action committees to collect contributions from members, shareholders, and managers to use for political purposes.

Later, when the Federal Election Campaign Act imposed dramatic contribution limits, parties and donors discovered "soft money"—unregulated contributions that could not be used directly for candidate advocacy, but could be used for "party-building" activities. Such party-building activities soon came to include "issue ads"—thinly veiled attacks on the opposition, or praise for one's own candidates—that stopped just short of urging people to vote for or against a candidate (instead typically ending with "Call Congressman John Doe, and tell him to support a better minimum wage for America's workers"). When the McCain-Feingold bill banned soft money, the parties—especially the Democrats—effectively farmed out many of their traditional functions to activist groups such as ACORN and MoveOn. When McCain-Feingold sought to restrain interest-group "issue ads" by prohibiting ads that mention a candidate from appearing within 60 days of an election, groups responded by running ads just outside the 60-day window. The National Rifle Association responded by launching its own satellite radio station to take advantage of the law's exception for broadcasters. Citizens United began to make movies.

Preventing this type of "circumvention" of the law has been a fixation of the "reform community" from the outset. Yet each effort has led to laws more restrictive of basic rights, more convoluted, and more detached from Madison's insights. Each effort also appears to be self-defeating, since the circumvention argument knows no bounds. As Madison would have appreciated, every time we close off one avenue of political participation, politically active Americans will turn to the next most effective legal means of carrying on their activity. That next most effective means will then become the loophole that must be closed.

This is how the Citizens United case found its way to the Supreme Court. When the case was reargued in September, solicitor general Elena Kagan—taking poor Malcolm Stewart's place at the podium—assured the Court that the government had never taken action against a book, and presumably never would. But in fact, after the election of 2004, the Federal Election Commission had conducted a two-year investigation of George Soros for failing to report as campaign expenditures the costs of distributing an anti-Bush book. The agency ultimately voted not to prosecute, but its authority to do so was never in question. And Kagan did not back away from the government's position that it had the authority to ban books should they, at some point, become a problem.

As the Supreme Court ponders whether campaign-finance restrictions assault Americans' First Amendment rights, academic champions of such "reform" efforts are laying the groundwork for yet more regulation. Legal scholars such as Harvard's Mark Tushnet, Ohio State's Ned Foley, and Loyola Law School's Richard Hasen—publisher of the "Election Law Blog"—have all argued that true reform will require open censorship of the press in order to assure political equality. Yale law professor Owen Fiss has argued that "we may sometimes find it necessary to 'restrict the speech of some elements of our society in order to enhance the relative voice of others,' and that unless the [Supreme] Court allows, and sometimes even requires the state to do so, we as a people will never truly be free."

Until *Citizens United*, such Orwellian newspeak was largely buried in obscure academic journals. Malcolm Stewart's sin was to state openly the implications of campaign-finance reform—and, in doing so, to strip away the veneer of "good government" and moral authority so carefully cultivated by reform advocates (and so important to their power). As a result, Stewart might have launched the beginning of the end for America's failed experiment to limit factions by destroying the liberty that allows for them in the first place. When the Supreme Court decides the case, it will have the opportunity to reassert the wisdom of Madison's deep insight into human nature—and to protect those liberties that, while they may make factions possible, also define the republic designed to contain them.

*Bradley A. Smith is the Josiah H. Blackmore II / Shirley M. Nault Designated Professor of Law at Capital University Law School in Columbus, Ohio, and chairman of the Center for Competitive Politics. He served on the Federal Election Commission from 2000 to 2005.

Bradley A. Smith. "The Myth of Campaign Finance Reform." *National Affairs*, Winter 2010. Copyright 2009. All rights reserved. See www.NationalAffairs.com for more information.

DISCUSSION QUESTIONS

1. Smith argues that "the effect of campaign-finance regulations has been to help the people who passed them and to strengthen special interests." Is this always the case? Can the government restrict election speech and expenditures without taking sides?

2. Smith contends that there is no evidence that campaign contributions corrupt legislators or influence their voting—and most political science literature backs him up on this point. Why is it so hard to find any link between campaign contributions and legislators' actions in office?

3. Is it fair for Smith to equate money with political skill, celebrity, or other resources that candidates can draw upon?

Part 2:
Campaign Finance Law and American Federal Elections

This section begins with a look at the most basic decision in campaign finance, the decision by individuals to contribute. The section then moves to a consideration of the decisions of interest groups to spend money, and it then looks at the ways in which American presidential and congressional candidates raise money. Taken collectively, these four articles provide a snapshot of American politics in the years between the passage of the Bipartisan Campaign Reform Act and the Supreme Court's *Citizens United* decision striking down part of that act. These articles do not all reference the Bipartisan Campaign Reform Act or *Citizens United*, but they show the effects of legal change as well as the effects of technological change and the fund-raising innovations of individual politicians. In contrast to the pieces in Part 1, these articles are primarily descriptive in nature. They should, however, provide enough context for the reader to measure the successes and failures of past reform laws and to consider the effects future reforms might have on the American political system.

It is difficult to identify the incentives of those who contribute to political candidates. Few Americans make campaign contributions at all, so public opinion data is of limited use. One approach to this problem is shown in Bertram Johnson's piece. In his article, Johnson compares the size and sources of contributions to different types of members of Congress. Johnson concludes that ideologically extreme members of Congress tend to raise a greater percentage of their money in small individual contributions, while more centrist members and members with more power in Congress tend to rely more on large individual contributions and on contributions from organized interests. These findings correspond to observations many have made about the fund-raising success of insurgent left-wing candidates such as 2004 Democratic presidential candidate Howard Dean and of conservative candidates such as 2008 Republican candidate Ron Paul, and, before him, Virginia Senate candidate Oliver North. Such findings also have direct bearing upon the ideological polarization that has developed within Congress over the past 30 years. Although Johnson stops short of linking his findings to campaign finance reforms, his conclusions raise a host of questions about the wisdom of raising or lowering contribution limits, the growth of the Internet as fund-raising tool, and restrictions on the ability of groups to contribute to candidates.

There has been little consensus regarding how the Bipartisan Campaign Reform Act has influenced the activities of organized interests over the past decade, and there has been even less consensus about how much the Supreme Court's *Citizens United* decision will affect the role of interest groups in elections. Michael Franz, the author of several studies of interest groups' advertising expenditures, argues here that many commonly voiced concerns about interest-group influence in elections have not come to pass. Instead of worrying about interest groups' activities in elections, Franz argues, we should concern ourselves with interest groups' lobbying expenditures, which are far larger and fall outside the purview of most campaign finance regulations. This piece was originally published in 2009; the author has revised it to include data on interest groups' contributions and independent expenditures in the 2010 election.

The chapter here on "networked campaigns" is excerpted from a report co-written by Anthony J. Corrado, Michael J. Malbin, Thomas E. Mann, and Norman J. Ornstein, members of three highly regarded Washington, D.C.–based public policy institutes—the Campaign Finance Institute, the Brookings Institution, and the American Enterprise Institute. Even before Barack Obama's record-setting fund-raising in the 2008 presidential election, several of these authors had been predicting that new communications technology was rapidly making many issues in the American campaign finance debate obsolete. In this article, the authors place the Obama presidential campaign into historical context—they show how Obama's fund-raising success was both a refinement of techniques used by previous candidates and a savvy use of new communications methods. They argue that many of the features of the Obama campaign that allowed him to raise so much money may be difficult to replicate, but that the campaign has at least opened up the possibility that we should be more concerned about encouraging small donations than about limiting overall spending.

Finally, while many analyses of campaign finance look at the motives of contributors, one of the biggest changes in the past several decades in American politics has been the increased effort by politicians to raise money. As Marian Currinder describes matters, money is not merely a necessity for winning office, but also a necessity for ambitious members of Congress seeking to gain power within the House or Senate. Because control of the House and Senate has been at stake in most elections since the early 1990s, both the Democrats and Republicans have sought to spread money around from safe districts to competitive ones. For decades, many students of Congress have argued that the need to raise funds tended to interfere with the ability of Congress to legislate; in recent years, some have also alleged that the need to raise money increases polarization between the parties and privileges the sorts of politicians who are best at raising money—politicians who are not necessarily the best legislators. Currinder's history of congressional fund-raising shows how these perceptions have arisen.

Individual Contributions: A Fundraising Advantage for the Ideologically Extreme?

by Bertram Johnson

Does ideological extremism give some candidates a fundraising advantage? If so, the advantage could appear in one of two ways: first, extreme candidates might do better than other candidates in the aggregate, raising more funds than their moderate peers; or second, extreme candidates might focus their fundraising efforts on extremist contributors, raising a greater proportion of money from them, even as they raise similar aggregate amounts as other candidates. Previous research has found no evidence that the first possibility is true. In this article, I present evidence that supports the second.

Candidates with policy positions outside the mainstream sometimes seem to thrive by raising money from enthusiastic individual contributors. Libertarian Republican Ron Paul took in $34 million in the 2008 Republican primaries, even as voters shunned him in favor of his rivals. Howard Dean's 2004 presidential campaign—characterized by antiwar positions that were unusual at the time—set records in collecting small individual contributions over the Internet.

There is an intuitively pleasing explanation for cases like these. People who are passionate about issues are more likely to take extreme positions than those who do not care much, and the passionate are more likely to become active in politics than others. Contributions from individuals, therefore (especially the smaller ones, which are too individually insignificant to buy any material rewards), are likely to come from extremists. As a result, extremist candidates will be more successful than moderates at raising money from small individual donors.

But there has thus far been little systematic evidence that candidates such as Ron Paul and Howard Dean are representative of any broader phenomenon. Moderate and extreme members of Congress raise similar amounts of money. Does candidate ideology have nothing to do with fundraising?

I propose that the equivalent aggregate amounts raised by extreme and moderate candidates mask very different donor coalitions. Candidates for office, like other people who organize for collective action, must offer their contributors selective incentives for working for the collective good (in this case, election victory). But different members of Congress are in positions to offer different types of incentives. A seasoned committee chair may provide her contributors with access, whereas a freshman representative with little clout in the chamber is better off catering to his donors' ideological concerns. The committee chair might rely on a small group of wealthier Washingtonians, each of whom can donate the maximum $2,400 to the campaign, whereas the freshman might have to raise funds in increments of $100 or less. Both may raise the same amount of money, but each has chosen a different fundraising strategy.

If extremism affects fundraising this way, the consequences for representation are more narrowly focused, but still significant. Junior members of Congress or those without a network of wealthy connections may find that it pays to be outside the mainstream. A sizeable group of representatives may feel pressured to cater to a passionate minority in order to remain competitive.

I test for this possibility by examining data on House campaigns from 1984 to 2004. I use a multilevel model to predict the proportion of incumbents' funds that come from individuals—and from small individual contributions in particular. More extreme incumbents collect a greater proportion of their funds from individual contributions—funds that are more likely to be given by ideologically motivated (rather than access-motivated) contributors. For individual contributions of all amounts, this phenomenon appears to be stable over time. For the smallest contributions—those below $200—there appears to be a closer relationship between contributions and extremism in recent years, suggesting that new fundraising technologies may have made it easier to appeal to small contributors.

POLARIZATION AND CAMPAIGN CONTRIBUTIONS

Politicians take more extreme positions on issues than do members of the general public (Fiorina, Abrams, & Pope, 2006; Jacobson, 2007; McCarty, Poole, & Rosenthal, 2006). One common explanation for why this is the case is that campaign contributors are passionate liberals or conservatives, and their concerns therefore shape candidate concerns. If a candidate slips toward moderation, contributors lose interest and go elsewhere. The "purists," as Fiorina puts it, who are more likely to contribute, therefore hold more sway with candidates (Fiorina et al., 2006, p. 191). Schier (2000) argues that restrictive campaign finance regulations have exacerbated the problem (see also Smith, 2001):

> National campaign finance law limits the amounts individuals and
> political action committees (PACs) can contribute, so candidates must

constantly scrape up new funds from new people, rather than relying on a few "fat cat" supporters or party coffers as they did in the old days. This need for contributors further empowers the more ideologically extreme partisan elites. (Schier, 2000, p. 93)

Contributors do appear to be more extreme than the general population. According to National Election Studies data, only around 10% of U.S. adults contribute to campaigns, and these people—like other activists—are likely to be idealists who are motivated primarily by ideological appeals (Fiorina, 2002). Francia, Green, Herrnson, Powell, and Wilcox (2003) found that 69% of individual contributors surveyed said a candidate's liberalism or conservatism was "always important" in making their decision to contribute—a consideration that ranked higher than partisanship, closeness of the race, and individual business and professional interests (Francia et al., 2003, p. 46).

Individuals who donate small amounts appear to be less materially self-interested and more ideologically motivated than those who donate more. The Institute for Politics Democracy & the Internet found in 2004, for example, that the larger donors surveyed were more likely to donate for reasons concerning their own companies or careers, whereas the smaller donors more often mentioned issue positions or that "the candidate's opponent is unacceptable" (Institute for Politics Democracy & the Internet, 2006).

Faced with this pool of donors, it seems natural that candidates with more extreme ideological positions should thrive, and more moderate candidates should find it difficult to mount effective campaigns. Congressional patterns of polarization are consistent with this supposition, with members of Congress becoming increasingly more extreme since the 1970s, when new campaign regulations made it tougher for candidates to raise money in large sums from a few (materially self-interested) people or organizations.

But this evidence is circumstantial. Systematic tests of whether campaign finance links extremist activists to extremist candidates have thus far not established such a connection. A second set of surveys of individual contributors, including an impressive ongoing effort by the Campaign Finance Institute, have found that small individual contributors to state-level campaigns are no more ideologically extreme than are other contributors (Joe, Malbin, Wilcox, Brusoe, & Pimlott, 2008). Similarly, Francia et al. (2003) find little difference in partisanship between contributors and the rest of the population.

Other studies that do not rely on survey data have also found no connection between candidate extremism and fundraising success. One of the most creative such efforts was conducted by McCarty et al. (2006), using their Nominate ideological scores for incumbent members of Congress. Restricting their contributor sample to people who have donated to at least eight different members of Congress, they calculate the mean and standard deviation of the Nominate score of the recipients of each contributor's funding.[1] Access-oriented contributors—caring little about ideology—should have a mean somewhere in the middle of the ideological spectrum and a large standard deviation; ideologically motivated contributors should have an off-center mean and a small standard deviation. Using this method, the authors show that the number of extremist contributors is significant and grew substantially between 1982 and 2002 (McCarty et al., 2006, chap. 5).

The growing number of extreme contributors does not appear to have affected candidate fundraising, however. Ideologically extreme candidates do not collect more money than other candidates do—not even if we leave out PACs and focus on individual contribution totals alone. Figure 1 confirms McCarty et al.'s (2006) analysis of this point. The horizontal axis represents extremism calculated as a member of Congress's distance from the median Nominate score for his or her Congress. The vertical axis is the natural logarithm of the total amount of money raised from individuals in constant 2004 dollars.[2] The lowess

Figure 1. Logarithm of total receipts 1984-2004 by ideology, with lowess smoother

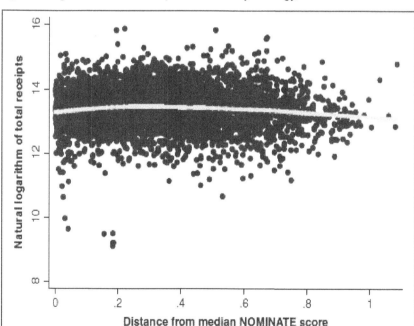

line of best fit is essentially flat, suggesting that extremist incumbents raise about as much total money from individuals as do moderates. McCarty et al. suggest that any gains from being extreme are offset by losses among the "access-oriented" contributors, for whom extremists are distasteful.

Political scientists and policymakers could be forgiven for discounting the importance of the growing number of extremist contributors if these contributors are not affecting the way candidates run their campaigns. Do extremist contributors really have no effect, or might they still be changing how candidates campaign in ways that are not visible in the aggregate analysis?

SELECTIVE INCENTIVES AND FUNDRAISING STRATEGIES

I propose that the effects of contributor extremism may be dependent on candidates' fundraising strategies, which in turn depend on candidates' relative abilities to provide contributors with what they want. Candidates for office are like interest group organizers: They must convince a large group of people to take action in pursuit of a collective good, even if it is not strictly in anyone's self-interest to contribute (Olson, 1965). To solve this problem, organizers typically offer selective incentives that can take the form of material benefits, social rewards, or "purposive" ideological gratification (Wilson, 1973).

Francia et al. (2003) confirm via survey data that campaign contributors give money to candidates for varied reasons: "Investors" seek material benefits, "intimates" enjoy socializing with other political activists, and "ideologues" are motivated by issues and ideology. Like other organizers, candidates are likely to try to do their best to match each contributor with an appropriate selective incentive.[3]

Not all candidates are equal, however. Senior members of Congress and committee chairmen are in positions that make "access" more valuable and therefore make material benefits easier to confer. These officeholders have a comparative advantage in pursuing contributions from materially oriented givers. Newer members of Congress, nonincumbents, and those without key committee positions are less able to credibly offer material incentives and may not be as successful in attracting this type of contributor. Similarly, an outspoken liberal or conservative member of Congress has a comparative advantage over moderates in seeking purposive contributions. Among liberals who care deeply about issues, it is more satisfying to contribute to Russ Feingold than to Joe Lieberman, for example.

Similar fundraising totals may therefore mask very different donor coalitions.

If there is a sizeable number of candidates for who pursuing purposive contributors is a relatively advantageous strategy, extremist contributions may have a significant effect on campaigns and elections.

The analysis that follows depends on one final point about the difference between materially oriented and purposive contributors: Individual contributions (as opposed to PACs) and smaller contributions (as opposed to larger ones) should be likely to come disproportionately from purposive contributors. Studies of PACs find that they mostly give for access rather than for ideological reasons (see, e.g., Franz, 2008; Grier & Munger, 1993). Survey data (cited above) shows that small donors are more likely to cite issues or ideology than are larger donors.

Larger contributors and PACs may also contribute for ideological reasons—indeed, research by McCarty et al. (2006; for individuals) and Franz (2008; for PACs) confirms that they sometimes do—but smaller individual contributions are likely to be more concerned with ideology than larger individual contributors, who in turn are likely to be more concerned with ideology than PACs. At the extreme, materially oriented givers are unlikely to contribute small amounts for two reasons.[4] First, candidates are less likely to take note of the identity of small contributors because the Federal Election Commission (FEC) does not require campaigns to collect detailed information about them. Second, contributors may reasonably assume that larger contributions may result in a greater chance of access than small contributions.

In summary, junior members of Congress without positions of authority within the chamber are likely to have a comparative advantage in gathering purposive, as opposed to materially oriented contributions. Smaller contributions are more likely to be purposive than larger contributions. Therefore, for these members, a larger proportion of funds ought to come from small individual contributors. More senior members of Congress are likely to have a comparative advantage in soliciting access-oriented contributors and will be more likely to rely on larger contributions for the bulk of their fundraising. Therefore, even if both types of representatives raise the same aggregate amount of money, the interplay of ideology and campaign finance may affect campaign fundraising.

DATA ANALYSIS

To test this hypothesis, I rely on pooled data from 1984 to 2004 on the proportion of funds incumbent members of Congress raise from individuals and, in particular, from small individual contributions. [...]

The key independent variable in this analysis is a "folded" first dimension DWNominate score (Poole & Rosenthal, 1997). Based on Poole and Rosenthal's exhaustive analysis of Congressional voting patterns, the first dimension DWNominate score represents an incumbent's position on a liberal–conservative continuum. I transform this variable simply by calculating an incumbent's distance from the median value of this score for the Congress in which he or she is serving. The resulting measure varies between 0 and 1.09 in the period studied; the closer to zero it is, the less extreme (or more moderate) the representative relative to the median.[5]

The use of the DWNominate score as the critical independent variable in the analysis that follows restricts the cases to incumbents running for reelection. [...]

A second set of independent variables measures other factors that might affect an incumbent's comparative advantage in raising money from different sources. I include dichotomous variables indicating whether a representative sits on any of the five committees most often cited as being "power" committees in the House: Appropriations, Ways and Means, Commerce, Budget, and Rules. An incumbent on one of these committees may have a comparative advantage in PAC fundraising and therefore may raise a smaller proportion of funds from individuals. The number of years that a candidate has spent in office is included to provide a measure of a member's seniority, a factor that may also make it relatively easier for a member to attract contributions from access-seeking PACs. Finally, I include the logarithm of the median income in the district (as recorded in the 1990 census).[6] Candidates from poorer districts may find it more difficult to raise the same proportion of their funds from individuals, because those with little money are less likely to donate (Verba, Schlozman, & Brady, 1995).

Other independent variables represent other factors that might affect an incumbent's fundraising calculations. A dummy variable that equals 1 if a candidate is a Democrat accounts for possible partisan differences in fundraising patterns. A dichotomous indicator accounts for the (rare) instances in which incumbents are defeated in primaries. I also control for two variables that serve as proxies for an incumbent's assessment of how much total money he or she will need to raise: first, the (logarithm of) the incumbent's total receipts for the campaign and second, the percentage of the vote that the incumbent receives in the general election. The lower the percentage the more likely an incumbent will fundraise vigorously to avoid defeat. In high-cost, highly competitive races, it is possible that incumbents may alter their fundraising strategies as they go beyond their traditional donor coalitions.[7]

[...]

Table 1 reports the results of two multilevel models predicting the proportion of funds that candidates raise from individuals. The first column reports results of a model predicting the proportion of total funds raised from all individual contributions of any amount; the second column represents a model predicting the proportion of total funds raised from small individual contributions (those below $200—an FEC threshold for itemized reporting).[8] Candidates with more extreme ideologies (as measured by their distance from the median DWNominate score) do in fact raise a greater proportion of their funds from individuals. On average, varying ideology from the median member of Congress to the most extreme can be expected to increase the proportion of funds raised from individuals by $(.13) \times (1.09) = .14$ (holding all else equal). For the average incumbent in the data set, who spent about $800,000 in 2004 dollars, this represents a shift of more than $113,000 in funds raised. Figuring the effect more modestly, even a shift in extremism from the congressional median to the third quartile affects about $67,000 of fundraising for the average incumbent. Focusing only on small individual contributions—those below $200—a shift from least to most extreme results in a shift in the source of $69,000, and changing from the chamber median to the third quartile affects about $33,000. These results are consistent with the hypothesis that more extreme incumbents have a comparative advantage in raising funds from individuals and therefore focus their efforts more on individual fundraising.

The comparative advantage hypothesis is also supported by the effects of other key variables on individual fundraising. Membership on three out of the five "power committees" is predicted to have a negative effect on overall individual fundraising. In the case of the Ways and Means and Commerce committees, these effects are large and statistically significant. This is consistent with the hypothesis that the members of these committees find it relatively easier to raise money from PACs and therefore focus less on fundraising from individuals. Similarly, the district's median income affects individual fundraising positively, as predicted. Members from wealthier districts apparently find it easier to raise money from individual contributors. A member's seniority appears not to matter independently of one's committee assignments.

Democrats raise a smaller fraction of their funds from individuals than do Republicans, a fact that may be the result of consistently high support for Democrats among labor PACs. A primary loss and a high amount of total receipts positively affect the proportion raised from individuals as a whole but not from small contributors in particular. Finally, the incumbent's percentage of the vote in the general election has no significant effect on whether funds come from individual or nonindividual sources.

Table I. The Effect of Extremism on the Proportion of Funds Raised From Individuals; Multilevel Models

Independent Variables	Dependent Variables	
	Proportion of Funds Raised From All Individuals	Proportion Raised From Individuals Giving Under $200
Extremism (distance from median dimension I DWNominate score)	.13 (.02)	.08 (.02)
Appropriations committee member	.02 (.01)	−.01 (.01)
Ways and Means committee member	−.09 (.01)	−.02 (.01)
Commerce committee member	−.07 (.01)	−.02 (.01)
Budget committee member	.02 (.01)	.00 (.00)
Rules committee member	−.03 (.02)	−.01 (.01)
Years in office	.00 (.00)	.00 (.00)
Ln(District median income)	.04 (.01)	.01 (.01)
Democrat	−.07 (.01)	−.06 (.01)
Lost primary	.06 (.02)	−.01 (.01)
Ln(total receipts)	.07 (.00)	.00 (.00)
Percent of vote in general election	.00 (.00)	.00 (.00)
Intercept	−.81 (.13)	.11 (.13)
Standard deviation for member intercepts ($\sigma_{\alpha j}$)	.12	.09
Standard deviation for state intercepts ($\sigma_{\alpha k}$)	.05	.02
Standard deviation for state slopes (σ_{Bk})	.09	.07
Group correlation parameter for states (ρ_k)	−.58	−.18
Standard deviation for election cycle intercepts ($\sigma_{\alpha l}$)	.02	.04
Standard deviation for election cycle slopes (σ_{Bl})	.04	.03
Group correlation parameter for election cycles (ρ_l)	−.69	−.89
Residual	.08	.06
Deviance	−7058.0	−7188.2
Total observations	4,364	3,153
Members of Congress	1,022	879
States	50	50
Election cycles	11	8

Note: Standard errors in parentheses.

One of the advantages of a multilevel model is that it enables us to examine separate (partial pooling) estimates for individual groups. In this case, this allows us to compare states and cycles. Figures 2 and 3 show the predicted effects of extremism for the six states in which the effect of extremism on the proportion of individual funds raised is the smallest (Figure 2) and the six states in which the effect is the largest (Figure 3).[9] In only one state, Utah, is the effect of extremism on individual fundraising predicted to be (slightly) negative. In all other states, the slope for the extremism variable is positive. In the six states pictured in Figure 3, the predicted coefficient for extremism is .21 or higher, indicating that for an incumbent spending $800,000, the most moderate incumbent is predicted to raise about $85,000 less from individuals (and more from other sources) than an incumbent at the third quartile. The pattern of state-level effects of extremism appears that it may be related to party organization. Of the six states with the largest predicted effects of extremism, four (Illinois, Louisiana, West Virginia, and New York) have been found to have historically powerful party organizations (see, e.g., Mayhew, 1986). The other two, Minnesota and Washington, have strong caucus systems that reward grassroots mobilization. The interaction between party activity and candidate fundraising would appear to offer fertile ground for future analysis.

An examination of the predicted effects of extremism by cycle provides a test of whether fundraising patterns have changed systematically over time. In particular, the Internet may have lowered the costs of raising money from individuals for all candidates (in which case the intercepts should increase over time), or it may have disproportionately advantaged extreme candidates by making it easier to reach out to ideologically polarized contributors (in which case the slopes should increase over time). Figure 4 graphs the predicted effects of extremism on the amount raised from individual contributions as a whole for all cycles in the analysis. There appears to be no particular pattern in the slopes or intercepts that would indicate a trend over time. Figure 5, however, graphs the predicted effects of extremism on the proportion raised in the smallest amounts (below $200). Here, there appears to have been a change in slope since 1996. The average coefficient for extremism prior to 1998 was .066. From 1998 to 2004, however, it was .10, with the largest coefficients (.11 and .12) appearing in the last two election cycles. The evidence is not definitive, but it is possible that the effect of extremism on fundraising from the smallest contributors has grown since the advent of the Internet and other new technologies in the late 1990s.

Figure 2. Estimated effects of extremism on fundraising by state, smallest slopes

(Republicans are higher lines, Democrats are lower lines)

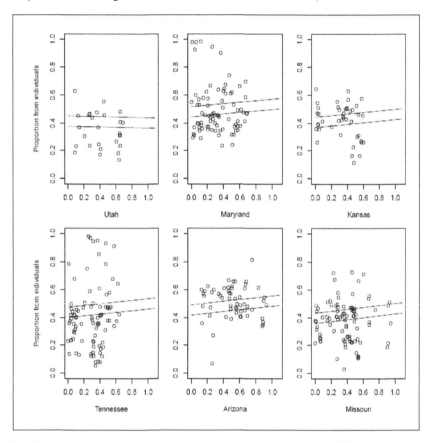

Note: X-axis in all graphs is "extremism" as operationalized with the first dimension DWNominate score (Poole & Rosenthal, 1997), folded at the chamber median.

Figure 3. Estimated effects of extremism on fundraising by state, largest slopes
(Republicans are higher lines; Democrats lower lines)

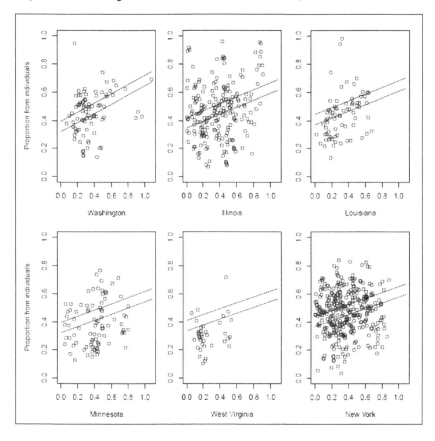

Note: X-axis in all graphs is "extremism" as operationalized with the first dimension DWNominate score (Poole & Rosenthal, 1997), folded at the chamber median.

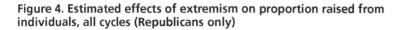

Figure 4. Estimated effects of extremism on proportion raised from individuals, all cycles (Republicans only)

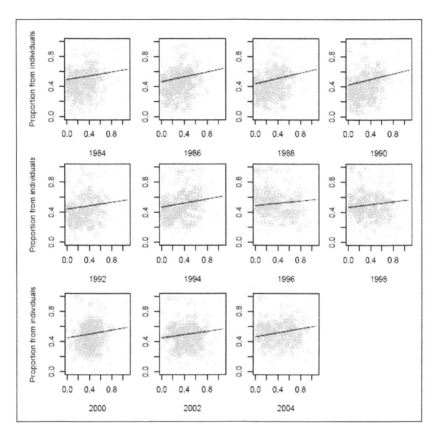

Figure 5. Estimated effects of extremism on proportion raised from small (<$200) contributions, by election cycle (Republicans only)

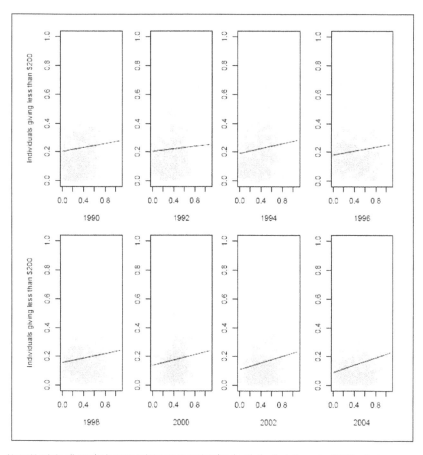

Note: X-axis in all graphs is "extremism" as operationalized with the first dimension DWNominate score (Poole & Rosenthal, 1997), folded at the chamber median.

DISCUSSION

The data presented above suggest that there is indeed a connection between candidate extremism and fundraising. Those who are less centrist are more appealing to a particular population of individual donors who, I have argued, are likely to be motivated by purposive incentives. At least three issues merit further discussion here and suggest avenues for future research.

First, are nonindividual donors shying away from ideologues? The above analysis focuses on individual contributions *as a proportion of all campaign receipts*. The dependent variable—this proportion—may change as a result of two factors. Individuals may increase or decrease their contributions, or *other* donors—PACs, for example—may increase or decrease their contributions. Could an increase in the proportion of receipts coming from individuals in fact be a decrease in contributions from PACs and parties? The distinctive patterns we observe here make it likely that being in a seat of power in Congress is a comparative advantage with PACs rather than that extremism makes it tougher to raise money from these organizations. In general, a seat on a power committee decreases the proportion of funds a member of Congress collects from individuals, suggesting that these members of Congress find fertile fundraising ground among Washington interest groups.

Second, has there been a change in the campaign finance regime in the period from 1998 to the present? National Election Studies data show that the number of (reported) individual contributors has increased dramatically in the last 10 years, so it is plausible that the effects of extremism on individual contributors have increased in the most recent cycles. New technology has reduced the cost of reaching potential donors. A few mouse clicks can now direct a donation to a candidate of one's choice. This may have made individual contributors more attractive as a fundraising option compared with PAC contributors, many of whom prefer to meet with candidates in person (Clawson, Neustadtl, & Weller, 1998). It has also become easier for potential contributors to track the statements, actions, and positions of candidates, allowing for more precise matches between candidate and contributor. If this is the case, the link between ideology and individual contributions could become even stronger in the future. Data on the most recent election cycles support this argument—at least for the smallest contributions.

Does ideological extremism help some candidates raise money? Based on the data presented here, the answer is a qualified "yes." An incumbent's ideological extremism improves his or her chances of raising a greater proportion of funds from individual donors in general and small individual contributors in particular. Extremism is not the only way to raise money—on the contrary, there are many members of Congress who rely on other sources of funding, such as "access-oriented" individual contributions, PAC funds, party campaign funds, and so on. But to some legislators, extremism is an advantage.

ACKNOWLEDGMENTS

I thank Matt Dickinson, Robert Van Houweling, Jeff Stauch, Steven Schier, Chris McGrory-Klyza, and anonymous reviewers for feedback that improved this article. I also thank Nick Campofranco for research assistance.

ENDNOTES

1. They weight these calculations by the dollar value of each contribution.

2. If each individual election cycle is considered in isolation, the pattern is the same.

3. To the extent possible within the law, of course.

4. A good definition of "small amount" is "below $200." This is because the FEC establishes that level as the threshold above which candidates must itemize contributions.

5. An objection to this approach might be that potential contributors care less about a member's extremism relative to other members of Congress than about a member's extremism relative to his or her district. One way to test for this would be to allow both slopes and intercepts for the "extremism" variable to vary by district (as opposed to the models reported, where only intercepts vary by district). In such a model (results not shown) the main effect for extremism is nearly identical (coefficient = .12, standard error = .02).

6. I use E. Scott Adler's Congressional District Data (available at http://sobek.colorado. edu/~esadler/Data.html) for these figures and thank him for making his data publicly available.

7. One objection to this approach might be that in including variables measured after the fundraising takes place, I inappropriately include causal variables that "occur" after my dependent variable occurs. In alternative models (not reported), I substituted lagged vote percentages and logged campaign expenditures from the previous election cycle. The substantive results in these models were the same as in the models reported here. Lagging variables results in a loss of a significant number of cases, however, so I report results from the unlagged models.

8. FEC data do not report the breakdown between above-$200 contributions and below-$200 contributions prior to 1990. The analysis of sub-$200 contributions therefore omits the earlier cycles.

9. All these figures show the effects for members of Congress who do not sit on a power committee, and all other variables are held at their means or modes.

REFERENCES

Clawson, D., Neustadtl, A., & Weller, M. (1998). *Dollars and votes: How business campaign contributions subvert democracy*. Philadelphia: Temple University Press.

Fiorina, M. P. (2002). Parties, participation, and representation in America: Old theories face new realities. In I. Katznelson & H. V. Milner (Eds.), *Political science: The state of the discipline* (pp. 511-541). New York: W. W. Norton.

Fiorina, M. P., Abrams, S. J., & Pope, J. C. (2006). *Culture war? The myth of a polarized America*. New York: Pearson Longman.

Francia, P. L., Green, J. C., Herrnson, P. S., Powell, L. W., & Wilcox, C. (2003). *The financiers of Congressional elections: Investors, ideologues, and intimates*. New York: Columbia University Press.

Franz, M. M. (2008). *Choices and changes: Interest groups in the electoral process*. Philadelphia: Temple University Press.

[...]

Grier, K. B., & Munger, M. C. (1993). Comparing interest group PAC contributions to house and senate incumbents, 1980-1986. *Journal of Politics, 55*, 615-643.

Institute for Politics Democracy & the Internet. (2006). *Small donors and online giving: A study of donors to the 2004 presidential campaigns.* Retrieved November 10, 2009, from http://www.ipdi.org/UploadedFiles/Small%20Donors%20Report.pdf.

Jacobson, G. C. (2007). *A divider, not a uniter: George W. Bush and the American people.* New York: Pearson Longman.

Joe, W. Y., Malbin, M. J., Wilcox, C., Brusoe, P. W., & Pimlott, J. (2008, April). *Who are the individual donors to gubernatorial and state legislative elections?* Paper presented at the 2008 Annual Meeting of the Midwest Political Science Association, Chicago.

Mayhew, D. R. (1986). *Placing parties in American politics: Organization, electoral settings, and government activity in the twentieth century.* Princeton, NJ: Princeton University Press.

McCarty, N., Poole, K. T., & Rosenthal, H. (2006). *Polarized America: The dance of ideology and unequal riches.* Cambridge: MIT Press.

Olson, M. (1965). *The logic of collective action: Public goods and the theory of groups.* Cambridge, MA: Harvard University Press.

Poole, K. T., & Rosenthal, H. (1997). *Congress: A political-economic history of roll call voting.* New York: Oxford University Press.

Schier, S. E. (2000). *By invitation only: The rise of exclusive politics in the United States.* Pittsburgh, PA: University of Pittsburgh Press.

Smith, B. A. (2001). *Unfree speech: The folly of campaign finance reform.* Princeton, NJ: Princeton University Press.

Verba, S., Schlozman, K. L., & Brady, H. E. (1995). *Voice and equality: Civic voluntarism in American politics.* Cambridge, MA: Harvard University Press.

Wilson, J. Q. (1973). *Political organizations.* New York: Basic Books.

*Bertram Johnson is an associate professor of political science at Middlebury College. His research interests include campaign finance and intergovernmental relations.

Bertram Johnson. "Individual Contributors: A Fundraising Advantage for the Ideologically Extreme?" *American Politics Research* 38 (5): 890–908, copyright © 2010, SAGE Publications.

DISCUSSION QUESTIONS

1. Do Johnson's conclusions suggest that contribution limits should be raised or lowered? What would the consequences of changing contribution limits be?

2. Do Johnson's conclusions suggest that limits on what organized interests can give should be changed?

3. Are there candidate characteristics other than ideology that might lead to success at raising money in small increments?

4. To what extent do Johnson's findings reflect the increasing role of the Internet in candidate fundraising?

The Interest Group Response to Campaign Finance Reform

*by Michael M. Franz**

Political scientist Marc Petracca observed in 1992 that scholars of interest groups often discuss changes in interest group politics as "explosions" (1992, 11–13). He noted this pattern before interest groups in the 1990s expanded their presence in American politics even further with soft-money party donations and with issue advocacy television ads. If interest groups "exploded" in the 1960s with their lobbying and advocacy, however, they surely went nuclear in the 1990s. Outside-group electioneering was so powerful a presence in the elections of 1994–2002 that Congress in 2002 was compelled to pass the first major campaign finance reform in a generation, the Bipartisan Campaign Reform Act (BCRA). The *New York Times* declared its passage "a victory for all Americans" (editorial, A36, March 21, 2002).

There were really two main concerns about interest groups that were addressed in BCRA: soft-money contributions by interest groups to non–federal party accounts, and issue advocacy advertisements by interest groups that featured federal candidates but avoided "magic words." So-called magic words were first established in a footnote in the Supreme Court's 1976 decision in *Buckley v. Valeo*. The court listed eight phrases that it believed clearly established an election message. These magic words are "vote for," "elect," "support," "cast your ballot for," "Smith for Congress," "vote against," "defeat," or "reject." By the 1990s, the presence of these words had developed into the legal bright line between regulated election ads (subject to restrictions on funding) and non-regulated issue ads.

BCRA eliminated the first concern with a near-complete ban on soft money for parties and attempted to handle the second with the establishment of the "electioneering communication." This category of election-related message (presumably) mandated that any interest-group ad aired within 60 days of a general election or 30 days of a primary *and* that featured or pictured a candidate for federal office be paid with hard-money dollars out of a regulated PAC account. PACs are committees most often formed by corporations and unions to collect regulated contributions from employees or members to be spent on federal electoral activity.[1]

As with all things campaign finance, however, these developments were merely prologue to yet another chapter in the "explosion" narrative. By 2004, the so-called 527s were nearly a household name (and a four-letter word to boot), and by 2010 (after two controversial decisions in *Federal Election Commission v. Wisconsin Right to Life* and *Citizens United v. Federal Election Commission*), the Supreme Court seemed intent on dismantling most of the BCRA regime (Hasen 2008). This raises the question posed here: Has BCRA failed relative to interest groups? More broadly, what's next in the realm of interest-group electioneering?

I begin with a discussion of soft-money contributions by interest groups, considering more broadly the role of interest groups as investors in parties and candidates. I then examine the nature and extent of issue-advocacy campaigns. In this second discussion, I wish to consider the possibility that concerns over interest groups as issue advocates may be misplaced. Even after the Court's decisions in *Wisconsin Right to Life* and *Citizens United*, one might argue that the most important problem relative to interest groups is not their public communications but the nature of their Washington lobbying, which is far more hidden from the American voter than the very public act of direct voter appeals on television.

INTEREST GROUPS AS INVESTORS

Interest-group contributions to parties and candidates are assumed to be part of a rational strategy in the pursuit of favorable governmental policy. This raises serious questions for reformers who presume that candidates and parties are happy to oblige special-interest demands in exchange for much-needed campaign dollars. While the evidence for such a nefarious relationship is mixed (Ansolabehere, de Figueiredo, and Snyder 2003), its potential is compelling and concerning. After seven years of tireless advocacy by Senators Russell Feingold and John McCain, BCRA did eventually pass in 2002 (see Green 2002, 73–83, for a concise history of the legislative struggle), and it contained specific provisions to blunt the role of interest groups as investors in public policy outcomes.

In addition to banning soft money for parties, BCRA also dealt a silent blow to PACs by doubling the upper limit on contributions from individuals to candidates (to $2,000, indexed for inflation) but retaining the same contribution limit of PACs to candidates (at $5,000). The law also increased the limit individuals could contribute in hard money to party accounts (from $20,000 to $25,000, also indexing the new limit to inflation) but left untouched the PAC limit on party contributions at $15,000. *Stated bluntly, in a post-BCRA world, in-*

terest groups play a significantly reduced role as contributors to parties and candidates. On this score, BCRA could be deemed a success.

Consider first the position of interest groups as contributors to parties. As it stands, after the elimination of soft money for parties, interest groups play no significant role in funding the Democrats' or Republicans' hard-money accounts. In Figure 1, I show the percentage of party money contributed by individuals from 1988 through 2008, a time span covering 11 elections. In 1988, individuals contributed over $105 million in itemized hard-money contributions (that is, contributions greater than $200 per donor) to all federal party accounts, representing 90 percent of itemized hard-money receipts. When including nonitemized contributions, individuals contributed over $241 million to parties that year. Compare this to PAC contribution totals to parties in 1988: just over $13 million for all PACs. In 2006, after the ban on soft money, individuals contributed over $418 million in itemized contributions to parties (82 percent of all itemized dollars), but PACs only accounted for just over $50 million.

During the 1990s, however, the story is largely different. It is apparent that the era of soft money significantly changed the funding structure of the Democratic and Republican parties. In brief, soft money was a creation intended to allow parties to build a party brand and to help nonfederal state candidates (Corrado 2005, 32). Parties argued, justifiably and successfully, that for spending on get-out-the-vote efforts or on generic "pro-Democratic" or "pro-Republican" appeals, it was unfair to force the funding of these activities with regulated hard money. Soft money developed, though, into a convenient method of avoiding the rules on hard money. Parties in the 1990s used soft money aggressively to air unregulated (non-magic-word) television advertisements on behalf of federal candidates. (I expand on this below.)

Using the Federal Election Commission reports of soft-money donations (the FEC first required parties to report itemized contributions of soft money in 1992), I split donors into individuals and interest groups. Interest groups in this scheme include any corporation, union, PAC, trade association, or membership group contributing to the parties' nonfederal accounts.[2] The graph demonstrates that between 1992 and 2002, parties steadily increased their reliance on *soft-money* donations by interest groups. Note, in particular 1998 and 2002, when interest-group soft money accounted for nearly 40 percent of all party receipts (hard and soft money combined).

These numbers are staggering. Interest groups donated over $255 million in soft money to parties in 2000 and over $276 million in 2002. This exceeds significantly the $176 million in individual contributions of soft money in 2000

Figure 1

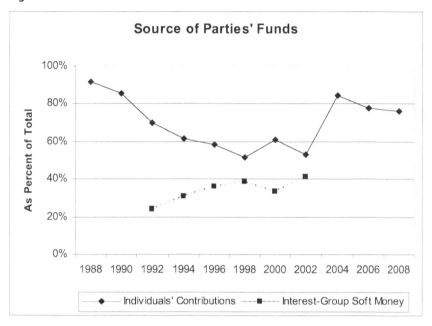

SOURCE: Federal Election Commission

NOTE: Figures for 1988 and 1990 do not include soft money in the denominator since soft-money totals were not reported to the FEC prior to 1992. Figures for 1992–2002 include hard and soft money in the denominator. All figures show only itemized contributions (>$200 per donor) in the FEC detailed contributor files.

and $171 million from individuals in 2002. In this sense, campaign finance reformers were correct to assert that the soft-money era was unique. It represented an unparalleled linkage between interest groups and parties. For example, McCarty and Rothenberg (2000, 292) note, "the use of so-called 'soft money' contributions [enhanced] the role of the party as an intermediary between groups and candidates: Interest groups [had] an incentive to channel large amounts of money to party organizations so it could be funneled into accounts where it could be spent directly on favored candidates." Former congressman Timothy Wirth affirmed the point in a 1997 affidavit for a campaign finance case:

> When I solicited contributions for the state party, in effect I solicited funds for my election campaign. I understood that solicitees who made contributions to the party almost always did so because they expected that the contributions would support my campaign one way or another. . . . In this fund-raising, I often solicited contributions to the DSCC [Democratic Senatorial Campaign Committee] from individuals or

Political Action Committees (PACs) who had already "maxed out" (contributed to my campaign committee the maximum amount allowed by federal law).[3]

At the same time, fund-raisers and party officials also acknowledged that soft money was used to purchase access to party leaders and federal policymakers. According to former senator Dale Bumpers in his 2003 affidavit for *McConnell v. FEC*,

> I believe that, in many instances, there is an expectation of reciprocation where donations to the party are made. . . . I do not think the tobacco industry gives the Republican Party a million and a half or two million dollars because they expect them to take a very objective view on tobacco issues. I think the tobacco industry got what they expected when, after they had given scads of money to both the Republican National Committee and the National Republican Senatorial Committee, a majority of Republicans killed the tobacco bill.[4]

In general, then, the presence of soft money allowed interest groups to contribute to parties with the goal of helping candidates in close races and to signal their loyalty to a party agenda. There can be no doubt that in the era of soft money, interest groups drew ever closer to parties, far closer than in any other period in the previous 100 years. With the passage of BCRA, however, individuals regained the primary status of party funders. Between 2004 and 2008, individuals accounted for around 80 percent of all party receipts. (The slight decline in 2006 and 2008 noted with the solid line in Figure 1 is the consequence of the party committees' extracting more donations from candidates, thereby lowering the percentage from individual citizens to just below 80 percent.)

Consider next the role of PACs as contributors to candidates. PACs have had a significant role in this regard since the passage of campaign finance reform in 1974. PACs increased significantly in the years after the 1974 reforms, and their presence as contributors has consistently engendered cynicism on the part of those worried about the power of special interests. Figure 2 shows the percentage of candidate contributions coming from individuals and PACs between 1988 and 2008. (Party and candidate contributions are included in the denominator here, but they represent only about 2 percent of all candidate receipts.) PACs play a more prominent role in this realm (as opposed to as party financers), but their status is still subordinate to contributions from individuals. More important, PACs account for a smaller share of candidate receipts after the passage of BCRA.

In 2004, for example, individuals contributed over $1 billion in itemized con-

Figure 2

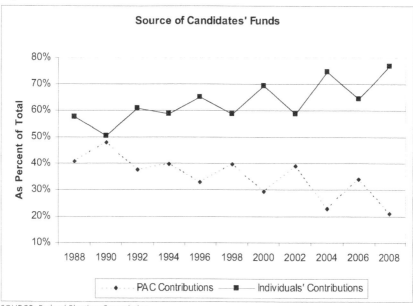

SOURCE: Federal Election Commission

NOTE: Contributions from individuals only include itemized contributions (>$200 per donor) in each cycle's FEC detailed file. Contributions to candidates from parties and other candidates are included in the denominator, though candidate transfers between committees and loans to candidate committees are not.

tributions to federal candidates, and PACs contributed just over $320 million. The huge individual presence in 2004 represented a near 70 percent increase in itemized donations from 2000, but the PAC commitment was only about 25 percent greater than four years prior. All told, individuals gave 75 cents of every dollar to federal candidates that year, the largest share of candidate budgets in over 20 years.[5] In 2006, PACs had their lowest share of candidate budgets in any of the five previous midterm elections. PACs accounted for only 34 percent of congressional candidate budgets that year, and the $724 million itemized contributions from individuals accounted for 64 percent of candidate war chests.

The chief message to draw from Figure 2 is that in 2004, 2006, and 2008, individuals were ever more important in candidate fundraising. Even without these post-BCRA years, however, there is an apparent trend between 1988 and 2002 away from PAC donations and toward individual contributions (Jacobson 2006 also notes this, p. 191). This is particularly true in presidential election years where PACs account for a lower share of candidate budgets in each subsequent election. The trend accelerates after BCRA's passage. For all those worried about PAC power, then, the evidence is clear: The problem is greatly alleviated with the doubling of the individual limits. This will likely become more apparent as these limits index to inflation and PAC limits do not.

Of course, there are those who would object to the implicit notion expressed here that contributions from individuals are "purer" than those from interest groups. The type of contributor who can give the individual maximum is still wealthier than most voters, and many of these individuals are powerful business and union leaders who might leverage significant influence with their hard-money donation.[6] Furthermore, individuals who bundle contributions (which is when an individual collects donations from others and delivers them in one large "bundle" to a candidate or party) might have particularly large influence with candidate and party beneficiaries. Whether wealthy individuals can leverage increased power over candidates is a controversial question, however. Ansolabehere and colleagues (2003), for example, observe that the average contribution from individuals to candidates tends to be small. They posit that individuals contribute not as a form of investment, which is more likely the motivation of interest groups, but as an act of democratic participation.

Ultimately, this point is unlikely to convince reformers, and as long as contributions are a legal form of political expression—a right that is surely here to stay—there will always be concerns about whether donors have more influence than nondonors. Furthermore, the current Supreme Court in *Randall v. Sorrell* (which in 2006 overturned Vermont's very low contribution limits at the state level) made clear that contributions are likely to remain high enough to warrant concern over the relationship between contributor and candidate. We can likely agree, though, that interest-group investment strategies are certainly not advantaged post-BCRA, and this should satisfy many reform advocates.[7]

Before moving on to a discussion of interest-group electioneering, I think the point can be extended even further. Consider the role of 527s. For many, 527s had the potential to become "shadow parties," where donors of soft money pre-BCRA were expected to shift to pro-party 527s post-BCRA (Skinner 2005). That is, some expected pro-Democratic groups such as the Media Fund, America Coming Together, and MoveOn.org—as well as pro-Republican groups such as Progress for America, Club for Growth, and Swift Boat Veterans—to become the primary organizations raising corporate and union soft money. On this, the evidence is mixed. Weissman and Hassan (2005), for example, show that many corporations did not move their soft money from parties to pro-party 527s.

Because 527s played such a prominent role in 2004, it's worth considering a bit more the donor bases of these active groups. What role did unions and corporations play in funding 527s in 2004? Do they sidestep the upper limits on donations of hard money with a prominent presence in the coffers of these new groups? In Figure 3, I show the contribution percentages of individuals, unions, and corporations to issue advocacy and federally oriented 527s in 2004.[8] I show these totals for each month in the year running up to the November election (October 2003 through October 2004). The graph demonstrates that in every month, individuals account for the largest percentage of donated money. This is particularly true for donations in the final few months of the election season, when individuals make up between 80 and 90 percent of these 527s' budgets.

The reason for this lies in the underlying exemption available for 527s in 2004 to air ads close to Election Day. In short, provided these groups received the bulk of contributions from individuals, and provided that they sidestepped "magic words" in their public communications, 527s were largely allowed to remain active until the very end of the election. It should be noted that this

Figure 3

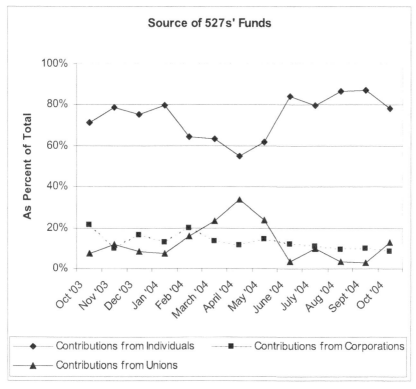

SOURCE: Internal Revenue Service

NOTE: Any 527 coded as federal oriented or issue advocacy is included here. State-level groups and non-federal candidate groups are excluded.

exemption was not necessarily intended by congressional reformers drafting BCRA; as with all legislation, there were some gray areas in the new law, and the allowance developed in the absence of clear guidance from the FEC. The figure shows how small a presence unions and corporations played in funding these groups, though. Even in this realm, general treasury money from unions and corporations was quite small in comparison to money donated by individuals out of their own bank accounts. Of course, unlike donations to candidate and party accounts, contributions to 527s are unlimited and often in the millions, even from individuals. This is justifiably a concern for many reformers, and one fight in recent years was over forcing many of these 527s to register as PACs.

All told, my point with this brief analysis is straightforward: Individuals are the primary funders of federal campaign activity. This is especially true post-BCRA, and has largely been true for the last 30 years. In a sense, then, BCRA was successful in minimizing the role of interest groups relative to party accounts, representing the most important victory for campaign finance reform advocates, and has moderately undercut the role of PACs relative to candidates. Even in the realm of 527s, individuals hold the most clout. This should ultimately temper the passions of many who assume that corporations and unions "buy" elections or "bribe" candidates.

INTEREST GROUPS AS ADVOCATES

The situation is noticeably different in the realm of interest-group direct advocacy, where BCRA reformers most hoped to stem the rising tide of pro-candidate spending. Indeed, in the world after *Wisconsin Right to Life* and *Citizens United*—which I'll discuss below—the wall erected by BCRA between election advocacy and issue advocacy seems to have crumbled.

In this sense, if "buying" votes or access is undermined by contribution limits, it is certainly possible that interest groups could alternatively work to elect candidates presupposed to help their policy agendas. At first glance, we might have less reason to worry. The number of groups who spend aggressively and independently of candidates is not significantly large. For example, in 1998, 84 PACs reported independent expenditure campaigns either for or against a candidate for federal office. Twenty-two groups aired television ads in the top 75 media markets that year. Of the 22, the AFL-CIO was the largest sponsor, while the League of Conservation Voters, the Sierra Club, and the Business Round-table were also on the list. Compare this to the over 2,800 PACs reporting contributions to federal candidates. In 2000, 159 groups reported independent expenditures to the FEC, and the Wisconsin Advertising Project captured ads from 103 distinct groups making television appeals, which again included the AFL-CIO, along with Planned Parenthood and Americans for Job Security. By contrast, 2,900 PACs made candidate contributions in 2000.

The larger issue, however, is the intensity of these appeals to voters. In Table 1, I show the level of expenditures in campaigns by parties and interest groups for all available data back to 1988. Party independent expenditures—which are public communications funded with hard money—were illegal prior to a 1996 Supreme Court case (*Colorado Republican Federal Campaign Committee v. FEC*) and in the elections of 1996–2002 were essentially irrelevant, as parties spent their huge war chests of soft money on unregulated candidate issue advocacy. In 2000, for example, parties spent well over $150 million on about 200,000 soft-money ads in the top 75 media markets. They spent nearly $100 million on such ads in the congressional elections of 2002. With the elimination of soft money, though, parties invested significant hard-money resources (overwhelmingly funded by regulated contributions from individuals) on independent expenditure campaigns.[9]

I illustrate these party numbers as a form of comparison with interest-group expenditures shown in the last three columns. First, PAC contributions always exceed any measured effort by interest groups and PACs to spend independently of candidates. For example, PAC independent expenditures (which use funds raised in small amounts from their members) are actually quite low between 1988 and 2002, never totaling more than $29 million. In that sense, the vast bulk of interest-group money in campaigns is in the form of regulated contributions to candidates and parties—and these have strict ceilings, as noted in the previous section.

After 2002, however, PACs nearly doubled their independent expenditure campaigns in hard money, with a significant jump to $150 million in 2008—though even that total still constituted about one-third the total for PAC contributions to candidates. From the perspective of the optimist, the spike in independent expenditures from both parties and PACs is a BCRA victory, since more candidate advocacy was being channeled through these regulated categories in the aftermath of the 2002 reforms.

Such optimism is short-lived, however, when we look at the far-right column in the table, which shows the amount spent by interest groups on television ads touting federal candidates. Political advertising by interest groups on television is quite high for the elections of 2004–2008, and most of this was outside the

Table 1—Party and Interest Group Electioneering Totals

	Party Independent Expenditures	Party Ads with No "Magic Words"	Party Coordinated Expenditures	PAC Candidate Contributions	PAC Independent Expenditures	Interest Group Pro-Candidate Television Advertising
1988	-	n/a	$40,689,308	$157,188,684	$21,465,566	n/a
1990	-	n/a	$19,553,001	$157,574,457	$5,647,859	n/a
1992	-	n/a	$62,950,765	$186,308,525	$11,035,701	n/a
1994	-	n/a	$42,834,872	$186,609,024	$5,200,081	n/a
1996	$12,345,461	n/a	$54,727,412	$213,883,248	$10,183,805	n/a
1998	$1,658,192	$25,302,728 (43,834)	$38,794,509	$219,528,697	$9,507,928	$6,610,365 (14,318)
2000	$3,612,127	$158,965,144 (224,698)	$52,164,188	$260,076,715	$28,802,075	$51,744,368 (79,295)
2002	$3,703,698	$96,698,140 (163,276)	$21,549,521	$300,658,557	$20,355,772	$20,054,608 (33,415)
2004	$269,462,574	-	$58,694,250	$320,273,768	$68,708,428	$122,106,322 (176,301)
2006	$225,461,770	-	$33,947,635	$380,389,934	$38,555,666	$45,640,890 (46,438)
2008	$280,523,392	-	$49,329,383	$425,331,761	$156,621,685	$70,800,955 (112,607)

Sources: Data in first, third, fourth, and fifth columns are from the FEC. Independent expenditures for parties were not legal before 1996. Data in the second and last columns are from Wisconsin Advertising Project estimates. Numbers in parentheses are the total number of ads broadcast fitting the description. Data in 1998 and 2000 are for the top 75 media markets, but the 2002–2008 numbers cover the top 100 markets. Data prior to 1998 are not available.

scope of federal election laws, as we will see below. Interest groups spent an estimated $51 million in 2000 to air nearly 80,000 political ads that mentioned federal candidates, and this level of activity is what finally compelled Congress to pass BCRA. After the passage of BCRA, though, 527s and other groups in 2004 spent over $120 million on political ads in the weeks leading up to the primaries and general election. As noted earlier, 527s were a new loophole that developed in the aftermath of the 2002 reforms. All told, interest groups in 2004 more than doubled their investment over 2000.

The trend continued past 2004, however. In 2006, the amount spent by groups doubled over the previous midterm cycle, and while there was less interest-group advertising in 2008 over 2004, interest-group ads still totaled $71 million, far more than in 2000. Is this "explosion"—the failure of BCRA to stem the tide of unregulated interest-group advertising—something to worry about? Perhaps. Keep in mind that prior to 1998 issue advocacy by interest groups was minimal. The AFL-CIO *did* spend significantly on issue ads in 1996 (Rozell and Wilcox 1999, 139), but before the mid-1990s, interest groups spent independently of campaigns with mostly hard money. And as Table 1 demonstrates, the level of such efforts (in the form of independent expenditures) was fairly modest.[10]

In this, it should be noted that I am excluding from these figures the totals devoted to the ground war (see Magleby and Monson 2004, Magleby and Patterson 2006), and there is some evidence that many groups have shifted tactics in recent years from TV to old-fashioned mail, phone calls, and door-to-door mobilization.[11] In this realm, interest groups are afforded greater opportunities to distort a candidate's record or spread character attacks. Such tactics are also less likely to foster media scrutiny. It is important to remember, then, that any figures for TV advertising by interest groups understate the overall level of group mobilization in campaigns.

The advertising totals suggest that interest groups were not stymied by congressional reform efforts, but simply devised new ways to sponsor campaign ads; 527s in 2004 are the clearest example of that. A powerful enabling factor after BCRA, though, was also the changing perspective of the Supreme Court.[12] Consider first the *Wisconsin Right to Life* decision from the summer of 2007, where the Supreme Court ruled that ads mentioning candidates should not be uniformly treated as election-related. Whereas the rules for 2004 permitted 527s to air unregulated ads for candidates close to Election Day (provided the ads were funded with contributions for individuals), *Wisconsin* permitted such messages from almost any interest group, even those funded with corporate or union money, provided the message is "reasonably" interpreted as issue related and not solely election related. Furthermore, the Court was clear that the context of the message (how close it airs to Election Day, for example) cannot be used as a determinative factor in its classification. That judgment is confined solely to the content of the ad.

In practical terms this reset the game to the pre-BCRA rules in the run-up to the 2008 elections. Groups were now free to run thinly disguised lobbying ads on TV and radio that supported or opposed federal candidates, and these could be funded with union and corporate dollars. We have all seen these ads. They attack a candidate's record, air in the weeks leading up to the elections, and end not by telling us how to vote but by urging us to "call candidate X and tell them to start working harder." The Court in *Wisconsin* said it is not apparent these ads should be uniformly considered electioneering. Maybe, the justices said, the group really wants viewers to take an interest in the legislative process. Richard Hasen, a campaign finance expert, made this astute observation after *Wisconsin*: "Note the breadth of this standard [as set out in *Wisconsin*]. What issue is unlikely to become the subject of legislative scrutiny by some Member of Congress in the near future? . . . Simply put, for most ads there *will* be a reasonable interpretation of even an ad likely to affect the outcome of an election that it is something other than an appeal to vote for or against a candidate" (2008, 29–30—emphasis in original).

The early evidence from the 2008 presidential primaries appeared to bear this prediction out too. Consider the headlines:
- "Stealthy Groups Shake Up Races," *Wall Street Journal*, February 4, 2008
- "Outside Groups Aid Obama, Critic of Their Influence," *New York Times*, January 30, 2008
- "After Ruling, Outside Groups Spend Heavily to Sway Races," *New York Times*, January 1, 2008
- "Nonprofits Become a Force in Primaries," *Washington Post*, December 5, 2007
- "A New Channel for Soft Money Appears in Race," *New York Times*, November 12, 2007

By February 2008, after the Iowa caucus and early primaries, interest groups had spent almost $7.5 million on television and radio advertising (as reported to the FEC) featuring candidates in presidential primary races.[13]

The *Wisconsin* case was merely the first of two key cases, however. In early 2010, the Supreme Court of the United States issued its ruling in *Citizens United v. FEC* that further changed the campaign finance system for organized interests. In the 5–4 vote, the Court sided with the claim of Citizens United—a non-profit advocacy group that in 2007 produced a documentary critical of Hillary Clinton—that all pro- or anti-candidate messages are protected speech under the First Amendment. In one sense, the Court ended the debate over what types of campaign messages from interest groups could be restricted or outlawed by Congress—an issue that tied knots for the Court in *Wisconsin Right to Life*. The Court in *Citizens United* said that so long as the messages were not coordinated with federal candidates, and absent a compelling and clear state interest, the First Amendment protects all interest-group speech, even when such speech attacks a candidate's character and avoids any policy debate.

The 2010 elections were the first test of this development, and the preliminary evidence is suggestive of an important effect. In Table 2, I list the proportion of all television ads aired in the election year that were sponsored by outside groups. In the last two columns I show the percentage of interest-group ads that made use of the "magic words" so important in the pre-BCRA period. (In those columns I am limited to two elections before BCRA and two after, since the coding for interest groups is not available in all years). The results show that 2010 saw more interest-group ads as a percentage of all ads aired than any previous election year—an all-time high for the Senate, in fact. In 2000, interest groups sponsored 17 percent of all House ads, but just under 6 percent of Senate ads. The totals never exceeded 10 percent in the House or Senate elections of 2002, 2004, or 2006. (Consider this side thought: Should we be worried about interest-group spending that constitutes such a small percentage of overall advertising dollars?) In 2008, after *Wisconsin*, outside groups more heavily invested in Senate races, but it was in 2010 that groups finally invested at noteworthy amounts (more than 10 percent) in both contexts.

Moreover, interest groups used express advocacy messages at a much higher rate in 2010, particularly in House races, where over one-fourth of all interest-group ads explicitly told viewers how to vote. This is a direct effect of *Citizens United*, where the Court finally said that all pro-candidate messages are permissible by any source. Note the low percentage of "magic word" usage in 2000, 2002, and 2008. This should put the advertising totals from Table 1 in better context. In the years before 2010, well over 90 percent of pro-candidate ads sponsored by interest groups avoided express calls to vote for or against a candidate, veiling themselves as advocacy concerned with issues, not elections, and putting most of that activity beyond the reach of campaign finance regulations. For many, these laxer rules are troubling and portened worse things to come. For one, 2010 may simply be a training ground for mobilization in the 2012 presidential elections. And because the Court seems unwilling to sanction

Table 2—Interest-Group Political Advertising in Congressional Elections

	% of Ads Aired		% Using "Magic Words"	
	House	Senate	House	Senate
1998	8.98%	0.65%	n/a	n/a
2000	17.13%	5.84%	2.50%	7.14%
2002	7.02%	4.53%	4.51%	2.89%
2004	2.91%	5.15%	n/a	n/a
2006	5.45%	5.65%	n/a	n/a
2008	6.29%	13.76%	7.05%	0.92%
2010	12.29%	14.76%	28.71%	10.13%

SOURCES: Data are from Wisconsin Advertising Project between 1998 and 2008, and from the Wesleyan Media Project for 2010.

NOTE: The data in the first two columns include all ads advocating for candidates in the election year in all available media markets.

aggressive limits on interest-group advocacy, the new campaign finance battle-ground has shifted to more-extreme disclosure laws. Although *Citizens United*-did not endorse political anonymity, one consequence of the decision was to remove the handcuffs on political groups who do not disclose donors to the Federal Election Commission. More to the point, all funds raised and spent by candidates, parties, and PACs, for example, are tracked and made public by the Federal Election Commission, and money raised and spent by 527s is made public by the IRS. These disclosed data are what allow me to present the trends in Figures 1–3. After *Wisconsin* and *Citizens United*, however, group efforts are increasingly funded through organizational forms that are *not* subject to disclosure, such as from 501c4, c5, and c6 organizations (501c4 groups are tax-exempt, social welfare nonprofits; 501c5 groups are labor unions; and 501c6 organizations are business groups, such as the Chamber of Commerce). Many interests in past cycles, especially 2010, used the 501c4 classification to hide their donors because these groups are easy to form and can use vague names—such as American Action Network and Crossroads GPS (two groups active in 2010)—to shield their intentions. With this development, my earlier argument about the primacy of individuals funding 527s is no longer verifiable with groups airing ads under the 501c section of the tax code. We have less knowledge, then, and will know less in future elections, about what role corporations and unions play in the air war.

On the one hand, disclosure requirements are some of the most accepted forms of campaign finance regulations, and it seems unlikely that current disclosure mandates are truly at risk, although the current Court seems eager to reconsider even long-accepted logics of campaign finance. But current disclosure rules are the not issue. Congressional attempts to expand disclosure to include 501c4 organizations have stalled, as many former defenders of disclosure now question their constitutional grounding. Expanded disclosure is no slam dunk, then.

All told, broader deregulation of interest-group campaign finance laws looms large on the horizon, and many expect interest groups to expand their electoral presence in future election cycles. Whereas BCRA was a success relative to interest groups as investors, the evidence is convincing that it has failed miserably relative to efforts at group advocacy. The oft-cited claim here about money in politics seems somewhat true: Whenever Congress shuts one avenue of entry for candidate advocacy by interest groups, another one emerges. Or, as is commonly said, money is like water on pavement, always finding the cracks. It is a notable addendum to this conventional wisdom that in recent years the Supreme Court has become an ally in that process.

For many, this is a sign of American decline. Even President Obama derided the *Citizens United* decision in his 2010 State of the Union, and there is a sense among reform advocates that the game is over. Should we worry about the state of American democracy when shadow groups are so active a player, though? Maybe not. In other words, I am not so sure that recent developments spell doom for American politics. I expand on this skepticism in the final section.

INTEREST GROUPS AS DEMOCRATS

There may be a trade-off for those reformers who want to remove interest-group money from electoral politics. It is, most likely, intense political competition between the Democrats and Republicans that motivates any expansion of electioneering by interest groups. Thus the polarized partisan politics after 1994 is undeniably the chief reason for the emergence of soft money and issue advocacy.[14] Attempts to constrain the flow of money in elections may work for a time, but as interest groups react to a consequential political context, they will mobilize to expand their resource base.

Indeed, the speedy explosion of 527s in the 2004 elections stands in contrast to the relatively slow emergence of issue advocacy, which took nearly two decades to "explode" onto the political scene. If the latter development is curious because it took so long, the former is intriguing because it happened so fast. Both changes are explained by the same mechanism, though: Interest groups and other political actors will find campaign finance loopholes when there is a political and electoral motivation to find them. I should stress that this tweaks the "water on pavement" analogy offered above. Instead, I would argue that absent the electoral impetus, there is little incentive for more money, in new and varied forms, to flow into the process.

On the other hand, here is the trade-off: Party theorists are thrilled to see a competitive political process where parties are polarized and differences matter. And although competitiveness has declined at the individual level in the last 20 years, meaning that fewer elections are close, competitiveness has increased at the macro or institutional level, meaning that polarized parties fight aggressively in a handful of races for majorities in Congress and for control of the policymaking agenda in Washington. Which do we value more? A competitive partisan context where interest groups continue to spend vast sums on elections, to the dismay of reform advocates? Or an electoral process where groups play a more limited role but where the outcome is pretty much known, to the dismay of many democratic theorists? Indeed, I am not sure that we can escape such a trade-off.

Consider a further question: Is interest-group money spent on electioneering worse for democracy than money spent on lobbying? Which *should* we prefer? Independent and uncoordinated interest-group electioneering that directly touches the voter? Or less visible lobbying by interest groups on K Street, fueled in part through contributions of hard and soft money? The bulk of empirical evidence suggests that PAC money almost never buys votes on the House and Senate floor, but it *does* buy access to policymakers at key moments of policymaking (Hall and Wayman 1990; Smith 1995). Even Bradley Smith, a persuasive critic of campaign finance regulation and a former FEC commissioner, admits that when it comes to legislating, the potential for corruption and influence peddling is far greater than in the world of electoral politics (2001, 76–77).

This concern extends far beyond the limited effect of regulated contributions. In 2007, Congress passed the Honest Leadership and Open Government Act, which contained provisions about lobbying gifts to elected officials, candidates' use of private airplanes, and disclosure for lobbying activity and budget earmarks. The act was motivated by a real concern that the relationship between lobbyist and legislator was too cozy and too invisible.

Of course, interest groups provide valuable information and expertise in the drafting and implementation of public policy—this should not be forgotten. But voters never know the true influence of lobbyists, and sporadic media coverage of lobbyist-funded golf trips and expensive meals do little to assuage the concerns of voters. In this sense, access politics presents real opportunities for consequential influence, and voters have few tools available to hold legislators accountable for any improper relationships.

In this light, the struggle over which groups can fund TV ads might not be so worrisome. After all, when interest groups try to persuade voters to support certain candidates, *voters keep the power.* If concerned citizens are worried about soft-money ads and who funds them, voters will discount the messages. If these voters dislike certain political products, like obvious electioneering disguised as issue advocacy, we might expect them to vote with their remote controls and turn the channel. And if voters care not about issue ads and soft money, which seems to be the case, since respondents in public opinion polls almost never list campaign finance as a major problem in American politics, then all the hand-wringing over finance reform may be misplaced energy.

Furthermore, there is considerable evidence that exposure to campaign advertising is a good thing. Recent scholarship has consistently uncovered a link between ads and increased campaign knowledge and interest (Franz et al. 2007), in addition to numerous null effects (Krasno and Green 2008). And meta-analytic assessments of negative advertising in particular find only sparse evidence that ads undermine the health of American democracy (with lower participation, for example: Lau, Sigelman, and Rovner 2007). The old line that TV ads are bad for America seems exactly that—an old line.

The question over how to regulate interest groups in the realm of electioneering is a critical one, however, and for powerful reasons. If we heed the call of many reformers and regulate activity with an expansive standard on what constitutes electioneering, we come close to unreasonable restrictions on free speech. For example, is it reasonable to mandate that Planned Parenthood (which has waded into electoral politics in past years) fund its pro-choice citizen education, or the NRA (also a political powerhouse) fund its ads about gun safety, with hard money? How about forcing Evangelical churches that air ads promoting their ministry—making appeals to faith that find favor disproportionately among Republicans—to fund this activity with hard dollars and to report collection basket totals to the FEC? Both are possible if we define anything even remotely political and said close to an election as implicit candidate advocacy.

On the other hand, with a vigorous defense of speech rights close to Election Day comes the possibility for a complete dismantling of distinctions between election and issue advocacy. The Supreme Court has maintained for more than a generation that regulations on election advocacy are acceptable if they help limit the "appearance of corruption." In this sense, an acceptable goal of campaign finance laws is to prevent actual corruption, but also to keep the process clean enough so as to inspire confidence among citizens that nothing shady is happening behind the scenes. The Court seems now to have abandoned that rationale, but very few people want the complete elimination of campaign finance restrictions. Many still believe powerfully that corruption of the political system, and the decline in trust in our political leaders, is inevitable if money is allowed to flow freely.

Once you dismantle at least some regulations on election-related speech, however—as was done by the Supreme Court in 2007 and 2010—it becomes harder to defend against further dismantling. The candidate-mention test in BCRA was designed to be a workable standard to fix the porous "magic word" standard, but that met with immediate criticism and set in motion a powerful resistance to all existing campaign finance regulations. The resistance caught fire with the Supreme Court and is quickly spreading to other restrictions on money in elections, from the soft-money ban for parties to clean election laws in the states (both recently litigated in federal courts).

I have no answer for what are "good" campaign finance restrictions. There may be no answer, in fact, only spirited dialogue, with one side winning more often than the other. The pendulum is sure to swing back in due course, and this is probably the most we can ever hope for.

CONCLUSION

Electioneering by interest groups has entered a new phase. The *Wisconsin* and *Citizens United* cases have guaranteed this. At the same time, however, I caution against embracing the reflexive pessimism of the most vocal advocates of reform. As a proportion of all funds, investments by interest groups in candidates and parties are lower now than in the previous 20 years, and advocacy by interest groups is largely bankrolled by a relatively small number of groups. Even if this were greatly expanded, though, voters remain the gatekeepers of any success by interest groups in this realm. This is important. Should voters worry about the funding source of ads from groups with strange-sounding names, it would behoove the citizen to ignore the message. Democrats in 2010, for example, made a campaign issue out of the aggressive advertising blitz on behalf of Republicans from the Chamber of Commerce. Who is funding their ads, Democrats asked? When voters do their due diligence in vetting the information they use to make decisions, it weakens the influence of information from shadow groups. This is unlike the far-more-hidden politics of lobbying, where interest groups can hold considerable power over the drafting and implementation of legislation, and in ways unknown to citizens. We would be better served to focus more energy on lobbying by interest groups. Demanding more disclosure in this regard and extending regulations on impermissible lobbying practices would do far more to limit influence by interest groups than any attempt to limit or prevent clever TV ads.

The future of campaign finance regulations is unknown. While there are some areas of concern—I am no Pollyanna when it comes to the consequences of deregulation—is it not time to focus on the points of access that sidestep citizens and remove power from voters?

ENDNOTES

1. It is beyond the scope of this chapter to outline all of the rules relative to interest groups and elections, but for much more information on the legal dos and don'ts I recommend *The New Campaign Finance Sourcebook* (Corrado et al. 2005). In particular, chapters 1 and 2 offer the best history available of the evolution of campaign finance laws.

2. There is an important conceptualization point worth making here. The FEC stores all soft-money donations to parties (for 1992 through 2002) in its Detailed File for contributions from individuals. To sort out whether the soft-money donor is an individual or interest group requires an examination of the specific donor name; there is no unique contributor code as in the PAC contribution files. There are over 50,000 soft contributions in 2002, for example, meaning that the donor classifications require some detailed recoding. Alternatively, the Center for Responsive Politics, at www.opensecrets.org, reports soft-money totals for interest groups in a much-easier-to-digest format. Unfortunately, in its summary reports, it includes soft-money contributions from certain individuals (CEOs and spouses and children of CEOs) in the total for different groups. This approach artificially increases soft-money totals for these groups. In my scheme, a more conservative one, I only show soft-money contributions directly from interest groups, excluding these affiliated individual totals.

3. Document accessed from a web archival search on relevant campaign finance cases. The affidavit was submitted for *Federal Election Commission v. Colorado Republican Federal Campaign Committee*. The electronic version is no longer online, but a hard copy is available from the author on request.

4. Accessed from Key Documents section of www.democracy21.net.

5. One should note, in addition, that PACs have historically given very little to presidential candidates (because of the general-election public funding system), which explains why the disparity between PACs and individuals in Figure 2 is always greater in presidential election years.

6. For example, we most certainly must be worried about the Jack Abramoffs of the world, but as I'll discuss below, their influence is primarily in the lobbying realm, on K Street in Washington. In my view, this is probably the place to be chiefly worried about the influence of individuals and interest groups, as opposed to the highly regulated role of candidate and party contributor.

7. I am not making a zero-sum argument here. Just because individuals under BCRA can contribute more money to candidates with higher limits does not preclude PACs from compensating by finding the means to invest more aggressively in candidates (as bundlers, for example).

8. These numbers are from reports to the IRS by 527s, which must report receipts and

expenditures to the IRS if they do not report to the FEC or conform to state-level reporting requirements. When initially reporting to the IRS, 527s must state the explicit purpose of the group. I examined each stated purpose and coded each group into one of four categories: issue advocacy, state and local, federal, and unclear. Issue advocacy groups, in my coding scheme, are those groups whose stated purpose is to educate voters or to get out the vote. State and local groups are those whose stated purpose is to contribute to or aid candidates for nonfederal office. Federal 527s are groups whose stated purpose includes either a specific reference to helping federal candidates or a generic reference to aiding candidates. Finally, unclear groups are 527s whose stated purpose is too vague to be classified.

9. Note that coordinated expenditures by parties—hard-money communications that are coordinated with candidate campaigns—have remained fairly consistent for the last 20 years. Coordinated expenditures are subject to certain limits, making them less attractive as an option for parties. In addition, the rules for coordinated expenditures have not changed during this period. This is unlike party independent expenditures, which were legal only after 1995 and now represent the chief way for parties to advocate for candidates without limit. Corrado (2006), however, discusses the Republicans' innovative use in 2004 of a hybrid form of party expenditure that was neither independent nor coordinated. One other point is relevant in comparing columns 1 and 2 in Table 1. The first column shows expenditures as reported to the FEC, which might include costs for producing and buying radio or airtime (or print space) for a pro-candidate message. The number in column 2 is an estimate of what the airtime cost and *excludes* production costs and consultant fees related to the message.

10. Consider specifically two major electoral controversies involving interest groups in the 1980s: John Dolan's National Conservative PAC (Sabato 1984) and the National Security PAC with its Willie Horton ads. These were largely hard-money fights on a modest scale.

11. I am usually suspicious of those announcing the apparent death of television advertising (see *New York Times*, A1, September 5, 2002, and *New York Times*, A1, April 6, 2004). It is true that the Internet electioneering is cheaper, and door-to-door efforts are comparatively more effective (Gerber and Green 2000), but television affords an interest group the chance to reach thousands of voters instantly. In addition, because there are always more TV ads with every successive election, I assume that TV advertising is here to stay.

12. One component of the regulatory environment that I do not mention is the behavior of the Federal Election Commission. The FEC is always staffed with three commissioners of each party, but the behavior of the commissioners is more partisan now than in previous decades. Because any regulatory action requires the approval of at least four commissioners, the FEC is often deadlocked on party lines. This will, without question, compel candidates, parties, and interest groups to push the limits on permissible electioneering.

13. This represents the largest presidential primary mobilization by interest groups in the modern era. Keep in mind, though, that presidential candidates through the end of January 2008 had spent over $100 million in television advertising alone (as reported by Wisconsin Advertising Project in its February 1, 2008, press release).

14. I discuss this in much more detail in Franz (2008).

Bibliography

Ansolabehere, Stephen, John de Figueiredo, and James Snyder. 2003. "Why Is There So Little Money in U.S. Politics?" *Journal of Economic Perspectives* 17(1):105–130.

Corrado, Anthony. 2005. "Money and Politics: A History of Campaign Finance Law," in *The New Campaign Finance Sourcebook*, ed. Anthony Corrado, Thomas Mann, Daniel Ortiz, and Trevor Potter. Washington, D.C.: Brookings Institution Press.

Corrado, Anthony. 2006. "Party Finance in the Wake of BCRA: An Overview," in *The Election after Reform: Money, Politics and the Bipartisan Campaign Reform Act*, ed. Michael J. Malbin. Lanham, Md.: Rowman & Littlefield.

Corrado, Anthony, Thomas Mann, Daniel Ortiz, and Trevor Potter. 2005. *The New Campaign Finance Sourcebook*. Washington, D.C.: Brookings Institution Press.

Franz, Michael M. 2008. *Choices and Changes: Interest Groups in the Electoral Process.* Philadelphia: Temple University Press.

Franz, Michael, Paul Freedman, Kenneth Goldstein, and Travis Ridout. 2007. *Campaign Advertising and American Democracy.* Philadelphia: Temple University Press.

Gerber, Alan S., and Donald P. Green. 2000. "The Effects of Canvassing, Telephone Calls, and Direct Mail on Voter Turnout: A Field Experiment." *American Political Science Review* 94(3):653–663.

Green, Mark. 2002. *Selling Out: How Big Corporate Money Buys Elections, Rams Through Legislation, and Betrays Our Democracy.* New York: Regan Books.

Hall, Richard, and Frank Wayman. 1990. "Buying Time: Moneyed Interests and the Mobilization of Bias in Congressional Committees." *American Political Science Review* 90(4):797–820.

Hasen, Richard. 2008. "Beyond Incoherence: The Roberts Court's Deregulatory Turn in FEC v. Wisconsin Right to Life." *Minnesota Law Review.* 92: 1064.

Jacobson, Gary. 2006. "The First Congressional Elections after BCRA," in *The Election after Reform: Money, Politics, and the Bipartisan Campaign Reform Act,* ed. Michael J. Malbin. Lanham, Md.: Rowman & Littlefield.

Krasno, Jonathan, and Donald Green. 2008. "Do Televised Presidential Ads Increase Voter Turnout? Evidence from a Natural Experiment." *Journal of Politics* 70(1): 245–261.

Lau, Richard, Lee Sigelman, and Ivy Brown Rovner. 2007. "The Effects of Negative Political Campaigns: A Meta-Analytic Reassessment." *Journal of Politics* 69(4):1176–1209.

Magleby, David, and J. Quin Monson. 2004. *The Last Hurrah? Soft Money and Issue Advocacy in the 2002 Congressional Elections.* Washington, D.C.: Brookings Institution Press.

Magleby, David, and Kelly Patterson. 2006. "Stepping out of the Shadows? Ground War Activity in 2004," in *The Election after Reform: Money, Politics, and the Bipartisan Campaign Reform Act,* ed. Michael J. Malbin. Lanham, Md.: Rowman & Littlefield.

McCarty, Nolan, and Lawrence Rothenberg. 2000. "Coalitional Maintenance: Politicians, Parties, and Organized Groups." *American Politics Quarterly* 28(3):291–308.

Petracca, Mark, ed. 1992. *The Politics of Interests: Interest Groups Transformed.* Boulder, Colo.: Westview Press.

Rozell, Mark, and Clyde Wilcox. 1999. *Interest Groups in American Campaigns.* Washington, D.C.: CG Press.

Sabato, Larry. 1984. *PAC Power.* New York: W. W. Norton.

Skinner, Richard. 2005. "Do 527's Add Up to a Party? Thinking about the 'Shadows' of Politics." *The Forum* 3(3), Article 5. Available at http://www.bepress.com/forum/vol3/iss3/art5.

Smith, Bradley. 2001. *Unfree Speech: The Folly of Campaign Finance Reform.* Princeton, N.J.: Princeton University Press.

Smith, Richard. 1995. "Interest Group Influence in the U.S. Congress." *Legislative Studies Quarterly* 20(1):89–139.

Weissman, Steve, and Ruth Hassan. 2005. "BCRA and the 527 Groups," in *The Election after Reform: Money, Politics and the Bipartisan Campaign Reform Act,* ed. Michael J. Malbin. Lanham, Md.: Rowman & Littlefield.

*Michael M. Franz is associate professor of government at Bowdoin College and the author of *Choices and Changes: Interest Groups in the Political Process* (Temple University Press, 2008).

Michael M. Franz. "The Interest Group Response to Campaign Finance Reform." *The Forum* (2010) 6:1, Article 10. Revised by the author.

Used by permission.

DISCUSSION QUESTIONS

1. Did BCRA restrict interest-group expenditures too much?

2. What are the consequences of the lack of inflation indexing for PAC contributions? Should they be indexed?

3. Do we have a right to know who the contributors to interest groups are?

4. Consider the author's claim that limiting interest groups' election-related spending would reduce the competitiveness of elections. Would you be willing to make this trade-off?

Reform in an Age of Networked Campaigns

*by Anthony J. Corrado, Michael J. Malbin, Thomas E. Mann, and Norman J. Ornstein**

The political world has been arguing about campaign finance policy for decades. Unfortunately, what was once a rich conversation has devolved into a two-sided battleground, with the debate's underlying structure looking much as it did in the 1970s. One side argues that restraining the role of money through contribution or spending limits is essential to restraining corruption, or the appearance of corruption, or the "undue influence" of wealthy donors. The other side resists any such limits in the name of free speech. Despite dramatic changes in the political world, and despite some court cases that have been coming down on the speech side of these debates, the arguments on each side remain largely unchanged.[1]

The time has come to leap over this gulf and, as much as possible, move the dispute from the courts. Each of the old perspectives contains insights, but each is also partial. Preventing corruption and protecting free speech should each be among the key goals of any policy regime, but they should not be the only objectives. This report seeks to change the ongoing conversation. Put simply, instead of focusing on attempts to further restrict the wealthy few, it seeks to focus on activating the many.

The report is not a brief for deregulation. Its co-authors support limits on contributions to candidates and political parties. But we also recognize the limits of limits. Contributions may be limited, but even before the most recent court cases were decided, it was clear that the Constitution protected independent spending by wealthy individuals, parties, and political committees.

As a result, restraint-based approaches do not substantially reduce participation by the determined wealthy, nor do they have a major effect on the competitiveness of election campaigns. Thus, even though we consider some limits important, they cannot resolve the key questions about equality, participation and competition—no matter where the Courts may draw the precise constitutional lines.

This chapter is excerpted from "Reform in an Age of Networked Campaigns: How to Foster Citizen Participation Through Small Donors and Volunteers," published in 2010 by the Campaign Finance Institute. The full report includes a detailed set of recommendations regarding ways to increase citizen participation in campaigns.

This report, therefore, seeks to redirect the public's attention toward expanding the playing field. It argues that the role of interactive communications technology points toward a level of engagement that potentially can transform the political calculus. But the report also argues that technology alone cannot do the trick. Sound governmental policies are essential to protecting the conditions under which a politically beneficial technology may continue to flourish. And government policies can and should help foster incentives to encourage more candidates—particularly those below the top of the national ticket—to reach out to small donors and volunteers.

We focus on participation for two reasons. First, if enough people come into the system at the low end, there may be less reason to worry about the top. Much of the current policy debate, and of political reality, has until recently been built on a universe in which a relatively small handful of donors supply most of the money. A significant increase in small donors therefore could shift these assumptions.

Second, we consider heightened participation to be healthy for its own sake. A more engaged citizenry means a greater share of the public following political events, participating in public life, and expressing their views to others—including to those who represent them in government. And the evidence seems to suggest that giving and doing are reciprocal activities: volunteering stimulates giving, but giving a small amount once also seems to heighten nonfinancial forms of participation by people who feel more invested in the process.

For these reasons, we aim to promote equality and civic engagement by enlarging the participatory pie instead of shrinking it. The Supreme Court has ruled out pursuing equality or civic engagement by constraining speech. But the Court has never ruled out pursuing those goals through policies that do not constrain speech.

This report will show how to further these ends. The first half surveys current conditions. It begins with a discussion of the opportunities created by new campaign technologies, as illustrated by President Obama's campaign and others. The report then explains why, despite these opportunities, the best promises of the new technology will not be self-fulfilling. This section draws upon the data from congressional campaigns, state elections, and most of the presidential candidates other than Obama. We argue that government regulations and incentives must continue to play a future role for the democratic potential of the Internet to be fulfilled.

NEW COMMUNICATIONS

Campaigns are about communications—candidates, parties and others, including outside groups, communicating with voters. A campaign's financial needs, and campaign finance rules, are inevitably driven by the nature of communications tools and the costs of communicating. Thus, it is appropriate and necessary for us to focus first on the dramatic changes in telecommunications technology that have already transformed the political world.

In only twelve years, the Internet has moved from the periphery to the center of communications. The digital revolution and the rise of Web 2.0—the collective term used to capture the wide range of online activities and applications that provide network-enabled interactive services—have dramatically altered the means by which individuals receive and use political information. Broadcast media remain the major means of communication in electoral campaigns, but traditional media outlets are losing their audiences and their authoritative role as they are being replaced or supplemented by the more decentralized, collaborative, and participatory information sharing facilitated by online communications and networked services such as blogs, social networking sites, wikis, and real time messaging.

Technological advances are creating a world in which communications are more personal, more mobile, and more global. Surveys conducted by the Pew Internet & American Life Project estimate that 75 percent of adults and 90 percent of teenagers were online by the beginning of 2008, and at least 80 percent of all adults had cell phones.[2] By March of 2008, 62 percent of all Americans had some experience with mobile access to digital data or services. More than half of those with a computer, cell phone, or personal digital assistant or PDA (who together amounted to 41 percent of all Americans) had used a wireless connection at least once to go online when they were away from home or work.[3] For many of these users, Internet access is now a multiplatform affair, moving beyond desktop or laptop computers to a variety of devices that offer online access.

The expansion of broadband availability has also spurred the use of interactive services and web-accessible information. Broadband is penetrating the populace more quickly than either the computer or cell phone, its nearest kin.[4] In fact, the 2008 election was the first election in which more than half of all Americans had broadband access at home.[5] Broadband has acted as a "force multiplier" in the creation of a more distributed computing environment. This environment should continue to expand significantly as broadband's reach increases, and as smart phones and cloud computing applications (in which everything is done online) gain wider use.

While technology increases access, it does not change the *logic* of political participation. Potential donors still have to perceive the benefits of participating, and the perceived costs of participating must not outweigh benefits. Political campaigns and organizations still have to identify and reach out to individuals, persuade and mobilize supporters, create a sense of community among their followers, generate visibility, and find ways to connect with those who are less involved, the "inadvertent audience" that is not specifically seeking political information.

Traditionally, the high costs of participation, combined with the resource needs of campaigns, have favored citizens with time and/or money. Political communication and mobilization have depended upon such expensive or labor-intensive techniques as broadcast advertising, direct mail, and telephone or door-to-door canvassing money has also been costly and time-consuming. Generally, the process favored those who had fundraising experience, well-established contacts, relationships with key fundraisers, an ability to solicit donations from those willing to give large sums, or the time needed to build a broad base of support. While some insurgent or lesser-known candidates lacking these capacities have succeeded, as have some who self-financed their campaigns, these contenders have been the exceptions.

The digital revolution is altering the calculus of participation by lowering the barriers to entry into the political process. Web-enabled communications have reduced the costs of both individual and collective action. Citizens can access information and become involved in a campaign or political organization more easily than ever before, while candidates and political groups have access to more cost-efficient methods for outreach and mobilization. In addition, interactive communications can enhance the benefits of participation by facilitating a sense of community and a stronger connection between individuals and candidates or groups. For example, according to one 2008 survey, 28 percent of Internet users reported that they felt more personally connected to the candidate or campaign of their choice as a result of their online activities, while 22 percent felt that they would not have been involved without the Internet.[6] Thus, the new communications environment facilitates greater participation by both reducing the perceived costs of participating and enhancing the prospective benefits.

The digital revolution's importance in enhancing civic participation was evident in 2008. Millions of Americans went online to access campaign materials, comment on news reports, watch videos, share information with friends, and respond to surveys. Individuals also posted their own views or videos on blogs, YouTube, Facebook, MySpace and other websites; organized or joined independent online political groups or affinity groups associated with a candidate; communicated with campaigns through email and text messaging; received volunteer tasks and reported their status online; and initiated or coordinated user-generated activities in support of the candidate of their choice.

These individual actions highlighted the beginning of an age of electronic interaction in American politics. While grassroots organizing has always been an important part of electoral politics and group politicking, the means and techniques now available for accomplishing this end are qualitatively different. The ready availability of user-generated content and interactive information sharing is empowering individuals, allowing them to move beyond sound bites, campaign ads and traditional information gatekeepers. They can now make their own information choices and produce information and action from the ground up, not simply receive them from the top down. Individuals or groups can share their views with a mass audience, which is a capacity once limited to broadcast media. They need no longer depend upon the command-and-control methods used by candidates and political parties. Now the many can communicate with the many without the intervention of elites or centralized organizations.

This capacity has enabled innovative forms of collective action. In the past, grassroots mobilization efforts or broad-based outreach programs typically were conducted by well-established organizations with the significant resources needed to finance such initiatives. These organizations, including parties, interest groups, trade associations, and unions, were also responsible for much of the money used to finance electioneering activities. But digital communications have made possible the formation of new types of political organizations or networked communities. These group entities can form quickly, mobilizing online around a particular candidate, issue, or common view. They can take any of a variety of legal forms, ranging from an online affinity group or political organization to an offline PAC or nonprofit advocacy corporation. In some instances they may emerge in response to timely issues or events, as in the case of Vote-Vets.org, a pro-military organization founded by veterans of the wars in Iraq and Afghanistan. Such groups may prove to be limited to the duration of their purpose, as in the case of Swift Boat Veterans and POWs for Truth in the 2004 election, or evolve into more permanent entities, as in the case of MoveOn.org or the independent progressive fundraising site, Act Blue.

Finally, candidate campaigns can achieve scales of engaged participation—whether measured in terms of the number of individuals in direct contact, the number of volunteers assisting, or the number of donors contributing—that were not feasible a short time ago. Digital communications make it easier to identify and incorporate supporters. This is partly because it is much easier now for individuals to take the first step, initiating contact. Once there has been some form of initial contact, it is also much easier now for candidates to keep the lines open, by tracking visitors to their websites and using email and other forms of inexpensive communications outreach to keep them engaged, rather than having to rely solely on expensive direct mail and telephone prospecting.

Moreover, once supporters are recruited, it is easier to personalize future communications. In essence, candidate campaigns increasingly will be able to communicate and establish a relationship with potential supporters and then to involve them in campaign activities if they are willing to volunteer.

THE OBAMA CAMPAIGN: A NEW MODEL?

No example to date better illustrates this potential than Barack Obama's 2008 presidential campaign. From the outset, Obama recognized the value of online communications and social networking tools, making them cores of his outreach and mobilization efforts. The campaign built a state-of-the-art website that featured a social networking hub, My.BarackObama.com, which became known as MyBO. This hub was used to build an "online relationship" with individual supporters and encourage them to share information and ideas, contribute to the campaign, undertake volunteer activities, and vote.

MyBO was established not as an afterthought, unconnected to the campaign's core, but as the center of all campaign-related Internet activity. The campaign sought out potential supporters where they were already online by linking to an array of social networking sites, including Facebook, MySpace, AsianAve, MiGente, BlackPlan, and Twitter.[7] These platforms helped the campaign drive supporters to the official website, where they could build individual supporter profiles and generate grassroots, bottom-up activity among networked groups of supporters. By Election Day, more than 2 million MyBO profiles had been created and Obama had 3.4 million Facebook supporters. The campaign also had an email list of 13 million, one million text message subscribers, and the most popular Twitter account, with more than 123,000 followers.[8]

From a campaign finance perspective, MyBO set a new standard for using the Internet to recruit and engage a vast network of financial supporters. In all, Obama, who decided to forgo public funds in both the primary and general election, raised a total of $746 million during the 2008 election cycle, a record sum that far surpassed the amount received by any other presidential contender.

Obama raised more than twice the amount taken in by his general election opponent, Republican John McCain, who refused public funds during the primaries but accepted the general election public funding grant. McCain raised a total of $350 million, including $84 million of public funds. During the primary campaign alone, Obama raised $409 million, which was more than the rest of the Democratic field combined, and $215 million more than his principal rival, Hillary Clinton. Even more notable, a significant share of Obama's total—$500 million according to one estimate—was raised through donations made online.[9]

MyBO offered individuals ways to participate in campaign fundraising that went beyond such standard online tools as a "donate" button for credit card contributions. Individuals who made a contribution were regularly solicited by email and often were asked to make an additional contribution that would be matched by another donor. Contributors could sign up for a "recurring gift" program that allowed them to make donations of as little as $25 on regular basis by charging the amount to a credit card. Supporters could also establish their own fundraising pages or affinity groups to solicit their friends or contacts to contribute, and then watch their personal web-page "fundraising thermometer" climb as those individuals gave in response to their requests. To promote such volunteer efforts, the campaign established a grassroots fundraising committee that helped train supporters online in how to collect donations from friends, relatives, or coworkers. This tactic was so successful that by the end of the general election, the Obama campaign had created a corps of 70,000 individuals who were willing to solicit their own networks for campaign dollars.[10]

In these ways, the Obama campaign personalized its fundraising appeals and emphasized the importance of small contributions. Empowering those who were willing to give small amounts led to an outpouring of small donations. These small donations were essential to Obama's financial success. According to an analysis of primary campaign funds conducted by the nonpartisan Campaign Finance Institute, Obama amassed $217 million from small contributions of $200 or less by the end of August of 2008, which was more than any previous presidential candidate and a sum that exceeded the small contribution receipts of all other candidates in both parties combined.[11] Small contributions of $200 or less constituted 50 percent of the total funds that Obama raised from individuals through August 31, compared to 36 percent ($64 million) of the total for Clinton and 31 percent ($62 million) for McCain. The one other candidate with noteworthy small contribution receipts was conservative Republican Ron Paul, who relied almost exclusively on online contributions from his coterie of supporters to raise almost $22 million from small gifts, which represented 64 percent of his money from individual contributions.

In addition to the sheer amount of money raised from small contributions, what distinguished Obama's campaign was the scope of citizen participation it was able to achieve. Obama's online strategy allowed him to benefit from the scalability offered by the Internet to recruit an unprecedented number of donors. By February of 2008, one million individuals had given money to his campaign, a mark that then-President George Bush, running unopposed for re-nomination in 2004, did not reach until May of that year.[12] As Obama continued to maintain his lead throughout the hard-fought nomination campaign against Clinton, his financial base continued to expand. By the end of the election, hundreds of thousands more had joined these ranks, bringing his total number of donors during the pre-nomination phase of the campaign to about 3 million.[13] No prior presidential candidate had ever mobilized such a broad base of donors.

Obama's emphasis on small contributions thus provided him with a large pool of individuals who could give repeated contributions without approaching the maximum contribution limit of $2,300. And thousands did give repeatedly. This ability to solicit multiple contributions was one of the major strategic advantages of his approach.

An analysis by the Campaign Finance Institute of the 405,000 individuals who donated at least an *aggregate* of $200 or more by August 31 (and thus had their names disclosed in filings with the Federal Election Commission) revealed that at least 212,000 were repeat donors who began by making an undisclosed small contribution of less than $200. About 93,000 of these repeat donors gave a total of $400 or less; 106,000 gave more than $400 but less than $1,000; and 13,000 gave $1,000 or more. These repeat donors ended up giving about $100 million to the campaign.

Thus, another way of assessing Obama's fundraising is on the basis of the *aggregate* amount given by individual *donors* instead of on the basis of the separate *donations* made by individuals. Such an analysis provides a clearer depiction of the role of small *donors*, defined here as those who gave no more than $200 in aggregate during the course of the campaign. This information is provided in Table 1.

When the multiple contributions from the same donors are aggregated, the differences between Obama and other candidates are narrower, although the importance of small donors to his campaign is still evident. Obama received 30 percent of his money during the primaries from donors who gave a total of $200 or less. This percentage was greater than Clinton's 22 percent and McCain's 21 percent as well as Bush's 26 percent or Kerry's 20 percent in 2004. Obama

Table 1: Sources of funds for presidential candidates
Pre-nomination: 2007–2008

| Candidate | Individual contributions | From donors aggregating in the primaries to ... | | | | | |
| | | $200 or less | | $201–$999 | | $1000 or more | |
	Total net $ million	$ million	%	$ million	%	$ million	%
DEM							
Obama	409.2	121.2	30%	113.1	28%	174.4	43%
Clinton	194.0	42.5	22%	43.8	23%	107.7	56%
Edwards	38.6	11.8	31%	8.5	22%	18.3	47%
Richardson	21.8	3.5	16%	4.0	18%	14.3	65%
Dodd	11.8	1.0	9%	0.9	8%	9.8	83%
Biden	9.6	1.6	17%	1.3	13%	6.7	70%
Kucinich	4.4	2.5	56%	1.1	26%	0.8	19%
Gravel	0.5	0.3	52%	0.1	24%	0.1	24%
Dem subtotal	735.5	184.4	25%	178.1	24%	373.0	51%
REP							
McCain	203.5	42.2	21%	40.2	20%	121.2	60%
Romney	59.8	4.7	8%	7.9	13%	47.1	79%
Giuliani	55.0	3.5	6%	5.6	10%	45.9	83%
Paul	34.3	13.4	39%	9.6	28%	11.3	33%
Thompson, F.	23.2	8.9	39%	4.2	18%	10.1	43%
Huckabee	16.0	4.6	29%	3.7	23%	7.7	48%
Tancredo	4.0	2.2	55%	1.1	28%	0.7	18%
Brownback	3.5	1.2	34%	0.8	22%	1.5	43%
Hunter	2.3	1.1	45%	0.4	19%	0.8	36%
Thompson, T.	1.0	0.1	8%	0.1	15%	0.7	77%
Gilmore	0.3	0.0	9%	0.0	9%	0.3	83%
Rep subtotal	403.1	81.9	20%	73.7	18%	247.4	61%
Pre-nomination total, 2008	1,138.5	266.3	23%	251.8	22%	620.3	54%

Major party nominees of 2004

Kerry	215.9	43.6	20%	51.1	24%	121.3	56%
Bush	256.1	66.4	26%	37.7	15%	153.3	60%

General election, 2008

| Candidate | Individual contributions | From donors aggregating in the general election to | | | | | |
| | | $200 or less | | $201–$999 | | $1000 or more | |
	Total net $ million	$ million	%	$ million	%	$ million	%
Obama	336.9	114.1	34%	79.2	23%	143.1	42%

Note: Because Obama is the only candidate who raised and spent private funds money for his general election campaign committee, these tables present his aggregate contributions per donor separately for the primaries and general election. This permits a direct comparison of Obama's primary fundraising to those of other candidates and Obama's general election to his own primary fundraising. Under this procedure, a donor who gave $150 in the primaries and $150 in the general election would be characterized as being in the separate "200-and-under" aggregates for the primary and general election. Recalculations based on combining the primary and general election figures into running two-year aggregates are available separately from The Campaign Finance Institute.

also depended less on contributors of $1,000 or more than Clinton or McCain, receiving 43 percent of his primary funds from such donors, as compared to 56 percent for Clinton and 60 percent for McCain.

So Obama successfully raised funds from all parts of the contributor spectrum, showing particular strength among donors of both smaller and larger sums. His share from those who gave an aggregate of $1,000 or more, however, was smaller than that of any other major contender in recent elections. In the general election, Obama's percentage from small donors was even higher: he raised $114.1 million, or 34 percent of his general election total, from donors whose general election contributions aggregated to $200 or less. At the same time, his percentage from donors who aggregated to $1,000 or more dropped slightly to 42 percent of his general election total (including funds raised for his campaign through joint fundraising committees), while contributions of those in the $201–$999 midrange was 23 percent.

SMALL DONORS' SMALL ROLE: THE NEED FOR BROADER PARTICIPATION, EVEN AFTER OBAMA

The Obama campaign points to a model of campaign finance that offers the prospect of reducing the relative influence of large donors by expanding the role of small donors. But whether Obama presents a model that most other candidates can implement successfully is an open question. Will technological and behavioral trends alone eventually resolve some of the major concerns that are commonly associated with campaign funding? Or will fundamental changes in campaign finance require more than simply the structural capabilities offered by digital technology?

Although Obama enjoyed remarkable success in generating small contributions, he benefited from factors other than technological change that will be hard to replicate. He was an inspiring and charismatic candidate, who emerged as a major contender relatively early in the race, and was seeking to make history as the first African American nominee of a major party. He was running as a candidate promising change, in an election defined by an electorate anxious for change. And he received substantial support from a new generation of online activists and young voters who fervently participated in his campaign.

That the Obama candidacy was in some ways unique is evident from the broader financial patterns in 2008. Most of the major contenders for the presidential nominations, except for Obama, raised a majority of their campaign funds from large contributions of $1,000 or more, even before aggregating.

Among Democrats, Clinton, Edwards, Richardson, Dodd and Biden each raised more than half of their campaign money from large contributions of $1,000 or more. Among the Republicans, McCain raised 54 percent of his funds in contributions of $1,000 or more, Romney 74 percent, and Giuliani 82 percent. Even Mike Huckabee and Fred Thompson, who raised less than $25 million each, took in at least 40 percent from donations of $1,000 or more. Ron Paul was the only Republican to raise a substantial amount of money ($34 million) without relying heavily on $1,000 donors. Paul received 18 percent in large contributions and 33 percent from donors who aggregated to $1,000 or more (see Table 1).

These overall figures, however, do not tell the whole story. The importance of large contributions as a source of campaign funding becomes clearer when campaign fundraising is considered over time during the campaign season. Presidential candidates file reports with the Federal Election Commission on a quarterly basis during the off year and monthly during the election year. An examination of the fundraising that took place during the beginning phase of the presidential contest reveals that all of the candidates—even Obama—started by relying heavily on large donors. In the first nine months of 2007, Obama raised 60 percent of his money in amounts of $1,000 or more. Even Ron Paul, who received half of his money during the first nine months of 2007 from small contributions, started during the first quarter by getting more than half of his funding from those who gave contributions of $1,000 or more. In every instance, the candidates who were able to mount viable campaigns started by emphasizing large contributions.

In general, candidates who eventually received substantial numbers of small contributions did not do so until they had gained name recognition and emerged as likely contenders for the nomination. For example, through the first three quarters of 2007, Obama received only 28 percent of his money from contributions of $200 or less. In the third quarter alone, he received only 24 percent of his funds from small contributions. But by the fourth quarter, he had emerged as a principal challenger, along with Edwards, to presumed frontrunner Hillary Clinton, and experienced a surge in small-donor giving, garnering 46 percent of his fourth-quarter funds from contributions of $200 or less. Thereafter, following his victory in Iowa and emergence as the leading candidate for the nomination, small contributions to his campaign grew dramatically, accounting for half of the money he brought in during the election year up to the time of the national convention. Similarly, Democratic challenger John Edwards and Republican Mike Huckabee did not begin to raise substantial sums from small contributions until the fourth quarter of 2007, while Hillary Clinton, who raised 69 percent of her money in the fourth quarter from large contributions, did not experience a jump in small donations until the first two months of the election year.

This reliance on large contributions during the early phase of the presidential contest is not surprising. It follows the practice of most candidates in recent elections, regardless of the office being sought. Given the financial demands of modern campaigns, candidates—whether seeking the presidency, a congressional seat or statewide office—face great pressure to raise as much money as possible as quickly as possible.

This strategic imperative is a result of both the anticipated costs of a campaign and the widely held perception of fundraising strength as an indicator of a candidate's viability, especially during the early phase of a contest. In other words, the best way for a candidate to generate visibility and be viewed as a major contender is to rank among the top fundraisers. This is especially true in a presidential race, but also applies to congressional and state contests. The most efficient way to accomplish this objective is to focus on large contributions. Candidates therefore have a strong incentive to focus on large donors.

The rising tide of online activity may alter this pattern in future elections. With new means available for generating visibility and communicating with the public, candidates may find it possible to launch a campaign without having to raise large amounts from a relatively small group of donors. The Internet makes it easier for candidates to disseminate information broadly, which may serve to engage voter interest and thereby produce more small contributions early in an election cycle.

But the lessons to date indicate that broad-based small-donor fundraising, in most cases, is only likely to occur after a candidate attains a certain level of public visibility and credibility. While a lesser-known or underdog candidate may not have to gain as much recognition as past candidates to engage in mass fundraising, public support still has to reach some kind of critical mass before small-donor fundraising is likely to produce substantial amounts of money. An underdog candidate for president would either have to develop a following within a viable niche, as Howard Dean did as the antiwar candidate in 2004 or as Ron Paul did as the libertarian Republican in 2008, or he or she would have to be seen as a credible alternative to a frontrunner, as Obama did in 2008. And the higher the amount garnered by the leading fundraisers, the more money it will take to be perceived as a credible challenger.

But even if citizen participation in presidential campaigns does improve and candidates are able to increase their reliance on small donors, such an outcome is unlikely in less visible elections. Currently, small donors play a relatively insignificant role in most federal and state legislative races. As a general rule, movement down the ticket is accompanied by a decline in the level of citizen participation in campaign funding. The lower the level of the race, the lower the level of small-donor participation. Consequently, the role of small donors is much smaller in U.S. Senate and House races than in the presidential. In many state gubernatorial and legislative contests, small donors are also responsible for only a tiny portion of campaign funding.

Candidates for the U.S. Senate and House have not experienced the growth in small contributions that has been seen in some presidential campaigns. Congressional candidates do not receive as much media coverage or public attention as presidential aspirants. They also operate within much smaller constituencies. They therefore tend to rely on relatively small numbers of large donors to finance their campaigns. This is especially true for established incumbents who have proven donor bases and access to PAC money and well-heeled donors.

The lower level of small-donor funding in congressional campaigns is evident from the financial patterns of the 2008 general election candidates. Senate candidates received 14 percent of their funding from individual donors who gave an aggregate of $200 or less. For incumbents, the percentage was only 9 percent. In contrast, 40 percent of the funds raised by Senate candidates came from those who gave an aggregate of $1,000 or more, with another 20 percent coming from PACs and 17 percent from all other sources, including self-financing. (See Table 2.)

In House general election contests, which typically feature candidates who are less well known and given less media coverage than Senate contenders, only 8 percent of the funding came from small donors who gave an aggregate of $200 or less (see Table 3). Among incumbents, the percentage was only 6 percent, which meant that, on average, incumbents received less than $85,000 from small donors out of $1.4 million raised. Instead, House candidates emphasized large donations and PAC money, receiving more than a third (35 percent) of their funding from donors who gave an aggregate of $1,000, more than another third (36 percent) from PACs, and 10 percent from other sources, including self-financing. (For incumbents, individuals who gave $1,000 or more were responsible for 34 percent and PACs another 45 percent.) In short, large donors and PACs were more than eight times as important as small donors for all House candidates, and twelve times as important for incumbents.

Determining the scope of small-donor participation at the state level is more complicated than at the federal level, due to variations in campaign finance

Table 2: Sources of funds for U.S. Senate candidates, 1999-2008

	Total receipts	From individual donors aggregating to...						PACs		Other inc. self-finance	
		$200 or less		$201–$999		$1000 or more					
	$ million	$ million	%	$ million	%	$ million	%	$ million	%	$ million	%
All candidates											
2007–2008	391.7	56.6	14%	33.4	9%	157.9	40%	77.6	20%	66.1	17%
2005–2006	517.0	84.9	16%	46.5	9%	218.3	42%	69.9	14%	97.5	19%
2003–2004	371.2	62.9	17%	39.4	11%	163.5	44%	64.5	17%	40.9	11%
2001–2002	288.3	49.1	17%	34.2	12%	102.3	35%	57.1	20%	45.6	16%
1999–2000	367.7	64.0	17%	36.1	10%	102.5	28%	50.7	14%	114.3	31%
Incumbents											
2007–2008	233.8	20.8	9%	17.8	8%	94.3	40%	59.4	25%	41.4	18%
2005–2006	278.0	43.2	16%	25.1	9%	133.4	48%	50.6	18%	25.7	9%
2003–2004	171.1	29.0	17%	17.2	10%	75.6	44%	38.9	23%	10.4	6%
2001–2002	122.5	20.9	17%	15.5	13%	43.1	35%	33.3	27%	9.8	8%
1999–2000	128.8	24.7	19%	15.0	12%	40.0	31%	32.6	25%	16.5	13%

Source: Campaign Finance Institute analysis of FEC records.

Table 3: Sources of funds for U.S. House candidates, 1999–2008

	Total receipts	From individual donors aggregating to...						PACs		Other inc. self-finance	
		$200 or less		$201–$999		$1000 or more					
	$ million	$ million	%	$ million	%	$ million	%	$ million	%	$ million	%
All candidates											
2007–2008	853.6	72.1	8%	94.6	11%	295.5	35%	307.7	36%	83.7	10%
2005–2006	779.5	71	9%	89.2	11%	265.3	34%	287.8	37%	66.3	9%
2003–2004	626.3	62.7	10%	80.8	13%	207	33%	229.4	37%	46.4	7%
2001–2002	555.3	66.5	12%	63	11%	142.1	26%	207.1	37%	76.6	14%
1999–2000	538.4	82.1	15%	66.3	12%	131.7	24%	193.2	36%	65.1	12%
Incumbents											
2007–2008	575.3	36.6	6%	57.2	10%	194.8	34%	257.3	45%	29.4	5%
2005–2006	527.2	33.2	6%	53.5	10%	176.2	33%	237.1	45%	27.1	5%
2003–2004	454	39.1	9%	56.8	13%	149.9	33%	191.7	42%	16.5	4%
2001–2002	367.4	42.3	12%	42.4	12%	96.3	26%	164.3	45%	22.1	6%
1999–2000	357.6	53.3	15%	42.4	12%	86.4	24%	150.3	42%	25.1	7%

Source: Campaign Finance Institute analysis of FEC records.

policies, disclosure requirements, and political environments. But an analysis of contributions in all states with gubernatorial and legislative elections in 2006, which was conducted by the Campaign Finance Institute based on data available from the National Institute of Money in State Politics, provides insight into the role of small donors at the state level, as well as the rules that may influence small-donor giving.

Small donors are not a significant source of funding in most elections found further down the ticket. In state gubernatorial or legislative elections in some of the largest states, small-donor participation falls below the levels in congressional contests. In 5 of the 33 states with gubernatorial and state legislative elections in 2006, small donors were responsible for less than 10 percent of the monies received by candidates from contributors, even when donors of up to $250 are included (as opposed to the $200 cutoff that is used in federal elections).* In another 16 states, donors who gave aggregates of $250 or less accounted for 10 to 18 percent of funds (see Table 4).

In several states, however, the proportional role of small donors was well above the levels for U.S. House and Senate races, as well for most presidential campaigns. Minnesota led the way with the highest levels of participation, with donors of $250 or less accounting for 60 percent of the candidates' money. The likely explanation for Minnesota's uniqueness lies in its campaign finance laws. The state had low contribution limits, offered donors a state rebate of up to $50 for contributions, and offered partial public funding to candidates.** About 5 percent of Minnesotans contributed to candidates under this set of policies.

This examination of campaign funding beyond the presidential race suggests that most candidates are not likely to be able to rely on small donor participation to launch a bid for office. In most instances, acquiring the initial funding to get a campaign off the ground will continue to depend on persuading a relatively small group of supporters to give larger amounts. Only then will a candidate be in a position to successfully expand his or her fundraising downward and outward.

---

* There is no uniform standard for determining what constitutes a small contribution or small donor. Under the provisions of federal law, contributions of less than $200 are known as "unitemized contributions," since they are considered small enough that they do not have to be itemized on disclosure reports. Donor information is disclosed when an individual's aggregate contributions to a candidate or political committee reach the $200 threshold. Unitemized contributions or donations of less than $200 thus can be used as a practical standard for identifying small contributions for the purposes of analysis. No such uniform standard for reporting donations or defining what constitutes an unitemized contribution exists in state law; instead, disclosure requirements vary depending of the provisions of state law. Thus, for the purposes of examining state contributions, differentiation of contributions up to $100 and contributions from $101 to $250 are used.

** In 2009, the Governor eliminated funding for contribution rebates in the state budget. [...]

Table 4. Sources of Funds for Candidates in State Elections in 2006

(Gubernatorial and Legislative Candidates in 33 States*with Gubernatorial Elections in 2006)

State	% from Individuals Who Gave Aggregate Amounts per Candidate of ...			% from Organizations		Totals	
	$1–$250	$251–$999	$1,000 or more	Non-Party	Party	Percent	Dollars
AL	4%	4%	17%	73%	2%	100%	$70,206,321
CA	5%	3%	47%	34%	11%	100%	$230,821,374
OR	5%	1%	47%	41%	6%	100%	$39,418,135
NY	7%	5%	33%	45%	10%	100%	$87,811,035
NV	9%	4%	14%	63%	10%	100%	$30,482,171
FL	10%	28%	5%	37%	20%	100%	$75,064,156
WY	11%	9%	29%	48%	3%	100%	$3,193,107
OH	11%	7%	37%	19%	27%	100%	$68,795,128
IL	11%	3%	10%	61%	15%	100%	$87,622,060
IA	12%	7%	37%	28%	16%	100%	$30,447,171
NM	12%	6%	38%	11%	32%	100%	$18,028,816
SC	13%	7%	39%	36%	4%	100%	$17,779,583
GA	13%	6%	38%	38%	4%	100%	$45,703,869
MI	13%	9%	45%	22%	10%	100%	$56,547,344
PA	14%	7%	43%	25%	10%	100%	$79,698,776
AR	15%	13%	39%	29%	4%	100%	$18,024,307
TN	16%	11%	37%	29%	8%	100%	$18,455,210
MD	17%	12%	35%	35%	1%	100%	$46,439,970
ID	17%	9%	25%	43%	6%	100%	$6,477,352
KS	17%	8%	28%	46%	1%	100%	$10,872,285
OK	18%	11%	49%	0%	22%	100%	$19,079,657
RI	20%	24%	36%	18%	3%	100%	$5,888,571
CT	21%	19%	41%	14%	5%	100%	$16,120,357
AK	21%	19%	28%	21%	11%	100%	$11,607,931
HI	22%	9%	40%	26%	3%	100%	$8,548,758
NH	22%	11%	37%	25%	4%	100%	$4,475,429
MA	27%	32%	34%	4%	3%	100%	$62,937,571
CO	28%	21%	25%	19%	7%	100%	$14,324,767
SD	29%	2%	32%	19%	18%	100%	$5,154,670
WI	36%	14%	39%	7%	3%	100%	$23,371,146
NE	38%	8%	28%	25%	2%	100%	$8,487,080
VT	40%	14%	17%	19%	10%	100%	$3,052,483
MN	60%	11%	17%	6%	6%	100%	$16,793,445

*Totals exclude public financing (where it exists) and candidate self-financing. The table also excludes two states with full public funding systems (AZ, ME) and one whose disclosure records do not permit comparable analysis (TX).
Source: Campaign Finance Institute, based on data from the National Institute on Money in State Politics.

Might this change as citizens come to make greater use of the technologies now available? With the remarkable pace of change in communications now underway, this is a possibility that should not be dismissed. But it would also be imprudent to count on it. While some congressional candidates and others have raised substantial amounts from small donors, these challengers have been involved in high-visibility races that were essentially "nationalized" because they represented targeted seats that were being contested in the context of a battle for majority control of the legislature. These candidates thus became a focus of well-viewed weblogs like Daily Kos or Red State, or of third-party fundraising efforts conducted by organizations like Act Blue. In this manner, the candidates gained the visibility they needed to raise large numbers of small donations successfully. But such a path is likely to be open for only a few dozen races—at best—in each election cycle. Until and unless a substantial change occurs in the system, the emergence of viable candidates in all other instances will depend on an established constituency, support from those who can give a lot, or the ability to finance a campaign out of one's own pocket.

But we also conclude from these data that public policy can play a beneficial role in offering an alternative to the current system by modifying incentive structures. At present, candidates have little incentive to seek out larger numbers of small donors because the process favors concentrations of wealth. It is more efficient for most candidates—especially incumbents or well-known contenders with established bases of donor support—to amass funds by emphasizing donations at the upper end of the range established by contribution limits. There is also a strong incentive to seek out the support of large, well-funded PACs, or of other organizations that can encourage their members to make contributions or can spend significant sums directly to assist a candidate's electoral chances. In these ways candidates and groups can concentrate their efforts on a smaller universe of donors and raise significant amounts of money quickly.

If broader civic participation in campaign funding is to be achieved, candidates and political groups must expand their outreach to citizens of average means. They must reach out to small contributors and emphasize their importance. The donors, in their turn, must perceive the benefits of participating and believe that their contributions, no matter how small, can make a difference.

Instead of focusing on further restraints, the law should offer incentives—either through public subsidies or other means—to encourage citizen participation by small donors. As the experience in the states demonstrates, policies that promote small-donor giving or enhance the value of small contributions can increase the benefits of small-donor fundraising for candidates. This opens an alternative means for potentially strong candidates to launch an effective campaign. This would improve candidate competition and voter choice, while strengthening civic participation in the electoral process.

WHAT SHOULD BE DONE?

Despite the successes of 2008, the authors of this report remain skeptical that technology's best promises will be self-fulfilling. For one thing, the communications environment of 2008 was in some ways a lucky accident. The conditions underlying this accident are bound to change along with communications platforms. The continuation and dispersion of the Internet's promise therefore will require governmental monitoring and support. The report's main recommendations accordingly begin with ones focused on using regulation to foster open access to communications, to lower the information costs of participation, and to improve transparency.

But we also remain skeptical that the "small-donor revolution" will be replicated down the ticket without support. Our skepticism is fueled by the results of new Campaign Finance Institute analyses of state and federal campaign finance records. Tables in the full report show that the typical congressional or state candidate is still being bankrolled by thousand-dollar donors and interest groups, with only a trickle coming in from those who give small amounts. To counter this, we recommend government incentives to engage and expand the role of small donors. Specifically, we recommend partial public financing for elections at all levels, in primaries as well as general elections.

- We favor systems in which public money goes to participating candidates in the form of multiple matching funds, but only for small contributions.
- Lower contribution limits should replace spending limits as a condition of eligibility for the receipt of public funds. There should also be a maximum ceiling on the amount of public money a candidate may receive.
- As a supplement, we also support tax credits or rebates targeted at lower-income donors.

Finally, to improve accountability and enhance the role of political parties in competitive elections, we support unlimited coordinated party spending, but the spending must be paid out of funds raised from small donors.[14]

ENDNOTES

1. See Michael J. Malbin, "Rethinking the Campaign Finance Agenda," *The Forum*, 6:1 (2008), www.bepress.com/forum/vol6/iss1/.

2. Susannah Fox, *Privacy Implications of Fast, Mobile Internet Access*, Pew Internet & American Life Project, February 13, 2008, www.pewinternet.org/Reports/2008/Privacy-Implications-of-Fast-Mobile-Internet-Access.aspx.

3. John Horrigan, *Mobile Access to Data and Information*, Pew Internet & American Life Project, March 5, 2008, www.pewinternet.org/Press-Releases/2008/Mobile-Access-to-Data-and-Information.aspx.

4. John Horrigan, *Why We Don't Know Enough About Broadband in the U.S.*, Pew Internet & American Life Project, November 14, 2007, www.pewinternet.org/Reports/2007/Why-We-Dont-Know-Enough-About-Broadband-in-the-US.aspx.

5. John Horrigan, *Home Broadband 2008*, Pew Internet & American Life Project, July 2, 2008, www.pewinternet.org/Reports/2008/Home-Broadband-2008.aspx.

6. Pew Internet & American Life Project, *The Internet and the 2008 Election*, June 15, 2008, www.pewinternet.org/Reports/2008/The-Internet-and-the-2008-Election.aspx.

7. Jose Antonio Vargas, "Obama's Wide Web," *Washington Post*, August 20, 2008.

8. Jose Antonio Vargas, "Obama Raised Half a Billion Online," *washingtonpost.com*, November 20, 2008, voices.washingtonpost.com/the-trail/2008/11/20/obama_raised_half_a_billion_on.html; and David Talbot, "The Geeks Behind Obama's Web Strategy," *Boston Globe*, January 8, 2009.

9. Vargas, "Obama Raised Half a Billion Online."

10. *Ibid.*

11. Campaign Finance Institute, "After Holding Financial Advantage in Primaries, Obama Likely to Achieve Only Parity with McCain in General Election," press release, September 25, 2008, www.cfinst.org/pr/prRelease.aspx?ReleaseID=205.

12. Kristin Jensen and Jonathan D. Salant, "Obama Began February with $10 Million Cash Advantage," *Bloomberg.com*, February 21, 2008, www.bloomberg.com/apps/news?pid=20601087&sid=aze.Uqi5D79Q&refer=home; Jonathan D. Salant and Kristin Jensen, "Obama Raised $40 Million in March, Twice Clinton's $20 Million," *Bloomberg.com*, April 3, 2008, www.bloomberg.com/apps/news?pid=20601103&sid=aYFVO4QlZuL0&refer=us; and Paul Farhi, "In April, Kerry's Fundraising Nearly Doubled Bush's; President Has Spent $130 Million on Race," *Washington Post*, May 21, 2004.

13. Michael J. Malbin, "Small Donors, Large Donors and the Internet: The Case for Public Financing after Obama," Campaign Finance Institute Working Paper, April 2009, p. 17. See also, Vargas, "Obama Raised Half a Billion Online."

14. For a full list of the authors' recommendations, see Anthony J. Corrado, Michael J. Malbin, Thomas E. Mann, and Norman Ornstein, "Reform in an Age of Networked Campaigns," Campaign Finance Institute, 2010. On line, http://www.cfinst.org/Press/PReleases/10-01-14/Reform_in_an_Age_of_Networked_Campaigns.aspx.

*__Anthony J. Corrado__ is Charles A. Dana Professor of Government at Colby College. He is a Nonresident Senior Fellow of The Brookings Institution and serves as Chair of the Board of Trustees of the Campaign Finance Institute.

__Thomas E. Mann__ is the W. Averell Harriman Chair and Senior Fellow in Governance Studies at The Brookings Institution.

Michael J. Malbin is a professor of political science at the State University of New York at Albany and the founder and executive director of the Campaign Finance Institute.

Norman J. Ornstein is a resident scholar at the American Enterprise Institute for Public Policy Research.

Excerpted from Anthony J. Corrado, Michael J. Malbin, Thomas E. Mann, Norman J. Ornstein. *Reform in an Age of Networked Campaigns: How to Foster Citizen Participation through Small Donors and Volunteers.* A Joint Project of the Campaign Finance Institute, American Enterprise Institute, and Brookings Institution. Washington, DC: The Campaign Finance Institute. January 2010.

DISCUSSION QUESTIONS

1. Will other presidential candidates be able to replicate Barack Obama's success in raising money, or was there something unique about Obama's campaign?

2. To what extent can the fundraising techniques of the Obama campaign be replicated by candidates at other levels of government?

3. How important is it for presidential candidates to raise money from small donors? That is, is a campaign that raises a large proportion of its money in small contributions necessarily "better" than a campaign that relies mainly on large contributions?

Paying to Play: Fundraising in the U.S. House of Representatives

*by Marian Currinder**

Three months before the November 2010 mid-term elections, then–Minority Leader John Boehner (R-Ohio) quietly launched a "Boehner for Speaker" fundraising committee. All signs suggested that Republicans would win majority control of the U.S. House and that John Boehner would become the next Speaker of the House. But rather than coast to victory, Boehner pledged to spend the final months of the campaign raising millions for Republican candidates. To bring in a lot of money quickly, Boehner set up a joint fundraising committee that allows individual contributors to give more because the money is divided between several accounts (in this case, contributions were divided between the Boehner for Speaker account, Boehner's reelection account, and a Republican campaign committee account). Lobbyists and other major donors who gave the maximum contribution of $37,800 or helped raise $100,000 for the new committee were promised meetings with Boehner, updates from Boehner's senior aides, and VIP access to a number of Republican briefings and events. By Election Day, Boehner had contributed over $5 million to GOP candidates and headlined hundreds of fundraising events. His efforts paid off when Republicans won majority control of the House and he was named Speaker (Hooper 2010; Jacobs 2010; Martin 2010).

In addition to raising millions of dollars every two years, House leaders are responsible for overseeing congressional party fundraising efforts. At a September 2010 House Republican Conference meeting, then–Minority Leader Boehner pledged to contribute $1 million to the National Republican Campaign Committee (NRCC) if his colleagues would pledge to contribute $3 million. The NRCC is the campaign committee for House Republicans and works to help the party gain or retain majority status. The committee's strategies depend on a number of factors but today center primarily on fundraising. The committee raises money to help Republican incumbents in close races and to fund promising Republican challengers and open-seat candidates. The Democratic Congressional Campaign Committee (DCCC) is the campaign committee for House Democrats and, like the NRCC, focuses on gaining or retaining majority status, primarily through fundraising.[1] As Boehner began calling on individual members to pledge, he pointed to a colleague standing by the door and said, "Block the doors. Nobody's leaving." Within 35 minutes, he had secured $3 million in pledges; several lawmakers, eager to impress Boehner, even committed to raising six-figure sums (Hooper 2010). For party leaders to persuade members to give for the good of the whole, they must lead by example.

Persuading members to spread the wealth, however, is sometimes easier said than done. While Boehner was appealing to a united minority, then–House Speaker Nancy Pelosi (D-California) faced a divided majority. Representative Raúl Grijalva (D-Arizona), co-chairman of the Congressional Progressive Caucus, said he had decided against contributing to the DCCC because the money would likely be funneled back out to conservative Democrats whose seats were at risk. "I hate to think the money that I and any progressive or any member of the Hispanic caucus gives goes directly to the most vehement anti-immigrant people on the [DCCC] list" (Newmyer 2010). Pelosi, who raised and contributed more than $43 million during the 2010 election cycle, also struggled to persuade senior Democrats to follow her lead. Three months before Election Day, Pelosi demanded that committee chairs and other high-ranking Democrats contribute to the DCCC or risk defeat in November. "Your money was budgeted for," she told them. "You owe us this money" (Palmer and Dennis 2010).

House members today operate in a highly ideological and highly competitive political environment; persuading these members to contribute to their party organizations and to their colleagues in need is one of the most challenging tasks House leaders confront. Members who resist, however, do so at their own risk because leaders have the power to reward and punish. An aide to Speaker Pelosi warned that anyone sitting on more than $1 million after Election Day could have a hard time competing for leadership, chairmanships, or seats on "A-level" committees (Palmer and Dennis 2010). Fundraising has become a means by which House leaders communicate their expectations to members, and members communicate their loyalty to leadership.

FOR THE GOOD OF THE WHOLE

Campaign money has figured prominently in electoral party politics for decades, but it became central during the 1990s and remains so today. As the margins between parties in the House shrank and electoral competition increased, party leaders sought out new sources of money for the congressional campaign committees (CCCs). In addition to requesting money from individual contributors and political action committees (PACs), the CCCs began asking incumbent members to contribute their excess campaign funds. They reasoned that retaining or gaining majority status was a group goal, and that all members who could afford to give should do so for the good of the whole. They also believed that incumbent giving would inspire potential outside contributors to support the party. Today, both parties count on contributions from their members for about one-third of their campaign committee funds.

As more and more members began to participate in the CCC's fundraising efforts, party leaders began to view member fundraising as a sign of party loyalty. The presence of real competition in the House meant that leaders had to enforce strict party discipline in order to pass (or block) policy. By rewarding loyalty, leaders could maintain some degree of control over members who were eager to promote their own political and policy agendas rather than the party's. Eventually, members understood that their ability to successfully pursue their own ambitions depended upon their willingness to vote with their leaders and raise money for their parties.

Members can contribute to the CCCs using funds from their personal campaign committees and from their leadership PACs. Members typically use their personal campaign committees to raise money for their own election and reelection campaigns. Leadership PACs are generally created to promote the politicians who establish them. Like other PACs, leadership PACs solicit donations and make contributions to candidates and party committees. Members also use leadership PAC funds to pay for travel, and for a broad range of campaign-related expenses. Members can make unlimited transfers from their personal campaign committees to party committees, but they can only contribute a total of $15,000 per election cycle from their leadership PACs to the national party committees.

Member contributions to the CCCs have increased dramatically since 1990. House Democrats contributed $300,000 to the DCCC during the 1990 election cycle, then upped that amount to $7.8 million during the 2000 cycle. In 2006, House Democrats contributed approximately $34 million to the DCCC, and in 2008 they contributed $48 million. House Republicans gave $1,000 to the NRCC during the 1990 election cycle and $14.7 million during the 2000 cycle. In 2006, they gave approximately $32 million to the NRCC, and in 2008, member contributions to the NRCC dropped to $25 million.[2] These figures reflect the escalating cost of running competitive campaigns, but they also reflect significant changes in the way that parties compete for majority status.

House members also have increased their efforts to raise money for each other and for same-party candidates. Members can give $2,400 per candidate, per election out of their personal campaign committees and $5,000 per candidate, per election out of their leadership PACs. In 1990, House Democrats contributed a total of $1.8 million to incumbents, challengers, and open-seat candidates; 10 years later, they contributed $7.8 million. In 2006, House Democrats gave candidates for the House $11.5 million. House Republicans contributed $700,000 to incumbents, challengers, and open-seat candidates in the 1990 elections and $9.6 million in the 2000 elections (Bedlington and Malbin 2003, 134). In 2006, House Republicans gave $22.4 million to Republican House candidates.[3] These figures have continued to rise as members have become more attuned to the collective and individual returns such contributions can provide.

The increasing amount of money that House members contribute to the CCCs and to other members and candidates is one of the most significant developments in congressional party politics over the past decade. As the CCCs' fundraising activities have become more important, congressional party leaders have moved from encouraging members to contribute money to the committees to requiring them to do so through dues systems and commitment contracts. Top Democratic leaders must contribute $800,000 per two-year cycle; exclusive committee chairs are required to contribute $500,000; second-tier leaders must pay $300,000; committee chairs and exclusive subcommittee chairs are obligated to give $250,000; members who sit on exclusive committees must contribute $200,000; subcommittee chairs on nonexclusive committees must give $150,000; and junior members are expected to pay $125,000 (Palmer and Dennis 2010). House Republicans have a similar party dues structure. While these party-orchestrated fundraising programs promote the collective goal of majority status, redistributing money also can help members promote themselves—a strategy that became more important following the 1970s House reforms.

How Did This System Evolve? Spreading Wealth the Old-Fashioned Way

In 1940, Lyndon B. Johnson (D-Texas) organized a massive fundraising campaign on behalf of his House colleagues. Democrats were short on funds and at risk of losing majority control of the House, so Johnson called on his Texas oil industry allies for help. Oil money flowed into the campaign coffers of House Democrats, and the party managed not only to maintain control of the House, but to pick up an additional eight seats. Johnson acted as a conduit for contributions and always made sure that the recipients understood the role he played. As a result of his efforts, Johnson quickly gained prestige in the chamber; in fact, his reputation as an influential and powerful politician was largely built on his ability to raise and distribute large sums of campaign money (Caro 1982; Baker 1989).

Johnson's fundraising activities in the 1940s were technically associated with the DCCC, but his relationship with the committee consisted of little more than his handing over money he had raised. He worked out of his own office and with his own staff. The concept of financing congressional races across the country from a single source was not new, but Democrats had never implemented such a plan. "No one before had ever worked at it," said James Rowe, a Roosevelt White House insider. "Johnson worked at it like hell. People running for Congress in those days never had much money; it had been that way for years, but Lyndon decided to do something about it; he got in it with both feet, the way he did everything, and he raised a hell of a lot of money." In effect, according to reporter Robert S. Allen, Johnson was "a one-man national committee for congressmen" (Caro 1982, 662).

Though Johnson's fundraising activities were on a scale never before seen, southern members with excess personal campaign funds had made cash-on-hand contributions to their more vulnerable colleagues for decades. Former majority whip Hale Boggs (D-Louisiana) is credited with formalizing this practice (Drew 1983). Such contributions were generally viewed as friendly gestures with no strings attached because they were given by members who simply had more cash on hand than they needed for their own reelection efforts. "It was an effort to help people who needed a little help," according to former congressman Richardson Preyer of North Carolina. "If you raised more money than you needed to spend in your campaign, you'd give some to a couple of other members of your delegation who were hard up for funds. This early form of giving was not directed to any particular purpose such as gaining control of a committee or anything of that sort. It was generally sort of good-will giving and in fairly small amounts" (Baker 1989, 17–18). But as the demand for campaign contributions grew, politically ambitious members who faced little or no competition in their own districts began to recognize the strategic value in raising excess campaign money. By virtue of simply having surplus campaign funds, members could prove they had the clout to attract donors. By sharing their campaign wealth with other members, they could prove they were team players.

Before the passage of campaign finance reforms in the early 1970s, no law required the reporting of these transactions. According to former representative Richard Bolling (D-Missouri), "a good deal of money moved around but it was not illegal to have long green. Nobody ever talked about it. Even later on in my career when I was more 'in,' I heard very few specific details. The reason it was legal was because there weren't any laws and a lot of it moved around in cash" (Baker 1989, 23). Whether member-to-member giving during this era played a role in leadership races, committee assignments, or other House proceedings is unknown because such contributions were not documented. However, because the House leadership structure at that time was largely determined by seniority, members who aspired to leadership positions generally had to wait their turn, regardless of their generosity.

THE 1970S REFORM ERA

The passage of the Federal Elections Campaign Act in 1971 strengthened campaign reporting requirements and restricted campaign spending. In explicitly requiring PACs to file quarterly reports of receipts and expenditures, the act acknowledged that such committees played a role in campaigns and in effect authorized their establishment. Prior to passage of the Federal Elections Campaign Act, groups made campaign contributions through political committees, but there was no formal means for tracking these contributions.

Public outrage over the Watergate scandal and campaign abuses in the 1972 elections convinced Congress that more regulation was necessary. The Federal Elections Campaign Act amendments of 1974 largely replaced the 1971 act. The amendments significantly strengthened disclosure requirements, set limits on contributions and expenditures in federal elections, created the Federal Election Commission, and established a system of public financing for presidential candidates. The amendments also set contribution limits of $5,000 per candidate, per election on PACs.

Two months after the 1974 amendments were passed, the constitutionality of contribution and expenditure ceilings was challenged in federal court. In *Buckley v. Valeo*, the Supreme Court declared that the government cannot restrict the speech of the wealthy in order to enhance the relative voice of the poor, and invalidated all restrictions on campaign expenditures. Yet limits on campaign contributions were left intact. The Court reasoned that contribution limits were justified in order to prevent the appearance (and possibly the reality) of corruption.

House reformers believed that stricter campaign finance, lobbying, and ethics laws would constrain the influence of outside interests. They also pushed for changes to constrict the powers of entrenched committee chairs and empower Congress as an institution. Progressive members of the House Democratic caucus—many of whom were elected in the 1960s and 1970s—led these reform efforts. By the mid-1970s, the House began to move away from the seniority rule and changed the procedures whereby committee and subcommittee chairs were chosen. Once the power of the House's longstanding committee chairs was dislodged, newer members began to seek their party leaders' help in pursuing their political and policy goals (Price 1992). Junior members thus became more active in their congressional party organizations and moved to strengthen the power of party leaders. Because the reforms required caucus approval by secret-ballot vote of committee chairs and party leaders, these positions became more attainable for junior members than they had been under the seniority system, and ambitious members began to pursue them. As a consequence of the reforms, the playing field between junior and senior members became more level and the political environment became more competitive.

Junior members also were enterprising when it came to promoting themselves; eager to impress their constituents, these members sought the help of professional campaign consultants and strategists. Pollsters, media advisers, policy consultants, and direct-mail experts—a group of specialists collectively known as the "elections industry"—were by-products of the 1970s reforms and the new kind of politics the reforms inspired (Mitchell 1998). Changes in the way campaigns were run meant that the average cost of running a campaign increased dramatically during the 1970s. Mean campaign expenditures for House candidates in 1974 amounted to $53,384. By 1978, mean expenditures were $109,440, and by 1980, House candidates spent an average of $153,221 (Malbin 1984, 278). Over the course of six years, campaign expenditures for House candidates nearly tripled. Gone were the days of all-volunteer, grassroots campaigns. In order to compete, candidates needed to raise a lot of money.

As the community of organized interests rapidly expanded, members actively began to seek out the PAC money many of these groups could provide. Because PACs could contribute $5,000 per candidate, per election, their donations were more attractive than those from individuals, who at that time could only contribute $1,000 per candidate, per election. The campaign finance reforms of the early 1970s authorized PACs in order to better regulate outside contributions to candidate campaigns. While this provision was intended to constrain the influence of organized interests, it ultimately advantaged self-interested members who needed to raise campaign money.

Attuned to the increasing value that members placed on campaign contributions, House leaders began helping members raise money with the expectation that members would repay the favor by supporting the party's agenda. The strategy was mutually beneficial in that it gave leaders a new way to promote party cohesion and gave members a new way to raise money. The ongoing quest for campaign funds thus gave leaders a new way to balance members' individual goals with the party's collective goals.

Under the seniority system, one member's aggressive networking did not trump another member's rank. While the reforms made it possible for more-junior members to pursue committee chairmanships or leadership posts, successfully doing so required building support in the chamber. Members with leadership aspirations typically pursued a strategy of building support networks in the chamber, but some also engaged in member-to-member giving. Ross Baker describes several cases during the 1970s where senior members raised money, then distributed it to their colleagues for the purpose of securing support for their own leadership bids. The 1976 majority whip race set a new standard in member-to-member contributing in that three of the four challengers gave campaign money to their colleagues for the express purpose of winning their support. One of the challengers, California Democrat Phil Burton, is credited with devising the strategy, which two of his competitors then copied. Texas Democrat Jim Wright won the position by one vote (Baker 1989, 24–26). By the end of the 1970s, House members began to redistribute money in a more strategic fashion.

The Rise of Leadership PACs

In 1978, Representative Paul Rogers (D-Florida) retired as chairman of the Energy and Commerce Committee's Subcommittee on Health and the Environment, sparking an unprecedented battle. Although the House reforms had made subcommittee chairmanships elective within committee, the most senior subcommittee member of the majority party was typically still recognized as next in line. But in this case, the most senior subcommittee member was Representative David Satterfield (D-Virginia), a member who was so far to the ideological right of his Democratic colleagues that the caucus refused to consider him for the chairmanship. Richardson Preyer (D-North Carolina), the next member in line behind Satterfield, announced his candidacy for the chairmanship and was expected to win committee approval easily.

Soon after Preyer declared his intentions, Representative Henry Waxman (D-California), a two-term member who was fourth in seniority on the subcommittee, announced that he too would seek the subcommittee chairmanship. Waxman actively lobbied his committee colleagues for the position and called upon his allies in the organized-labor community to lobby, on his behalf, committee members with large working-class constituencies. He also publicly suggested that Preyer's financial ties to pharmaceutical firms and his representation of a tobacco-steeped North Carolina district were jurisdictional conflicts of interest that might affect his ability to be impartial.

Waxman then did something that no member of Congress had ever before done—he established a leadership PAC and contributed $24,000 to his Energy and Commerce Committee colleagues. After a large number of last-minute vote switches, Waxman defeated Preyer by a 15–12 vote. "Friends of Henry Waxman," the first leadership PAC established by a member of Congress, was considered instrumental in Waxman's ascension to subcommittee chair (Baker 1989, 29–32).

While most Democrats, including Preyer, considered Waxman to be an extremely bright and competent member, many were dismayed by the way he competed for the subcommittee chairmanship. Because member-to-member giving had only been practiced by senior members and party leaders, many members thought Waxman's adoption of the strategy was disrespectful. Other members accused Waxman of simply buying the chairmanship. Rules Committee Chairman Richard Bolling (D-Missouri), one of the House's lead reformers, angrily denounced Waxman's appointment as chair, claiming that "what Waxman did was an institutionalization of something that I think was pernicious when it was hidden. It was clear, however, that it was going to be a precedent" (Baker 1989, 31).

Even though the innovation was not widely imitated at first, Waxman's PAC was an early indicator of what would eventually become a standard strategizing tool for enterprising politicians. True to Bolling's prediction, Waxman's leadership PAC set the standard for those who aspired to leadership positions or committee chairmanships, and for the leaders and chairs themselves. In 1988, 10 years after Waxman became the first member of Congress to establish a leadership PAC, there were 45 active leadership PACs affiliated with members of Congress (Wilcox 1990). By 1998, 81 members of Congress had established leadership PACs, and by 2000, that number climbed to 141. The growth in leadership PAC contributions is even more remarkable. In 1978, fewer than 10 leadership PACs gave political candidates a total of $62,485; in 1988, they contributed a total of $3.7 million, and by 1998, leadership PAC contributions totaled $11.7 million. The proliferation of leadership PACs in the wake of the reform era suggests that members began to view leadership positions as increasingly attractive (Canon 1989) and that members were seeking new ways to ingratiate themselves with their colleagues.

Leadership PACs also were part of the broader trend toward greater member autonomy in that they provided ambitious members with a way to promote their own self-interests. Member-to-member giving in the pre-reform era emphasized party building; politicians like Lyndon Johnson certainly understood that they would benefit personally by helping their colleagues, but the contributions they made were more about securing majority control for the party. Post-reform contributors gave to colleagues more for the purpose of advancing their own personal ambitions than for building the party.

While the party organizations focused on the collective goal of getting candidates elected, House members continued to concentrate on their own, individual ambitions. In the decade or so after Henry Waxman established "Friends of Henry Waxman," most congressional leadership PACs were formed by liberal Democrats who held safe congressional seats (Baker 1989, 35). Democrats had presided over the House since 1954, so it is not surprising that they would be the first to form leadership PACs, as they controlled all the top leadership posts and committee chairmanships. Most Democrats who formed leadership PACs followed Waxman's example and used them for the purpose of garnering colleague support for their own ambitions.

Money played a prominent role in the 1986 majority whip race, which pitted California Democrat Tony Coehlo against Charles Rangel of New York and W. G. (Bill) Hefner of North Carolina. Coehlo was the early favorite, having raised tremendous amounts of money for Democratic House candidates during his tenure as chair of the DCCC. He also was a member of the California Democratic delegation, which was populated by a number of strong fund-raisers like Phil Burton and Henry Waxman. Many California Democrats were alumni of the California state legislature, and in that system, party leaders were traditionally chosen based on their ability to raise campaign money for party members (Jacobson 1985-86, 623). Charles Rangel, one of the leading African American House members, was Coehlo's primary competition. Rangel was a well-respected and well-liked member of the Democratic caucus who was supported by the Speaker, as well as the Congressional Black Caucus. However, Coehlo had one advantage: a leadership PAC. Rangel claimed he was personally and politically opposed to leadership PACs and refused to compete with Coehlo on those grounds. He also suggested that giving members money was akin to buying votes and claimed he did not want to embarrass his colleagues by putting them in an awkward position.

As the whip's race heated up, Rangel changed his mind and established the "Committee for the 100th Congress" leadership PAC. In doing so, he set out to compete with Coehlo on grounds where Coehlo was virtually unbeatable. Coehlo contributed $570,000 to 245 Democratic House campaigns and Rangel contributed a total of $225,000 to about 100 candidates. Coehlo won the whip's race by a comfortable margin, despite some grumbling about the role fundraising played in the race's outcome (Baker 1989, 35–36).

Two years later, Pennsylvania Democrat William Gray established a new precedent in member-to-member giving when he ran for chair of the House Democratic Caucus. When he ran for chair of the House Budget Committee in 1984, Gray had established a leadership PAC and contributed $27,000 to 75 Democratic incumbents and challengers. The caucus selected Gray in a three-way contest for the chairmanship, naming him to a prestigious position from which he could raise even more campaign money for his colleagues. House rules limit Budget Committee chairs to two two-year terms, so Gray announced his intentions to seek the caucus chairmanship in 1987, approximately one year before his budget chairmanship was set to expire. Mary Rose Oakar of Ohio and Mike Synar of Oklahoma also declared themselves candidates in the race and, like Gray, began campaigning for the post one year in advance. In the few months after announcing his candidacy, Gray used excess campaign money he had raised as budget chair to give $35,750 in contributions to his colleagues. Oakar contributed to five Democrats (at the request of the leadership), and Synar did not give any campaign money to his colleagues.

As the election drew closer, Gray's self-promotion campaign became even more pronounced. In early 1988, he hosted an extravagant dinner for his colleagues at Occidental, a posh D.C. restaurant, and used the occasion to promote his candidacy. In addition to enjoying an expensive dinner, members of the Pennsylvania delegation were singled out and given $1,000 campaign checks. Just as they were recovering from their astonishment over the dinner he hosted, Gray then surprised his colleagues again. This time he established a new leadership PAC called the "Committee for Democratic Opportunity" and solicited outside contributors to help him in his quest to become caucus chair. This marked the first time a member of Congress had actively sought outsider help in a leadership race. Gray also hosted a breakfast meeting for lobbyists and asked them to contact other Democrats and urge them to support his bid to become caucus chair. In the end, Gray's rigorous campaigning paid off, and he was elected caucus chair. His campaign for the chairmanship revealed that, in addition to establishing leadership PACs, members had numerous options for influencing their colleagues (Baker 1989, 37–40).

William Gray's strategy of incorporating outside interests into leadership races inaugurated a new tactic for leadership aspirants, which House Republicans soon adopted. In 1994, after Republicans won majority control of the House for the first time in more than 40 years, Republican members were finally in a position to pursue leadership posts and committee chairmanships. During the 1970s and 1980s, House Republicans did not establish leadership PACs at the same rate as House Democrats, but that equation changed in the 1990s.

Republicans who were interested in one day running for a leadership post or a committee chair now understood the value of helping themselves by helping their colleagues.

THE CONGRESSIONAL CAMPAIGN COMMITTEES TAKE CENTER STAGE

House Democrats in the 1970s and 1980s rarely worried about losing their majority status, as their party had controlled the chamber since 1954. The Republican outlook was quite different; they had been out of power for so long, it was difficult for them to imagine things any other way. Democrats held comfortable margins over the Republicans throughout the 1970s and 1980s—another factor that contributed to the Republicans' lack of enthusiasm. When there is a realistic opportunity to win majority control, the minority party is typically better able to pull together as a team because its members are highly motivated by their desire to take charge of the chamber. Once the majority party begins to fragment as members pursue their own political and policy agendas, a unified and organized minority party can exploit the majority party's weaknesses and promote its alternative agenda.

Competition for House seats increased substantially in the 1990s due to a number of factors. The percentage of incumbents winning with 60 percent or more of the vote dropped from a postwar high of 89 percent in 1988, to 76 percent in 1990, to 66 percent in 1992, then to 65 percent in 1994. The competitive balance between Democrats and Republicans also shifted so that in the 1990s, Republicans began to regularly win more seats than they had between 1946 and 1990. Voting behavior changed as well; the percentage of districts where voters elected a presidential candidate of one party and a House member of another declined considerably after 1984. Reapportionment after the 1990 census also shifted the electoral dynamics in a number of districts, creating more-favorable conditions for House Republicans. The post-reform southern realignment led to more ideologically homogeneous parties, as many conservative Democrats left their party for the Republican Party. These changes were apparent in the House, where Democrats and Republicans fought their political and policy battles in increasingly partisan terms. Republicans also took advantage of President Bill Clinton's high unfavorable ratings and successfully challenged a number of vulnerable Democrats who were elected in 1992. In addition, 27 House Democrats decided to retire in 1994 and left open many formerly safe seats. Despite all the evidence to suggest otherwise, Democrats still believed they would retain majority status in 1994 (Kolodny and Dwyre 1998, 277–279). Instead, the Republicans finally ended four decades of Democratic control of the House.

The 1994 elections signaled a new era of electoral competitiveness. For the next 12 years, Republicans would remain in the majority but hold very small margins over the Democrats. Real party competition was a phenomenon House Democrats and Republicans had not experienced for decades. This new dynamic dramatically strengthened the role of the congressional parties in that ambitious members—one-time independent actors—began turning to their party organizations for help in pursuing their personal goals (Kolodny and Dwyre 1998, 278; Schlesinger 1991). Enhanced competitiveness enables party leaders to leverage more control over members because a member's ability to attain power closely depends on the party's ability to maintain majority control. While this is always the case in theory, members are much more likely to abide by leadership directives when the margin between parties is small, simply because their status hangs in the balance every two years.

The CCCs had made fundraising appeals to incumbent members throughout the 1980s, but most members chose not to contribute for the good of the whole (Jacobson 1985–86, 616). The presence of real electoral competition throughout the 1990s swayed members to see the value in contributing to the party committees. In addition to forming leadership PACs and contributing money to their colleagues, ambitious members began contributing money to and raising money for the congressional party committees. While the collective goal of majority status drove members to contribute, so did the desire to impress party leaders.

Following their success in 1994, Republican leaders believed that if the party was to maintain majority control, it needed to maintain its vigorous fundraising efforts. In 1993, the NRCC broke new ground by convincing members that the party could gain majority status in 1994 if members would contribute money to the committee and to other candidates. NRCC directors Bill Paxon and Newt Gingrich reasoned "that the collective goal of majority status was more valuable to these incumbents than the few extra thousand dollars" they asked them to contribute (Kolodny and Dwyre 1998, 289). Gingrich established a formula for "voluntary contributions" by each incumbent; unless they were in financial trouble themselves, members were expected to contribute (Gimpel 1996, 10). The strategy was hugely successful—members donated just under $13 million to Republican candidates and to the NRCC. Money was targeted to outside challengers who were running against vulnerable Democratic incumbents and to open-seat candidates (Kolodny and Dwyre 1998, 289). Gimpel notes that the "1994 campaign signaled the coming of a Republican revolution both in terms of message and money" (1996, 11).

Following the 1994 elections, Republican leaders confronted the Madisonian dilemma of how to channel individual ambition for the good of the whole by enforcing party discipline and rewarding members who supported the leadership's agenda. Gingrich believed that fragmentation was the root cause of the Democrats' defeat and that strong, centralized leadership was necessary to keep members in line. By rewarding party loyalty over longtime service, leaders discovered that ambitious members would act in service to the party organization as they pursued their own political and policy goals. Though there are a number of ways members can demonstrate party loyalty, fundraising and party-line voting rank high on the list.

Upon taking majority control, House Republicans adopted a number of institutional reforms; of particular importance were the six-year term limit placed on committee and subcommittee chairs and the enhanced power the leadership was given in the chair selection and committee appointment process. Committee chair selection was at Speaker Gingrich's discretion, and his main goal was to appoint loyalists. All except four of the newly appointed chairs had contributed to the NRCC during the 1994 cycle, and five of the incoming chairs also gave to other candidates. A staff person for then–Majority Leader Dick Armey explained that the decision to appoint party loyalists "ended up sending a very clear signal that you just don't rely on seniority; you've got to prove yourself as someone willing to pursue . . . our agenda" (Owens 1997, 250).

Fundraising for the party and its candidates was central to the leadership's agenda. The newly appointed committee chairs understood that they were expected to raise and contribute campaign money, and most upped their overall contribution amounts in the 1996 cycle and again in the 1998 cycle. Of the four chairs who failed to contribute, one ran for Senate, one retired in 1998, and two retired in 2000. As the six-year term limit on chairs appointed in 1994 inched closer, competition among Republican members who wished to replace them grew fierce. Many committee chair aspirants took a cue from the sitting chairs and began contributing money to GOP candidates and to the NRCC.

Dennis Hastert, who replaced Gingrich as Speaker in 1998, decided that any member who wanted to be considered for a committee chairmanship would be interviewed by the party's steering committee. While chair aspirants were free to highlight whatever qualifications they chose, most focused on their party-based fundraising efforts. Twenty-nine potential committee chairs appeared before the steering committee in December 2000; steering committee members voted by secret ballot, then presented their recommendations to the full Republican Conference for ratification.

Seniority was violated in 6 of the 10 competitive chairmanship races. Geography, party unity scores, and ideology did not seem to affect the chair races in any detectable way. The fundraising efforts of the chair aspirants, however, did seem to matter. In five of the six cases where seniority did not prevail, the member who had raised the most money won. And in 7 of the 10 competitive races, the chairmanship went to the "highest bidder" (see Brewer and Deering 2005). Two years later, at the beginning of the 108th Congress (2003–2004), five Republicans were tapped to fill vacant chairs on the Armed Services, Resources, Government Reform, Agriculture, and Homeland Security committees. Of the five new chairs, only two held seniority. Together, the five new chairs had contributed more than $1 million to the NRCC and nearly $500,000 to Republican candidates during the 2002 election. Joel Hefley (R-Colorado), who was passed over to chair the Resources Committee, said, "Fundraising evidently was an enormous part of it. It's unseemly. It's like buying seats and we shouldn't do that" (Kratz 2003).

Term limiting committee chairs proved extremely profitable for House Republicans. Once the individual goal of power in the chamber was linked to the collective goal of majority status, members understood that if they wanted to advance in the chamber, they had to act in service to the parties. Anne Bedlington and Michael Malbin have documented how House members are now giving a higher proportion of their personal campaign committee money to the CCCs rather than to other candidates. They also document the CCCs' increased reliance on member contributions as a source of campaign funds (2003, 133–136). In the contemporary Congress, members who raise money for the party and toe the party line have considerable opportunities to advance in the House's power structure (Schickler and Pearson 2005, 220).

Conclusion

The career trajectory of ambitious members changed significantly following the 1970s House reforms. Under the seniority system, House members moved up the chamber's "power ladder" through extended service. Committee chairs were the majority party members who served on the committees the longest, and party leaders earned their posts by slowly progressing up through the ranks. The contemporary House operates under a dramatically different set of rules. Both parties permit all members to compete for leadership posts, chairmanships, and even committee seats. When the margins between parties are narrow and the political atmosphere is fiercely partisan, party loyalists are favored for higher positions in the chamber. Ambitious members can demonstrate their loyalty through party-line voting, but they also can distinguish themselves by raising money for the party and its candidates. Those who raise money for the good of the whole demonstrate that they are loyal, team players—qualities that members want to see in their leaders.

Because more money is raised at the ideological extremes, House members at the far ends of the liberal and conservative spectrum tend to attract more money than centrists. And the ability to raise large amounts of money propels these members to leadership posts that they otherwise might not have won (Heberlig, Hetherington, and Larson 2006). Since winning election to Congress in 1987, Nancy Pelosi (a self-proclaimed liberal) has proven herself a prodigious fundraiser. In 1998, her leadership PAC, PAC to the Future, was second in receipt growth among all PACs. In 2000, she contributed more money to her colleagues than did any other member of the House or Senate. Her ability to raise money helped propel her to the position of minority whip in 2001, minority leader in 2002, and Speaker of the House in 2006. Her fundraising skills also helped her hold on to her party leadership post, even after Democrats suffered major losses in the 2010 midterm election. Likewise, John Boehner (a self-proclaimed conservative) is one of the most prolific Republican fund-raisers in Congress. Between his leadership PAC and reelection committee, he raised over $13 million and was the top contributor to the NRCC in 2010.

Wealthy connections can also jump-start the careers of new members. When Debbie Wasserman Schultz (D-Florida) was elected to the House in 2004, she began her congressional career by contributing $100,000 in leftover campaign funds to the DCCC before she was even sworn into office. She was appointed to the Democratic whip organization during her first term and by her third term was named a chief deputy whip and landed an appropriations subcommittee chairmanship. During the final weeks of the 2010 campaign, several Republican freshmen-to-be took a page out of Wasserman Schultz's playbook and funneled thousands of dollars to the NRCC and to GOP candidates. "It's a way for people in the conference to get noticed," said Carl Forti, a former top NRCC staffer. "In a crowded freshman class, it's a way to differentiate you from other members." Some of the incoming House Republicans who directed their excess campaign funds to the NRCC were rewarded with seats on the exclusive Appropriations and Ways and Means committees (Isenstadt 2010).

For members who regularly face hotly contested races or lack the connections needed to raise large amounts of campaign money, fundraising for the party and its candidates presents a challenge. Members who represent poor constituencies or constituencies with expensive media markets may also find it difficult to raise money beyond what they need for their own campaigns. Other members simply find fundraising a distasteful distraction. According to Diane Watson (D-California), the pressure to raise money prevents members from focusing on the issues. "For anything up over $100,000, you've got to focus full-time on fundraising. . . . We're going to have to come to grips with this some way. I understand to win these national races, there's a cost to it. . . . Money should not be the only driving force" (Hearn 2007).

Due to their fundraising obligations, members have less time to spend on policy. Most committee hearings are poorly attended, and floor debates often feature just a handful of members. House leaders have even adjusted the chamber's floor schedule to make more time for members to raise money. The link between a member's ability and willingness to fund-raise for the party and that member's ability to obtain more power in the chamber also raises important questions about the criteria by which potential leaders are judged. If fundraising skills are deemed as important as policy expertise and institutional experience, are there still benefits to developing an expertise or to long-term service? Whose interests are prioritized in a system that requires policymakers to focus constantly on fundraising and rewards those who raise the most?

Endnotes

1. See the preface of Robin Kolodny's *Pursuing Majorities* (1998) for a discussion of how different variables affect the strategies the congressional campaign committees use to pursue majority status.

2. Figures can be found at http://www.cfinst.org/pdf/federal/parties/MemberContribs_ NationalParty-Committees_1998-2008.pdf. Also see Anne H. Bedlington and Michael J. Malbin (2003, 134).

3. The 2006 figures are through November 2006.

BIBLIOGRAPHY

Baker, Ross K. 1989. *The New Fat Cats*. New York: Priority Press.

Bedlington, Anne H., and Michael J. Malbin. 2003. The Party As an Extended Network: Members Giving to Each Other and to Their Parties. In *Life after Reform*, ed. Michael J. Malbin, 121–140. Lanham, Md: Rowman & Littlefield.

Brewer, Paul R., and Christopher J. Deering. 2005. "Musical Chairs: Interest Groups, Campaign Fundraising, and Selection of House Committee Chairs." In *The Interest Group Connection*, ed. Paul S. Herrnson, Ronald G. Shaiko, and Clyde Wilcox, 141–163. Washington, D.C.: CQ Press.

Canon, David T. 1989. "The Institutionalization of Leadership in the U.S. Congress." *Legislative Studies Quarterly* 14, no. 3:415–443.

Caro, Robert A. 1982. *The Years of Lyndon Johnson*. New York: Vintage Books.

Drew, Elizabeth. 1983. *Politics and Money: The New Period of Corruption.* New York: Macmillan.

Gimpel, James G. 1996. *Fulfilling the Contract: The First 100 Days.* Boston: Allyn & Bacon.

Hearn, Josephine. 2007. "DCCC Raises $24 M, Asks Members for More." *Politico*, June 20.

Heberlig, Eric S., Marc Hetherington, and Bruce Larson. 2006. "The Price of Leadership: Campaign Money and the Polarization of Congressional Parties." *Journal of Politics* 68, no. 4:992–1005.

Hooper, Molly K. 2010. "Boehner Blocks Doors, Secures Millions in Campaign Pledges from Colleagues." *The Hill*, September 29.

Isenstadt, Alex. 2010. "GOP Freshmen-to-Be Shared Wealth." *Politico*, December 21.

Jacobs, Jeremy P. 2010. "Boehner Gives NRCC $3 Million in October." *National Journal's Hotline*, November 1.

Jacobson, Gary C. 1985–1986. "Party Organization and Distribution of Campaign Resources: Republicans and Democrats in 1982." *Political Science Quarterly* 100, no. 4:603–625.

Kolodny, Robin. 1998. *Pursuing Majorities: Congressional Campaign Committees in American Politics.* Norman: University of Oklahoma Press.

Kolodny, Robin, and Diana Dwyre. 1998. "Party-Orchestrated Activities for Legislative Party Goals." *Party Politics* 4, no. 3:275–295.

Kratz, Vikki. 2003. "The House Money Built." *Capital Eye*, January 16.

Malbin, Michael J. 1984. "Looking Back at the Future of Campaign Finance Reform: Interest Groups and American Elections." In *Money and Politics in the United States: Financing Elections in the 1980s*, ed. Michael J. Malbin. Chatham, NJ.: Chatham House Publishers.

Martin, Jonathan. 2010. "The Cash-for-Speaker Program." *Politico*, July 29.

Mitchell, Alison. 1998. "A New Form of Lobbying Puts a Public Face on Private Interests." *New York Times*, September 30.

Newmyer, Tory. 2010. "Members Urged to Open Wallets to the DCCC." *Roll Call*, June 30.

Owens, John E. 1997. "The Return of Party Government in the US House of Representatives: Central Leadership—Committee Relations in the 104th Congress." *British Journal of Political Science* 27, no. 2:247–272.

Palmer, Anna, and Steven T. Dennis. 2010. "Pelosi Puts Heat on Chairmen." *Roll Call*, September 28.

Price, David. 1992. *The Congressional Experience: A View from the Hill.* Boulder, Colo.: Westview.

Schickler, Eric, and Kathryn Pearson. 2005. "The House Leadership in an Era of Partisan Warfare." In *Congress Reconsidered*, ed. Lawrence C. Dodd and Bruce I. Oppenheimer, 207–226. Washington, D.C.: CQ Press.

Schlesinger, Joseph A. 1991. *Political Parties and the Winning of Office.* Ann Arbor: University of Michigan Press.

Wilcox, Clyde. 1990. "Member to Member Giving." In *Money, Elections, and Democracy*, ed. Margaret Latus Nugent and John R. Johannes. Boulder, Colo.: Westview.

*Marian Currinder** is a senior fellow at the Government Affairs Institute at Georgetown University and the author of *Money in the House: Campaign Funds and Congressional Party Politics* (Westview Press, 2009).

DISCUSSION QUESTIONS

1. Has the setting of fundraising quotas for party members been helpful or harmful to party unity? To the ability of Congress to legislate?

2. Should success at raising money be an important consideration for the parties in choosing their leaders?

3. How have the campaign finance reforms of the past decade influenced fund-raising by members of Congress?

Part 3:
Campaign Finance Law in State Elections

In many policy areas, the American states have been referred to as "laboratories of innovation." This is certainly the case for state campaign finance laws. The diversity of laws regarding contribution limits, public financing, and other aspects of campaign finance have provided researchers with valuable information on how reforms have worked in practice. The two articles presented here are examples of this research.

The first of these articles, by Donald A. Gross, Robert K. Goidel, and Todd G. Shields, concisely explains the reasons why comparative study of the American states can provide insight into how proposed federal campaign finance reforms might work. The authors demonstrate that different types of regulations can interact to produce results that no individual regulation might produce on its own, and they discuss the importance of the precise amounts set for spending or contribution limits. Limits that are set too low may disproportionately benefit incumbents, yet limits set too high may have little effect on candidate spending or election outcomes. Several states have changed their campaign finance laws since the publication of this piece—in particular, the conclusions the authors draw here about the effects of public funding have been substantially revised by scholars looking at newer public funding systems in states such as Connecticut and Maine. Nonetheless, this article has had a substantial influence on the study of money in state politics for the past decade. Portions of this article ultimately appeared in Donald A. Gross and Robert K. Goidel's book *The States of Campaign Finance Reform*.

One of the strongest arguments made by proponents of campaign finance reform has been that the need to raise large amounts of money deters many potential candidates. Not only are some candidates who might be excellent legislators discouraged from running, but their decision not to run can reduce the diversity of choices offered to voters. Keith Hamm and Robert E. Hogan address this issue in the second article of this section, studying the relationship between state campaign finance laws and the number of contested legislative elections. As Hamm and Hogan point out (and as Gross, Goidel, and Shields point out as well), the precise dollar amounts set as contribution and spending limits are important to candidates' success and to their decisions to run. Hamm and Hogan conclude, however, that lower contribution limits can benefit challengers and encourage competition. As the authors show, however, campaign finance laws are only part of the puzzle—this article is valuable not only because of its attention to campaign finance laws, but also because of its discussion of other campaign laws, such as term limits or ballot access laws, in bringing about contested elections. Unlike many of the other American pieces in this book, this article also assesses the consequences of campaign finance laws for minor-party candidates.

Many of the most intriguing state-level innovations are too new for their consequences to be adequately measured. Several states, most notably Maine, Connecticut, and Arizona, have introduced systems of almost complete public financing of elections. While some states are far more lenient than the federal government in their restrictions on campaign contributions, others have enacted far tougher laws. The Supreme Court, at times, has been hesitant to interfere with state-level campaign finance law. In its 2000 *Nixon v. Shrink Missouri Government PAC* decision, the court upheld a Missouri law that placed substantial restrictions on campaign contributions; but in its 2006 *Randall v. Sorrell* decision, it struck down a Vermont law that featured even stricter limits. And in June 2011 the Court struck down a provision of Arizona's campaign finance system that allowed publically funded candidates to receive state funding to match the spending of privately funded opponents. The courts, then, have placed some restrictions on what states can do, but there is still substantial room for states to experiment with options that are not politically feasible at the federal level. The articles here capture the effects of some of this variation, but the jury is still out on the consequences and the legality of many other state programs.

State Campaign Finance Regulations and Electoral Competition

by Donald A. Gross, Robert K. Goidel, and Todd G. Shields*

How do campaign finance laws affect electoral outcomes and campaign spending levels? In the 25 years following the passage of the most comprehensive campaign finance legislation in U.S. history, numerous studies have been conducted, yet little can be said with certainty regarding the electoral consequences of campaign finance laws (Malbin & Gais, 1998). Works studying the effects of reform at the national level have provided contradictory, and often controversial, assessments regarding the electoral consequences of campaign finance laws. Whereas some works emphasize the negative consequences of reform (Abramowitz, 1991; Jacobson, 1980; Sorauf, 1992), others provide a more positive assessment (Goidel & Gross, 1994, 1996; Goidel, Gross, & Shields, 1999; Green & Krasno, 1988; Gross, Shields, & Goidel, 1997; Krasno & Green, 1993). Aside from the controversy, these studies also are plagued by limited variance in the key variable of interest: Federal campaign finance laws have remained virtually unchanged for the past 25 years.

Works at the state level avoid this particular problem but suffer from their own set of limitations. First, until quite recently, most of the work has focused on either a single state or limited number of states and a limited time frame (Donnay & Ramsden, 1995; Mayer & Wood, 1995; Redfield, 1996). More recent studies have expanded the scope of the analysis and provided considerable insight into the "lost world" of state-level campaign finance (Hogan, 1999, 2000; Malbin & Gais, 1998; Mayer, 1997; Thompson & Moncrief, 1998) but also have been limited in terms of their ability to provide a comprehensive assessment of state reform efforts. For example, writing the conclusions for the most exhaustive study of state legislative campaign finance to date, Jewell and Cassie (1998, p. 226) observe that there is not enough evidence "to conclude that public financing would succeed or fail in meeting the goals of reformers." A recent analysis by Robert Hogan (2000) concludes that although campaign finance laws have a statistically significant impact on campaign spending in state legislative elections, the impact is relatively modest compared with other factors. Along these lines, Hogan (2000, p. 14) finds that both contribution limits and public funding reduce campaign spending, but that "these effects are limited primarily to incumbents."

Second, most of what we know about campaign finance has been derived from work on campaign spending in legislative elections (see, e.g., Goidel & Gross, 1996; Hogan, 1999, 2000; Jacobson, 1980; Krasno & Green, 1993; Thompson & Moncrief, 1998), the findings of which may or may not be applicable to gubernatorial campaigns.[1] For example, looking at the effects of candidate spending on electoral competition, Partin (1999, p. 19) found that gubernatorial elections are "a horse race of a different color" in that, unlike legislative elections, incumbent spending matters almost as much as challenger spending.[2] In addition, gubernatorial elections are more visible, generate greater media coverage, attract more experienced candidates, and are generally more competitive than legislative elections (Kahn, 1995; Squire, 1992; Squire & Fastnow, 1994). As such, campaign finance reforms may have a much different effect in gubernatorial than in legislative campaigns.

As this brief review illustrates, the literature on campaign finance reform has developed into two separate strands. Literature at the national level has been methodologically sophisticated but suffers from limited variance in the key variable of interest. The state-level literature, which has the potential to say much more about the electoral consequences of campaign finance laws, has, until quite recently, tended to be limited in scope because of practical limitations in data collection and research design.[3] This study attempts to bridge the gap between these separate strands of the literature by focusing on the impact of campaign finance laws on candidate spending and electoral competition in gubernatorial elections. We improve on prior work in several ways: First, using data on gubernatorial elections, we are able to account for the variance in state campaign finance laws across all 50 states and are able to do so over a considerable time frame (1978–1997). Because state legislatures have been more willing to impose reform on gubernatorial candidates than on themselves, there is considerably more variance in public financing schemes (and spending limits) for gubernatorial elections than for state legislative elections. Second, by paying greater attention to the measurement of state reform efforts, we are better able to distinguish between the effects of contribution limits, spending limits, and public financing on the electoral process. Third, with these improved measures of the state legal framework, we are able to make stronger, more convincing inferences regarding the effects of campaign finance reform on candidate spending and electoral competition—at least within the context of gubernatorial elections.

MEASUREMENT AND HYPOTHESES

Most laws distinguish between at least three different components of campaign finance regulations—contribution limits, public financing, and spending limits. Each component has a different set of intended purposes and as such should also have a different set of effects on the electoral process. Contribution limits, for example, are intended to reduce public perceptions of corruption by reducing the influence of large contributors. They are also intended to make the process of campaign fund-raising more democratic by forcing candidates to raise money from smaller contributors. Despite this stated intent, many critics of reform argue that increasing contribution limits would increase competitiveness by reducing the fund-raising burden on nonincumbent candidates. From this, we can suggest the following hypotheses:

Hypothesis 1: Campaign spending by nonincumbent candidates should be lower in states with more restrictive contribution limits.

Hypothesis 2: Differences in campaign spending should be larger in states with more restrictive contribution limits.

Hypothesis 3: Gubernatorial elections should be less competitive in states with more restrictive contribution limits.

To measure the restrictiveness of state contribution limits, we first examined whether the state imposed limits on contributions from individuals, family members, candidates, unions, political action committees (PAC), and corporations. Each state was coded 1 if it imposed the particular type of limit and 0 if there were no limits. We did this for each of the six categories (individuals, family, candidate, unions, PAC, and corporations) and then created an index based on the number of categories limited by the particular state. In the index, lower values indicate less restrictive states, whereas higher values indicate more restrictive states.[4] As can be seen in Table 1, the most common type of restriction involves limitations on corporate contributions followed by unions, individuals, PAC, family members, and candidates.[5]

Of course, this scale does not reflect the differences that may exist among the states that have a particular type of contribution; for example, is the limit on individual contributions set at $500 or $1,000? However, three important considerations lead us to use this particular measurement. First, in terms of an individual's or group's potential to contribute a total number of dollars, the differences among the states that limit a potential type of contribution is small compared with the difference between those states that limit a potential type of contribution and those that do not establish a limit. In ANOVA terminology, the between-category variance is much greater than the within-category variance. Second, the inclusion of all six contribution limit variables separately would have created a number of methodological problems, including severe multicollinearity.[6] Finally, we would argue that from a theoretical perspective, the overall regulatory environment is more important to potential contributors and candidates than the specific level of any particular contribution limit. So, for example, if a state does not limit PAC contributions, it makes little difference to a corporation or union whether a state places a $500 limit on corporate/union contributions or prohibits such contributions altogether because they can filter money to a candidate through PAC (Redfield, 1996; Sorauf, 1988).

TABLE 1

Percentage of Races With Spending Limits, Public Financing Provisions, and Contribution Limits

	Percentage of Races With (n)	
Spending limits	14.1	(36)
Public financing	36.2	(95)
Public financing to parties	20.2	(53)
Public financing to candidates	16.0	(42)
Contribution limits		
Individuals	54.0	(142)
Political action committees	42.6	(112)
Unions	60.1	(158)
Corporations	70.3	(185)
Family members	37.3	(98)
Candidates	8.4	(22)

Other reforms, such as public financing, are not only created to deal with perceptions of "election buying" but also are intended to increase electoral competition by providing money to challengers. They are, in this sense, intended to level the playing field of electoral politics. In terms of distributing public funds, states have opted either to give directly to candidates, to the political parties, or to both. Where public funds are distributed to candidates, the funding is generally used to entice compliance with associated spending limits. Where funding is distributed solely to political parties, no spending limits apply. Reformers believe that spending limits help to control the costs of political campaigns and—in combinations with public financing provisions— serve to enhance electoral competition. In direct contrast, opponents contend that when combined with spending limits, public financing serves to reduce nonincumbent candidate spending and, because of this reduction in spending, electoral competition. In addition, with Democrats generally supporting and Republicans generally opposing campaign reform, one would suspect that, operating under a principle of self-interest, Democrats would fare better under candidate-based public financing schemes than Republicans. Overall, we would offer the following hypotheses:

Hypothesis 4: Candidate spending (particularly incumbent spending and Republican spending) should be significantly lower in states with candidate-based public funding mechanisms and associated spending limits.

Hypothesis 5: The effect of spending limits on campaign spending should depend on the level of the associated spending limits. Campaign spending should be higher in states with less restrictive limits (on per citizen basis) than in states with more restrictive limits.

Hypothesis 6: Absolute differences in candidate spending should be significantly smaller in states with candidate-based public funding mechanisms.

Hypothesis 7: Gubernatorial elections should be less competitive in states with candidate-based public funding mechanisms and associated spending limits.

Unlike candidate-based public funding, party-based mechanisms have not been tied to spending limits, and, subsequently, have been less controversial. By providing a stable source of funding for political parties, party-based funding is thought to be particularly beneficial to minority parties and the out party (Jewell & Olson, 1988; Jones, 1984). In addition, whereas public funding is generally used for organizational maintenance, this frees up other money for electoral activity. Subsequently, party-based public funding mechanisms should have a positive effect on candidate spending and electoral competition.

Hypothesis 8: Candidate spending should be significantly higher in states with party-based public funding mechanisms.

Hypothesis 9: Absolute differences in candidate spending should be smaller in states with party-based public funding mechanisms.

Hypothesis 10: Gubernatorial elections should be more competitive in states with party-based public funding mechanisms.

To measure public financing, we created two dummy variables. The first is coded 1 if the state provided public funding directly to candidates and is coded 0 otherwise. The second is coded 1 if the state provided public funding to the parties, 0 otherwise. As can be seen in Table 1, 36% of the gubernatorial elections from 1978–1997 had some form of public financing. Over this time period, more gubernatorial elections provided public financing through the political parties (20%) than directly to the candidates (16%). To measure spending limits, we included a variable indicating the level of spending limits on a per citizen basis for those states that imposed limits. Because spending limits are inevitably entwined with candidate-based public financing, this measure has to be interpreted within the context of the candidate-based public financing dummy variable. The candidate-based public financing variable should indicate the change in the intercept that results from a state having spending limits (in combination with public funding), whereas the second variable should then serve as an interactive effect, indicating the effect of the level of the limits for those states that have spending limits.

DATA AND ANALYSIS

To investigate these hypotheses, we utilize spending data on gubernatorial elections from 1978–1997 provided by Thad Beyle (see, e.g., 1983, 1986, 1992). These spending data were then supplemented with data on state-level demographics, partisan voting behavior, and state campaign finance regulations. [...]

Control Variables

Beyond state legal restrictions, candidate fund-raising efforts are also affected by the level of competition within the state, whether the incumbent is running for reelection, the political experience of nonincumbent candidates, the size of the state, and the level of competition in the primary. To measure competitiveness, we first created a variable indicating the level of competition in the contemporary gubernatorial campaign. Margin is defined as the absolute value of the Republican nominee's vote in the general election minus the Democratic nominee's vote in the general election. To measure the general level of competition within the state irrespective of the current gubernatorial campaign, we first created an index of state partisanship based on the Democratic vote for presidential and senatorial campaigns during the most recent elections and the Democratic percentage of the state Senate and state house.[7]

Because candidates also spend money to win the primary election, we included a measure of financial competition based on spending by losing primary candidates. As with the other spending variables, candidate spending by the losing candidates was first converted to real 1992 dollars and then divided by the total voting age population in the state. In addition, to account for differences in spending created by geographical differences across states, we included a measure of the size of the state in square miles. Holding state population constant, it is often more expensive to campaign in states where voters are more geographically spread out than in states with a higher population density.[8] To make the coefficients more visually appealing and more consistent in size with the other regression coefficients, we divided the size of the state in square miles by 10,000. Finally, both candidate fund-raising and electoral competition are affected by electoral context (Jacobson & Kernell, 1983). To control for electoral context, we include dummy variables for each of the years included in the analysis.[9]

[…]

Dependent Variables

The dependent variables in this portion of the analysis, various indicators of candidate campaign spending, were first deflated to real 1992 dollars and were then divided by the state's voting age population.[10] Because separate spending totals for primary and general election campaigns can be obtained in only some of the states, candidate campaign spending is measured as total candidate spending that includes spending in both the primary and general election (Svoboda, 1995). As various indicators of campaign spending, we included total candidate campaign spending (defined as the total spending of the two party nominees), as well as spending by partisanship (Republican vs. Democratic) and candidate type (incumbent vs. challenger). The results of the regression analysis are presented in Table 2.

Results

As can be seen in Table 2, spending in gubernatorial elections largely reflects differences in competition in the current election, the size of the state,[11] and the level of financial competition in the respective primary elections. The underlying level of competition is also significant but in the opposite direction of what one would expect. Less competitive states are more expensive than more competitive states. Although the finding is somewhat counterintuitive, candidate spending may serve as a means of compensating for an unfavorable party balance.

What can states do to affect spending in gubernatorial elections? For one, they can provide a combination of candidate-based public financing and spending limits. To gauge the effects of reform, one has to look both at the coefficient for the variable indicating whether a state provided candidate-based public financing and the coefficient for the variable indicating the effect of spending limits on a per citizen basis. Overall, the effects of such a reform depend greatly on the level of any associated spending limits. For example, in an election with

TABLE 2

Regressions of Candidate Spending per Voting Age Citizen on State Campaign Finance Regulations

	Total Spending	Republican Spending	Democratic Spending	Incumbent Spending	Challenger Spending
Margin	−0.02 (0.008)***	−0.01 (0.003)***	−0.011 (0.006)*	−0.01 (0.007)*	−0.011 (0.005)**
Competition	0.02 (0.009)***	0.005 (0.003)*	0.02 (0.007)***	0.02 (0.01)*	0.012 (0.005)***
Incumbent seeking reelection	0.15 (0.22)				
Democratic incumbent		−0.46 (0.11)***	0.40 (0.18)**	−0.09 (0.19)	−0.28 (0.12)**
Republican incumbent			0.16 (0.11)	0.11 (0.19)	
Size of state (square miles)	0.09 (0.02)***	0.05 (0.01)***	0.05 (0.01)***	0.05 (0.02)***	0.03 (0.01)**
Spending by losing candidates in Democratic/incumbent primary	0.73 (0.24)***			0.53 (0.19)***	0.35 (0.70)
Spending by losing candidates in Republican/challenger primary	0.20 (0.19)	0.16 (0.08)*			0.28 (0.17)
Spending limits	−0.92 (0.31)***	−0.52 (0.16)***	−0.39 (0.21)*	−0.93 (0.43)**	−0.40 (0.23)*
Spending limits per voting age citizen	1.31 (0.39)***	0.79 (0.28)***	0.50 (0.27)*	1.86 (0.84)**	0.15 (0.29)
Contribution limits	0.09 (0.06)	0.02 (0.02)	0.08 (0.04)*	0.12 (0.06)*	0.04 (0.03)
Public financing to parties	0.12 (0.24)	0.04 (0.11)	0.10 (0.17)	0.03 (0.27)	0.25 (0.17)
Constant	0.93 (0.38)*	0.74 (0.17)***	0.12 (0.28)	0.35 (0.29)	0.56 (0.22)**
R^2	.47	.53	.35	.25	.47

NOTE: For the purposes of presentation, year variables are not included in the table. Standard errors are in parentheses. The full regression estimates are available upon request from the authors.

*$p < .10$. **$p < .05$. ***$p < .01$.

candidate-based public financing and spending limits set at $0.50 per voting age citizen, total spending would be expected to decrease by $0.27 per voting age citizen. With limits set at a $1.00 per voting age citizen, however, total spending would be expected to increase by approximately $0.39 per voting age citizen. Based on these estimates, in those states with candidate-based public financing and spending limits, total spending would have been expected to increase in about 39% of the gubernatorial elections but would have decreased in 61% of these elections.[12]

Interestingly, a cursory glance at the coefficients might also suggest that incumbents are hurt more by reform than challengers, but working out the implications of the coefficients suggests a different story. In fact, if limits were set at $0.25 per citizen, incumbent spending would decline by approximately $0.47 per citizen. However, incumbents quickly make up for any lost ground as spending limits increase. With limits set at $0.50 per citizen, incumbent spending would be roughly equal to incumbent spending in states without candidate-based public financing provisions. And with limits set at more than $0.50 per citizen, incumbent spending would be expected to increase, rather than decrease. In terms of practical implications, in just more than half the states with spending limits, incumbent spending would be expected to increase, whereas in just less than half those states incumbent spending would be expected to decrease. Challenger spending, on the other hand, would be expected to decrease regardless of the level of any associated limits (approximately $0.32 with $0.50 per citizen limits and approximately $0.25 with $1.00 per citizen limits).

Spending limits also have partisan implications, but these implications are not what one would expect. Democratic rather than Republican spending is more likely to be affected negatively by the imposition of spending limits. In this respect, Republican spending would be expected to decline by $0.13 under a $0.50 per citizen limit but would increase by $0.27 under a $1.00 per citizen limit. A similar pattern is found for Democrats, who would see their spending decline by $0.14 with a $0.50 per citizen limit but increase by $0.11 with a $1.00 per citizen limit. Contrary to expectations, in most scenarios, Republican candidates benefit relative to Democratic candidates.[13] Looking specifically at states with candidate-based public financing and spending limits, the patterns for Republican and Democratic spending are very similar. Both Republican and Democratic spending would be expected to increase in roughly 39% of the cases and decrease in 61% of those cases.

Contribution limits do not seem to have a significant effect on total spending, Republican spending, or challenger spending. Somewhat surprisingly, however,

Democratic and incumbent spending increases in states with more restrictive contribution limits, defying our expectation that more restrictive regulatory environments would make the fund-raising process more burdensome, particularly for nonincumbent and out-party candidates. According to the results, challengers do not spend significantly less in states with more restrictive contribution limits, but both Democratic and incumbent spending increase. In states that restrict each category of contribution, Democratic spending would be expected to be $0.48 per voting age citizen higher than in states with no limits at all. Under a similar scenario, incumbent spending would be expected to be $0.72 per citizen higher. As such, Democrats and incumbents gain a relative advantage over nonincumbent and Republican candidates in states with more restrictive limits, but restrictive contribution limits do not appear to limit nonincumbent spending. As a final note, we find little evidence that party-based public funding increases candidate spending.

Absolute Spending Differences

Although campaign finance reform is intended to control the expense of election campaigns, it is also intended to level the playing field by reducing the differential in candidate spending. The difference in candidate spending is measured as the absolute value of the difference in Republican and Democratic spending per voting age citizen. It was then regressed on the state campaign finance provisions as well as the various controls included in Table 2. The results are presented in Table 3.

As can be seen in Table 3, the difference in candidate spending is affected by both spending limits (in combination with candidate-based public financing) and contribution limits. In this respect, spending limits generally work to reduce the disparity in candidate spending, although as before the effect is contingent on the level of the spending limit. For example, with spending limits set at $0.50 per citizen, the difference in candidate spending would be reduced by $0.14 per citizen. With limits set at a $1.00 per citizen, the difference in spending would be expected to increase by approximately $0.23 per citizen. In terms of practical implications, the findings are remarkably similar to those presented in Table 1. The difference in candidate spending would be expected to increase 39% of those elections with candidate-based public financing and spending limits but would decrease in 61% of those elections. Contribution limits also affect absolute differences in spending, but they do so by increasing rather than decreasing differences in candidate spending. In states that restrict each category of contribution, the difference in spending would, on average, be $0.54 higher than in states without any contribution limits.

TABLE 3

Regressions of Spending Difference on State Campaign Finance Regulations		
	Absolute Spending Difference	
Margin	0.006	(0.005)
Competition	0.013	(0.006)**
Incumbent seeking reelection	0.23	(0.14)*
Size of state (square miles)	0.01	(0.01)
Spending by losing candidates in Democratic primary	0.12	(0.15)
Spending by losing candidates in Republican primary	0.02	(0.09)
Spending limits	−0.50	(0.19)***
Spending limits per voting age citizen	0.73	(0.26)***
Contribution limits	0.09	(0.04)**
Public financing to parties	0.05	(0.13)
Constant	−0.20	(0.23)
R^2	.20	

NOTE: For the purposes of presentation, year variables are not included in the table. Standard errors are in parentheses. The full regression estimates are available upon request from the authors.
*$p < .10$. **$p < .05$. ***$p < .01$.

PARTISAN AND ELECTORAL COMPETITION

Democratic Percentage of the Vote

If reform serves to effectively limit spending, what is the impact on electoral outcomes? To answer this question, we begin by considering the partisan consequences of campaign finance reform. Does reform help Democratic candidates? Or is it neutral in terms of its partisan consequences? We then consider the consequences of reform for electoral competition, defined as the margin of victory for the winning gubernatorial candidate. Finally, we consider the effects of reform on the electoral prospects of incumbents and challengers.

We begin by considering the effects of state campaign finance systems on the Democratic percentage of the vote. As explanatory variables, we include measures of Democratic and Republican campaign spending, dummy variables indicating whether a Republican or Democratic incumbent was running for reelection, interactions between candidate spending and incumbency, the underlying partisan division of the electorate, and the measures tapping into various aspects of the state campaign finance system (spending limits, contribution limits, and public financing). As in the previous analysis, we also included dummy variables for each of the years included in the analysis. The results are presented in column 1 of Table 4.

TABLE 4

Regressions of Partisan Competition and Democratic Vote on State Campaign Finance Regulations

	Democratic Percentage of the Vote		Margin of Victory (absolute value)	
Democratic spending per voting age citizen	3.43	(0.81)***	1.68	(0.98)
Republican spending per voting age citizen	−3.80	(0.67)***	−4.68	(1.18)***
Democratic incumbent	11.76	(1.53)***	10.46	(2.28)***
Republican incumbent	−7.58	(2.31)***	10.09	(3.40)***
Democratic Spending × Democratic Incumbent	−3.84	(0.74)***	−3.09	(1.19)***
Republican Spending × Republican Incumbent	1.47	(1.37)	−0.03	(2.09)
Partisanship/competition	0.23	(0.05)***	0.25	(0.06)**
Spending limits	−2.53	(2.36)	0.68	(3.55)
Spending limits per voting age citizen	3.91	(2.35)**	−1.38	(3.25)
Contribution limits	−0.29	(0.27)	−0.23	(0.37)
Public financing to parties	−1.62	(1.18)	−2.07	(1.77)
Constant	38.64	(3.18)***	8.83	(2.67)***
R^2	.50		.30	

NOTE: For the purposes of presentation, year variables are not included in the table. Standard errors are in parentheses. The full regression estimates are available upon request from the authors.

$**p < .05. ***p < .01.$

Looking first at column 1, the Democratic percentage of the vote is largely a function of candidate spending, incumbency, and state partisanship. In terms of affecting electoral outcomes, Republican spending appears to be more effective than Democratic spending regardless of whether the candidate is a nonincumbent or an incumbent. For Republican nonincumbents, an increase of $1.00 per citizen in spending yields 3.8% of the vote. Democratic nonincumbents, by comparison, yield only 3.4% of the vote for each additional dollar per citizen spent. The Republican advantage in spending holds for incumbents as well. Republican incumbents, on average, receive 2.3% of the vote for each dollar per citizen spent, whereas Democrats can expect a 0.41% reduction for the same level of spending.

Other than through their impact on candidate spending, campaign finance laws appear to have little direct effect on the Democratic percentage of the vote. Only the variable indicating the per citizen level of state spending limits is significant, suggesting that as spending limits are increased, the Democratic percentage of the vote increases as well. For example, in a state with limits set at $0.50 per citizen, the Democratic share of the vote would be expected to decrease by approximately 0.57%. In contrast, in states with limits set at $1.00 per citizen, the Democratic share of the vote would be expected to increase by approximately 1.4%.

In addition to the direct effects of reform, reform should also have indirect effects through its impact on candidate campaign spending. The partisan implications of these indirect effects depend a great deal on the scenario in question. For example, with limits set at $0.50 per voter and assuming an open seat election, Democratic spending would be expected to decrease by approximately $0.14, whereas Republican spending would be expected to decrease by $0.13 per citizen. The net effect in terms of the Democratic percentage of the vote is a very slight advantage to Democrats (0.03%). With limits set at $1.00 per citizen, however, the Republican candidate would be expected to win an additional 0.7% of the vote. Notably, in both the scenarios, the overall anticipated effects of reform appear to be fairly marginal.

Margin of Victory

If spending limits are associated with higher candidate spending and spending is associated with the partisan vote, one might reasonably infer that higher spending limits also would be associated with more competitive elections. To consider this possibility, we created a measure of the margin of victory in gubernatorial elections defined as the absolute value of the Democratic percentage of the vote subtracted from the Republican percentage of the vote. We then regressed the margin of victory on candidate spending, incumbency, competition, our measures of the state campaign finance regulations, and the dummy variables for each year. The results of this analysis are presented in column 2 of Table 4.

As can be seen in column 2, the margin of victory is largely a function of candidate spending, electoral competitiveness within the state, and incumbency. Although the effects of the various measures of state campaign finance reform are in the expected direction, none of these measures has a significant, direct effect on electoral competition.

Incumbency Effects

Because Table 4 lumps incumbents and nonincumbents together, one might suspect that the effects of campaign finance laws would be different in those races in which incumbents seek reelection. To account for this possibility, we ran additional analyses on the incumbent percentage of the vote and the incumbent margin of victory including only those races in which the incumbent sought reelection. It is worth noting that although, in the previous analysis, the margin of victory variable failed to differentiate between Democratic and Republican winners, the incumbent margin of victory variable is defined as the incumbent share of the vote minus the challenger share of the vote. Negative values then indicate races in which the incumbent lost his or her bid for reelection. The results of this analysis are presented in Table 5.

Looking at Table 5, several findings merit discussion. We find no significant direct effects of public funding, spending limits, or contribution limits on the incumbent share of the vote. In terms of the indirect effects, spending limits generally work to the disadvantage of challengers. For example, in a scenario in which a state limited spending to $0.50 per voting age citizen, incumbent

TABLE 5

Regressions of Incumbent Percentage of the Vote and Incumbent Margin of Victory on State Campaign Finance Regulations				
	Incumbent Percentage of the Vote		Incumbent Margin of Victory	
Incumbent spending per voting age citizen	−0.23	(0.50)	0.35	(1.02)
Challenger spending per voting age citizen	−5.21	(1.18)***	−10.58	(2.17)***
Democratic incumbent	0.38	(1.72)	1.04	(2.92)
Competition	0.15	(0.06)**	0.26	(0.11)**
Spending limits	−1.82	(3.21)	−7.47	(6.38)
Spending limits per voting age citizen	−0.38	(4.25)	4.91	(8.24)
Contribution limits	−0.14	(0.45)	−0.24	(0.70)
Public financing to parties	0.17	(2.22)	1.58	(3.28)
Constant	56.47	(2.42)**	16.58	(4.23)**
R^2	.32		.37	

NOTE: For the purposes of presentation, year variables are not included in the table. Standard errors are in parentheses. The full regression estimates are available upon request from the authors.
**$p < .05$. ***$p < .01$.

spending would be expected to remain stagnant while challenger spending would be expected to decrease by $0.32. Under this scenario, the incumbent margin of victory would be expected to increase by 1.7%. With limits set at $1.00, incumbent spending would be expected to increase by 1.09%.

CONCLUSIONS

In this analysis, we have attempted to provide a comprehensive assessment of the impact of campaign finance reform on the electoral process. The work improves on prior research by examining a larger, more comprehensive time frame (1978–1997) and by examining the impact of several different components of reform (contribution limits, public financing, and spending limits) within a single analytic framework. Unfortunately, although a comprehensive assessment of reform remains more elusive than we had imagined, we can derive several lessons for reform.

First, if the intent of reform is to limit candidate spending or to create parity in candidate spending levels, spending limits (in combination with candidate-based public financing) will serve this purpose. The effect of spending limits on candidate spending, however, differs according to candidate type, partisanship, and the level of the spending limits. In states with candidate-based public financing and relatively high spending limits, candidate spending (as well as differences in candidate spending) may in fact increase. As such, if the purpose of reform is to limit candidate campaign spending, more restrictive limits serve this purpose.

Second, it has been argued that by increasing contribution limits, states could help reduce the fund-raising burden on nonincumbent candidates. The evidence from this analysis provides a mixed verdict on the impact of contribution limits. In this respect, although there is no significant effect of contribution limits on challenger spending, more restrictive contribution limits are associated with increased incumbent spending. More restrictive contribution limits also are associated with increased disparities in candidate spending. At least in gubernatorial elections, however, there is no evidence that contribution limits hinder the fund-raising efforts of nonincumbent candidates. Relatively speaking, incumbents and Democrats are advantaged under systems with more restrictive limits but because they are raising more money, not because nonincumbents and challengers are raising less.

Third, the effects of reform on electoral competitiveness are primarily indirect, meaning that reform affects electoral competition through its effects on the level of spending in gubernatorial elections. In terms of partisan implications, in most scenarios reform appears to benefit Republican candidates, although overall the effects are relatively marginal. Reform also appears to place challengers at a disadvantage, because challengers raise less money in states with candidate-based public financing. Oddly, however, raising spending limits appears to do little to offset the decline in challenger spending. Overall, the results suggest that we should resist the temptation to over-generalize about the electoral consequences of campaign finance reform. The electoral consequences of reform on the electoral process depend very much on the version of reform enacted in each individual state.

ENDNOTES

1. In fact, until recently, there has been very little research examining the impact of gubernatorial campaign spending on either electoral outcomes or voter turnout. Patterson (1982) and Patterson and Caldeira (1983) are notable exceptions. More recently, Craig Svoboda (1995) has examined the effects of spending on electoral outcomes and voter turnout in gubernatorial elections.

2. It should be noted that in the congressional elections literature, the marginal effect of incumbent campaign spending remains in dispute (Green & Krasno, 1988).

3. See Gierzynski (1998) for a discussion of the problems in obtaining data on state legislative campaign finance and creating comparable data records.

4. The measure is similar to one employed by Hogan (1999, 2000) in his analysis of the impact of state campaign finance laws in state legislative elections.

5. Although there are some violations, the contribution limits index conforms, for the most part, to a Guttman scale. The cumulative Guttman scale created from the six types of contribution limits can be seen as a unidimensional measure of the restrictiveness of state contribution limits in a given state for a given year. The Coefficient of Reproducibility is .98, and the Coefficient of Scalability is .93 (McIver&Carmines, 1981). Thirty-one percent of the cases received a score of 0. In these cases, the states simply had no limit on any of the six types of contributions making up the scale. The percentages of the cases in the remaining six categories, from least restrictive to most restrictive, were 10%, 6%, 11.2%, 5.3%, 28.5%, and 8.4%, respectively.

6. For any of the contribution limit variables to be included in the equations, an arbitrarily high value would have to be assigned to those states that did not have a contribution limit. And, the designation of such a value would have made all six of the contribution limit variables highly collinear, with the resultant estimates being highly unstable.

7. Most often in analyses of this sort, competition is measured as a lagged Democratic or incumbent percentage of the vote or by the percentage of the vote received in the president's party in the most recent presidential election. In this analysis, we use an index, based on the Democratic percentage of the vote in the most recent presidential and Senate campaigns and the Democratic percentage of the state house and state Senate. The index is similar to the Ranney index (1976), as well as other measures of electoral competition, but has been modified for the purposes of this analysis. Because we are interested in examining the impact of competition in contemporary gubernatorial election as well as the more general level of competition within the state, we could not use the Ranney index because it includes the Democratic percentage of the vote in the gubernatorial election as one of its indicators of

competition. Moreover, later in the analysis, we consider the direct effect of campaign finance laws on the Democratic percentage of the vote, controlling for electoral competition. The Democratic presidential vote is the Democratic presidential candidate's percentage of the two-party vote in the presidential election coterminous with the gubernatorial election or in the presidential election most closely preceding the gubernatorial election. In the case of the two U.S. Senate races, we use the Democratic candidate's percentage of the two-party vote in the two Senate races coterminous or most immediately preceding the gubernatorial election. The final two components of the partisanship variable are the Democratic percentages of the state Senate and state house. The partisanship variable represents, therefore, the average level of Democratic success in these five settings. In the case of Nebraska, we only included the presidential and U.S. Senate votes. The competition variable is coded such that low scores indicate high levels of competition. The correlation between margin and competition is .21. The separate indicators of state partisanship were first summed and then divided by 5. To measure competitiveness, we then folded that index, such that

Competition = absolute value [partisanship − (100 − partisanship)],

where lower values indicate more competitive states and higher values indicate less competitive states. Again, the folded index is similar to other folded measures of electoral competition, including the Ranney index. For a review of the literature on electoral competition, see Holbrook and Van Dunk (1993).

8. In the gubernatorial elections literature, Ransone Coleman (1982) has noted that the geographic configuration of the state is important determinant of campaign costs. More broadly, in the literature on political campaigns, it is widely noted that the geographical spread of the district affects candidate campaign activities (see, e.g., Shea, 1996).

9. Including the dummy variables for separate years also controls for differences in presidential versus nonpresidential years, as well as for states that hold gubernatorial elections in odd-numbered years. For ease of presentation, we have not included the estimates for the year dummy variables in the tables. However, these results are available from the authors upon request.

10. All spending figures reported in this article only include monies spent by the candidates. As such, independent expenditures, soft money, and party spending are not included in the analysis. "Real 1992 dollars" are used to control for the effect of inflation. Spending figures are also divided by the state's population to control for the strong relationship that is often found between candidate spending and population (see, e.g., Beyle, 1996; Sorauf, 1988). In the data, the correlation between total spending and a state's population is .74, whereas the correlation between total spending in the general election and a state's population is .83.

11. It is important to remember that spending figures have already been divided by the state's population so the argument is that, controlling for population, it is more expensive to campaign in geographically larger areas. For example, once one controls for population size, it ought to more expensive to campaign in Alaska and Montana than it is to campaign in New Jersey or Maryland.

12. These percentages are derived by first finding the level of spending limits on a per voting age basis at which spending would be expected to be the same with or without limits. We then simply computed the number of states with spending limits above and below this limit. For total spending, with candidate-based public financing and limits set at $0.70 per voting age citizen, spending with limits (and public financing) would be expected to be the same as spending without limits. Of the 36 elections with some combination of candidate-based public financing, 14 (roughly 39%) had limits above $0.70 per voting age citizen, whereas 61% set limits below this number. For Republican spending, limits needed to be set at $0.79 per voting age citizen, and Democratic spending limits needed to be set at $0.78. Finally, for incumbents, spending limits needed to be set at $0.50 per voting age citizen. Challenger spending would be expected to decline almost regardless of the level of limits.

13. Of the races in which an incumbent sought reelection, 58% involved a Democratic incumbent. This may also reflect the fact that Republicans may be more inclined to disregard

voluntary spending limits. Malbin and Gais (1998) contend that Republicans are more likely to opt out of voluntary spending limits. In our analysis, however, we found no significant difference between the proportion of Republicans who spend more than the voluntary limit and the proportion of Democrats who spend more than the limit. This may, however, reflect a difference in candidates who accept the limits but then violate the limits versus candidates who disregard the limits altogether. Unfortunately, we do not have data on the number of candidates who opt out of the voluntary spending limits.

REFERENCES

Abramowitz, A. (1991). Incumbency, campaign spending, and the decline of competition in U.S. House elections. *Journal of Politics, 53,* 34–56.

Beyle, T. (1983). The costs of becoming governor. *State Government, 56,* 74–84.

Beyle, T. (1986). The cost of becoming governor. *State Government, 59,* 95–101.

Beyle, T. (1992). Big spending in the quest for the governors' chair. *State Government, 65,* 15–20.

Beyle, T. (1996). Governors: The middlemen and women in our political system. In V. Gray and H. Jacob, *Politics in the American States.* Washington, DC: CQ Press, 207–252.

Coleman, R. (1982). *The American governorship.* Westport, CT: Greenwood.

Donnay, P.,&Ramsden, G. (1995). Public financing of legislative elections: Lessons from Minnesota. *Legislative Studies Quarterly, 20,* 351–364.

Gierzynski, A. (1998). Data-gathering issues. In J. A. Thompson & G. F. Moncrief (Eds.), *Campaign finance in state legislative elections.* Washington, DC: CQ Press.

Goidel, R.,& Gross, D. (1994).A systems approach to campaign finance in United States House elections. *American Politics Quarterly, 22,* 125–153.

Goidel, R., & Gross, D. (1996). Reconsidering the "myths and realities" of campaign finance reform. *Legislative Studies Quarterly, 21,* 129–150.

Goidel, R., Gross, D., & Shields, T. (1999). *Money matters: Consequences of campaign finance reform in United States House elections.* Boulder, CO: Rowman & Littlefield.

Green, D., & Krasno, J. (1988). Salvation for the spendthrift incumbent. *American Journal of Political Science, 32,* 844–907.

Gross, D., Shields, T., & Goidel, R. (1997). Campaign finance reform and the 1994 congressional elections. *Policy Studies Journal, 25,* 215–234.

Hogan, R. (1999). Campaign spending in state legislative primary elections. *State and Local Government Review, 31,* 214–220.

Hogan, R. (2000). The costs of representation in state legislatures: Explaining variations in campaign spending. *Social Science Quarterly, 81.*

Holbrook, T., & Van Dunk, E. (1993). Electoral competition in the American states. *American Political Science Review, 87,* 955–962.

Jacobson, G. (1980). *Money and congressional elections.* New Haven, CT: Yale University Press.

Jacobson, G., & Kernell, S. (1983). *Strategy and choice in congressional elections* (2nd ed.). New Haven, CT: Yale University Press.

Jewell, M., & Cassie,W. (1998). Can the legislative campaign finance system be reformed? In J. A. Thompson & G. F. Moncrief (Eds.), *Campaign finance in state legislative elections.* Washington, DC: CQ Press.

Jewell, M., & Olson, D. (1988). *Political parties and elections in American states.* Chicago: Dorsey Press.

Jones, R. (1984). Financing state elections. In M. J. Malbin (Ed.), *Money and politics in the United States: Financing elections in the 1980s.* Chatham, NJ: Chatham House.

Kahn, K. (1995). Characteristics of press coverage in Senate and gubernatorial elections: Information available to voters. *Legislative Studies Quarterly, 20,* 1–23.

Krasno, J., & Green, D. (1993). Stopping the buck here: The case for campaign spending limits. *Brookings Review,* 17–21.

Malbin, M., & Gais, T. (1998). *The day after reform: Sobering campaign finance lessons from the American states.* Albany, NY: Rockefeller Institute Press.

Mayer, K. (1997). *Campaign finance reform in the states: A report to the governor's Blue Ribbon Commission on Campaign Finance Reform.* Available from: http://www.polisci.wisc.edu/~kmayer/

Mayer, K., & Wood, J. (1995). The impact of public financing on electoral competitiveness: Evidence from Wisconsin, 1964–1990. *Legislative Studies Quarterly, 20,* 69–88.

McIver, J., & Carmines, E. (1981). *Unidimensional scaling.* Beverly Hills, CA: Sage.

Partin, R. (1999, April). *Assessing the impact of campaign spending in governor's races.* Paper presented at the annual meeting of the American Political Science Association, September 2–5, Atlanta, GA.

Patterson, S. (1982). Campaign spending in contests for governor. *Western Political Quarterly, 35,* 457–477.

Patterson, S., & Caldeira, G. (1983). Getting out the vote: Participation in gubernatorial elections. *American Political Science Review, 77,* 675–699.

Ranney, A. (1976). Parties in state politics. In H. Jacob & K. Vines (Eds.), *Politics in the American states* (3rd ed.). Boston: Little, Brown.

Redfield, K. (1996). The good, the bad, and the perfect: Searching for campaign finance reform in Illinois. *Spectrum: Journal of State Government, 69,* 38–42.

[...]

Shea, D. (1996). *Campaign craft: The strategies, tactics, and art of political campaign management.* Westport, CT: Praeger.

Sorauf, F. (1988). *Money in American elections.* Glenville, IL: Scott, Foresman.

Sorauf, F. (1992). *Inside campaign finance: Myths and realities.* New Haven: Yale University Press.

Squire, P. (1992). Challenger profile and gubernatorial elections. *Western Political Quarterly, 45,* 125–142.

Squire, P., & Fastnow, C. (1994). Comparing gubernatorial and senatorial elections. *Political Research Quarterly, 47,* 703–720.

[...]

Svoboda, C. (1995). *How and why voters vote in gubernatorial elections.* Unpublished doctoral dissertation, University of Wisconsin–Milwaukee.

Thompson, J., & Moncrief, G. (1998). *Campaign finance in state legislative elections.* Washington, DC: Congressional Quarterly.

Authors' Note: An earlier version of this article was presented at the 1999 annual meeting of the Midwest Political Science Association, Palmer House Hilton, Chicago, IL. We would like to thank Thad Beyle, without whom this article would not have been possible, for generously sharing the data on gubernatorial campaign spending. He, of course, bears no responsibility for any errors.

*Donald A. Gross is a professor of political science and chair of the Political Science Department at the University of Kentucky.

Robert K. Goidel is associate professor of political science and director of Public Policy Research at the Manship School of Mass Communication, Louisiana State University.

Todd G. Shields is interim associate dean of academic affairs at the Clinton School of Public Service and director of the Diane D. Blair Center of Southern Politics and Society at the University of Arkansas, Fayetteville.

DISCUSSION QUESTIONS

1. What are some of the normative concerns involved in setting the dollar amounts for spending limits and contribution limits? How should these vary across states?

2. The authors measure the effects of campaign finance regulation on total spending in state elections. Should campaign finance laws aim to reduce this amount?

3. The authors also investigate the consequences of campaign finance regulation for electoral competition. Again, should campaign finance regulations be evaluated based on whether they encourage or discourage competition?

4. The authors draw a distinction between party-based and candidate-based public funding systems. What is the difference, and which is more desirable?

5. Is a finding that campaign finance regulation has few measurable effects on election outcomes an argument for or against campaign finance reforms?

Campaign Finance Laws and Candidacy Decisions in State Legislative Elections

by Keith E. Hamm and Robert E. Hogan*

This article examines the influence of campaign finance laws on patterns of candidacy in state legislative elections. Fundamental to electoral competition are the decisions by candidates to seek elective office; however, few studies consider the influence of various legal conditions that may serve to inhibit or enhance candidacy. Several factors on both the state and district levels will be taken into account; however, one of the most important for this analysis is the potential effect of campaign finance laws. Previous studies demonstrate that restrictions on campaign contributions vary dramatically from state to state (e.g., Alexander 1991; Gross and Goidel 2003; Jones 1984; Malbin and Gais 1998; Schultz 2002; Thompson and Moncrief 1998; Witko 2005), and such variation affects levels of campaign spending (Hogan 2000) and electoral competition (e.g., Gross, Goidel, and Shields 2002; Stratmann 2002). But how do such conditions influence the likelihood that candidates will decide to run? Do restrictions on funding sources have any effect on the probability that elections are contested? The present analysis considers this question in a district-level analysis of lower house elections to the state legislature across three election cycles in the 1990s.

Effects on Candidacy Decisions

The major candidacy decision examined in this analysis is the choice to challenge a sitting incumbent. Given the frequency with which incumbents seek to retain their seats, this type of election would appear to be a logical first step in determining the effects of campaign finance laws. Indeed, a variety of studies have identified a number of factors that affect the likelihood of challenger emergence, ranging from institutional characteristics and district-level conditions (e.g., Squire 2000; Van Dunk and Weber 1997) to candidate characteristics (Pritchard 1992; Holbrook and Tidmarch 1993) and campaign war chests (e.g., Hogan 2001). The general finding from these studies is that district and institutional factors play a large role in influencing candidacy decisions.

In the present analysis, the concern is with campaign finance laws as they may influence candidates' potential fundraising efforts. Many candidates in state elections report that the onerous task of fund-raising is a major deterrent to running for office (Faucheux and Herrnson 1999; Maisel, Stone, and Maestas 2001; Moncrief, Squire, and Jewell 2001). What is unclear is how campaign finance laws might play a role in this process, particularly among those thinking of challenging a sitting incumbent. Do campaign finance laws make it more or less likely that a contested race will occur? One school of thought suggests that challengers are less likely to emerge in states where contribution limits are low. Challengers nearly always have difficulty raising money to defeat incumbents, and contribution limits will simply make their jobs that much harder. Another school of thought, however, suggests that challengers are more likely to emerge in states where contribution limits are low, since this puts all candidates more or less on equal footing. We believe that this latter perspective is more accurate, given that incumbents are the major recipients of contributions from organizations (Cassie and Thompson 1998; Jones and Borris 1985; Sabato 1985). Low limits are likely to benefit challengers who very often have difficulty matching the fundraising prowess of well-connected incumbents. We expect that potential challengers recognize how their particular state's campaign finance laws would affect their campaigns, and this influences their entry decision. Specifically, we expect to observe higher rates of challenger emergence in those states where campaign finance laws are more stringent, all other factors held constant.

Few studies have looked very closely at the potential effects of campaign finance laws on candidacy decisions. An analysis by Mayer and Wood (1995) finds that the public financing mechanism available in Wisconsin does not have much of an impact on the number of candidates who decide to run. But an analysis by Stratmann and Aparicio-Castillo (2003) finds that individual contribution limits increased the number of candidates who run in single-member districts. The present analysis continues this line of inquiry by examining the likelihood that challengers emerge to run against sitting incumbents. We consider the possible effects of these laws in both primary and general elections to determine how they might influence the emergence of major party challengers as well as minor party and independent candidates.

The first two dependent variables are dichotomous and indicate whether a sitting incumbent is challenged initially in the primary and then in the general election by a major party candidate. Each of these variables takes the value of either 1 or 0 (1 = yes, 0 = no). A third dichotomous dependent variable indicates whether an independent or minor party candidate decides to run against an incumbent in the general election (1 = yes, 0 = no). For those who expect stringent campaign finance laws to have deleterious effects on the chances that major party candidates will mount challenges, such effects are probably exacerbated among potential independent and minor party candidates. However, since we believe that stringent laws hamper incumbents' fundraising prowess, the presence of such laws is expected to increase the likelihood that independent and minor party candidates emerge. By considering the impact of campaign finance laws on two distinct stages of the election process, as well as on major party and other types of candidates (minor party and independents), we hope to obtain a more thorough understanding of their overall effects.

Gauging the Impact of Campaign Finance Laws

As indicated earlier, states provide an excellent venue for determining the impact of campaign finance laws, given the wide assortment of legal contexts that are present (Alexander 1991; Gross and Goidel 2003; Jones 1984; Malbin and Gais 1998; Schultz 2002; Thompson and Moncrief 1998). Such interstate variation provides a natural laboratory for determining how laws influence various parts of the electoral process. However, one must be aware that each state's regulatory regime is quite complex and is an amalgam of statutory provisions, regulatory rulings, and court decisions. Attempting to categorize the states on the basis of their campaign finance regulations is fraught with difficulty. In the present analysis, we recognize the complexity of these laws and focus on what we believe are some of the most influential and fundamental elements of state campaign finance laws.[1]

There are a variety of different limits that states place on where candidates may obtain campaign funding. We believe that limits on sources of funding are likely to influence a potential challenger's decision to run. Specifically, greater limits are likely to result in a higher likelihood of challenger emergence. A large number of states either limit or prohibit direct contributions from corporations and labor unions. Some states also place limits on the amounts that political action committees (PACs), individuals, and political parties contribute. To gauge the effect of these limits, an additive index is created that sums the number of sources (of five) that are limited or prohibited: corporations, labor unions, PACs, individuals, and political parties. The score for each state can range from 0 (no limitations from any of these sources) to 5 (some limits imposed on all five sources). This variable will be used in multivariate analyses to determine if limits serve to enhance the likelihood of candidate emergence.

In addition to laws that limit contributions, a small number of states also have public financing systems in which candidates agree to abide by relatively low spending and contribution limits in exchange for a public subsidy. Because such systems are probably attractive to potential challengers who have difficulty raising large sums of cash, we expect the probability of a challenge to be higher in these states. Only a handful of states provide public funds to candidates (in the states analyzed here, there are only three: Hawaii, Minnesota, and Wisconsin); however, this may be a strong incentive to potential challengers considering a run for office.[2] A dichotomous indicator is used to control for this potential influence (1 = public funding system, 0 = no public funding system). Does the presence of such a system make it more or less likely that a candidate will emerge?

Control Factors

Previous studies demonstrate that many elections to the state legislature go uncontested on a regular basis (Moncrief, Squire, and Jewell 2001), and a number of factors have been identified to explain variation in contestation for both primary and general elections (e.g., Hogan 2003; Squire 2000; Van Dunk and Weber 1997). To adequately assess the impact of campaign finance laws, it is necessary to control for a wide assortment of these statewide and district-level conditions.

Filing Requirements

An initial hurdle that all candidates must overcome is simply getting on the ballot. In addition to qualifications such as age and residency, there are often required filing fees or a specific number of voter signatures. Previous studies of congressional elections demonstrate that petition requirements and fees can have an effect on rates of contesting (Ansolabehere and Gerber 1996). For example, Ansolabehere and Gerber (1996, 259) find that "in states with neither fees nor petitions, the predicted frequency of uncontested seats is 6.9%; in states requiring $1,000 fees and 1,000 signatures, the predicted frequency of uncontested seats jumps to 24.7%." A study of state legislative elections from 1998 to 2000 finds a similar effect for filing fees and signature requirements (Stratmann 2005). For example, Stratmann (2005, 68) finds that "a $1,000 increase in the filing fee leads to a 4% decrease in major party candidates." In addition, Stratmann finds that "the entry decision of minor-party candidates is much more sensitive to monetary barriers to entry than major-party candidates" (p. 69). Recent work by Lem and Dowling (2006) shows that ballot access restrictions limit the number of minor party candidates who run for governor.

Given these findings, we therefore control for ballot access restrictions in each state as they apply specifically to major party and independent candidates. We use a measure that places states into one of three categories based on the stringency of their ballot access laws (low = 0, medium = 1, and high = 2). A state is put into the *low* category if the signature requirements or filing fees are nominal (e.g., Alaska's filing fee is $30; in Rhode Island, a candidate needs only 50 signatures; and in Indiana, a candidate merely signs a declaration of candidacy). States in the *medium* category are those that require a moderate number of signatures or dollar amount for filing fees (e.g., in Michigan, candidates must collect 200–400 signatures or pay a $100 filing fee). Finally, for states in the *high* category, a substantial effort to collect signatures (more than 500) or a relatively high filing fee (in excess of $250) is required. For example, in Florida, the filing fee is set at 6 percent of the salary for the office sought and the signature requirement is 1 percent of registered voters in the district. During the mid-1990s, this amounted to a filing fee of more than $1,000 or 600 signatures. While these examples are applicable to major party candidates, similar, if not more onerous, hurdles confront independent candidates. A comparable categorization scheme (low = 0, medium = 1, and high = 2) is created for restrictions that apply to independent and minor party candidates.[3]

Other State- and District-level Conditions

Previous studies demonstrate the influence of several state- and district-level factors on contestation in state legislative elections. At the state level, a major factor that should be controlled for is legislative professionalism. The higher pay and status associated with more professional legislatures result in a greater number of contested seats in both primary and general elections (Hogan 2003; Squire 2000). A measure of professionalism developed by Squire (2000) based on characteristics of legislative institutions in the mid-1990s is included in the models.

The presence of term limits is another state-level condition that might influence the likelihood that incumbents are challenged. Past studies indicate that term limits do not influence the likelihood that incumbents win reelection (Niemi et al. 2006), but it is not clear how such limits might affect challenger emergence. Because term limits reduce the attractiveness of a legislative seat, we might expect fewer incumbents to be challenged. However, because incumbents can no longer spend a large amount of time developing a personal vote within their districts, they may be more vulnerable and therefore at greater risk to be challenged. To control for term limits, a dichotomous measure is used to indicate the presence of term limits.[4]

Party competition at the chamber level is also included in the multivariate models. As chamber competition increases, both parties would appear to have an incentive to field candidates in as many districts as possible in hopes of either retaining or gaining control of the chamber. Previous studies find this to have an influence on measures of general election contestation (Van Dunk and Weber 1997). Here, the variable is measured as the minority party's percentage of chamber seats held prior to the election.

Constituency-level conditions are also expected to affect the likelihood that incumbents are challenged. District competitiveness should have a strong influence on the probability that a challenger emerges in both primary (Grau 1981; Jewell 1967) and general elections (e.g., Pritchard 1992; Van Dunk 1997). This variable is calculated as one hundred minus the winner's percentage of the two-party vote in the previous general election. If past support for the incumbent is high, challenger emergence is less likely, particularly in the general election.

Another constituency-level characteristic that is expected to have an influence is social diversity. We would expect to find challenger emergence to be greater in more heterogeneous districts than in more homogenous ones, all other things being held constant. Previous studies find such a variable to have an effect in congressional primary elections (Herrnson and Gimpel 1995). Patterned after an index developed by Lieberson (1969) and used by Sullivan (1973), higher values of the measure indicate that citizens in the district share fewer common characteristics.[5] Greater diversity is therefore expected to increase the likelihood of candidacy.

Other district-level conditions are also included as control variables. Previous studies demonstrate a positive relationship between election competition and population (Barrilleaux 1986; Patterson and Caldeira 1984); therefore, a variable measuring average district population (in thousands) is included. In addition, a dichotomous measure for district urbanism is controlled for in the models. A district is considered urban if it overlaps a standard metropolitan area (SMA) as defined by the U.S. Census.

DATA

The data used in this analysis consist of district-level information collected for lower house legislative elections in 1994, 1996, and 1998. Several criteria were used in choosing the states included in this study. First, we selected states where only single-member districts are used for elections to the lower houses.[6] Such similarity facilitates comparisons and analyses of factors believed to affect incumbent challenge. Second, we chose states where substantial redistrict-ing occurred only once after the 1990 election but prior to the 1992 elections, thereby making demographic features and past competition measures consistent across three time periods.[7] And third, because we want to include primary infor-mation, it was necessary to limit the analysis to states that actually use primaries as a means of choosing party nominees. Therefore, states such as Connecticut, New York, Utah, and Virginia are excluded.[8] In addition, states using blanket primaries during the time period (Alaska and Washington) as well as those with nonpartisan (Nebraska) and open-election systems (Louisiana) are also exclud-ed.[9] Given these criteria, the election data set contains 25 states: Arkansas, California, Colorado, Delaware, Florida, Hawaii, Idaho, Illinois, Indiana, Iowa, Kansas, Michigan, Minnesota, Missouri, New Mexico, Nevada, Ohio, Okla-homa, Oregon, Pennsylvania, Rhode Island, Tennessee, Texas, Wisconsin, and Wyoming.

While no group of states can be representative of all fifty, this list contains a wide assortment from all regions of the country. There is also considerable varia-tion on important state-level variables of interest (legislative professionalism and chamber competition between parties) as well as on district-level features (such as district population and urbanism). Most important, there is variation on the critical aspects of the campaign finance laws.

Information used to construct the dependent and independent variables was obtained from a variety of sources. Election data came from the relevant agen-cies in each state. Demographic characteristics of the districts are primarily from *State Data Atlas: Almanac of State Legislatures* (Lilley, DeFranco, and Diefender-fer 1994) and the U.S. Census.

ANALYSIS

We begin by examining how often incumbents face challenges in primary and general elections. Table 1 lists the percentage of incumbents in each state who faced a challenge in either election, a challenge in the primary, and a challenge in the general election. The last column shows the percentage fac-ing an independent or minor-party challenge in the general election. Previous research demonstrates that a large percentage of seats held by incumbents go uncontested on a regular basis (Moncrief, Squire, and Jewell 2001), and the results presented in Table 1 clearly support this conclusion. Only 65 percent of incumbents in these twenty-five states faced a challenge in either the primary or the general election. Approximately 23 percent of incumbents had a primary challenge, while 59 percent faced a general election challenge. Only 11 percent of candidates faced at least one independent or minor-party opponent in the general election.

Table 1 demonstrates that there is substantial variation across the states on all four indicators of contestation. Arranged in order of highest to lowest percentage of incumbents challenged in either type of election, we see that more than 90 percent of incumbents faced challengers in Michigan, California, and Minnesota, while fewer than half did in Rhode Island, Delaware, Texas, and Arkansas. In Arkansas, only 38 percent of incumbents running for reelection were challenged. Dramatic differences between the states can also be observed within the columns calculated separately for primary and general elections. For example, only 7 percent of incumbents in Iowa were challenged in a primary, while about half were challenged in Michigan (49 percent) and Hawaii (51 percent). In general elections, only 24 percent of incumbents in Arkansas were challenged, while over 90 percent in California and Minnesota faced an opponent. As for independent and minor-party challenges, 1 percent or fewer of the incumbents in Illinois, Oklahoma, and Florida faced such opposition. In California districts, however, independent or minority-party contestants were challenged in 60 percent of the districts where incumbents ran.

Overall, there is a large amount of variation across the states on these various indicators of incumbency challenge. The question we now address is: What explains these differences? Specifically, what effect might campaign finance laws have once a number of state- and district-level conditions are controlled?

Table 2 provides the results of logistic regression analyses of factors believed to affect the likelihood that incumbents are challenged in primary and general elections. The dependent variable is dichotomous and indicates the presence of a major-party opponent in each election. Three different models are presented separately for primary and general elections to test the effects of two indicators of campaign finance laws along with the control factors. Model 1 includes the results when using only the limitations index, model 2 includes only the dichotomous indicator for public financing, and model 3 uses both measures simultaneously. Because logistic regression coefficients are not directly interpretable, we have calculated a change in probability score to indicate the percentage point difference in the likelihood of a contested election for each of the coefficients listed in model 3. For the dichotomous variables (e.g., urban, presence of public financing, etc.), the difference is between the values of 0 and 1. For continuous variables (e.g., past electoral competitiveness, social diversity, etc.), the value is the difference between one standard deviation below the mean to one standard deviation above the mean. For the categorical measures

Table 1

Among Races Involving an Incumbent: Percentages of Contested Primary and General Elections in the 1994–1998 Elections in Twenty-five States					
State	(N)	Primary or General Election Contest	Primary Election Contest	General Election Contest	Independent or Minority Party Contest
Michigan	(222)	97	49	89	22
California	(105)	94	37	91	60
Minnesota	(342)	93	13	92	9
Ohio	(254)	90	21	86	14
Hawaii	(126)	88	51	79	11
Oregon	(117)	79	31	74	25
Nevada	(95)	79	33	77	27
Colorado	(143)	71	10	71	15
Illinois	(310)	69	27	59	1
Indiana	(271)	66	21	61	13
Kansas	(309)	65	26	58	7
Missouri	(411)	64	25	56	13
Pennsylvania	(558)	64	20	58	10
Iowa	(244)	62	7	61	5
Oklahoma	(268)	61	29	52	1
New Mexico	(167)	60	28	44	4
Wisconsin	(263)	60	17	56	14
Tennessee	(251)	56	28	40	10
Idaho	(173)	52	20	41	8
Wyoming	(143)	52	15	46	6
Florida	(303)	51	25	39	1
Rhode Island	(261)	47	15	37	14
Delaware	(111)	46	11	43	18
Texas	(388)	44	21	30	7
Arkansas	(206)	38	18	24	2
All twenty-five states	(6,041)	65	23	59	11

Note: Data for California are from the 1994 and 1996 election periods only. Numbers in all cells are rounded to the nearest percentage. Numbers in parentheses are total elections examined per state for the three-year period.

of campaign finance laws and filing requirements, the change score represents the difference between the lowest and highest values of each variable.

The results of these tests demonstrate that many of the control variables perform as expected, although the effects are not always consistent across elections. Among the district-level control variables, we find that past electoral competitiveness has a positive effect on competition but only in the general election. Here we find that a movement in past competition from one standard deviation below the mean to one standard deviation above the mean results in an increase in the probability of challenger emergence by nearly 37 percentage points. Such a finding is consistent with past literature showing that district competitiveness plays a large role in candidacy decisions. Whether the district is an urban district or not also influences the likelihood of challenge but only in the primary election. Here we find that the likelihood of a challenger emerging in the primary is about 5 percentage points higher in urban districts. Neither social diversity nor total district population has an influence on challenger emergence in the primary or general election.

Among the system-level effects, we find that legislative professionalism has a positive effect on candidate emergence in both types of elections. Moving from one standard deviation below to one standard deviation above the mean in professionalism increases the likelihood of a primary challenge by about 8 percentage points and a general election challenge by more than 16 percentage points. Chamber competition also has a statistically significant effect in both primary and general elections, but interestingly, the effects are in opposite directions. While chamber competition reduces the likelihood of a primary contest, it increases the odds of a general election challenge. Such a differential effect is not too surprising, given the incentives for party leaders who are working to gain or regain control of the chamber. In situations where control hangs in the balance, party organizations will likely do their best to discourage intraparty competition while at the same time stimulating as many challenges as possible to the opposing party's incumbents.

Term limits also have an effect but only in the general election. As indicated earlier, term limits might decrease the likelihood of a challenge, as potential opponents simply wait until the incumbent is ineligible to run for reelection. Or such limits may serve to increase vulnerability, as fewer incumbents have the time or incentives to build a "personal" vote among their constituents. The positive effect for term limits in the general election would appear to support this latter proposition. The likelihood of a general election challenger is about 10 percentage points higher in states that have term limits than in those that do not.

The dichotomous indicators for election context also have influence in each type of election. As these differences indicate, the particular election year affects the likelihood that challengers emerge. Such differences no doubt reflect state and national forces that make the prospects for particular parties look bright or dim, depending on altered political conditions.

The more interesting aspects of Table 2 are those related to the effects of the

Table 2

Logistic Regression Analyses of Factors Affecting the Probability of a Major Party Challenge to an Incumbent in Primary and General Elections in Twenty-five States (1994–1998)

	Primary Elections				General Elections			
	Model 1	Model 2	Model 3	Change	Model 1	Model 2	Model 3	Change
Campaign finance laws								
Limitation index	0.015	—	0.022		0.069***	—	0.047*	+.057
Public funding	—	-0.304**	-0.316**	-.053	—	0.776***	0.736***	+.164
Filing requirements	-0.036	0.001	-0.011		-0.286***	-0.328***	-0.355***	-.172
District-level factors								
Past electoral competitiveness	0.001	0.001	0.001		0.043***	0.042***	0.042***	+.368
Social diversity	-0.053	0.099	0.186		1.320+	0.475	0.704	
Population	0.001	-0.001	0.001		-0.001	0.001	0.002	
Urban	0.343***	0.333***	0.326***	+.055	-0.055	-0.005	-0.019	
System-level conditions								
Legislative professionalism	1.602***	2.113***	1.989***	+.082	3.952***	3.189***	2.974***	+.165
Chamber competition	-0.008*	-0.009***	-0.008*	-.031	0.014***	0.010**	0.013***	+.063
Term limits	0.063	0.030	0.032		0.332+	0.412*	0.423*	+.097
Election context								
1996	-0.131+	-0.117	-0.134+	-.024	0.367***	0.417***	0.382***	+.091
1998	-0.376***	-0.354***	-0.376***	-.065	-0.273***	-0.219**	-0.268***	-.065
Constant	-1.430***	1.432***	-1.542***		-2.407***	-1.841***	-2.094***	
N	6,120	6,120	6,120	Base Prob.	6,041	6,041	6,041	Base Prob.
Pseudo R²	0.02	0.03	0.02	.232	0.19	0.20	0.20	.595
Correctly predicted	77.4	77.4	77.4		57.9	57.9	57.9	

+$p < .10$. *$p < .05$. **$p < .01$. ***$p < .001$.

state's legal context. Beginning with the filing requirements measure, we see that the coefficients are statistically significant only in the general election, but their effects are quite large. If we compare a state where such requirements are quite weak to where they are strong, we see a 17-percentage point difference in the likelihood that an incumbent is challenged. Such differences suggest that challenger emergence is greatly influenced by this legal contextual feature. The monetary and signature requirements are clearly a deterrent to candidacy even when a host of state- and system-level factors are controlled.

Campaign finance laws also have a large influence, and again, the effect is mainly in the general election phase. In the general election, more restrictive campaign finance laws increase the likelihood of challenger emergence. The difference in challenger emergence between states where there are no restrictions (limitations index equals 0) and where there are many (limitations index equals 5) is nearly 6 percentage points. The presence of a public funding mechanism also has a positive influence in the general election. Having such a system increases challenger emergence in these elections by more than 16 percentage points. In primary elections, contribution limits have no statistical influence, but the presence of public financing actually leads to a reduced likelihood of challenger emergence by about 5 percentage points. Such a finding is unexpected and may be reflective of other conditions present in these three states that reduce intraparty competition.[10]

So far, these results demonstrate that election laws have an influence on candidacy decisions, especially in general elections. Greater contribution limits increase the likelihood of challenger emergence, while more restrictive filing requirements reduce the incidence of challenger opposition. The effects of public financing are less clear, given that only three states utilize such systems during this time frame, but they lead to a greater likelihood of a challenger in the general election but a lower likelihood of an opponent in the primary. In assessing the overall impact of campaign finance laws, we can say that their impact is substantial, although not overwhelming, and there are other conditions that also have a large influence. For example, the other legal condition examined, filing requirements, has quite a large effect in general elections. Legislative professionalism also has a large influence. Furthermore, consistent with previous findings, electoral competitiveness dramatically affects the likelihood of challenger emergence in general elections.

Having assessed the influence of such factors on the emergence of major-party challenges, how do these variables affect the likelihood that an independent or minor-party candidate emerges? Do campaign finance laws deter these candidates from running in the general election? Table 3 presents the results of logistic regression analyses in which the dependent variable is the presence of at least one independent or minor-party candidate. As one can see, many of the variables that affected the emergence of a major-party challenge are also statistically related to independent challenger emergence. For example, past competition, legislative professionalism, and term limits all have a positive influence on the emergence of at least one independent or minor-party candidate. In addition, we find that social diversity, district population, and urban setting also have a positive influence on the likelihood of such a candidate's running.

The most interesting elements to Table 3 are those related to election laws. Similar to findings regarding major-party candidates in the general election, we find filing requirements having a statistically significant negative influence. Emergence of minor or independent candidates is nearly 8 percentage points higher in those states where such requirements are quite minor compared to where they are rather onerous. Campaign finance laws also have an influence in a manner that we would expect. The limitations index has a positive and statistically significant effect—the difference between strict and relatively lax restrictions is about 3 percentage points. Interestingly, public funding mechanisms also have a positive influence on independent and minor party candidacies—the difference between high and low categories moves the likelihood more than 5 percentage points.

Overall, the results in Table 3 demonstrate that various factors influence the emergence of independent and minor-party challenges. Filing requirements as well as the stringency of campaign finance laws have an effect even after a wide range of state- and district-level factors have been controlled.

CONCLUSIONS

Do more stringent campaign finance laws increase the likelihood that a challenger emerges to contest a seat currently held by an incumbent? Analyses reported here from elections involving incumbents from twenty-five states across three election cycles indicate that they do. Financing laws that limit where candidates may raise funding increase the likelihood that major-party as well as minor-party and independent challengers emerge in the general election. These results hold even after a number of district- and state-level indicators have been taken into consideration. The presence of public financing may also increase the likelihood of major-party challenger emergence; however, further study using a wider number of states that utilize such systems is needed before any definitive conclusions can be reached.

Table 3

Logistic Regression Analyses of Factors Affecting the Probability of an Independent or Minor Party Challenge to an Incumbent in General Elections in Twenty-five States (1994–1998)				
	Primary Election		General Election	
	Model #1	Model #2	Model #3	Change
Campaign finance laws				
Limitation index	0.079**	–	0.078**	+.031
Public funding	–	0.562***	0.553**	+.054
Filing requirements	-0.386***	-0.483***	-0.508***	-.077
District-level factors				
Past electoral competitiveness	0.005*	0.005*	0.005*	+.016
Social diversity	3.910***	3.419**	3.668**	+.025
Population	0.004**	0.004**	0.005***	+.034
Urban	0.549***	0.604***	0.579***	+.042
System-level conditions				
Legislative professionalism	1.604***	1.436**	0.890+	+.017
Chamber competition	-0.003	-0.007	-0.001	
Term limits	1.065***	1.112***	1.132***	+.140
Election context				
1996	0.353***	0.411***	0.346**	+.030
1998	0.138	0.204+	0.123	
Constant	-4.715***	-4.212***	-4.606***	
N	6,041	6,041	6,041	Base
Pseudo R^2	0.04	0.04	0.05	Probability
Correctly predicted	89.5	89.6	89.6	.090
$+p < .10.$ $*p < .05.$ $**p < .01.$ $***p < .001.$				

These results provide insight into the effects of campaign finance laws that were designed, in part, to produce higher rates of election competition. Contrary to those who believe low limits might impose a significant burden on challengers, these findings suggest that restrictions make the prospects of running against an incumbent more attractive to potential candidates. We believe the causal mechanism responsible for this finding involves the perceptions of potential challengers in assessing their ability to raise money relative to the incumbent. Where limits are more stringent, challengers perceive they have a better chance of keeping pace with an incumbent's fundraising and are more likely to make a run for office. The fact that the influence is observed in the general but not in the primary election certainly provides support for this interpretation. Because primary elections involve smaller amounts of money and are less often funded by PAC and party donations, expectations about funding probably plays less of a role in the minds of potential primary candidates.

The findings from this analysis are a first, but important, step in understanding the influence of campaign finance laws. While these legal conditions may ultimately affect the amounts of money that candidates raise and the degree of competition observed, we find here that they have a strong influence on this very initial stage in the electoral process—the decision to run. Future work will want to continue this line of inquiry into how laws affect not only the likelihood that a candidate emerges but also the characteristics of those who decide to run. For example, might low limits result in the emergence of different types of candidates, perhaps those who have fewer ties to financial and economic power? Do low limits ultimately produce a more diverse pool of candidates with regard to their occupation and background? In addition to examining how laws affect aspects of the electoral process, future research should more closely examine features of the laws themselves. Attention in this analysis has fallen on just a few legal dimensions; however, there are other aspects of the laws that may prove to have an even greater influence than those examined here.

ENDNOTES

1. We used various editions of *Campaign Finance Law* (Feigenbaum and Palmer 1994, 1996, 1998) published by the Federal Election Commission to obtain the basic information on state campaign finance laws for this article. Clarification concerning some details of the laws was obtained in a few states directly from the oversight agencies themselves.

2. One could argue that Hawaii has, in practice, only a nominal public financing system. The system requires such low spending limits that few candidates are willing to accept public funding. Given that it is used so infrequently, separate analyses were conducted (but not shown) in which Hawaii was counted as not having public financing. The results of those analyses (strength and statistical significance of the coefficients) are very similar to those presented in the Analysis section of the article.

3. It is important to note that different rules often apply to independent and minor-party candidates regarding requirements for ballot access. In addition, requirement for minor parties often vary depending on whether the minor party is officially recognized by the state (parties that are not recognized must meet additional requirements). In this analysis, where the emergence of either an independent or minority-party candidate is the dependent variable, the ballot requirements applicable to recognized minor parties are used. Such an approach is justified because the vast majority of these candidates are minor-party candidates rather than independents. Separate analyses (not shown) indicate that distinct measures that apply specifically to independent and minor-party candidacies have similar effects when used in analyses conducted separately for the presence of independent or minority-party candidates.

4. Only five of the states in the analysis had term limits in one or two of the election cycles

examined (Arkansas in 1998; California, 1996 and 1998; Colorado, 1998; Michigan, 1998; and Oregon, 1998). This small number of states reduces our ability to draw conclusions about the effects of term limits. But such a variable is important to include as a control variable nonetheless.

5. Sullivan (1973) uses the following formula to compute social diversity scores:

$$A_w = 1 - \left(\sum_{k=1}^{p} Y_{k^2}/V\right)$$

where

A_w = the social diversity measure for the district,

Y_{k^2} = the proportion of the district within a given category for each variable,

V = the number of variables, and

p = the total number of categories within each of the variables.

The five demographic characteristics used include family income (percentage $100,000 or greater; percentage less than $100,000 but greater than $50,000; percentage $50,000 or less), occupation (percentage in manufacturing, percentage in service industry, percentage in government, percentage in farming), education (percentage with at least a two-year degree, percentage with less than a two-year degree), age (percentage age 55 years old and older, percentage younger than 55), and race–ethnicity (percentage White, percentage Black, percentage Hispanic, percentage Asian).

6. Several states are excluded because they elect many or all of their members in multimember districts: Arizona, Maryland, New Hampshire, New Jersey, North Carolina, North Dakota, South Dakota, Vermont, and West Virginia. Note that Idaho is included even though the lower house has a designated post system (two members elected per district). For purposes of this analysis, these elections are simply treated as single-member districts.

7. This requirement excluded Georgia, Kentucky, Maine, Massachusetts, Montana, and South Carolina. Alabama and Mississippi were excluded because their four-year terms and odd-year election cycles meant that only one election cycle fell within the time frame.

8. Note that not all states that use convention methods to select party nominees are excluded. For example, Colorado and Delaware are included here because their threshold for a challenge primary is relatively low, making them very similar to states that use primaries exclusively.

9. Note that the 1998 data from California are also excluded, given the use of the blanket primary for that one time period in our study.

10. Caution must be exercised in interpreting the results for the public financing variable, given that only three of the states examined employ public financing of legislative elections. These observed differences may be because of some other unmeasured condition present in these particular states.

REFERENCES

Alexander, Herbert E. 1991. *Reform and reality: The financing of state and local campaigns.* New York: Twentieth Century Fund Press.

Ansolabehere, Stephen, and Alan Gerber. 1996. The effects of filing fees and petition requirements on U.S. House elections. *Legislative Studies Quarterly* 21:249–64.

Barrilleaux, Charles J. 1986. A dynamic model of partisan competition in the American states. *American Journal of Political Science* 30:822–40.

Cassie, William E., and Joel A. Thompson. 1998. Patterns of PAC contributions to state legislative candidates. In *Campaign finance in state legislative elections,* eds. Joel A. Thompson and Gary F. Moncrief, 158–84. Washington, DC: Congressional Quarterly Press.

Faucheux, Ron, and Paul S. Herrnson. 1999. See how they run: State legislative candidates. *Campaigns and Elections* August:21–26.

Feigenbaum, Edward D., and James A. Palmer. 1994. *Campaign finance law 1994: A summary of state campaign finance laws.* Washington, DC: Federal Election Commission.

Feigenbaum, Edward D., and James A. Palmer. 1996. *Campaign finance law 1994: A summary of state campaign finance laws.* Washington, DC: Federal Election Commission.

Feigenbaum, Edward D., and James A. Palmer. 1998. *Campaign finance law 1994: A summary of state campaign finance laws.* Washington, DC: Federal Election Commission.

Grau, Craig. 1981. Competition in state legislative primaries. *Legislative Studies Quarterly* 6:35–54.

Gross, Donald A., Robert K. Goidel, and Todd G. Shields. 2002. State campaign finance regulations and electoral competition. *American Politics Research* 30:143–65.

Gross, Donald A., and Robert K. Goidel. 2003. *The states of campaign finance reform.* Columbus: The Ohio State University Press.

Herrnson, Paul S., and James G. Gimpel. 1995. District conditions and primary divisiveness in congressional elections. *Political Research Quarterly* 48:101–16.

Hogan, Robert E. 2000. The costs of representation in state legislatures: Explaining variations in campaign spending. *Social Science Quarterly* 81:941–56.

Hogan, Robert E. 2001. Campaign war chests and challenger emergence in state legislative elections. *Political Research Quarterly* 54:815–30.

Hogan, Robert E. 2003. Sources of competition in state legislative primary elections. *Legislative Studies Quarterly* 28:103–26.

Holbrook, Thomas M., and Charles M. Tidmarch. 1993. The effects of leadership positions on votes for incumbents in state legislative elections. *Political Research Quarterly* 46: 897–909.

Jewell, Malcolm E. 1967. *Legislative representation in the contemporary south.* Durham, NC: Duke University Press.

Jones, Ruth S. 1984. Financing state elections. In *Money and politics in the United States: Financing elections in the 1980s,* 172–213. Chatham, NJ: Chatham House.

Jones, Ruth S., and Thomas J. Borris. 1985. Strategic contributing in legislative campaigns: The case of Minnesota. *Legislative Studies Quarterly* 10:89–106.

Lem, Steve B., and Conor M. Dowling. 2006. Picking their spots: Minor party candidates in gubernatorial election. *Political Research Quarterly* 59:471–80.

Lieberson, Stanley. 1969. Measuring population diversity. *American Sociological Review* 34:850–62.

Lilley, William, Laurence J. DeFranco, and William M. Diefenderfer. 1994. *The almanac of state legislatures.* Washington, DC: Congressional Quarterly.

Maisel, L. Sandy, Walter J. Stone, and Cherie Maestas. 2001. Quality challengers to congressional incumbents: Can better candidates be found? In *Playing hardball: Campaigning for the U.S. Congress,* ed. Paul Herrnson, 12–40. Upper Saddle River, NJ: Prentice Hall.

Malbin, Michael J., and Thomas L. Gais. 1998. *The day after reform: Sobering campaign finance lessons from the American states.* Albany, NY: Rockefeller Institute.

Mayer, Kenneth R., and John M. Wood. 1995. The impact of public financing on electoral competitiveness: Evidence from Wisconsin, 1964–1990. *Legislative Studies Quarterly* 20: 69–88.

Moncrief, Gary F., Peverill Squire, and Malcolm E. Jewell. 2001. *Who runs for the state legislature?* Upper Saddle River, NJ: Prentice Hall.

Niemi, Richard G., Lynda W. Powell, William D. Berry, Thomas M. Carsey, and James M. Snyder Jr. 2006. Competition in state legislative elections, 1992–2002. In *The marketplace of democracy: Electoral competition and American politics,* ed. Michael P. McDonald and John Samples, 53–73. Washington, DC: Brookings Institution.

Patterson, Samuel C., and Gergory Caldeira. 1984. The etiology of partisan competition. *American Political Science Review* 78:691–707.

Pritchard, Anita. 1992. Strategic considerations in the decision to challenge a state legislative incumbent. *Legislative Studies Quarterly* 17:381–93.

Sabato, Larry J. 1985. *PAC power: Inside the world of political action committees.* New York: Norton.

Schultz, David. 2002. *Money, politics, and campaign finance reform law in the states.* Durham, NC: Carolina Academic Press.

Squire, Peverill. 2000. Uncontested seats in state legislative elections. *Legislative Studies Quarterly* 25:131–46.

Stratmann, Thomas. 2002. *Contribution limits and competitiveness: An analysis of how state campaign finance laws affect challengers and incumbents.* Boston: U.S. PIRG Education Fund.

Stratmann, Thomas. 2005. Ballot access restrictions and candidate entry in elections. *European Journal of Political Economy* 21:59–71.

Stratmann, Thomas, and Francisco Aparicio-Castillo. 2003. Competition policy for elections: Do campaign contributions limits matter? Paper presented at the American Economic Association meetings, Washington, DC.

Sullivan, J. L. 1973. Political correlates of social, economic, and religious diversity in the American states. *Journal of Politics* 35:70–84.

Thompson, Joel A., and Gary F. Moncrief. 1998. *Campaign finance in state legislative elections*. Washington, DC: Congressional Quarterly Press.

Van Dunk, Emily. 1997. Challenger quality in state legislative elections. *Political Research Quarterly* 50:793–807.

Van Dunk, Emily, and Ronald E. Weber. 1997. Constituency-level competition in the U.S. states, 1968–1988: A pooled analysis. *Legislative Studies Quarterly* 22:141–59.

Witko, Christopher. 2005. Measuring the stringency of state campaign finance regulation. *State Politics and Policy Quarterly* 5:295–310.

Authors' Note: This research is based on work supported by grants from the National Science Foundation (SES-0215450 and SES-0215604). Any opinions, findings, and conclusions or recommendations expressed in this material are those of the authors and do not necessarily reflect the views of the National Science Foundation.

*Keith E. Hamm is professor of political science at Rice University.

Robert E. Hogan is an assistant professor of political science at Louisiana State University.

DISCUSSION QUESTIONS

1. Hamm and Hogan look primarily at whether elections are contested, not at what types of candidates decide to run. Do their results suggest that different types of candidates emerge in states with different types of campaign finance systems?

2. How might a proponent of deregulating campaign finance, such as Bradley Smith, respond to Hamm and Hogan's findings?

3. The authors distinguish between candidate emergence in the primary election and in the general election. Should campaign finance laws be designed to encourage competition in primaries as well as in the general election? How might they do this?

4. The authors find that public financing actually reduces the likelihood of contested general elections. Do you agree with them that this is a quirk specific to the states they studied, or is there something about public financing that may actually deter candidates from running?

Part 4:
Campaign Finance Law in Comparative Context

As noted in the introduction, the study of American campaign finance is limited in part because many of the changes reformers have sought have never been adequately tested in the American context. The nations considered in this section have implemented reforms that run the gamut from nearly full public financing of elections (in the case of Canada) to almost complete deregulation of campaign spending (in the case of Australia). Beyond simply focusing on the success or failure of these campaign finance regimes, however, the chapters in this section highlight the role of national political culture in bringing about reforms and encouraging or discouraging the implementation of reforms.

Lisa Young has argued that the campaign finance system in Canada gives an idea of what the American system might look like in the absence of the *Buckley v. Valeo* decision. As she explains here, Canada has gone from a relatively deregulated system to one in which individual contributions are sharply limited, group contributions are prohibited, and the parties receive substantial public funding. In her chapter, Young evaluates Canada's reforms with reference to the goals of accountability, transparency, integrity, and equity. Like many of the other authors in this volume, she believes that political parties will only seek to implement campaign finance reforms when they believe that they can benefit from them. This does not mean, however, that parties have accurate foresight; the Canadian reforms have clearly not helped the Liberal Party, which implemented many of them. And the self-interested behavior of politicians also does not mean that we cannot step back from the politics surrounding campaign finance laws and evaluate their effect on citizens and on democracy. It should be noted that the pre-vote public fund subsidy that Young discusses was eliminated following the Conservative Party's victory in the 2011 election.

In most democratic polities, elections involve two stages—the selection of candidates by the parties, and the choices made between parties by the voters. As Menachem Hofnung notes, the first of these stages has not traditionally involved very much input from the public, and hence has traditionally not been regulated by campaign finance laws. As democratic parties have begun to involve the public more in candidate selection, however, the need to regulate spending in intraparty contests has increased. In "candidate centered" systems, where candidates actively run for their party's nomination, this need has been met with stricter regulation of candidate expenditures. In more party-centered systems, however, spending during the candidate selection process is often not very transparent. This can lead to corruption and to public dissatisfaction with the choices provided. Hofnung describes the problem of regulation of intraparty elections and discusses the manner in which Israel (and its party-centered system) has sought to regulate the candidate selection process.

There are few studies of campaign finance in Latin America. Eduardo Posada-Carbó offers an explanation for this scarcity. Prevailing conceptions of democracy in Latin America, he claims, have more to do with the substance of government policy and less to do with electoral procedures. Corruption has flourished in many nations in part because politicians simply do not regard campaign finance as an important enough issue to command their attention. Posada-Carbó offers a history of Latin American campaign finance, a study of how attitudes toward campaign finance have influenced Colombian politics, and a look at the recent adoption of public subsidies in many Latin American countries. Despite the poor track record for public funding in Europe, Latin America's very different political culture and institutional arrangements may enable public funding to play a more important role there than it has in other parts of the world.

Australia has adopted far fewer restrictions on campaign spending than have most other democratic nations. Whatever the political issues raised by the Australian approach, it is clear that the less-regulated Australian system allows researchers to test hypotheses about campaign contributions that they could not test in other countries. Specifically, Iain McMenamin takes advantage of the ability of Australian corporations to contribute, and the lack of restrictions on the size of corporate contributions, to explore the "access versus influence" paradigm as it pertains to Australian businesses. He explores hypotheses regarding the relationship between the political clout of the Australian political parties and the timing of corporate contributions. He differentiates corporations according to their size and their sector of the economy. McMenamin's analysis shows how one might differentiate between the pragmatic and the policy goals of businesses by considering their campaign contributions.

The literature on comparative campaign finance is vast, and these articles provide only a small sample of that literature. Collectively, however, they demonstrate that there is no "one size fits all" campaign finance regime. To the extent that particular values matter in the financing of elections, the priority politicians give these values is strongly affected by the institutional structures of individual nations and the history of different nations' democratic regimes.

Regulating Campaign Finance in Canada: Strengths and Weaknesses

by Lisa Young*

The regulation of political finance in Canada is extensive. The basic frame-work for the regulatory regime was established in 1974 with the passage of the Election Expenses Act, which limited campaign expenditures, required trans-parency in contributions, and offered partial public subsidies for election ex-penditures. In subsequent years, Parliament amended elements of the regime, as did the courts in response to a series of challenges to the constitutionality of various elements of the legislation. In 2004, new legislation came into ef-fect that added significant new elements to the regulatory regime, most notably limits on the size and source of contributions, and extensive public funding of political parties.

This chapter offers an evaluation of the strengths and weaknesses of the Ca-nadian regulatory regime, using as criteria four basic requirements for an effec-tive regulatory regime: accountability, transparency, integrity, and equity. *Ac-countability* means that parties and candidates must be held responsible for their actions and actions taken in their name, and be subject to penalties if they fail to do so. It implies that parties and candidates should be accountable to voters because the purpose of democratic elections is to allow the voters to select rep-resentatives by casting fully informed votes (Adamany 1990, 95). *Transparency* refers to full disclosure of the source of money used in election campaigns, as well as to the amounts spent. For a system to be fully transparent, this informa-tion must be made available to the public in a timely fashion. Disclosure of political financing information equips citizens with the information they need to make decisions about the integrity and trustworthiness of candidates. Know-ing that financial transactions will be open to public scrutiny may discourage parties or candidates from accepting contributions in return for which they will be obligated to favor the contributor's interests. *Integrity* refers to limiting the potential for undue influence over political decision makers. Like fairness, *equity* is a more complex concept. At a minimum, equity requires that all parties or candidates be treated in a similar fashion in legislation. This criterion does not mean that distinctions cannot be made between parties that win a substantial proportion of the vote and those that win very little support; rather, it means that the same set of rules are applied to all parties, and none are subject to arbitrary reward or punishment. A more expansive understanding of equity would involve measures intended to level the playing field for political competition or to make the political process more accessible to citizens who are not wealthy.

In addition to these four basic requirements for a regulatory regime, two additional objectives are worth considering. Unlike the four requirements, which focus on the behavior of and competition between contestants in elections, the two additional objectives relate to enhancing democratic participation. These two objectives are *strengthening political parties* and *encouraging citizen participation*. The first objective rests on the premise that political parties are essential to democratic life. Political parties offer voters political alternatives; they organize the electoral process, and they provide a mechanism through which citizens can participate in the political process. The second objective, encouraging citizen participation, assumes that democracy is strongest when citizens are actively engaged in the democratic process. As Nugent and Johannes (1990, 11) argue, citizen participation "provides a mechanism for citizen control of government, decreases the likelihood that certain interests are being overlooked in policy-making process, and enhances the perceived legitimacy of government."

In this chapter, I argue that the greatest strength of the Canadian regime is the limits placed on candidate and party spending. A secondary strength is the availability of public funding. Neither the spending limits nor the arrangements governing public funding are perfect, and the expansion of public funding in 2004 has proven somewhat problematic in some regards. Nevertheless, the combination of spending limits and public funding has reduced the pressure on candidates and parties to raise large amounts of money, thereby reducing the incentives to solicit large amounts of money, and thereby reducing the incentives to circumvent limits on the source of contributions. While these are significant strengths of the Canadian system, there are nonetheless notable weaknesses as well. These weaknesses include untimely disclosure requirements and possible distortions to electoral competition introduced by the 2004 public-funding regime.

Any discussion of the Canadian regulatory regime must take note of the particular context of Canadian politics. The Canadian political system employs Westminster-style parliamentary institutions, characterized by cohesive political parties and concentration of power in the hands of the executive. Among Westminster-type systems, Canada stands out for its tight party discipline and concentration of power in the hands of the prime minister (Savoie 1999). As a consequence of this system, Canadian elections tend to be contests between rival political parties to a greater extent than among rival candidates. The "personal vote" is not unknown in Canada, but its significance is substantially less than is the case in the United States. As a consequence, political parties, rather than candidates, are the most significant players in Canadian elections, and much of the regulatory effort focuses, appropriately, on them.

REGULATION OF POLITICAL FINANCE IN CANADA, 1974–2003

In 1974, Parliament established the regime governing electoral finance in Canada until 2003 with the adoption of the Election Expenses Act (RSC 1974 [1st Supp.] c. 51). In subsequent years, legislation has altered some of the details of the legislative regime, but its basic elements have remained in place. They are as follows:

- Party registration and agency: The act recognized political parties as legal entities, limited their spending, and provided them with public funding. As a result, it was necessary to create a process of registration for political parties. To qualify as a registered political party, it was necessary to run candidates in 50 (of 264 at the time, now 308) electoral districts. Aspects of the registration requirements were later amended, but the amendments were struck down by a court decision discussed in greater detail below.
- Spending limits for parties: The legislation created limits for spending by political parties during the campaign period. The limit was initially set at $0.30 per elector in each electoral district in which the party was running a candidate; the per-elector amount was indexed to inflation for subsequent years. The legislation excluded volunteer labor and grants from the party to candidates. Subsequently, the chief electoral officer, in consultation with an ad hoc committee composed of representatives of the major parties, interpreted the spending limit not to include a number of other expenses, including the cost of opinion polling.
- Spending limits for candidates: The legislation imposed spending limits for candidates. The limit in each electoral district was calculated according to a formula based on the number of eligible electors in the district.
- Limits on "third party" or independent expenditures: In an effort to avoid circumvention of the spending limits for parties and candidates, the legislation prohibited groups and individuals other than parties or candidates from spending during elections to promote or oppose candidates, unless the expenditures were intended to gain support for a policy stance or to advocate the aims of a nonpartisan organization. This word-

ing was so broad that it allowed most interventions. In 1983, the legislation was amended to prohibit anyone other than parties or candidates from spending money to support or oppose candidates or parties. This provision was successfully challenged in court (*National Citizens Coalition Inc. v. Canada* [1984] 5 WWR 436). There were two subsequent efforts to legislate, the second of which was upheld by a decision of the Supreme Court of Canada in 2004 (*Harper v. Canada*) and which limits the spending of third parties at both the national and electoral district levels.

- Disclosure: The legislation established disclosure requirements for both parties and candidates. Political parties were required to file annual reports disclosing the names and amounts of contributions greater than $100 and detailing the party's revenues and expenditures. Candidates were required to file election expense reports with similar information during the campaign period. All disclosure reports are filed months after the election campaign or fiscal year ends and are subsequently made public by the office of the chief electoral officer. The threshold for disclosure was subsequently increased to $200.

- Reimbursement of election expenses for parties: The 1974 legislation established a practice of reimbursing registered political parties for 50 percent of their election expenses on television and radio advertising. In 1983, the legislation was changed to reimburse parties for 22.5 percent of their total election expenses, provided that they had spent at least 10 percent of their limit. In 1996, the legislation was changed again, requiring that a party receive either 2 percent of the valid votes cast nationally or at least 5 percent of the valid votes cast in the electoral districts in which it ran candidates to be eligible for the 22.5 percent reimbursement.

- Reimbursement of election expenses for candidates: Candidates who won at least 15 percent of the votes in their electoral district became eligible for partial reimbursement of their election expenses. In the 1974 legislation, the amount of the reimbursement was based on a formula taking into account the number of electors in the district; subsequently, the legislation was changed to make the reimbursement equal to 50 percent of the candidate's total election expenditures.

- Broadcasting: The 1974 legislation amended the Broadcasting Act to require radio and television stations to make available up to 6.5 hours of prime time for paid advertising or political broadcasts by registered parties during the election campaign (RSC 1970, c. B-11; Section 17 of the Elections Expenses Act altered the Broadcasting Act). The broadcast arbitrator allocated this time among the parties based on their success in the most recent general election. This requirement ensured that parties would be able to purchase prime media time and at the same time limited the amount they could purchase. The legislation also required networks to make free-time programming periods available to registered parties, allocated among the parties according to the same formula as paid advertising (Stanbury 1991, 37–38).

• Political contribution tax credit: Finally, the legislation established the political contribution tax credit, which allowed individuals and corporations to deduct a portion of contributions to parties or candidates from their taxes payable. The tax credit was worth 75 percent of amounts contributed up to $100, plus 50 percent of amounts contributed between $100 and $550, plus 33 percent of amounts contributed exceeding $550, up to a total tax credit of $500. The thresholds of the tax credit remained unchanged until 2000, when they were increased so that the 75 percent credit could be claimed on contributions up to $200, and so on.

Spending Limits

Limits on spending by parties and candidates formed a central element of the 1974 reforms to election finance. Unlike their American counterparts, the constitutionality of Canadian spending limits has not been challenged.[1] When Parliament adopted these spending limits, the established parties "essentially entered into an agreement to put an end to the upward spiral of election spending" that had been driven by increasing television advertising costs through the 1960s and early 1970s (Carty, Cross, and Young 2000, 134).

Although the primary impetus for adopting spending limits was to stop the upward spiral of spending, many Canadian observers argue that the limits also reflect the principle of fairness. In 1991, the Royal Commission on Electoral Reform and Party Financing, or the Lortie Commission, concluded that spending limits "constitute a significant instrument for promoting fairness in the electoral process. They reduce the potential advantage of those with access to significant financial resources and thus help foster a reasonable balance in debate during elections. They also encourage access to the election process" (Royal Commission on Electoral Reform and Party Finance 1991, 336). Finally, the Lortie Commission maintained there was no evidence that the presence of spending limits in any way reduced the competitiveness of Canadian elections, pointing to the high rate of turnover in Canadian election campaigns.

Any analysis of the merits of spending limits for parties must start with the observation that the limits are not watertight. The spending limits imposed on political parties in 1974 covered only parties' election expenses as defined by the Canada Elections Act (RSC 1970 [1st Supp.] c. 14; Sections 1 to 16 of the Elections Expenses Act altered the Canada Elections Act) and interpreted by the chief electoral officer on advice of a committee composed of representatives of the major political parties. The definition of election expenses that emerged from this process excluded costs associated with public opinion polling, a major campaign expenditure. This definition has meant that some costs parties incurred during election campaigns were not limited. This omission was corrected by the 2003 legislation, which broadened the definition of election expenses and increased the parties' spending limits by 13 percent.

Even more significant, however, is the parties' ability to spend without limits during the weeks and months prior to an election. Spending limits apply only during the 36-day campaign period, but spending—including spending on television and radio advertising—outside this period is not subject to any limitations. While this time limit certainly constrains the effectiveness of the legislation, it would be very difficult to design spending limits that encompassed the pre-election period. Elections in Canada are not held on fixed dates. The prime minister has almost complete discretion in selecting the date of the election and is not obligated to reveal the date in advance of dropping the writ.

It is quite apparent that parties spend more in election years than during non-election years. Table 1 breaks down average expenditures for each party in election and non-election years between 1975 and 2000 and shows that all parties' non-election expenditures are higher in election years. This pattern is most pronounced for the two right-of-center parties—the Progressive Conservatives and Reform / Canadian Alliance—with average differences of $6.3 million and $4 million, respectively.[2] If we assume that the entire difference is election-related expenditures, then the worst offenders—the Progressive Conservatives—have spent about 50 percent more than their legal limit in election years between 1974 and 2000.

Table 1: Mean Non-Election Expenditures, 1974–2000 (2000$)

Party	Non-Election Years ($million)	Election Years ($million)	Difference ($million)
Progressive Conservative	12.0	18.4	6.3
Liberal	11.9	13.6	1.7
New Democratic	13.9	14.7	0.7
Reform / Canadian Alliance	5.6	9.6	4.0
Bloc Québécois	1.3	2.6	1.3

Source: Calculated from Elections Canada data.

Given that the limits are not watertight, it is not surprising that their introduction did not entirely halt the upward spiral of total party spending. The lower line in Figure 1 tracks all major parties' election expenses; the upper line tracks total spending (election and non-election) by major parties, both in real dollars. It should be noted that the number of major parties increases to include Reform / Canadian Alliance and the Bloc Québécois in 1993. Total spending levels by the three major parties remained similar in the elections of 1979 and 1980 but then increased substantially in the 1984 campaign, when the governing Liberals were defeated by a massive Progressive Conservative majority. After 1984, however, total spending remains at levels similar to or less than those of the 1984 election, even when the number of parties increases from three to five. The absence of increases in overall spending between 1984 and 2000 could be taken as evidence that spending limits for parties have been effective in keeping election-related spending in check.

Figure 1: Parties' Total Expenses and Election Expenses, for Election Years (in 2000$)

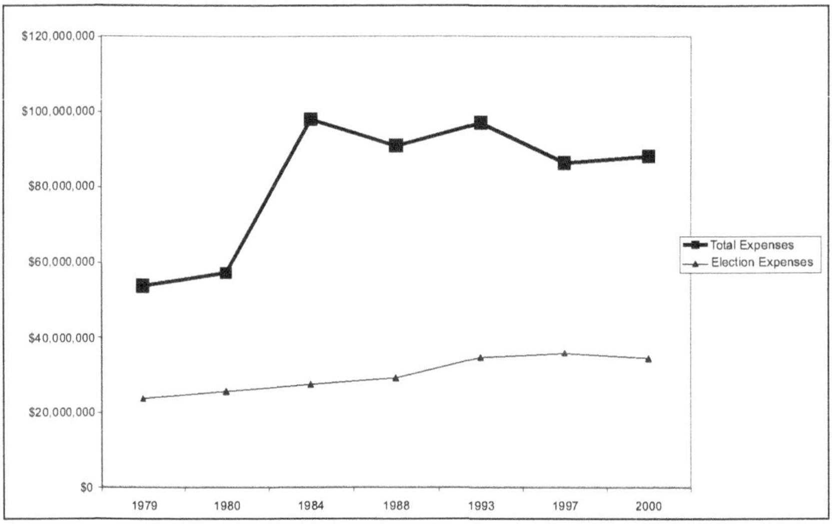

Source: Calculated from Elections Canada data.

It is not entirely clear, however, that we can attribute the absence of increases to total spending to the effect of the spending limits for parties. In fact, Table 2 suggests that, with the exception of the governing Liberal Party, parties have in recent years had difficulty raising sufficient funds to spend the maximum legal amount during elections. Facing much-reduced political circumstances, the Progressive Conservatives and New Democrats spent less than half their allowed amount. Even the two larger opposition parties—the Bloc Québécois and Canadian Alliance—spent only 58 percent and 77 percent respectively of their limit in 2000. In short, changing political circumstances have contributed to the flattening of the line in Figure 1, possibly to a greater extent than the presence of spending limits.

Table 2: Party Spending as a Proportion of Limit, 2000 Election

Party	Party Spending
Progressive Conservative	32%
Liberal	99%
New Democratic	50%
Reform / Canadian Alliance	77%
Bloc Québécois	58%

Source: Calculated from Elections Canada data.

Spending limits appear to have a greater impact at the level of candidate spending. Competitive candidates at the local level have little difficulty raising the funds they need to spend up to the amount of the limits. In the 2000 federal election, a substantial proportion of competitive candidates could have spent more, had limits not been in place. A total of 193 candidates raised more money in contributions than they could spend under the spending limit in their electoral district. These 193 candidates represent 11 percent of the candidates for whom complete financial information is available,[3] or 15 percent of the 1,263 candidates run by the five major parties.[4] In fact, a majority of candidates did not spend all the money they raised: Fully 77 percent of candidates had total contributions that equaled or exceeded their total expenditures. Given the relative affluence of candidates, it comes as little surprise that 362 candidates, or 21 percent of all candidates for whom information was available, spent at least 75 percent of their limit. Of these 362 candidates, 120 spent between 95 percent and 110 percent of their limit.[5]

If our purpose is to determine whether the existence of the spending limit prevents candidates from excessive spending, it is perhaps more helpful to examine the candidates who raised the most money. Of the 300 candidates with the highest total contributions, 97 spent between 95 and 110 percent of their limits. Of these 97, all but 15 had contributions greater than their expenditures—in other words, they could have spent more in the absence of limits. In short, it appears that spending limits for candidates are an effective means of capping the amounts spent by the candidates with the largest political war chests.

It is more difficult to determine whether the presence of spending limits has increased the accessibility of the political system. The number of women and visible minorities elected to the House of Commons has increased substantially over the period since 1974, but this has coincided with a period of considerable social change, with women entering many professions in greater numbers and barriers to members of visible minority groups being substantially decreased.

It is, however, evident that the use of spending limits has not created insurmountable barriers for new challengers to achieve electoral success in federal elections. A comparative study of electoral volatility in 18 OECD member states since the 1950s found that Canada has the fourth-highest rate of per annum increase in electoral volatility over the period from 1953 to 1997. Comparing average rates of volatility in national elections in the 1990s, Canada places second only to Italy in its volatility (Dalton, McAllister, and Wattenberg 2000, 41).[6]

From this analysis, it is fair to conclude that the spending limits for candidates and parties in Canadian elections are imperfect instruments for controlling the costs of elections and equalizing opportunities among contestants. That said, these imperfect instruments have achieved significant successes both in terms of controlling costs and leveling the political playing field. As such, they should be considered an overall success. Spending limits have created three benefits for the Canadian political system. First, by controlling parties' total expenditures on advertising during the crucial election campaign period, the spending limits have ensured that one party cannot entirely dominate the airwaves. This creates at least a modicum of balance between competitors during the campaign period.[7] Second, when combined with a reasonable level of public funding, spending limits reduce the pressure for parties and candidates to raise funds. This should not be interpreted to mean that parties face no such pressures. Rather, the pressure to raise money is reduced so that candidates do not find themselves devoting as significant a portion of their time to fundraising as do their American counterparts. By lessening the pressure to raise funds, spending limits are believed to reduce the temptation for parties and candidates to offer a quid pro quo for large contributions. Of course, such unsavory practices do occur from time to time, but the combination of spending limits and public funding in all probability reduces the frequency of such incidents. Finally, spending limits for candidates appear to have been fairly effective in preventing incumbents, particularly Cabinet ministers who are able to raise substantial sums of money, from vastly outspending challengers. This prevents the scenario found in the United States, where vast imbalances in spending between incumbents and challengers may have contributed to high rates of incumbency in both the Congress and Senate (Malbin 2003, 19).

PUBLIC FUNDING

The second key element of the regulatory regime established in 1974 was public funding for candidates and registered political parties. Prior to 2004, public funding was delivered in three ways:

- A reimbursement of 50 percent of all election expenses to candidates who won at least 15 percent of the vote in their electoral district.
- A reimbursement of 22.5 percent of election expenses of registered political parties (with thresholds for eligibility changing during the period).
- The political contribution tax credit that subsidizes the cost of relatively small individual contributions to candidates and registered political parties.[8]

In addition to these more direct forms of public funding, registered parties also benefit from a provision requiring broadcasters to make airtime available for free-time political broadcasts during the campaign. In evaluating the public-funding provisions, I examine the magnitude of public funding, the forms in which it was provided, and the formulas for its allocation.

When we evaluate the magnitude or extent of public funding, two competing concerns come into play. First, the funding must be extensive enough to achieve its intended objectives of reducing the barriers to entry into the political system, leveling the playing field for political competition, and strengthening political parties as intermediary institutions (see RCERPF 1991). Second, the funding must not be so extensive as to turn political parties into stage agencies with little need to seek financial support from voters (see Katz and Mair 1996; Committee on Standards in Public Life 1998, 92).

The public-funding provisions in place from 1974 to 2004 created an admirable balance between these two objectives. Estimates of public subsidies as a proportion of expenditures in election years between 1979 and 1988 suggest that public funding accounts for no more than 40 percent of parties' and candidates' spending (Young 1998, 354). This rate of public funding is insufficient to trigger concerns about Canadian political parties relying on the state rather than the electorate for financial support, as the public sector remains the minority funder. It is, however, sufficient to make parties with fewer financial resources more competitive in electoral contests, and to ease significantly the burden of fundraising for candidates.

The second set of criteria on which to evaluate public finance provisions is the form in which public funding is provided. The form of public funding most costly to the public purse is the political contribution tax credit (PCTC). All registered political parties and, during elections, candidates are able to issue tax receipts to donors. The PCTC is available to registered political parties in both non-election and election periods, and as such has been the only source of public financing between elections. As Table 3 shows, the PCTC is the largest single source of public funding even in an election year, with a cost of some $19 million in 2000.

As a mode of public funding, the PCTC has considerable merit. First, it helps parties solicit small contributions from individuals by subsidizing their cost to the contributor. In so doing, the PCTC "has arguably strengthened . . . ties between civil society and registered parties" (Young 1998, 354). Although there has been no comprehensive study of the impact of the political contribution tax credit on propensity to donate in Canada, research on a similar tax credit in Ohio suggests that when citizens are aware of the existence of political contribution tax credits, there is potential to expand the number of small contributors and bring about a donor pool more similar to the general public than it would otherwise be (Boatright and Malbin 2005). Second, the tax credit is sensitive to a party's public support, as an unpopular party will find it more difficult to solicit individual contributions.

Table 3: Cost of Public Funding to Parties and Candidates, 2000

Form of Funding	Total Cost in 2000
PCTC	$19,290,000* (n = 167,140)
Reimbursements to candidates	$15,574,812 (n = 684)
Reimbursements to parties	$7,680,358 (n = 5)
* The total cost of the PCTC is an estimate that the CCRA produces based on a stratified sample of tax returns filed.	

Sources: Canada Customs and Revenue Agency, Income Statistics 2002–2000 Tax Year, Final Basic Table, and Elections Canada data.

Of course, unequal distribution of wealth within the population inevitably means that affluent individuals will be more able to make contributions and thus benefit from the tax credit. Examining the breakdown of filers by income category (Table 4), this is clearly the case. The almost half of all Canadian tax filers whose incomes fall into the lowest bracket make up only 10 percent of all PCTC claimants, while the 3 percent of tax filers in the highest bracket make 18 percent of all claims. The pattern is even more skewed when one compares the value of the tax credit for low- and high-income earners, as the latter are prone to make larger contributions. Despite its other merits, then, the PCTC reinforces an inequitable pattern of giving to parties and candidates.

The remainder of public funding comes in the form of reimbursements to candidates and to political parties. Jenson (1991) points out that there are flaws

Table 4: Filers, Filers Claiming the PCTC, and Value of PCTC, by Income Bracket, 2000

Income Bracket	All Returns Filed As % (n in millions)	Filers Claiming PCTC as % (n)	Value of PCTC As % (value in $thousands)
Under $20K	48% (10.6)	10% (16,460)	6% (1,100)
$20K–$40K	27% (6.1)	28% (47,620)	25% (4,824)
$40K–$60K	14% (3.1)	23% (39,070)	21% (4,024)
$60K–$100K	8% (1.8)	21% (34,700)	22% (4,271)
Over $100K	3% (0.6)	18% (29,300)	26% (5,070)
TOTAL	100% (22.2)	100% (167,150)	100% (19,290)

Source: Calculated from Canada Customs and Revenue Agency, Income Statistics 2002–2000 Tax Year, Final Basic Table.

inherent in a system of public funding that rewards spending rather than electoral success. In Jenson's view, such a system lacks an element of fairness because it ties reimbursements to a candidate's or a party's ability to spend rather than that candidate's or party's electoral support. In addition, by tying public funding to expenditures, the system creates a "built-in escalator pushing up election expenses overall" as candidates who expect to win at least 15 percent of the vote are effectively spending 50-cent dollars.

There is certainly merit to Jenson's arguments. Reimbursement of candidates' expenditures has in all probability encouraged higher rates of spending, particularly among candidates. Moreover, a system based on reimbursements allows for the possibility of providing greater public funding to parties with wealthy backers and little electoral support than to parties with modest funds but considerable electoral appeal. Some attempts have been made to mitigate this by imposing thresholds of electoral support that must be crossed before reimbursements can be made, but these are admittedly crude instruments.

The rates at which candidate and party expenses are reimbursed have, however, created an imbalance between cash-strapped national parties and candidates' substantial surpluses (RCERPF 1991, 305–7). Even though the national parties shoulder the costs of the leader's tour and extensive national advertising campaigns, their reimbursements are at a much lower rate than candidates'.

This imbalance has forced parties to devise mechanisms for taxing back portions of candidates' reimbursements in order to pay for the national campaign and maintenance of the national party organization.

Despite these flaws, the practice of reimbursing candidates' and parties' election expenses has at least moved in the direction of leveling the playing field for political competition and ensuring that both candidates and parties can mount competitive election campaigns. Moreover, in an analysis of large contributions to candidates in the 1988 election, Padget (1991, 354–55) concludes that "tax credits, expenditure limits and reimbursement have lessened the amount of money needed from private sources to run a competitive campaign. This creates conditions conducive to the financial independence of candidates from large private donors."

The other form in which public funding is provided for Canadian parties is in-kind: a requirement that networks provide free broadcasting time to all parties and candidates during an election. In the 2000 election, this meant that 428 minutes of free-time broadcasting was available on English-language television, 410 minutes on French-language television, and 120 minutes on both English and French public radio. This time is allocated among registered political parties by the broadcasting arbitrator, following the formula for allocation of paid time. As a result of this allocation, the governing Liberal Party received 29 percent of the time allocated, the opposition Canadian Alliance 15 percent, the Progressive Conservatives 12 percent, and the New Democratic Party and Bloc Québécois 10 percent each. Parties without seats in the House of Commons received only 4 percent of the time, each, and newly registered parties only 1.5 percent of the time (or three minutes on each English-language television network).

As a mode of providing public support for political parties, provision of free broadcast time can be judged a success. Its cost to the public purse is relatively small (as private broadcasters must assume the costs of revenue forgone), and it allows parties to deliver their message to voters, often in formats longer than a 30-second advertisement. This encourages parties to develop more-thoughtful messages than those crafted for traditional television advertisements. Less beneficial, however, is the formula for allocating time among parties. Even the revised allocation, which sets aside one-third of all time for small and new parties, does little to provide these organizations, which are usually less affluent than the established parties, with an opportunity to get their message across. Moreover, the method for allocation among the major parties serves to reinforce the governing party's incumbency advantage. An allocation that mirrored the spending limits for parties (that is, one based on the number of candidates a party was running) would be infinitely more equitable.

Disclosure

The disclosure requirements governing parties and candidates in Canada are, for the most part, thorough. Both registered political parties and candidates are required to disclose their election expenditures, broken down by category of expenditure. After an election, candidates are required to disclose the names and addresses of all contributors who gave more than $200. Registered political parties are required to file annual returns that list the same information for all contributors who gave more than $200, and to detail their expenditures, assets, and debts.

There are three notable gaps in the disclosure requirements. The first is the absence of a requirement for electoral district associations of political parties to file returns. After an election, candidates are required to transfer their surplus to their electoral district association. These surpluses can be substantial and usually include public money from the reimbursement of candidate expenses. Until 2004, however, there was no requirement for electoral district associations to disclose the amounts they held or how the funds were spent. Moreover, as Stanbury (1991) points out, electoral district associations could raise money on behalf of their organization, incumbent MP, or prospective candidate, and as long as the money was not to be tax receipted, they would not have to disclose the size or source of the donor. These gaps led Stanbury to refer to electoral district associations as the "black holes" of Canadian political finance. The 2003 reforms remedied this by establishing a requirement for registration of and disclosure by electoral district associations.

A second gap is party leadership campaigns. The only disclosure provisions that governed leadership campaigns were guidelines for Cabinet ministers contesting their party's leadership. Introduced in 2002 while the governing Liberal Party was in the midst of a leadership contest, the guidelines for Cabinet ministers require disclosure of the names of contributors to leadership campaigns (Office of the Ethics Counsellor 2002, appendix 6). There is no requirement for candidates for the leadership of other parties to disclose the identity of their supporters. Given that a newly elected leader of an opposition party may become prime minister not long after winning his or her party's leadership, it is alarming that there is no public record of who contributed to his or her leadership campaign. The 2003 legislation addresses this problem by extending reporting requirements to leadership campaigns, including weekly interim reports of contributions during the last four weeks of the leadership contest.

Finally, the Canadian system of disclosure is less timely than is ideal. Candidates and third parties are required to submit their election expense and contribution reports four months after Election Day. Parties file their election expenses report six months after Election Day and their annual fiscal returns three months after the end of their fiscal year. This means that 15 months could pass between the time a contribution to a party was made and the time when it was disclosed to the public. Ideally, voters should have access to information about the source of major contributions to parties, candidates, and third parties prior to Election Day. The American experience shows that it is possible to design a disclosure system that achieves this objective. The advent of computerized record keeping makes such a system far more viable than it would have been when Canadian disclosure requirements were first implemented. To lessen the administrative burden on parties, it would be possible to increase the threshold for disclosure from $200 to $1,000 but require more timely disclosure reports. Registered political parties in all probability have the capacity to meet such a requirement. Candidate organizations, which tend to be short-lived ad hoc organizations established for the election period, may not.

THIRD-PARTY SPENDING

The question of third-party (or, in the American parlance, independent) expenditures in elections has been highly contentious. The first effort to regulate came in 1974, with legislation prohibiting groups and individuals from spending during elections to promote or oppose candidates unless the expenditures were intended to gain support for a policy stance or to advocate the aims of a nonpartisan organization. The wording of this legislation was so broad as to permit almost any sort of intervention, so in 1983 the government passed legislation prohibiting anyone other than parties and candidates from spending money to support or oppose candidates or parties. The next year, the National Citizens Coalition, an advocacy group active in election advertising, successfully challenged the constitutionality of the law. The Alberta Court of Queen's Bench ruled that the government had not demonstrated a clear need for the spending regulations, so the legislation could not be justified under section 1 of the Canadian Charter of Rights and Freedoms.[9] The government did not appeal the ruling, so there were no restrictions on third-party spending in either the 1984 or 1988 federal elections.

The 1988 federal election campaign centered on the very contentious issue of free trade with the United States. The uncharacteristically controversial campaign issue prompted an unprecedented level of third-party expenditures.

Of the estimated $4.7 million spent on third-party advertising on the issue, over 75 percent was spent by proponents of the free-trade agreement (Hiebert 1991). The government subsequently adopted legislation limiting third-party spending directly supporting or opposing a candidate or party to $1,000 per group. The National Citizens Coalition once again challenged the constitutionality of the law, and once again the Alberta courts struck it down as an unjustifiable restriction on freedom of speech and the right to an informed vote (*Somerville v. Canada (Attorney General)* [1996] 8 WWR, 199). Yet again, the federal government did not appeal the ruling, choosing instead to make another attempt at legislating.

In 2000, the federal government made another attempt to legislate limits on third-party advertising. In this effort, the regulated activity was defined as "the transmission to the public by any means during an election period of an advertising message that promotes or opposes a registered party or the election of a candidate, including one that takes a position on an issue with which a registered party or candidate is associated" (Canada Elections Act RSC 1970 [1st Supp.] c. 14). The legislation placed spending limits on this activity of $150,000 overall, and $3,000 in a given electoral district. The legislation also imposed disclosure requirements on third-party advertisers. The National Citizens Coalition once again challenged the constitutionality of the legislation, and the Alberta courts once again struck it down.[10] The federal government appealed this ruling to the Supreme Court of Canada, which upheld the constitutionality of the legislation in its 2004 ruling in *Harper v. Canada*.

REGULATION OF CONTRIBUTIONS

The regulatory framework put into place in 1974 used the policy instruments of spending control, public funding, and disclosure provisions to govern the conduct of political finance and left the matter of who could contribute how much to parties and candidates essentially unregulated. When the Royal Commission on Electoral Reform in 1991 revisited the decision not to restrict the size or source of contributions, it did so on the grounds that there was little evidence that large contributions led to undue influence on parties or candidates, that disclosure served as an adequate check on the relationship between contributors and politicians, and that restrictions on the size and source of contributions are difficult to enforce.[11]

Although there have been allegations in recent years that some advertising firms were receiving lucrative government contracts in return for substantial campaign contributions, allegations of unethical behavior related to campaign contributions have been small in number. In its report, the Royal Commission on Electoral Reform and Party Financing (1991, 437) concluded that "there are few instances in Canadian candidate and party financing where a contribution's size relative to total revenue would reasonably give rise to suspicion that a donor may acquire undue influence." In the last election year in which these contributions were permitted (2000), the largest single contribution to a political party came from the Canadian Labour Congress, an organization representing trade unions. The group gave almost $700,000 to the New Democratic Party (or NDP, as it is called). The next five largest contributions were from the national offices of trade unions, again with the NDP as recipient. These large contributions are fairly routine events, as the New Democratic Party is officially affiliated with organized labor. The largest single corporate contribution was from the Canadian Imperial Bank of Commerce, which gave just over $150,000 to the Liberal Party. The Liberals received only three contributions greater than $100,000, while the opposition Canadian Alliance received nine. The sources of large contributions tended to be fairly consistent, with chartered banks and financial services companies frequently appearing among the largest donors.

THE NEW REGULATORY REGIME GOVERNING POLITICAL FINANCE IN CANADA

Parliament made significant changes to the regulation of political finance in Canada in legislation passed in 2003 and 2006. The 2004 changes, often referred to as the Bill C-24 changes, were part of an ethics package introduced by the Liberal government in 2003. This legislation extended government regulation to cover spending in nomination contests and applied annual disclosure requirements to registered political parties' electoral district associations and leadership campaigns. Its most significant provisions, however, were an almost total ban on corporate and union contributions, a $5,000 annual limit for individual contributions, and an infusion of substantial public funds to support registered political parties. In 2006, the newly elected Conservative government made further changes as part of its Accountability Act, banning all corporate and union contributions and limiting individual contributions to $1,000 (indexed to inflation).[12]

The new regulatory regime was based on the principle employed in several Canadian provinces that only eligible electors should be able to make political contributions. Its key provisions in this regard are as follows:

- Only individuals may make contributions to registered political parties.
- Each citizen or permanent resident of the country will be allowed to

contribute up to $1,000 per year to each registered party and its affili-
ated entities, registered electoral district associations, candidates, and
nomination contestants.

• Individuals will also be allowed to contribute up to $1,000 per leadership
contest.

These restrictions on the size and source of contributions had clear implications for parties' finances: They reduced the income from nonpublic sources of
all but one of the political parties with seats in the current House of Commons.
The only exception to this was the Bloc Québécois, which received only very
limited funding from corporations and trade unions.

Despite the ban on corporate and union contributions, the new legislation
did not render Canadian political parties cash-poor. The new sources of public
funding have for the most part compensated for revenues lost through the legislation. This public funding took the following forms:

• Registered political parties receive an annual allowance calculated at a
rate of $1.75 (indexed to inflation) for each vote the party won in the
most recent general election. To qualify, parties must receive at least 2
percent of all votes cast nationally, or 5 percent of all votes cast in electoral districts where the party is running a candidate.

Figure 2: Proportion of Revenue Derived from Quarterly Allowance

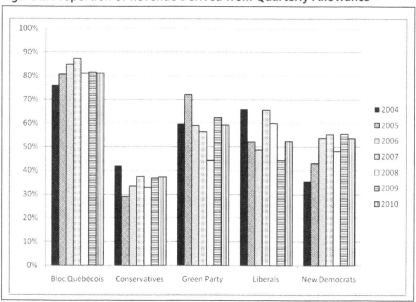

Source: Jansen and Young 2011.

- The rate of reimbursement for registered political parties' election expenses increased from 22.5 percent to 50 percent.
- The threshold for reimbursement of candidates' election expenses was lowered from 15 percent to 10 percent of the valid votes obtained.
- The 75 percent PCTC was increased from $200 to $400.

Public funding, most notably the quarterly allowance, has become an essential source of income for Canadian political parties in the new regime. As Figure 2 shows, the quarterly allowance has become the major source of revenue for the Bloc Québécois, and a significant source of revenue for the Liberal and New Democratic parties. One of the unanticipated consequences of the new regulatory regime was the ability of the Green Party of Canada to meet the 2 percent national threshold for funding, which has given the party (which holds no seats in the House of Commons) a new source of income, thereby making it more electorally competitive than it was prior to the changes.

Figure 3: Revenue from Individual Fundraising (constant 2009$)

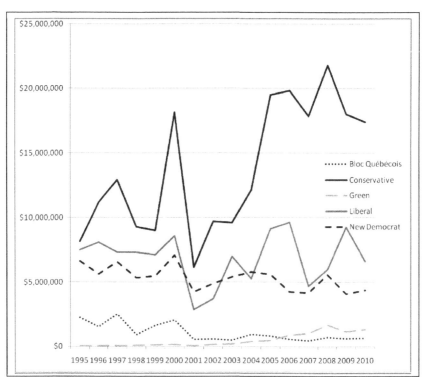

Source: Jansen and Young (2011).

With the ban on corporate and union contributions, parties faced the challenge of recasting their fundraising strategies to emphasize relatively small (under $1,000) contributions from individuals. The only party to successfully accomplish this, however, has been the Conservative Party, which has developed an impressive fundraising program since 2004. Figure 3 shows that the Conservatives are the only party whose fundraising has shown a consistent increase, in constant dollars, since 2004.

When the 2003 legislation was introduced, there was some concern that the virtual ban on corporate and union contributions would lead to efforts to circumvent the legislation or to increased third-party spending. To date, these concerns appear to have little ground. Parties and candidates have been able to raise sufficient money from individual donors to supplement their public funds and have been able to keep up with the financial demands of frequent federal elections held because of a series of minority governments (in 2004, 2006, and 2008). This suggests that the combination of public funding plus the limits on campaign spending have been sufficient to limit the demand for money on the part of political contestants.

CONCLUSION

Returning to the criteria set out at the beginning of the article, it is fair to say that the regulatory regime put in place in 1974 established reasonable levels of accountability and transparency in political finance in Canada. Integrity, understood as limiting the potential for undue influence, was at least partially achieved with the introduction of disclosure in 1974, and has certainly been achieved with the limits on the size and source of political contributions in the past decade.

Equity is, of course, a more difficult concept to operationalize. Certainly, the use of spending limits for both parties and candidates has leveled the playing field to some extent during the electoral period. Public funding likewise can bolster a party whose supporters are not affluent, although the formula employed for delivering the quarterly allowance does create additional advantages for the winning party, as it will receive the most public funding. That said, the party that has arguably been the greatest beneficiary of the introduction of the quarterly allowance is the Green Party, which holds no seats in the House of Commons.

Finally, turning to our alternative considerations of strengthening political parties and encouraging citizen participation, the Canadian regime can be judged a modest success. Certainly, Canadian political parties are financially very solid as a result of the quarterly allowance. There is little evidence, however, that parties have leveraged their financial stability into forms that would make them more participatory organizations.

ENDNOTES

1. In all probability, this reflects a consensus among the major parties over the desirability of spending limits. In a series of decisions striking down limits on third-party, or independent, expenditures, Canadian courts have made reference to the U.S. Supreme Court's decision in *Buckley v. Valeo*, in particular the notion that in politics, money is speech. These rulings, the most recent of which is currently before the Supreme Court of Canada, could conceivably open the door to a challenge of the constitutionality of spending limits for candidates and parties.

2. All figures reported in this article are in Canadian dollars.

3. For the 2000 election, Elections Canada released machine-readable tab-delimited files of candidates' financial information. These files are available at http://www.elections.ca. The files list the names of 1,798 candidates, but complete financial information is available for only 1,726 of them. Because of the format in which the files are made available, the author was not able to break down any of the candidate financing information by the candidate's political party.

4. This statistic should not be interpreted to mean that all the candidates whose total contributions exceeded their spending limit were affiliated with one of the five major parties—this could not be determined from the data set provided by Elections Canada.

5. According to the statistics in the Elections Canada file, two candidates spent more than 100 percent of their limit.

6. The figure for Canada included the 1993 federal election, in which the governing Progressive Conservative Party was reduced from a majority to only two seats in the House of Commons. The rate of volatility in this election would certainly skew the average for the 1990s in an upward direction.

7. For several elections after 1974, the Canada Elections Act established a cap on the number of minutes of paid advertising time a party could purchase during an election. Under this provision, each broadcaster was required to make available 390 minutes at the lowest equivalent rate, even if this preempted other broadcasting. The 390 minutes were allocated among the parties according to their number of seats in the House of Commons and their proportion of the popular vote in the most recent general election. In 1995, however, the Reform Party successfully challenged the constitutionality of this law. The Alberta Court of Appeal's decision in *Reform Party of Canada et al. v. Attorney General of Canada* struck down provisions that effectively transformed this entitlement into a cap, preventing a party from purchasing more than its allocated time on any station. In the 1997 and 2000 elections, parties were free to purchase more time than was allocated to them under the act, as long as broadcasters were willing to sell them time over and above the allocation (Broadcasting Arbitrator 2001, 3). In the 2000 election, the Liberal Party reported some $7.7 million in advertising expenditures, while the second-place Canadian Alliance reported about $7.5 million.

8. The provision of public funding via the tax credit and reimbursement of election expenses for registered parties necessitates a legal definition of a "registered party." When these provisions were first introduced, the legislation required that a political party run 50 candidates in a federal election in order to qualify as a registered political party. This was intended to

discourage "frivolous" and regionally based parties. The constitutionality of the provision was challenged by the leader of the Communist Party of Canada, which was deregistered after failing to nominate 50 candidates during a general election. In its decision in *Figueroa v. Canada (Attorney General)* (2003) 1 SCR 912 , the Supreme Court of Canada struck down the 50-candidate threshold on the grounds that it infringed the constitutionally guaranteed right to vote and run for office. The government in October 2003 introduced legislation that lowered the registration requirement to running one candidate and collecting the signatures of 250 party members.

9. Canadian Charter of Rights and Freedoms, Part 1 of the Constitution Act, 1982, being Schedule B to the Canada Act 1982 (UK), 1982, c. 11, s. 1. Section 1 states, "The Canadian Charter of Rights and Freedoms guarantees the rights and freedoms set out in it subject only to such reasonable limits prescribed by law as can be demonstrably justified in a free and democratic society."

10. An Ontario court has also ruled against the legislation. In the aftermath of the 2000 election, the commissioner of elections prosecuted the National Citizens Coalition for failing to register prior to engaging in election advertising. An Ontario criminal court dismissed the charges on the grounds that the legislation was an unconstitutional intrusion on freedom of expression. See *Canada (Elections Canada) v. National Citizens Coalition* (2003) OJ no. 3420 for the Ontario Court of Justice's s. 2(d) analysis, and *Canada (Elections Canada) v. National Citizens Coalition* (2003) OJ no. 3939 for the Court's s. 1 analysis.

11. The Lortie Commission did recommend a ban on contributions from foreign sources, which Parliament subsequently implemented (RCERPF 1991).

12. For a discussion of the passage of these two legislative initiatives, see Young and Jansen (2011), chapter 1.

REFERENCES

Adamany, David. 1990. "The Unaccountability of Political Money." In Margaret Latus Nugent and John R. Johannes, eds. *Money, Elections and Democracy: Reforming Congressional Campaign Finance*. Boulder, Colo.: Westview Press.

Boatright, Robert G., and Michael J. Malbin. 2005. "Political Contribution Tax Credits and Citizen Participation." *American Politics Research* 33 (6): 787–817.

Canada Elections Act, RSC 1970 (1st Supp.) c. 14.

Carty, R. Kenneth, William Cross, and Lisa Young. 2000. *Rebuilding Canadian Party Politics*. Vancouver: UBC Press.

Commissioner of Elections Canada v. National Citizens Coalition. 2003. Ontario Court of Justice, October 15.

Committee on Standards in Public Life (UK). 1998. *The Funding of Political Parties in the United Kingdom*. London: Queen's Printer.

Cross, William. 2004. *Political Parties: A Democratic Audit*. Vancouver: UBC Press.

Dalton, Russell J., Ian McAllister, and Martin P. Wattenberg. 2000. "The Consequences of Partisan Dealignment." In Russell J. Dalton and Martin P. Wattenberg, eds. *Parties without Partisans: Political Change in Advanced Industrial Democracies*. New York: Oxford University Press, 37–63.

Drysch, Thomas. 1993. "The New French System of Political Finance." In Arthur B. Gunlicks, ed. *Campaign and Party Finance in North America and Western Europe*. Boulder, Colo.: Westview Press.

Eagles, Munroe. 1993. "Money and Votes in Canada: Campaign Spending and Parliamentary Election Outcomes, 1984 and 1988." *Canadian Public Policy* 19: 432–99.

Feasby, Colin. 2003. "Seems Our Entire Electoral System May Be Unconstitutional." *Globe and Mail*, July 3.

Figueroa v. Canada (Attorney General). 2003. 1 SCR 912.

Harper v. Canada (Attorney General). 2004. SCC 33 (2004) 1 SCR 827.

Heintzman, D. Keith. 1991. "Electoral Competition, Campaign Expenditure and Incumbency Advantage." In F. Leslie Seidle, ed. *Issues in Party and Election Finance in Canada*. Toronto: Dundurn Press.

Hiebert, Janet. 1991. "Interest Groups and Canadian Federal Elections." In F. Leslie Seidle, ed. *Interest Groups and Elections in Canada*. Toronto: Dundurn Press.

Jansen, Harold J., and Lisa Young. 2011. "Cartels, Syndicates, and Coalitions: Canada's Political Parties after the 2004 Reforms." In Lisa Young and Harold J. Jansen, eds. *Money, Politics, and Democracy: Canada's Party Finance Reform*. Vancouver: UBC Press, 2011.

Jenson, Jane. 1991. "Innovation and Equity: The Impact of Public Funding." In F. Leslie Seidle, ed. *Comparative Issues in Party and Election Finance*. Toronto: Dundurn Press.

Johnston, Richard, Andre Blais, Henry Brady, and Jean Crete. 1992. *Letting the People Decide: Dynamics of a Canadian Election*. Montreal: McGill–Queen's University Press.

Jones, Ruth S. 1990. "Contributing As Participation." In Margaret Latus Nugent and John R. Johannes, eds. *Money, Elections, and Democracy: Reforming Congressional Campaign Finance*. Boulder, Colo.: Westview Press.

Katz, Richard S. 1996. "Party Organizations and Finance." In Lawrence LeDuc, Richard G. Niemi, and Pippa Norris, eds. *Comparing Democracies: Elections and Voting in Global Perspective*. Thousand Oaks, Calif.: SAGE.

Katz, Richard, and Peter Mair. 1996. "Changing Models of Party Organization and Party Democracy: The Emergence of the Cartel Party." *Party Politics* 11 (1): 5–18.

Mair, Peter. 1994. "Party Organizations: From Civil Society to the State." In Richard S. Katz and Peter Mair, eds. *How Parties Organize: Change and Adaptation in Party Organizations in Western Democracies*. Thousand Oaks, Calif.: SAGE.

Malbin, Michael J. 2003. "Thinking about Reform." In Michael J. Malbin, ed. *Life after Reform: When the Bipartisan Campaign Reform Act Meets Politics*. Lanham, Md.: Rowman & Littlefield.

Massicotte, Louis. 1991. "Party Financing in Quebec: An Analysis of the Financial Reports of Parties, 1977–89." In F. Leslie Seidle, ed. *Provincial Party and Election Finance in Canada*. Toronto: Dundurn Press.

Mutch, Robert E. 1991. "The Evolution of Campaign Finance Regulation in the United States and Canada." In F. Leslie Seidle, ed. *Comparative Issues in Party and Election Finance*. Toronto: Dundurn Press.

Nassmacher, Karl-Heinz. 1993. "Comparing Party and Campaign Finance in Western Democracies." In Arthur B. Gunlicks, ed. *Campaign and Party Finance in North America and Western Europe*. Boulder, Colo.: Westview Press.

National Citizens Coalition Inc. v. Canada. 1984. 5 WWR 436.

Nugent, Margaret Latus, and John R. Johannes. 1990. "Introduction: What Is at Stake?" In Margaret Latus Nugent and John R. Johannes, eds. *Money, Elections, and Democracy: Reforming Congressional Campaign Finance*. Boulder, Colo.: Westview Press.

Office of the Ethics Counsellor. 2002. *The Report of the Ethics Counsellor on the Activities of the Office of the Ethics Counsellor to September 30, 2002*. Ottawa: Minister of Supply and Services.

Padget, Donald. 1991. "Large Contributions to Candidates in the 1988 Federal Election and the Issue of Undue Influence." In F. Leslie Seidle, ed. *Issues in Party and Election Finance in Canada*. Toronto: Dundurn Press.

Royal Commission on Electoral Reform and Party Financing (Canada). 1991. *Reforming Electoral Democracy*. Ottawa: Minister of Supply and Services.

Savoie, Donald. 1999. *Governing from the Center: The Concentration of Power in Canadian Politics*. Toronto: University of Toronto Press.

Somerville v. Canada (Attorney General). 1996. 8 WWR 199.

Stanbury, W. T. 1991. *Money in Politics*. Toronto: Dundurn Press.

Tanguay, Brian, and Barry J. Kay. 1998. "Third Party Advertising and the Threat to Electoral Democracy in Canada: The Mouse That Roared." *International Journal of Canadian Studies* 17: 57–79.

Young, Lisa. 1991. "Toward Transparency: An Evaluation of Disclosure Arrangements in Canadian Political Finance." In F. Leslie Seidle, ed. *Issues in Party and Election Finance in Canada*. Toronto: Dundurn Press.

———. 1998. "Party, State and Political Competition in Canada: The Cartel Model Reconsidered." *Canadian Journal of Political Science* 31: 2 (June 1998): 339–58.

Young, Lisa, and Harold J. Jansen. 2011. "Introduction." In Lisa Young and Harold J. Jansen, eds. *Money, Politics, and Democracy: Canada's Party Finance Reform.* Vancouver: UBC Press.

***Lisa Young** is professor of political science and associate dean of graduate studies at the University of Calgary. She is the author of *Feminists and Party Politics* (University of Michigan Press, 2000).

Lisa Young. "Regulating Campaign Finance in Canada: Strengths and Weaknesses." *Election Law Journal* (2010) 3 (3): 444–62. Revised by the author.

Used by permission.

DISCUSSION QUESTIONS

1. Do the public-funding provisions of Canada's new campaign finance regime prevent the entry of new parties?

2. Do expenditure limits prevent the entry of new parties or candidates?

3. Do the Canadian restrictions on the activities of "third parties" or non-party groups unduly restrict these groups' freedom of speech?

4. Would the types of reforms implemented in Canada work in a less party-centered system, such as the United States?

Unaccounted Competition: The Finance of Intra-Party Elections

by Menachem Hofnung*

Regulation of party finance traces its roots to the emergence of mass parties in the late nineteenth and early twentieth century. When parties ceased to be the business of small elites and notables, and opened their ranks to mass participation, the funding of general elections quickly became a burning issue. The relatively high cost of electoral campaigns, and the accumulated evidence that competitors for public office are willing to make all kinds of corrupt promises in return for their campaign expenditures being covered, has given rise to the idea that electoral funding should be provided by the state in return for the parties' acquiescence to subjecting themselves to certain minimal demands of accounting, auditing and reporting (Alexander, 1989: 3–7).

Several decades after the initial introduction of direct public funding, however, political corruption still runs high in many democracies. Although scandals related to the funding of electoral campaigns are frequently reported around the globe (Casas-Zamora, 2005: 39; Pinto-Duschinsky, 2002: 69; Smilov and Toplak, 2007: 16–19), not much is known about the financial dealings of individual candidates outside the circle of majoritarian systems in English-speaking, established democracies. In fact, in countries that employ proportional representation (PR) or mixed electoral systems, very little is known about the finance of pre-nomination periods or internal party races.

While general elections provide the grand show, significant political finance often begins, and is carried out, long before the formal opening of national campaigns. In many countries, such activity is either unregulated or regulated in a way that leaves exploitable loopholes for borderline practices and the manipulation of the electoral process. Thus, the question of funding candidate selection, although frequently treated as marginal, is in fact a significant question that cannot be avoided in any serious discussion of campaign finance.[1]

Intra-party elections refer to the selection processes that take place within a political party. Such selections may be carried out through different electoral forms including: primaries, votes of approval by a party convention, decisions by small nominating committees, meetings of regional councils, a vote taken by a central committee and the like. In short, the term applies to almost any form of internal selection in which candidates within a party can present and promote their own candidacy to an electoral office. In this study, the term applies to selection races within a party for nominating candidates to run on the party ticket for national executive or legislative office.

As parties form their ideological and organizational infrastructure for promoting candidates for senior political nominations, internal selection processes may limit the range of choices presented to the general public on election day. The issues of internal selection rules in general (Rahat and Hazan, 2001: 313), and candidate funding in particular, are for all practical purposes unregulated by the great majority of democratic states. Thus, the issue in question is whether a state should regulate the financial dealings of candidates in these intra-party nomination processes. If the answer to this question is in the affirmative, how far should regulations go? And in the event of a negative answer, what is the public cost of non-regulation and the absence of candidate selection monitoring?

This study claims that unclear regulation, lack of funding (from honest sources) and the absence of non-partisan oversight of intra-party races sends a clear message to candidates that it is acceptable to seek financial support from dubious sources, to build 'war chests' and to overspend on election campaigns. At the same time, this study acknowledges that a lack of controls of intra-party campaigns increases the electoral chances of candidates who possess the means and of those willing to engage in arguably corrupt fundraising practices. The consequences of irregularities in internal selection campaigns are accusations of corruption and growing public mistrust of the political process in general and of political parties in particular (Hofnung, 2004: 77).

This study begins by describing the trends in the regulation of parties, continues on to look at the objectives of regulating party finance as an extension of party regulation at the national and local levels, and then proceeds with a comparative analysis of financing intra-party selection races in different electoral settings.

Among the established democracies that use either PR or mixed electoral systems, Israel is the only one that carries out a detailed regulation of internal selection races, though even in Israel enforcement of the rules concerning the financing of intra-party campaigns is far weaker than enforcement of the rules for the general elections. Thus, this study compares Israel with other countries that employ non-majoritarian electoral systems in order to assess the consequences of ignoring the regulation of financial transactions of candidate selection.

REGULATION OF PARTIES

Political parties are the central institutional form through which mass participation in politics is organized and operates in the modern state. The constitutional treatment of parties, in areas such as elections and campaign financing, has important implications for the process of elections as well as the overall democratic governance of a given country (Pildes, 2004: 101).

For decades, parties were widely considered as voluntary associations, whose purposes included promoting an ideological agenda, engaging in social mobilization and educational efforts as well as presenting the prospective voter with policy alternatives and competing lists of candidates for public office. This approach, however, is no longer dominant. Parties nowadays are looked upon as semi-public institutions (van Biezen, 2004). Parties are understood not only in terms of their linkages with civil society, but rather in terms of their permanent relationships with the state, which has assumed increased responsibility in legitimizing the status of parties, regulating their activities and supplying them with resources (van Biezen and Kopecky, 2007: 237). In other words, parties are conceived as semi-public institutions, created as private associations, but treated as important democratic institutions (with an official legal status). The favourable normative overtones associated with the party as a political institution have served as justifications for legitimizing the direct intervention of the state in parties' internal affairs. Among other activities, political finance has ceased to be the exclusive domain of the parties as private associations (van Biezen, 2004: 705). The increasing legal demands imposed on parties led Richard Katz to state that 'party structures have become legitimate objects of state regulation to a degree far exceeding what would normally be acceptable in the past for private associations in a liberal democracy' (2002: 90).

Recent comparative research shows that almost all democracies have some form of regulation of political parties, and most of the countries regulate both party activities and party finances. In many countries, regulation is accompanied by public money extended to parties for covering their ongoing and campaign expenses (van Biezen and Kopecky, 2007: 238). Still, while regulating party affairs is becoming the norm in democratic countries, as far as competition between rival political parties is concerned, that type of regulation is often non-existent when it comes to looking at the electoral finances of candidates in intra-party races.

ELECTORAL SYSTEMS AND MODELS OF POLITICAL FINANCE

Regulation of political finance is widely regarded as tied to the regulation of parties, but apparently this is not always the case. In some countries, especially countries that employ single-member district (SMD) electoral systems, regulation of campaign finance is geared towards individual candidates rather than the parties. In other countries, the party is the recipient of state subsidies and is the legal entity responsible for allocation, use and reporting of financial dealings. Regardless of the type of electoral system, the general underlying objective of finance regulation is to ensure fairness and equality in elections. The purpose of such regulation is to maintain the principle of 'one person one vote' and to ensure that financials might is not the ultimate factor in deciding the outcome of the electoral process.

Two other important objectives of political finance regulation are transparency and accountability. Transparency is aimed at reducing corruption in political life by opening the process and increasing visibility in order to track financial transactions. An underlying assumption of financial regulation is that transparency and full disclosure can limit the clout of big money, as it sheds light on the web of prevailing inter- and intra-connections, and deters secret, corrupt deals exchanging money for favours.[2] While transparency provides for the electorate's right to know where the money comes from and where it goes, accountability addresses the political actors' responsibility to be answerable to the electorate and to the law for their actions (Davidson and Lapp, 2007: 4). A related aspect of regulating the finance of intra-party contests is placing limits on the ability of political bosses to maintain unaccountable control through their domination of financial resources (Pinto-Duschinsky, 2002: 70).

The prevailing tendency in electoral systems is to regulate the upper tier of political competition, namely the contestants (either parties or individuals) whose names appear on the ballot at a public election (Hofnung, 2006: 374). This observation may explain the difference between SMDs, on the one hand, and PR or mixed electoral systems, on the other.[3] In SMD systems, individual candidates appear on the ballot, while their parties maintain the infrastructure, support system and initial identification. Despite representing a party, the candidate must open a special account and be answerable for running financial matters and reporting to public authorities. In other words, the fact that several majoritarian countries subject candidates in their intraparty races to higher standards of transparency and accountability is not rooted in a legal philosophy emphasizing the importance of regulating intraparty affairs, but, on the contrary, views the candidate rather than the party as the legal entity answerable to the public. By contrast, in mixed and PR systems the obligations of individual candidates are either loosely defined or non-existent. The party is the legal entity responsible for reporting and running all financial matters.

At this juncture, a few words should be added about the differences between SMDs and mixed or PR electoral systems. It is difficult to identify two identical electoral systems, since almost every system has its own peculiar attributes and practices. However, in general we can identify three major types of electoral system: (1) in SMD plurality systems the country is divided into many electoral districts. The candidate who wins the contested office in each district is the one who obtains the most votes (for example, as in the United States and United Kingdom); (2) in mixed-member electoral systems, a certain proportion of parliamentary members are elected in SMDs, while the rest are elected according to the proportional share of the party among the electorate. The Federal Republic of Germany, Japan and Mexico are the major examples of such electoral systems; (3) in PR systems, the rationale is consciously to reduce the disparity between a party's share of the national vote and its share of parliamentary seats. In general, each party receives a number of parliamentary seats roughly corresponding to its relative strength within the electorate. The Netherlands and Israel represent the extreme end of this electoral method. In both states, the entire country is comprised of one electoral district.

The difference between these systems may help in explaining the lack of empirical research on the funding of internal races in non-plurality electoral settings, as summarized in Table 1. For example, there is a vast body of research on electoral rules, national campaign funding and party finance in mixed and PR systems.[4] There is a rich literature covering the electoral rules of the game of national campaigns and intra-party selection in SMD systems in which primaries serve as the prologue to national elections in the same district (Bardwell, 2002; Cooper, 2002; Hopkin, 2001; Stephenson, 2004; Thompson, 2002). A large volume of literature also covers the issue of the financing of intra-party races in SMD systems, in particular in North America (Ewing, 2003; Nassmacher, 2003a; Potter and Ryan, 2005; Young, 2004).

In addition, there is extensive research on intra-party competition, including leadership battles and candidate selection in all kinds of electoral systems (Bille, 2001; Caul Kittilson and Scarrow, 2003; Katz, 2001; Kenig, 2007). What has passed almost unnoticed in this vast volume of research is the way in which intra-party campaigns are financed in mixed and PR systems. Unlike the norm in SMD systems, the finance of internal campaigns in mixed or proportional systems is only rarely regulated. In fact, the greater proportion of comparative research on the finance of intra-party races is based on information emanating from the SMD systems of North America and Australia.

Intra-party races are salient both in SMD and in mixed or PR systems. In SMDs, winning the primary ensures a candidate a shot at a parliamentary seat with the backing of a national party. In districts that are usually won by a particular political party, selection as a candidate is more important for the would-be legislator than the subsequent election. In most SMD systems a loser can still opt to run independently and might eventually be elected to national (or regional) office. In a PR system with fixed lists of candidates in order of preference,[5] winning a top position in the internal race may secure a candidate a safe seat on the party list even before the start of the national campaign. If the party becomes part of the winning coalition, winning a high position on the list may provide a candidate with a better shot in seeking an executive ministerial post. In countries that use preference votes in addition to PR, winning or losing in intra-party races sends a strong message to the electorate about the electoral chances of a given candidate. In short, from the contestants' point of view, in PR systems internal elections may affect their future political career as much (if not more) than the general elections.

Table 1. Comparative knowledge of electoral and finance rules in different electoral systems

Electoral system	National elections		Intra-party races	
	Electoral rules and practices	Finance rules and practices	Selectoral rules and practices	Finance rules and practices
SMD	++	++	+	+
PR and mixed	++	++	+	−

Source: Updated from Hofnung (2006).

Elections provide a natural platform for partisans and the public to raise their passions and to express their frustrations with the existing status quo (Issacharoff, 2007: 1410). Thus, electoral campaigns often take the form of personal contests between rival candidates, but in most recorded cases a candidate is backed by a political party. While candidates supported by a political party exist in almost every electoral system, regulation of political finance can be found in either of two basic models. The first model, the 'candidate-centred' model of political finance, appears mainly in presidential systems. In several presidential systems that employ this model, the primacy of parties at the federal level is challenged by individual candidates. State funding is usually small or non-existent, candidates can seek large donations and use their own personal wealth to finance their own campaigns (Smilov and Toplak, 2007: 3). Parties assume a secondary role even in countries where they are active in the campaign. The main financial activity related to the campaign is carried out by the candidate, who is also a legal entity subject to political finance regulation.

The second model, the 'party-centred' model, appears mainly in parliamentary systems where strong cohesive parties form the legislative majority. Although this model is more prevalent in electoral systems that employ PR, it also appears in majoritarian systems like that in Canada and the UK. The 'party-centred' model acknowledges the role of parties as an important institution of democratic government, and national parties as the recipients of the state's financial aid. Parties are the legal entities subject to regulation. The parties raise funds and bear the burden of spending the money legally and submitting the reports (Smilov and Toplak, 2007: 4). There is a trace of regulation of candidates and *ad hoc* groups in this model, in terms of registration and fundraising for elections, but those provisions apply to independents or party-picked candidates who appear on the ballot on election day. It does not cover the financial dealings of candidates within their own party at the pre-nomination period in non-majoritarian systems. Here we reach the root of the problem. The 'party-centred' model of political finance that exists in most Western European countries was developed and adopted in the 1950s and 1960s, when decisions on leadership nominations and candidacy for parliamentary seats were made by a small group of party insiders in 'smoke-filled rooms'. In such circumstances, when the masses were called to express their preferences in general elections (but did not have any voice in the selection of candidates presented on the ballot), the party-centred model made sense. This logic hinged on the fact that individual candidacy within the party does not cost much (if it costs at all), while national elections require a fortune. This state of affairs, however, no longer holds true.[6]

As demonstrated in Figure 1, since the early 1980s more and more parties have opened up their intra-party races to selection by ever-growing electoral bodies (Scarrow et al., 2000: 139–44). The trend of moving to more inclusive electorates came as a reaction to decreasing political participation and as an attempt to lure younger voters to cast their vote for parties who appear to be more responsive to their supporters. This is especially the case with party leadership races (Caul Kittilson and Scarrow, 2003: 71–3; Kenig, 2007: 176). This tendency of moving to larger candidate selecting bodies presents a dilemma: the bigger the electorate, the more the resources needed to reach out and gain access to all eligible voters. Selection races in which millions of eligible voters are targeted by candidates and encouraged to cast their vote are neither funded by the state nor commonly financed by the party, leading to the financial dealings of candidates being kept in the dark.

As we shall see, the move to more inclusive candidate selection methods often has not translated into corresponding amendments to financial regulations. With the exception of a handful of English-speaking countries, the financial activity of candidates in intra-party campaigns still remains unregulated and unaccounted for.

INTRA-PARTY FINANCE IN DIFFERENT ELECTORAL SYSTEMS

We have greater knowledge of intra-party races under SMD than in mixed and PR electoral systems. This is so mainly because the SMD method is employed in the United States and Canada, countries where the most extensive research has been done. Primaries (or intra-party races) are considered part of the electoral campaign and as such they are subject to regulation, reporting and enforcement. Although infractions occur in many electoral campaigns, the volume of regulations and the degree of compliance are quite impressive. Much of the candidates' financial activity is presented online and is thus available for verification, comparison and research.[7]

In stable democracies (defined here as those having at least 15 years of uninterrupted regular and free elections) that use mixed or PR electoral systems and employ public finance of political parties, disclosure requirements of individual candidates are nominal or non-existent.[8] In several of the countries that employ

Figure 1: Exclusion and Inclusion in Party Candidate Selection Methods

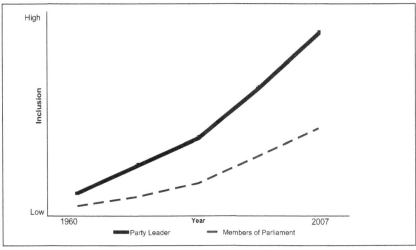

Figure 1 represents a rough picture rather than a detailed account of the general shift to more inclusive selectorates (*Sources*: Scarrow, et al., 2000; Caul Kittlison and Scarrow, 2003; Kenig, 2007).

a mixed electoral system, candidates are formally required to report their financial activity. These requirements, however, usually apply to financial transactions related to national elections and to the sources of their personal income.

Table 2 demonstrates the procedures applied to the finance of individual candidates in 34 established democracies that have a system of party finance, a system in which the parties, not the candidates, are the recipients of public funding.

From Table 2 it clearly appears that only Israel and several Eastern European countries have regulation (YES score) relating to all seven variables. Among the countries with free and recurring elections for a period of more than 30 years, only Belgium is close to Israel with five regulated areas, while all other Western European countries have very little regulation, ranging from 2.5 (Germany) to 0 (Switzerland). How such regulation in Eastern Europe is applied, as far as individual candidates are concerned, is unclear. Although the provisions appear in legislation, there is no indication of any enforcement in intra-party races.[9] However, had this table been created prior to 1992, before the introduction of direct elections for the office of prime minister, and voluntary adoption of mass primaries by several parties, Israel would have been exactly in the middle of the group. Thus, two questions come to mind: what were the causes for instituting extensive regulation in Israel? What general lessons can be learned from the Israeli case?

At this point, the Israeli experience becomes relevant for comparative purposes, owing to recent international trends of moving to large selection bodies; these bodies have been a feature of Israeli politics for several decades. Moreover, after experiencing regulation of finance in intra-party races in the past 15 years, the shortcomings of partial regulation that prevails in Israel have become clear. Thus, the Israeli experience can serve as a caution or warning to other countries embarking on a similar path.

ISRAEL: PUBLIC FUNDING OF PARTIES, PRIVATE FUNDING OF CANDIDATES

Until 1996, Israel used a strictly PR electoral system in 13 successive national electoral campaigns (1949–92). Electoral lists were drawn and closed at the outset of the campaign. Voters could cast a vote for one party and by doing so endorse its entire list of candidates. Until the late 1970s, electoral lists in all parties were drawn up by party leaders who picked and placed – rather than selected – candidates for the entire list to be presented to the public on elections day (Weiss, 1977: 49–56).[10]

Table 2. Public control of intra-party races in non-majoritarian electoral systems

Country	Electoral system	Finance law	Disclosure or reporting by candidates	Criminal sanctions for reporting violations	Limits on private donations	Limits/bans on corporate donations	Limits/bans on foreign donations	Limits on expenditures in internal races
Austria	PR	Yes	Yes	No	No	No	No	No
Belgium	PR	Yes	Yes	No	Yes	Yes	No	Yes (party and campaign)
Bulgaria	PR	Yes	Yes	No	Yes	Yes (limit)	Yes (ban)	Yes (campaign)
Costa Rica	PR	Yes	No	No	Yes (limit)	Yes (limit)	Yes (ban)	No
Croatia	PR	Yes	Yes	Yes	No	No	No	No
Czech Republic	PR	Yes	Yes	No	Yes (limit)	No	Yes	No
Denmark	PR	Yes	Yes	No	No	No	No	No
Estonia	PR	Yes	Yes		No	No	n/a	n/a
Finland	PR	No	Yes	No	No	No	No	No
Germany	Mixed	Yes	Yes	No	No	No	Yes (limit)	No
Greece	PR	Yes	Yes		Yes	Yes (limit)	No	Yes
Hungary	Mixed	Yes	Yes	No	No	No	Yes (limit)	Yes (campaign)
Iceland	PR	Yes	No	No	No	No	No	No
Ireland	PR	Yes	Yes	Yes	No	No	No	Yes (campaign)
Israel	PR	Yes	Yes	Yes	Yes	Yes	Yes (limit)	Yes
Italy	Mixed	Yes	Yes	No	No	No	No	Yes (campaign)
Japan	Mixed	Yes	Yes	No	Yes (limit)	Yes (ban)	Yes (ban)	Yes (campaign)
Latvia	PR	Yes	Yes		Yes	Yes (limit)	Yes (ban)	No
Luxembourg	PR	Yes	No	No	No	No	No	No
Macedonia	PR	Yes	Yes	Yes	Yes	Yes (limit)	Yes (ban)	Yes
Moldova	PR	Yes	Yes	Yes	No	No	Yes (ban)	No

Country	Electoral system	Finance law	Disclosure or reporting by candidates	Criminal sanctions for reporting violations	Limits on private donations	Limits/bans on corporate donations	Limits/bans on foreign donations	Limits on expenditures in internal races
Netherlands	PR	Yes	Yes	No	No	No	No	No
Norway	PR	No	Yes	No	No	No	No	No
Poland	PR	Yes	Yes	Yes	Yes (presidential)	Yes (presidential)	Yes (ban)	Yes (campaign)
Portugal	PR	Yes	Yes	Yes	Yes	Yes (limit)	Yes (limit)	Yes (party and campaign)
Romania	PR	Yes	Yes		Yes	Yes (limit)	Yes (limit)	No
Slovakia	PR	Yes	Yes	No	No	No	Yes (ban)	Yes (campaign)
Slovenia	PR	Yes	Yes	Yes	Yes	Yes (limit)	Yes (ban)	n/a
Spain	PR	Yes	Yes	n/a	Yes	Yes (limit)	Yes (limit)	Yes
Sweden	PR	No	Yes	No	No	No	No	No
Switzerland	PR	No	No	No	No	No	No	No
Taiwan	Mixed	Yes	Yes	Yes	Yes (limit)	Yes (limit)	Yes (ban)	Yes
Turkey	PR	Yes	No	Yes	Yes (limit)	Yes (limit)	Yes (ban)	No
Uruguay	PR	Yes	No	No	No	No	No	No

Sources: Updated from van Biezen (2004) with additions from Grant (2005); Hofnung (2006); Smilov and Toplak (2007).

In 1977, the Herut party (the main party in the Likud Bloc, which won the largest number of seats in the national election of that year) introduced a moderate reform by transferring the power to select its list of candidates to the party's Central Committee comprised of about 600 members (Goldberg, 1994: 68–82; Rahat and Sher-Hadar, 1999: 67).[11] The other major party, Labor, failing to win the 1981, 1984 and 1988 elections,[12] turned in 1992 to a radical reform: the introduction of mass party primaries among its 200,000 party members in order to select both the party leader and the list of candidates. Following Labor's decisive victory in 1992, other parties felt obliged to follow suit and democratize their internal procedures. Likud and Labor, as well as other parties, held primaries to select their candidates for city mayors and municipal council members before the local elections of November 1993. Within a year of the 1992 general elections, five of the six largest parties announced plans to introduce some form of primaries in selecting their candidates for local and national office.

Another electoral reform, incidentally also introduced in 1992, had a direct bearing on intra-party races. In March 1992 (two months before the general election of that year), the Israeli parliament amended the electoral system, installing direct elections for the prime minister, with the change to take effect in 1996. But, after five stormy years and three different individually elected prime ministers, this unique electoral system was laid to rest in 2001 in favour of its predecessor.

Several factors combined to change the way in which candidates approached intra-party races. The introduction of direct elections for prime minister, reports of large expenditure by candidates in the Labor primaries of spring 1992, and the costly and successful campaign of Benjamin Netanyahu to take over the leadership of the Likud party (after the party's defeat in the 1992 elections). Unlike other countries, where the move to more inclusive methods of selecting party leaders and candidates occurred gradually, while the national electoral system remained unchanged, Israel was faced with a situation in which within a single year (1992) several changes were made in an uncoordinated sequence (Hazan, 1997). Party activity began to be regulated by law; the electoral system was changed with the adoption of direct elections for prime minister, and both major parties voluntarily adopted mass primaries to select their leaders, parliamentary representatives and candidates for municipal and trade union positions.

Personal campaigns and financial reserves became a *sine qua non* in Israeli politics. Thus, in a vain attempt to regulate future races before costs turned politics into the playground of the wealthy, the Israeli parliament hastened in 1993 to amend the Parties Law and set up legal ceilings on individual donations to candidates, as well as limits on campaign expenditures.

In designing the new law, MPs did not have reliable data about the costs of running a personal electoral race among 200,000 or so party members spread throughout the country. Unwilling to face public resentment against the ever-growing public funding of political activity (Hofnung, 1996: 138), MPs opted for private funding of internal races. From the protocols of the debates, it is quite evident that MPs did not have a clue as to how much it might cost to run a primary campaign: the focus of attention was on placing limits on rich candidates and skilful fundraisers (Knesset Protocols 125, 3438–83, 3 August 1993).

The Israeli electoral system allows only for parties to compete in national elections. Candidates are recognized as individual competitors and may run their own campaigns only in intra-party races that select among contestants who compete for securing high positions on the party's electoral list. The Parties Law sets expenditure ceilings for internal elections that are adjusted yearly.[13]

The new arrangement has several loopholes and escape clauses that have made enforcement unattainable. Candidates were required to submit reports detailing their financial activity only during the nine months preceding the primaries.[14] Contributions and expenditures prior to that date were exempted from disclosure. Until 2006, the Parties Law entrusted the parties themselves with the monitoring and enforcing of reporting requirements. Given the fact that internal candidate selection generally takes place less than two months before the general elections, the desire to avoid public scandals prevents strict enforcement and disclosure of illegal activities.[15] Thus, despite ample newspaper reports and numerous complaints by the losing candidates of several parties regarding their opponents' heavy spending and campaign violations, not a single candidate in any party has ever been found guilty[16] by an internal auditing body of serious campaign violations.[17]

Thus, Israel presents a case where two systems of political finance, interparty and intra-party, exist in what seems to be two different electoral environments. Enforcement is fairly tight and effective when national parties and parliamentary party groups are concerned. In return for generous funding, parliamentary groups are subject to year-round monitoring by the office of the State Comptroller. Compliance is achieved by installing a system that sanctions violations with public reports and heavy fines. While not pretending to claim that the system works without infractions or abuses, compared to other political systems and even other electoral environments in Israel itself, enforcement is effective in the sense that parties are deterred from knowingly committing offences. In most cases parties prefer to comply with the guidelines published by the State Comptroller rather than paying fines for illegal violations.

The effectiveness of the national system, however, was not apparent in the other electoral settings. For example, enforcement at intra-party internal selection campaigns was for all purposes non-existent. How the 2007 provisions extending state supervision to cover intra-party races are implemented in future campaigns remains to be seen. In the past, without state surveillance, the parties were left to carry out their own inspection. This regime has proved to be ineffective and riddled with corruption. Many candidates who rose to national prominence, or secured a top position on the party's list, did so after exhibiting a blatant disregard for the provisions of the Parties Law and after raising illegal contributions and spending as much as they could afford.

COMPARATIVE IMPLICATIONS

Regulation of political parties, including internal party affairs, has become a worldwide trend in recent years. Parties are no longer regarded as private entities, free to engage in their own affairs without answering to the basic demands of public accountability. Strangely enough, this tendency, built on the notion that financially sound and transparent internal party procedures are essential for healthy democracy, has ignored the area most prone to corruption and sleazy practices – intra-party races. At least, this is the case in mixed and PR systems that comprise the great majority of national electoral systems around the globe. The simple fact that the finance of intraparty contests in mixed and PR systems is neither covered by regulation nor discussed in the literature went unnoticed because of the vast volume on funding intra-party selection races coming from countries that use SMD electoral arrangements. However, as more and more parties adopt nationwide leadership campaigns, in a manner resembling United States-style primaries, old practices seem to be out of date and unfit for modern realities.

Intra-party selection contests involve significant amounts of money. The more inclusive the party procedure is in selecting its candidates, the more costly the campaigns of contestants. The larger the geographical electoral area in which an intra-party campaign is held, the more expensive it becomes. Obviously, there are exceptions, but in general a primary leadership race to select the Socialist Party candidate for the office of President of France requires more resources than it takes to win the position on the Israeli Labor Party list 'reserved' to the city of Jerusalem. The fact is that we know more about the expenses of the Labor party contestants in Jerusalem in 2006 than we know of the financial dealings of the candidates who competed in the French Socialist primary to select its official candidate for president in 2007.

Retaining the old 'party-centred' model of political finance ought to be re-evaluated when parties in mixed and PR countries adopt intra-party selection methods imported from SMD systems, and do so without changing the regulations and reporting mechanisms that were tailored to earlier selection methods. This is not to say that SMDs are to be preferred over mixed or PR systems. What can be said is that adopting inclusive intra-party selection races without paying attention to the changing financial demands created by such reform can carry with it the potential of infusion of big money into intra-party races, thus changing the dynamics of party politics.

Despite the importance of democratic procedures and practices in intraparty everyday life, many old and new democracies prefer to turn a blind eye to the financial practices of competitors in the internal selection of party leaders and candidates for national offices. Most countries show a reluctance to ask for more than nominal demands of disclosure and reporting of financial dealings. The moral of the Israeli case is that attempts to regulate the selected areas of campaign finance without taking into consideration the electoral process as a unified whole can severely affect the entire political culture. The lack of finance enforcement in the internal party races can result in widespread contempt and the discrediting of the entire political process.

By hastily installing a porous system of intra-party financial regulation, it became difficult to ensure that Israeli candidates adhered to the rules. Although, despite the lack of enforcement, when compared to other nonmajoritarian electoral systems, the Israeli system ensures a limited degree of transparency as far as intra-party competition is concerned. Even such limited transparency paints an alarming picture, as it becomes clear that without effective enforcement and real sanctions any borderline opportunity will be exploited by one candidate or another. Politicians in other countries may not reach the extremes exhibited in Israeli primary races, but judging by what has been exposed in Israel, and the indifference towards financial dealings in internal races in European democracies, it would be rather premature to assume that such races are immune to corruption and manipulation by interested third parties.

NOTE

I am greatly indebted to my research assistants Avner Tal, Liora Norwich and Gil Hertshten for their valuable help. Reuven Hazan and Gideon Rahat, my colleagues at the Department of Political Science at the Hebrew University, have been especially kind in reading and commenting on earlier versions of this manuscript. I also thank Keren Weinshall and the anonymous reviewers for their valuable comments and suggestions. Support for this study was received from the Authority for Research and Development at the Hebrew University of Jerusalem.

Endnotes

1. Expenditures in intra-party elections can reach significant amounts of money. In the United States Presidential race of 2004 the eventual winners in both major parties, President George Bush and Senator John Kerry, opted out of the public funding programme, which imposes spending limits on candidates who accept matching funds and limits the total amount of public funds available. The $269.6 million raised by President Bush prior to the convention was nearly three times his fundraising total in 2000, when he also declined to accept public funds. John Kerry raised $234.6 million, nearly six times more than had ever been raised by a Democratic nominee under the public funding programme (Federal Election Commission, 2004 Presidential Campaign Financial Activity Summarized). Available at: http://www.fec.gov/press/press2005/20050203pressum/20050203pressum.html

2. Thus, in all Western European countries, with the exception of Sweden, there is a statutory obligation to disclose the identities of party donors. There is also a general practice of reporting on party funds and assets. Enforcement, though, varies from one political system to another (Nassmacher, 2003b: 129–36).

3. In a country like Germany, where a mixed system is used, and where half of the Bundestag members are elected in single-member districts, the party handles individual candidate accounts. The main reason is that donations to parties are partly tax-deductible, while a candidate who accepts donations has to pay donation taxes (Morlok and Streit, 2005).

4. See, for example, the special issue of *Party Politics* in 2004, vol. 10(6). (See also Alexander, 1989; Alexander and Shiratori, 1994; Austin and Tjernstrom, 2003; Casas-Zamora, 2005; Nassmacher, 2003a; Smilov and Toplak, 2007.)

5. In Israel, the parties submit lists of candidates five weeks before the national elections. Voters have the choice of electing any single party on the ballot, but they cannot change the order of candidates on any given list.

6. Enforcement of the 'party-centred' model is easier than that of the 'candidate-centred' model. Instead of tracking and auditing records of multiple candidates, the regulator deals with a dozen or so centralized organizations. It also allows the state to maintain the policy of non-interference in intra-party affairs.

7. See the websites of the main monitoring agencies in the United States and Canada. Available at: http://www.fec.gov/ (last accessed 3 October 2007); http://www.elections.ca/ (last accessed 3 October 2007). See also Davidson and Lapp, 2007; Kingsley, 2004; Simon, 2004.

8. In several electoral systems, the state extends funding to parliamentary parties or individual parliamentary members to carry out their legislative functions. Here, I refer to public funding extended to candidates for the purpose of competing in internal selection races. With the exception of Israel, I have not found any research specifically aimed at exploring financial regulation of intra-party races in mixed or PR electoral systems. Israel thus offers an interesting exception for reasons to be discussed later.

9. Information related to Eastern Europe is based on van Biezen (2004) and Smilov and Toplak (2007). In neither source are there clear indications of enforcement related to intra-party elections. Moreover, as Walecki notes, some of the provisions aimed at regulating the activities of parties in Eastern Europe were adopted under pressure from the European Union as preconditions imposed on the respective countries before they were admitted to the European Union. How much of that regulation is indeed implemented is open to debate (Walecki, 2007: 15).

10. Petitions against such practices reached the courts only on rare occasions before the 1980s. See CA 189/76 *Labor Party v. Levin*, 31(2) P.D. 265; AR 210/87 *Gruper v. Modai*, 5 Takdin

Elyon 512; CA 197/89 *Agudat Israel v. Schwartz*, 45(3) P.D. 320; HP (Tel Aviv) 150/90 *Shalev v. Likud*, 51(3) PM 99.

11. The initial attempt to introduce primaries also occurred in 1977. The newly founded Dash party had used a country-wide primary system to select its candidates (Bar, 1996: 151). Although Dash won 15 seats and became the third largest party in the 1977 general election, infighting and irreconcilable differences among the founding groups proved to be fatal, and the party ceased to exist as a political entity before the 1981 election.

12. Labor tried moderate reform in 1988, when candidates were asked to compete in several rounds at the Party's Convention. Ten candidates were placed on the national list in each round, with the losers and newcomers allowed to compete in the next round until the list was completed.

13. In October 2007, those internal campaign ceilings stood at NIS 400,000 per candidate ($100,000) for parliamentary primaries, and NIS 2,000,000 ($500,000) in primaries for party leadership and party candidate for prime minister.

14. The nine-month requirement takes full effect only if elections are held on time. In seven of the last eight general campaigns, elections were called early, before the parliament had completed its full four-year term.

15. After the Likud internal elections of December 2002, four Likud ministers and four Likud MPs failed to report donations they received for their internal campaign, in violation of the party by-laws. Even though 78 of the contestants never filed a report, no penalties were imposed (*Ha'aretz*, 15 December 2002).

16. In 2006, two former MPs were sentenced to jail terms for violations committed in intra-party races. Those offences, however, were not reported by the party, but rather came as a result of independent police investigations. Omri Sharon, a former MP and the son of a former Israeli prime minister, was sentenced to a jail term of 9 months for violations of campaign finance regulations committed while managing the primary campaign of his father, Ariel Sharon, in the 1999 Likud leadership race. It was established in court that campaign expenses reached 7.1 million NIS (about $1.7 million at the time). The legal ceiling in that race was 826,000 NIS or about 12 percent of the eventual spending. His appeal was rejected by the appellate court (*Criminal Appeal [Tel Aviv] 70509/06 Sharon v. State of Israel*). Another former Likud MP, Naomi Blumenthal, was sentenced to jail for bribery and obstruction of justice. Blumenthal was convicted of bribing 15 Likud activists and central committee members. She hosted them and their spouses in a luxurious hotel before the December 2002 selection process for the party's candidates, in the hope of gaining their votes in the elections (*Criminal Appeal [Tel Aviv] 70722/06 Blumenthal v. State of Israel*).

17. Just before the 2006 elections the Israeli parliament temporarily amended the Parties Law, 1992. The main provisions of the new law included: application of the Parties Law to all internal campaigns, regardless of whether the party's candidate slate is chosen by the entire party membership or its central committee; campaign funding for internal races are to be supervised by the State Comptroller rather than by the parties themselves; all candidates in internal campaigns are required to provide the Comptroller with a list of all contributions received during the previous year; a month after the internal selection race, candidates are required to submit a list of their expenditure. In 2007, those provisions were extended again (*Book of Laws* 2007 [2106], p. 414).

REFERENCES

Alexander, Herbert E. (ed.) (1989) *Comparative Political Finance in the 1980s*. Cambridge: Cambridge University Press.

Alexander, Herbert E. and Rei Shiratori (eds.) (1994) *Comparative Political Finance among the Democracies*. Boulder, CO: Westview.

Austin, Reginald and Maja Tjernstrom (eds.) (2003) *On Funding of Parties and Election Campaigns Handbook*. Stockholm: IDEA.

Bar, Aliza (1996) *Primaries and Other Methods of Candidate Selection*. Jerusalem and Tel Aviv: Israel Democracy Institute and HaKibbutz HaMeuchad [Hebrew].

Bardwell, Kedron (2002) 'Money and Challenger Emergence in Gubernatorial Primaries', *Political Research Quarterly* 55: 653–68.

Bille, Lars (2001) 'Democratizing a Democratic Procedure: Myth or Reality? Candidate Selection in Western European Parties', *Party Politics* 7: 363–80.

Casas-Zamora, Kevin (2005) *Paying for Democracy: Political Finance and State Funding for Parties*. ECPR Press: University of Essex.

Caul Kittilson, Miki and Susan Scarrow (2003) 'Political Parties and the Rhetoric and Realities of Democratization', in Bruce Cain, Russell Dalton and Susan Scarrow (eds.) *Democracy Transformed*, pp. 59–80. Oxford: Oxford University Press.

Cooper, Alexandra (2002) 'The Effective Length of the Presidential Primary Season: The Impact of Delegate Allocation Rules and Voter Preferences', *Journal of Theoretical Politics* 14: 71–92.

Davidson, Diane and Miriam Lapp (2007) *Political Financing in Canada: Achieving a Balance*. Paper presented at the Annual Meeting of the Law and Society Association, Humbolt University, Berlin, Germany.

Ewing, Keith (2003) 'Promoting Political Equality: Spending Limits in British Electoral Law', *Election Law Journal* 2: 499–524.

Goldberg, Giora (1994) *The Israeli Voter*. Jerusalem: Magnes [Hebrew].

Grant, Tom (ed.) (2005) *Foreign Corrupt Practices Worldwide: Navigating the Laws, Regulations and Practices of National Regimes*. New York: Oceana.

Hazan, Reuven Y. (1997) 'Executive–Legislative Relations in an Era of Accelerated Reform: Reshaping Government in Israel', *Legislative Studies Quarterly* 22: 329–50.

Hofnung, Menachem (1996) 'Public Financing, Party Membership and Internal Party Competition', *European Journal of Political Research* 29: 73–86.

Hofnung, Menachem (2004) 'Fat Parties – Lean Candidates: Funding Israeli Internal Party Contests', in Asher Arian and Michal Shamir (eds.) *Elections in Israel 2003*, pp. 63–85. New Brunswick, NJ: Transaction Press and the Israel Democracy Institute.

Hofnung, Menachem (2006) 'Financing Internal Party Races in Non-Majoritarian Political Systems: Lessons from the Israeli Experience', *Election Law Journal* 5: 372–83.

Hopkin, Jonathan (2001) 'Bringing the Members Back In? Democratizing Candidate Selection in Britain and Spain', *Party Politics* 7: 343–61.

Issacharoff, Samuel (2007) 'Fragile Democracies', *Harvard Law Review* 120: 1405–67.

Katz, Richard S. (2001) 'The Problem of Candidate Selection and Models of Party Democracy', *Party Politics* 7: 96–277.

Katz, Richard S. (2002) 'The Internal Life of Parties', in Kurt Richard Luther and Ferdinand Müller-Rommel (eds.) *Political Challenges in the New Europe: Political and Analytical Challenges*, pp. 87–118. Oxford: Oxford University Press.

Kenig, Ofer (2007) *Party Leaders Selection Methods and Their Political Consequences* (PhD thesis). Jerusalem: The Hebrew University [Hebrew].

Kingsley, Jean-Pierre (2004) 'The Administration of Canada's Independent, Non-Partisan Approach', *Election Law Journal* 3: 406–11.

Morlok, Martin and Thilo Streit (2005) 'The German System of Political Finances', in Grant Tom (ed.) *Foreign Corrupt Practices Worldwide: Navigating the Laws, Regulations and Practices of National Regimes*, pp. 123–40. New York: Oceana.

Nassmacher, Karl-Heinz (2003a) 'The Funding of Political Parties in the Anglo- Saxon Orbit', in Reginald Austin and Maja Tjernstrom (eds.) *On Funding of Parties and Election Campaigns Handbook*, pp. 33–52. Stockholm: IDEA.

Nassmacher, Karl-Heinz (2003b) 'Monitoring, Control and Enforcement of Political Finance Regulation', in Reginald Austin and Maja Tjernstrom (eds.) *On Funding of Parties and Election Campaigns Handbook*, pp. 139–56. Stockholm: IDEA.

Pildes, Richard (2004) 'The Constitutionalization of Democratic Politics', *Harvard Law Review* 118: 28–154.

Pinto-Duschinsky, Michael (2002) 'Financing Politics: A Global View', *Journal of Democracy* 13: 69–85.

Potter, Trevor and Paul Ryan (2005) 'United States Political System and Campaign Finance', in Tom Grant (ed.) *Foreign Corrupt Practices Worldwide: Navigating the Laws, Regulations and Practices of National Regimes*, pp. 557–93. New York: Oceana.

Rahat, Gideon and Neta Sher-Hadar (1999) *Intraparty Selection of Candidates for the Knesset List and for Prime-Ministerial Candidacy 1995–1997*. Jerusalem: Israel Democracy Institute [Hebrew].

Rahat, Gideon and Reuven Y. Hazan (2001) 'Candidate Selection Methods: An Analytical Framework', *Party Politics* 7: 297–322.

Scarrow, Susan, Paul Webb and David Farrell (2000) 'From Social Integration to Electoral Contestation: The Changing Distribution of Power within Political Parties', in R. Dalton and M. Wattenberg (eds.) *Parties Without Partisans: Political Change in Advanced Industrial Democracies*, pp. 129–55. Oxford: Oxford University Press.

Simon, Donald J. (2004) 'Current Regulation and Future Challenges for Campaign Financing in the United States', *Election Law Journal* 3: 474–87.

Smilov, Daniel and Jurij Toplak (eds) (2007) *Political Finance and Corruption in Eastern Europe*. Aldershot: Ashgate.

Stephenson, Donald Grier (2004) *The Right to Vote: Rights and Liberties Under the Law*. Santa Barbara, CA: ABC-CLIO, Inc.

Thompson, Dennis (2002) *Just Elections: Creating Fair Electoral Process in the United States*. Chicago, IL: University of Chicago Press.

van Biezen, Ingrid (2004) 'Political Parties as Public Utilities', *Party Politics* 10: 701–22.

van Biezen, Ingrid and Petr Kopecky (2007) 'The State and the Parties', *Party Politics* 13: 235–54.

Walecki, Marcin (2007) 'The Europeanization of Political Parties—Influencing the Regulations on Political Finance'. Paper presented at the Annual Meeting of the Law and Society Association, Humbolt University, Berlin, Germany.

Weiss, Shevach (1977) *The Knesset*. Tel Aviv: Achiasaf Publishing House [Hebrew].

Young, Lisa (2004) 'Regulating Campaign Finances in Canada: Strengths and Weaknesses', *Election Law Journal* 3: 444–62.

*Menachem Hofnung is an associate professor in the Department of Political Science at the Hebrew University of Jerusalem. He is chair of the IPSA Research Committee on Political Finance and Political Corruption.

Hofnung, Menachem. "Unaccounted Competition: The Finance of Intra-Party Elections." *Party Politics* 14 (6): 726–744, copyright © 2008, SAGE Publications.

DISCUSSION QUESTIONS

1. Hofnung draws a contrast between the regulation of candidate selection in single-member district systems (such as the United States) and the regulation of candidate selection in proportional representation systems. Should there by different types of campaign finance laws governing candidate selection in the two types of systems?

2. Hofnung attributes some of Israel's difficulties in regulating candidate selection to the speed with which the new regulations were written. Does this indicate that nations should exercise more caution than did Israel in writing campaign finance laws?

3. Hofnung distinguishes between the conception of parties as private associations and the more contemporary view of parties as public utilities. Is there still a compelling argument for viewing parties as private associations?

4. Does regulating money spent in the candidate selection phase penalize "outsider" candidates or parties?

Democracy, Parties, and Political Finance in Latin America[†]

by Eduardo Posada-Carbó*

On its 25th anniversary, the influential Spanish newspaper El País convened a forum of prominent intellectuals on the prospects for Latin American democracies in the new millennium. The Mexican novelist Carlos Fuentes gave a gloomy view of the future: Latin American democracy, he noted, was in "danger." The colonial legacy still weighed heavily on the region, as a "painful warning" of possible things to come. In addition to the Spanish past, Fuentes referred to the processes of state reform in the last decades, to the rise of civil society, and to the internationalization of the economy. Absent from his reflections on democracy were the political parties. There was no mention of electoral campaigns, nor were there any references to threats against political and civil liberties. Fuentes's analysis focused on the persistence of injustice and poverty in the region. If democratic institutions do not deliver prompt economic and social results, he concluded, Latin Americans run the risk of returning to their oldest and most rooted tradition: authoritarianism.[1]

Fuentes's predictions have not materialized, nor do they seem likely to do so, but the path of democracy in many Latin American countries remains crisis prone. My interest in Fuentes's reflections, however, is to illustrate the notion of democracy that still prevails in Latin America among significant sectors of public intellectuals[2]—a view that defines democracy as a system to deliver welfare to the majority, rather than a set of rules to form governments. It also serves as an introduction to one of the arguments that I would like to pursue here: In the face of a definition of democracy that prefers substantive over procedural issues, the debate among public-opinion makers on the financing of political parties takes second stage. And without the pressure from public opinion, the prospects for effective reform may be doomed.

Democracy in Latin America has attracted a great deal of scholarly attention, particularly since the early 1980s, as democratic regimes were reestablished in most countries suffering from military dictatorship in previous decades. But academic attention was initially centered above all on issues of democratic "transition" and "consolidation."[3] At present the focus has shifted to debates over the democratic processes and institutions themselves. Interest in the study of what for a long while were largely neglected topics, such as the organization of parties, electoral campaigns, voter alignments, the reshaping of party systems, judicial reforms, or the workings of Congress, is growing, though there is still a vast field to be explored.[4]

The revival of democracy throughout the region also initially encouraged a revaluation of the previously maligned notion of "formal democracy." However, minimalist, procedural definitions of democracy—closely linked to representative institutions—have long faced strong resistance from currents of thought favoring an ideal type of democracy that is predicated on the achievements of substantial social equality. Representative democracy in the region has been further challenged by demands for participation, in a context where social movements and civil society are favored over political parties and electors. In such a context, I will argue, the debate on the financing of political parties and electoral campaigns is not seen as a high-priority topic.

This does not mean that the subject of party funding has been ignored. Indeed, corruption has been a major preoccupation in most Latin American countries since the reemergence of democracy during the last two decades. It has been the concern with corruption, and its impact on democratic legitimacy, that has motivated most recent studies of political finance. Throughout the industrial world, the "third wave" of democratization has been accompanied by a growing attention to political finance and to the corrupting influence of money in democratic politics and to the question of fair electoral competition.[5] As outlined by J. Mark Mayne and Juan Cruz Perusia, the major concerns behind this new interest, and indeed the motivations for reforming political financing, have tended to be "promoting . . . equality in electoral competition; lowering financial barriers for individuals to run for political office; reducing the extent to which politicians' policy decisions are oriented toward appeasing their financial backers . . . and lowering the risk that dirty or illicit money will corrupt the system and undermine the rule of law."[6]

This effort has been fruitful in providing us with a comprehensive picture of the different legal frameworks and some of the major features of the funding of political parties and electoral campaigns in Latin America.[7] It has also shed some light on many of the funding challenges encountered in the recent processes of democratization—such as the risks of corruption and the needs for transparency.[8] And it has been useful in identifying a research agenda that merits further development, including the vexing and difficult questions of how much elections really cost and where exactly the money is coming from.[9]

What has been generally ignored in the discussion, however, is the impact that any political finance regime has on the nature and organization of political parties and their respective party systems.[10] The state of parties and party systems does not seem to figure high among the objectives of political financing reform outlined above by Mayne and Perusia. There is a need for reconsideration, particularly in the face of an overall trend in Latin America that seems to support an expanded role for public subsidies in the financing of parties and electoral campaigns.

This essay tries therefore to link the topic of political finance to the wider question of democracy and political parties in Latin America. By doing so, it aims at providing a conceptual framework within which the subject of political finance could acquire a centrality hitherto missing in both the academic literature and current debates. The next section examines the extent to which, in spite of renewed democratic developments in Latin America during the last two decades, dominant views of democracy in the region continue to neglect and even undermine the significance of political parties and elections in the workings of democracy. This is followed by a discussion of how prevalent concepts of democracy can impinge on the course of political reform. In the last section, I discuss how public funding—a trend visible in most Latin American countries, apparently adopted to fight corruption and to guarantee equality—may be affecting political parties and party systems in the region.

A central, underlying assumption of this essay is that ideas are paramount in shaping the course of policymaking, thus conditioning any process of political reform.[11] Perhaps no other concept is so significant to modern politics as that of "democracy," and it is precisely here where our inquiry should start.

THE SHORTCOMINGS OF "DEMOCRACY" IN LATIN AMERICA

The idea of "democracy" has been the focus of a long-standing and rich debate.[12] It is important to look at the dominant notions of democracy in Latin America, and the extent to which such notions might determine not just the level of public interest in political finance but the very prospects of reforming the existing state of affairs. This is not an easy task, as any examination of the subject could be held on at least three levels, taking into account the views of academics and public intellectuals, of legislators and policymakers, and of the public at large. Of course they are all closely interrelated in a democratic environment, where public opinion is a key component to the decision-making process. This section offers a brief outline of what I consider to be the major historical trends in the understanding of democracy in Latin America, trends that have often been echoed by scholars outside the region.

Following the recent wave of democratization, there was a perception that democracy defined in procedural rather than substantive terms was finally prevailing in Latin America. In the early 1990s, Scott Mainwaring observed that there was an increased intellectual commitment to democracy and a "notable shift" in how the concept was being employed by social scientists. The derogatory expressions "formal" and "bourgeois democracy" were abandoned; so was the insistence "that political systems with marked social and economic inequalities were not truly democratic." "To a considerable extent," Mainwaring concluded, "[Joseph] Schumpeter's definition . . . focusing on electoral competition among political elites and parties, has prevailed."[13]

It is true that after initial enthusiasm about the rediscovery of political liberties in the countries where the military ruled, many of the values of liberal democracy regained currency. There were, however, some paradoxical cases. In Colombia—one of the few countries that did not go through the harsh experience of dictatorship—a democratic regime persevered in spite of the dominant view among opinion makers that democracy was merely "formal," devoid of any real contents—a feeling that has persisted to this day. Furthermore, antiliberal and illiberal notions of democracy soon resurfaced elsewhere, accompanied by associated ideas that tend to undermine the primacy of representation.[14]

In the mid-1990s, the form adopted by some Latin American democracies prompted Guillermo O'Donnell to label them "delegative democracies"—a term that since then has become familiar in the literature.[15] The regimes in Argentina, Peru, Ecuador, or Bolivia were "democracies" in Robert Dahl's sense, but they did "not seem to be on the path toward becoming representative democracies." The "plebiscitary tendencies" of such regimes "were detectable . . . long before the . . . social and economic crisis" that had erupted at the time. O'Donnell noted that delegative democracies are "not alien to the democratic tradition," but they are "less liberal than representative democracy." And even if they belong to the democratic family, they "could hardly be less congenial to the building and strengthening of democratic political institutions."[16]

"What kind of democracy is emerging in Latin America?" Laurence Whitehead had asked in a similar skeptical note regarding the future of liberal democracy, as new forms of "plebiscitary" and "populist" democracy became visible.[17] According to Whitehead, no other term was more evocative in referring to the emerging situation in some countries than that of "*Cesarismo Democrático*," coined by Laureano Vallenilla Lanz in his classical study on the "sociological bases of the effective constitution of Venezuela," published in 1919. Vallenilla

Lanz's *Cesarismo Democrático* was a defense of a political system without media-tors between the ruler and the people. The "Democratic Cesar" was the uncon-scious expression of the will of the majority, supposedly the manifestation of social equality under a leader.[18] In his view, it was absurd to pretend that written constitutions or any form of impersonal laws were the rule: The personal power of the caudillos was the true, effective constitution of South America, as the caudillos embodied the people and, as such, were able to bring order into anar-chy. Stability, economic prosperity, and social order had only been possible in these countries when the popular masses were themselves involved, through the caudillos, in the management of public affairs.[19]

Vallenilla Lanz's antiliberal stand took place in Venezuela, a country under authoritarian rule. But elsewhere in Latin America, where liberal democracy had sometimes made significant inroads since the mid-19th century, the con-cept of democracy was also challenged and redefined during the first decades of the 20th century. Socioeconomic concerns gradually replaced the priority of liberal constitutional issues in the political debate, a trend that became even more prominent after the 1930s. Some influential political thinkers, like the Colombian Alberto Lleras Camargo, continued to favor a definition of democ-racy where elections, parties, Congress, and political liberties were paramount. His position increasingly was that of a minority, in the face of other compet-ing ideologies. Meanwhile, the rise of populism in countries such as Argentina and Brazil opened the way for a dominant discourse that conditioned political liberties to the achievements of "economic democracy."[20] This view was further reinforced by the ideological influences of the 1959 Cuban revolution.

The idea that political liberties—and therefore representative democracy—were meaningless without deep socioeconomic changes was echoed somewhat by a significant number of Latin America scholars abroad. Whenever they looked at democratic developments, more often than not they concentrated their attention on the shortcomings of "social democracy" in the region. In 1942, Kingsley Davis acknowledged that since the early adoption of representa-tive government after independence from Spain, political democracy had not been merely an "empty form" in Latin America.[21] But in his view the key prob-lem was the lack of social democracy, without which political democracy could not develop.[22] In fact, some social indicators seemed to have improved during the following decade. In Russell H. Fitzgibbon's view, there was accordingly ground for optimism. This was a conclusion that hardly fit with the observa-tion that other indicators in the political realm, "civilian supremacy over the military, freedom of party organization, the state of local government, and the nature of elections were thought to be in a bad way indeed."[23] In a later piece,

R. Fitzgibbon and K. H. Johnson noted that prevalent definitions of democracy in countries such as Great Britain, Switzerland, and the United States would not be generally accepted in Latin America: While the former countries were inclined "to regard the problem as one of political democracy . . . the approach in much of Latin America is likely instead to emphasize social democracy."[24]

Regardless of the definition, the "second democratic wave" in Latin America came to a halt. By the early 1980s, civilian regimes prevailed in only four countries—Colombia, Costa Rica, Venezuela, and Mexico—although the latter's democratic credentials, under firm one-party rule, were highly questionable. Latin America, John A. Peeler observed, was "not very hospitable to liberal democracy."[25] Peeler did recognize that it was "too easy simply to dismiss" those liberal institutions that the countries of Latin America had adopted since the early 19th century. However, he still considered democracy in Latin America to be an "anomaly." Peeler did not go as far as those like Howard Wiarda, who suggested that the very concept of democracy was probably out of place in Latin America: Here "the use of the 'democratic' label" implied, in Wiarda's view, "not just political and economic imperialism but cultural imperialism as well."[26] Nonetheless, in the end Peeler favored a reconceptualization of democracy supposedly more congruent with "Iberian traditions": a "developmental and participatory democracy," a "way of life . . . emphatically more democratic than liberal democracy."[27]

This brief historical survey shows why the initial enthusiasm with the rediscovery of representative democracy in the late 1980s was followed so soon by intellectual disenchantment. The bias against liberal democracy in Latin America has a long-rooted tradition—both within and outside the region. What the fall of the Berlin Wall meant for Latin America was perhaps the end of revolutionary illusions, although some guerrilla movements survived. It is also true that among those considered to be on the "left" of the political spectrum, there is today a better appreciation of the values of representative democracy, as acknowledged by Jorge Castañeda in his much-acclaimed *Utopia Unarmed*.[28] However, as Castañeda's account makes clear, there is still a reluctance to accept that liberal democracy in Latin America had been meaningful in the past. Furthermore, in his agenda for "democratizing democracy" there is an implicit notion of democracy that goes beyond a procedural definition.[29] And although Castañeda's *Utopia Unarmed* values the role of parties and other elements of representation, his overall emphasis is in the direction of participatory democracy.

Latin America's recent experience with democracy has been subject to a renewed criticism. Both intellectuals and political scientists are again questioning the quality of democracy along the lines of traditional arguments that aimed at distinguishing "formal" from "substantive" democracy, or "political" from "social" democracy.[30] When the bells are rung to call our attention to the threats faced by Latin American democracies today, the clamor is above all about the shortcomings of their social welfare programs and excessive income disparities. Moderate voices are heard.[31] However, radical voices dismissive of liberal democracy have also appeared, raising the familiar complaint that "democracy is fundamentally flawed unless it involves major socioeconomic change," while suggesting an alternative "model," based on participatory democracy, social movements, and "a holistic approach towards democracy."[32]

Of course the debate is far from being simple. Any attempt at generalizing ought to acknowledge significant national variations. Yet is it possible to discern certain trends in the current discussion. Consider, for example, some of the propositions of the recent United Nations Development Program report *Democracy in Latin America* (2004). This report accepts a definition of democracy where politics have a central place. It notes that "the crisis surrounding political parties is one of the greatest threats to democracy in the region." And it warns of the possible effects that "mechanisms of direct democracy"—which are increasingly popular—might have in undermining "the institutions of the political system." However, the concept of democracy embraced by the report is not limited to its procedural dimensions. It explicitly reiterates that its notion "includes, but goes beyond the electoral process," thus concluding that "we must move from electoral democracy to a democracy of citizens"—their full development "necessitating the complete exercise of political, civil, and social rights."[33] In the agenda proposed by the United Nations Development Program report, the reform of the political parties is a condition of the higher goal of moving "closer to a participatory democracy, in which civil society organizations can expand their involvement in the democratic process."[34]

While the tone of the U.N. report is one of compromise, the discourse from radical actors is often openly confrontational. When he signed the Organization of American States "democratic clause," President Hugo Chávez of Venezuela raised his hand and said, "We sign this but we have to reserve our vote from representative democracy: we believe in participatory democracy."[35] In Bolivia, as René Antonio Mayorga points out, representative democracy is facing hostile indigenous movements that "seek to destroy democratic institutions and replace them with utopian, ethnic-based, direct democracy and nationalist populism."[36]

Let me clarify my argument. I am not denying the significance that a participatory civil society may have for the quality of democracy. And of course any democracy gains in strength if it is capable of delivering public goods to satisfy citizens' demands. But what modern democracy has offered above all is an arrangement—a set of institutions and procedural rules—through which problems such as poverty can be addressed, and an environment of freedom in which civil organizations can proliferate, stimulating the participation of citizens in collective affairs.[37] The basic instruments of liberal democracies have been political parties and elections, which are decried as insufficient by advocates of alternative models of democracy. As Miriam Kornblith has observed regarding Venezuela, "The so-called participatory democracy enshrined in the 1999 constitution devalues representative democracy, [and] dilutes the prominence of parties as articulators of collective will."[38] By undermining such normal channels of interest aggregation in a democracy, the result is, in the end, a lower quality of democracy.

Parties and elections did not grow naturally in Western societies.[39] They historically underwent a sort of rite of passage, while proving to be indispensable in modern democracies. This requires, as Seymour Martin Lipset has noted, "the creation of a supportive culture that fosters the acceptance" of all the rules and procedures that have made them work toward an effective and stable democratic order. It also requires "an almost permanent base of support among a significant segment of the population."[40]

It is here—in the weakness of parties and party systems—where the shortcomings of Latin America democracy—exceptions like Chile (and surprisingly Mexico) aside—seem to lie. Indeed, it is here where some of the more severe recent crises of democracy in the region have clearly manifested: in countries such as Venezuela and Colombia, with relatively strong party systems in the past, or in Ecuador and Peru, whose parties have been traditionally weak.[41] And it is here—in the discussion of parties and their basic function in any democracy—where the debate on the financing of politics should take place.

Far from being abstract, notions of democracy do impinge on the way societies value the role of parties. They are particularly relevant to the whole question of political reform, in as much as they can condition the direction of public pressure, and therefore the behavior of governments and legislators. A climate of opinion under which substantive over procedural notions of democracy prevail may be less prone to accept the urgent need to count on strong parties. Debating parties and their organizations may not be considered a priority in the face of other issues, such as unemployment, health care, or education. Moreover, a public mood favorable to participatory democracy is usually accompanied by indifference or open hostility to parties. In such a context, the prospects for party reform are either left in the hands of politicians (generally unwilling to reform themselves), or the reform movement take turns that are detrimental to party structures.

It is not easy to establish with precision how and the extent to which dominant notions of democracy influence decisions regarding political parties and their organizations—including their financial regimes. However, a brief look at the recent Colombian experience serves to illustrate some of the general points raised so far in this section.

"DEMOCRACY" AND POLITICAL REFORM: A COLOMBIAN EXCURSION

Ever since its reestablishment in 1958, Colombian democracy has been subject to severe criticism. The achievements of the National Front (1958–74)—in which elections were regularly held and political liberties generally prevailed in an area of the world that had largely succumbed to military rule—were simply dismissed. Colombian representative democracy underwent a process of delegitimation among intellectuals.[42] The usual pejorative labels of "formal" and "bourgeois" were often applied to a democracy that was increasingly under siege by drug cartels and guerrilla groups.

Condemnation of liberal democracy was common at the time in Latin America and elsewhere. However, according to Eduardo Pizarro Leongómez, while in the rest of the continent intellectuals had rediscovered the values of liberal democracy by the 1980s, in Colombia they remained long attached to their critical, pejorative views.[43] The language condemning liberal democracy persevered among Colombian intellectuals, politicians, and academics. Leading figures such as Carlos Gaviria—former president of the Constitutional Court, 2006 presidential candidate, and the leader of the Polo Democrático Alternativo (Alternative Democratic Pole)—have repeated the idea that "in Colombia . . . democracy as such does not exist. There cannot be political democracy where there is no social democracy." Former president Alfonso López Michelsen expressed similar views.[44] Academic analyses have also questioned the validity of representative democracy—as shown in a recent essay by Andrés Hernández Quiñones, who in his critique of the various models of liberal democracy raises doubts about the effectiveness of periodic elections to guarantee the public interest. For philosophers such as Oscar Mejía and Jacqueline Blanco, the challenge is to move from a "restrictive democracy" to a "participatory democracy," supposedly a "different" democracy from both the European and the North American paradigms.[45]

As liberal democracy was held in low esteem, alternative notions—participatory or direct democracy—gained currency. In such a context, antiparty feelings prevailed in an ongoing process of political reform whose impact on the party system is still uncertain. And when the issue of political finance attracted some public attention, it was motivated by reasons other than the need to strengthen political parties. After several frustrated attempts, the country finally moved ahead with substantial reforms in the mid-1980s with the introduction of popular elections for city mayors—and more significantly, with the adoption of a new constitution in 1991. The 1991 constitution introduced a set of new electoral rules, with the purpose of undermining an already fragile two-party system, and various mechanisms to promote direct democracy.[46] It also introduced state financing of electoral campaigns and the ordinary activities of parties and movements, with the aim of bringing a level playing field to electoral competition.

In 1994, a serious scandal erupted after accusations that drug cartel money had gone into the coffers of the Liberal presidential candidate. As a result, the country was immersed into a deep crisis, which encouraged a wide and open debate on the financing of politics and other political reforms.[47] At the time, however, the debate was in general highly personalized around the president's role in the financing of his campaign. A report produced by an independent Commission on Political Reform—which, among other items, suggested that presidential campaigns should be fully financed by the state—passed almost unnoticed by opinion makers, and its proposals did not get the backing of Congress.[48] As new presidential elections approached in 1998, in spite of the scandal and the debate that followed, the legal regime on the financing of politics remained untouched.

Shortly after the election of Andrés Pastrana, his government (1998–2002) introduced a comprehensive project of political reform to Congress.[49] The same week in October 1998 that the project was officially admitted for discussion in the Lower Chamber, a significant number of so-called independent congressmen (opposed to both Liberals and Conservatives) expressed their dissatisfaction with the proposals, arguing that the reform project did not tackle the country's fundamental issues, such as social justice or unemployment.[50] Two months later, the president of Congress himself—a close ally of fellow Conservative Pastrana—undermined the significance of the project by pointing out that what the country needed was an "integral reform of the state . . . and above all an extensive social and economic reform."[51] These dismissals in themselves do not explain the failure of the project, finally voted down by the Senate in 1999. But they do serve to illustrate the point: In the dominant discourse there was little interest in the reform of the electoral system and the organization of parties. The emphasis was on "structural," socioeconomic change.

Public enthusiasm seemed to have been raised after the government, in another attempt to pursue a political reform, proposed to put the project to a referendum. Although the project seemed aimed at modernizing representative institutions, the minister of the interior backed the initiative by stating that this was the way forward to consolidate "participatory democracy."[52] The debate among opinion makers centered on the "participatory" mechanism—the use of the plebiscite, and the conflict that ensued between the president and Congress when the plebiscite was proposed. In the referendum, hardly any systematic attention was given individually to any of the project's 18 proposals—including major reforms to the electoral system and again full public funding of presidential campaigns.

In the face of mounting opposition from Congress that threatened to destabilize the regime, the president withdrew the proposal for the referendum. Yet a third initiative to go ahead with the reform project emerged, this time from a group of members of Congress itself. And this time the climate of opinion was even more indifferent and cynical about the issues at stake. "No one gives a damn" about the project, observed an influential columnist in the leading Colombian newspaper,[53] while others suggested that such a discussion only concerned the interests of politicians. Two former finance ministers also expressed the view that the discussion of a political reform should not be a priority in the face of an economic crisis and other social problems.[54] Surprisingly, the project made it through various hearings in Congress, but once again was voted down by the Senate.

The election of President Álvaro Uribe in 2002 has arguably been the most serious challenge the Colombian party system has faced since the mid-20th century. His unprecedented election (as a dissident Liberal candidate and with no competing presidential candidate from the Conservative party), followed by his reelection in 2006, may prove to be the final blow to the dominance of the two traditional parties.[55] Since his first election, the distance between the Liberal party and Uribe's government widened, although a significant number of Liberal members of Congress and former ministers shifted their loyalties to the Uribe camp. The president was at first reluctant to create a party of his own, though a political reform bill, passed somewhat unexpectedly by Congress in 2003, forced some of his political supporters to realign around various new parties, whose fates are in any case still uncertain.

Uribe's preference, from the start, was to call for a referendum that, similar to Pastrana's project, included a long list of questions on a wide array of topics. As in the previous debate, public discussion centered on the use of the referendum and its plebiscitary nature. One of the few questions that was hotly discussed was the proposal to introduce participatory mechanisms to approve the budget. Uribe's style of government tended to favor instruments associated with direct democracy, such as the regular practice of *Consejos Comunales de Gobierno*— town hall meetings where local authorities, the president himself, and members of his Cabinet discuss the government agenda with the local population.[56] To be sure, President Uribe's position toward representative democracy and political parties was not hostile. It can be best described as ambivalent, while his discourse tended to emphasize the benefits of participatory and direct democracy. Nonetheless, given his sympathies with participatory and direct forms of democracy, his critics label him "neopopulist."[57]

This brief account can hardly do justice to the complexities of the Colombian situation. Political parties have not disappeared. In the past few years, representative democracy has regained strong advocates.[58] Indeed, a growing concern with the fate of parties was behind the reform approved by Congress in 2003—though it is still too early to judge its final results. This section shows how during the last few decades the erosion of a formerly institutionalized party system went hand in hand with the intellectual depreciation and even abandonment of representative democracy.[59] As alternative models of democracy gained currency, political parties—and the very notion of party—were to some extent neglected as central democratic actors.[60] Perhaps this can explain the paradox posed by Bejarano and Pizarro Leongómez: that "efforts to strengthen democracy" in Colombia might have contributed "to its erosion rather than its consolidation."[61]

This relative lack of public interest in parties did not mean ignoring altogether the problem of political finance, but what motivated any interest in party finances were concerns with corruption and political equality rather than the need to put parties on a firmer footing. Amid the general indifference or even hostility of public opinion toward political parties, the idea that the state should generously provide for the financing of electoral campaigns gained favor among legislators. This was also the case elsewhere in Latin America. But what are the implications of public funding for the nature of political parties? Will public funding help to strengthen the parties, or will public funding encourage a divorce between parties and their respective societies? And how in general do political funding regimes relate to party organization?

THE LATIN AMERICAN TREND TOWARD STATE FUNDING

The adoption of state funding for political parties and electoral campaigns has been a general movement in Latin America, following a growing preoccupation with problems of political finance. In this last section, I look at the major motivations behind this trend. Rather than arguing for or against public funding, my interest is to ask questions and suggest ways to approach political finance issues, whose relevance should be seen in conjunction with that of parties and party systems in representative democracies.

Corruption scandals related to the role of money in politics have been at the center of public debate and new legislation across Latin America. Scandals in Colombia, Brazil, and Venezuela involved their respective heads of state—and in the latter two countries led to their impeachment and resignation. In Bolivia, accusations in 1994 that money from drug cartels had financed the 1987–89 electoral campaigns of one of the major parties involved a former president of the country.[62] Indeed, the fear that funds from the illegal narcotics trade would infiltrate the political system has been a focus of particular attention throughout the region.[63]

Public concern with corruption naturally went hand in hand with the process of democratization, as political and civil liberties made possible the open discussion of political affairs.[64] The reemergence of democracy brought to the fore the problem of electoral costs. In addition to the traditional spending, the reliance on political consultants, opinion polls, and the mass media have all added to what is perceived as ever-expanding campaign costs. Electoral costs also seem to have been fueled by a series of electoral reforms aimed at deepening democracy.[65] A significant number of countries have adopted the double ballot to elect presidents. Popular elections of city mayors and provincial governors are now the rule, and these local elections often take place on different dates than national elections. Plebiscites, referendums, and "consultas populares" (popular consultations) are becoming relatively frequent events.[66] Primary elections to select party candidates are now stipulated by law in nine countries, while they are held at least on occasion in five others.[67]

However, the real cost of electioneering in Latin America is still largely unknown. Fernando Collor de Mello's campaign for the presidency in Brazil in 1989 seems to have cost as much as Bill Clinton's in the United States in 1992—some US$120 million, a high figure in contrast with the estimated cost of President Luiz Inácio Lula da Silva's reelection campaign more than a decade later, US$42.4 million.[68] The 1994 presidential election in Colombia was not that expensive, but the estimated sum of US$32 million,[69] probably spent by all candidates, represented a substantial increase over the cost of previous campaigns. In January–October 1999, the three major presidential candidates in Argentina together spent some US$91 million just on campaign advertisements.[70] According to Daniel Zovatto, campaign cost for the 2000 presidential election in Mexico amounted to US$234 million. Kevin Casas Zamora has estimated that the total cost of all Uruguayan elections from 1999 to 2000 was close to US$40 million.[71] As these are all presidential systems, attention has been mostly centered on presidential campaigns. The problem of electoral costs would appear sometimes to be even more serious in local and congressional elections. In the Brazilian state of São Paulo, it has been estimated that "candidates for the Chamber of Deputies spent US$200,000 to $5 million on campaigns in 1990 and candidates for the Senate spent $10 million."[72] Thus, throughout the continent, the perception certainly exists that elections are becoming extraordinarily expensive. Closely related to the issue of cost is the lack of knowledge as to where the money is coming from. In some countries, such as Colombia, scandals related to campaign financing have resulted in revelations about the identity of major donors, and in further pressures from citizens' organizations for transparency in the managing of political financing. The 1994 scandal revealed significant funding from illegal-drug traffickers. But the publication of the names of contributors to the various presidential campaigns in 1998 confirmed what was already known: that a few big donors—including the major financial and industrial groups and companies with state contracts—were responsible for a large proportion of the electoral costs. Nevertheless, "opacity" is still the term commonly used to refer to the state of affairs in countries such as Chile, or Venezuela—where it was estimated that 76 percent of the funds for the 1993 elections came from unknown sources.[73]

In an atmosphere of perceived increasing campaign costs, fears of the corrupting influence of big donors, from both legal and illegal sources, have been the major driving force behind a wave of new regulations related to the financing of political parties and elections. These have been accompanied by a concern for guaranteeing fairness in the process of electoral competition.[74]

The pace and subject matter of the regulatory movement of course varies from country to country, and the new regulatory frameworks are often wide-ranging—including norms about disclosure, electoral authorities, access to the media, limits to expenditures and private donations, and public subsidies. What concerns us here is the impact that these regulations—the granting of state funds in particular—might have on the nature and organization of political parties and party systems in the region.

The public funding of parties is not a complete novelty in Latin America.

Indeed, some countries took an early lead on this front: Uruguay in 1928, Costa Rica in 1954, and Argentina in 1955—all preceding Western European nations, the earliest of which, West Germany, introduced public subsidies in 1959.[75] But while most Latin American countries had to wait for further movement, the trend continued elsewhere.

The introduction of subsidies in Western Europe, however, has not always produced the intended results. The subsidies were expected to combat corruption, control the power of lobbying, reduce expenditures, and encourage a level of equality in party competition.[76] Only the latter has probably occurred with some degree of success. As the experiences of Italy, Spain, France, and Germany clearly show, state generosity in the financing of politics is not a deterrent to corruption. State generosity has not deflated electoral costs; it might have helped to whet the appetite of politicians for more money.[77] And state generosity toward parties has had the unintended consequence of widening the gap between parties and electors. Parties need money, true, but they also need partisans.[78] The failures of generous public subsidies to political parties have encouraged a move in a different direction, to limit the levels of state support, although legislators have proved resilient to change.[79]

While some European countries, in the light of their experiences, reconsider the role of public subsidies in the financing of politics,[80] in Latin America the general trend seems to go in the opposite direction. There are of course significant variations. The system in Chile is clearly based on private funding (though there is public access to TV for candidates), in contrast to the one in Mexico, where 90 percent of political funding must come from the state. In Colombia, most of the attempts to reform the system since 1994 have included proposals for full state financial support for presidential elections. In 1997, the Argentine government presented a project in Congress banning private contributions to parties. Direct state support for the financing of politics is now accepted by 16 Latin American countries.[81] Up to 1997, the Dominican Republic was the only country whose laws did not allow the state to fund party activities and electoral campaigns.[82]

It is perhaps too early to judge the Latin American experience with public financing of politics. This should be done country by country, and it cannot be simply assumed that the effects that state funds have had in other Western democracies will be replicated elsewhere. However, rather than inviting a debate on the merits of public funding, what I am suggesting here is to reconsider the way we think about political funding regimes. The dominant trend in Latin America has been to devise regulatory systems aimed at combating corruption, controlling the power of big donors, and leveling the playing field. These aims should not be abandoned. But there is a need to discuss more systematically the subject in terms of the political parties. This is particularly relevant in some Latin American countries where democratic stability may be at risk as political parties fail to consolidate themselves as institutions with strong roots in society.

A regime of political financing is neither the only nor the most important variable in explaining the nature and organization of parties. However, in conjunction with other variables, political financing arrangements could weaken or strengthen party organizations, affect the way they operate, and therefore affect the way they relate to the political system as a whole. Consider, for example, the case of Brazil and its weakly institutionalized party system. There are surely historical and structural factors that help to explain the decentralized nature of Brazilian parties, and their generally weak social roots.[83] However, individual campaign financing in Brazil serves to perpetuate weak party organizations. Brazilian parties do not provide funds for electioneering: "the money spent by candidates is raised by the candidates."[84] That individuals and not parties are the major actors in the process of political financing is to some extent the reflection of a system that has developed around candidates and not parties. As David Samuels concluded, "Brazil's campaign finance law exacerbates the individualistic, personalistic, and antiparty tendencies in its electoral system by providing candidates with strong incentives to raise and spend money independently of their party's dictates and by restricting parties' ability to influence the sources and flow of funds."[85]

In contrast, changes in the financial regulations of electoral campaigns—channeling fundraising activities through a party central office, for example—might lead to a stronger role for the parties. The financial regulation of parties accompanied by ill-designed electoral and political reforms can have serious effects on parties and party systems.

Conclusion

The ultimate aim of this essay has been to provide a conceptual framework within which issues of political finance in Latin America might gain some salience. Hitherto, the relatively scarce attention paid to this topic has been largely caused by preoccupations with corruption and political equality. Without neglecting these valid concerns, I have suggested that there is a need to rethink the subject in terms of the role of political parties. And a reconsideration of the role of parties may imply a revision of deep-rooted notions of democracy in the region.

My point of departure, therefore, was a reexamination of the ways in which democracy has historically been defined in Latin America, where leading intellectuals and prominent politicians have very often favored plebiscitary over representative forms of government. Their views have had significant resonance in the academic debate abroad. Although procedural concepts of democracy did gain some acceptance beginning in the 1980s, they were soon challenged by calls for participatory and direct democracy, which undermine the role of parties and show little appreciation for the centrality of electoral processes. The drive for direct democracy, with its accompanying antipolitics stand, has been a worldwide phenomenon.[86] Yet its impact has probably been stronger in a region such as Latin America, where the very notion of representative democracy has in the past met and still meets with so much resistance. Thus a proper reevaluation of representative democracy is necessary in order to appreciate the centrality of parties and electoral processes. Only by appreciating their central role in democracies can we accept the subsequent key significance of the issues of party and campaign funding.

The implications here are twofold. Firstly, in societies where substantive concepts of democracy prevail over procedural concepts, concerns about the rules of representation—including political finance regimes—either take second stage or are ignored in the public opinion debate, thus diminishing the possibilities of effective political reform. Secondly, if parties are not considered central democratic actors, their fate may be ignored when adopting any political financing regime. Let me briefly touch upon both implications.

The extent to which "ideas" influence policy choices has long been a focus of inquiry in the field of historical institutionalism. Margaret Weir, for example, has suggested that "the influence of ideas on politics is strongest when programmatic ideas, tied to administrative means, are joined with a public philosophy" (or "broad concepts that are tied to values and moral principles").[87] I intended this paper's "Colombian excursion" to show how successive attempts at political reform in Colombia were conditioned by the overarching concept of participatory democracy. The evidence illustrates how the dominant, substantive notion of democracy in Colombia discouraged public interest in piecemeal reform with regard to party politics. And when concerns were raised about problems of political finance, they were mostly motivated by corruption scandals rather than by interest in modernizing political parties.

In the area of political finance, a visible trend in Latin America has been the adoption of state subsidies for political parties and electoral campaigns. My aim here has not been to question state funding regimes per se—I wish to raise awareness of the possible impact that any political finance regime has on parties and party systems. But parties and party systems do not seem to have been in the minds of most policymakers, whose regulatory measures have been rather a response to problems of corruption or to the need to level electoral competition. The variety of objectives is not irrelevant. As Michael Pinto-Duschinsky has noted, "a system that aims to control corruption in the funding of parties and election campaigns is likely to be different from a system that seeks mainly to promote 'fairness.'"[88] A different system should also be required if the aim is to strengthen the role of parties as major democratic protagonists.

The conceptual framework discussed here is above all crucial when considering the role of public opinion in any attempt at reforming democratic rules.[89] Without the pressure from public opinion, such rules either remain untouched by politicians or are changed in ways that are mostly beneficial to the politicians themselves. Back in 1896, discussing "money in practical politics," Professor J. W. Jenks warned that "no man [or woman] better understands the motives that guide men in daily life than the politician; and no man uses this knowledge to accomplish his own purposes with greater skill than he."[90] Any attempt to understand and reform the role of money in politics should bear this warning in mind.

Endnotes

†An original version of this paper was commissioned by the National Endowment for Democracy (NED) to be presented at a conference coorganized with the Sejung Institute on party finances in East Asia and held in Seoul, Korea, and later published in the Working Paper Series of the Kellogg Institute at Notre Dame University (No. 346, April 2008). I want to thank the NED, and Marc Plattner in particular, for authorizing its publication. This chapter is an edited version of the paper published by the Kellogg Institute. I wish to thank Robert Boatright for his encouragement and editorial advice.

1. Carlos Fuentes, "Democracia latinoamericana: anhelo, realidad y amenaza," *El País*, Madrid, May 15, 2001. I thank Carlos Malamud for calling my attention to this article; see his reply to Fuentes's article, "La democracia en América Latina: ¿una cuestión de votos o de botas?" and their further exchange of views in *El País*, July 1 and 18, 2001.

2. I borrow the term from Richard Posner, but while Posner restricts it mostly to academics, I use it in its broadest sense, to refer to those learned individuals who help to shape public opinion. See Posner, *Public Intellectuals: A Study of Decline* (Cambridge, MA, and London: Harvard University Press, 2003).

3. See Guillermo O'Donnell, Philippe C. Schmitter, and Laurence Whitehead, eds., *Transitions from Authoritarian Rule: Latin America* (Baltimore and London: Johns Hopkins University Press, 1986); J. Samuel Valenzuela, "Democratic Consolidation in Post-transitional Settings: Notion, Process and Facilitating Conditions," in Scott Mainwaring, Guillermo O'Donnell, and J. Samuel Valenzuela, eds., *Issues in Democratic Consolidation: The New South American Democracies in Comparative Perspectives* (Notre Dame, IN: University of Notre Dame Press, 1992); Juan Linz and Alfred Stepan, *Problems of Democratic Transition and Consolidation: Southern Europe, South America, and Post-Communist Europe* (Baltimore: Johns Hopkins

University Press, 1996). For a recent discussion see the special section "Debating the Transition Paradigm" in the *Journal of Democracy* 13:3, July 2002.

4. The relative neglect of some of these topics was noted by Scott Mainwaring, *Rethinking Party Systems in the Third Wave of Democratization: The Case of Brazil* (Stanford, CA: Stanford University Press, 1999), p. 137. For an assessment of the state of parties and party system by the mid-1990s, see Scott Mainwaring and Timothy R. Scully, eds., *Building Democratic Institutions: Party Systems in Latin America* (Stanford, CA: Stanford University Press, 1995).

5. See Robert Williams, ed., *Party Finance and Political Corruption* (Basingstoke: Palgrave Macmillan, 2000); Martin Rhodes, "Financing Party Politics in Italy: A Case of Systemic Corruption," *West European Politics* 20:1, 1997, pp. 67–97; Veronique Pujas and Martin Rhodes, "Party Finance and Political Scandal in Italy, Spain and France," *West European Politics* 22:3, 1999, pp. 41–63.

6. See J. Mark Payne and Juan Cruz Perusia, "Reforming the Rules of the Game: Political Reform," in Eduardo Lora, ed., *The State of State Reform in Latin America* (Palo Alto, CA, and Washington, DC: World Bank, 2007), p. 78.

7. See the volume edited by Pilar del Castillo and Daniel Zovatto, which includes 18 individual countries, *La financiación de la política en Iberoamérica* (San José, Costa Rica: IIDH-CAPEL, 1998); Steven Griner and Daniel Zovatto, eds., *Funding of Political Parties and Election Campaigns in the Americas* (San José, Costa Rica: DEA/OAS, 2005); and Carlos Malamud and Eduardo Posada-Carbó, eds., *The Financing of Politics: Latin American and European Perspectives* (London: Brookings Institution, 2005). See also Delia M. Ferreira Rubio, ed., *Financiamiento de partidos políticos* (Buenos Aires: Konrad Adenauer-Stiftung: CIEDLA, 1997); and *El financiamiento de las campañas electorales. Memoria* (Washington, DC, 1998). For a another recent general overview see Daniel Zovatto, "The Legal and Practical Characteristics of the Funding of Political Parties and Election Campaigns in Latin America," in Reginald Austin and Maja Tjernstrom, eds., *Funding of Political Parties and Election Campaigns* (Stockholm: International IDEA, 2003), pp. 95–116.

8. See, for example, the chapters by Maria D'Alva Kinzo on Brazil and Carlos Huneeus on Chile, in Peter Burnell and Alan Ware, eds., *Funding Democratization* (Manchester: Manchester University Press, 1998).

9. See Kevin Casas Zamora, "Paying for Democracy in Latin America: Political Finance and State Funding for Parties in Costa Rica and Uruguay" (unpublished DPhil dissertation, Oxford University, 2002), published under the title *Paying for Democracy: Political Finance and State Funding for Parties* by the European Consortium for Political Research (Colchester: ECPR, 2005). See also his "State Funding and Campaign Finance Practices in Uruguay," in Malamud and Posada-Carbó, eds., *Financing of Politics*, pp. 189–236; and David Samuels, "Money, Elections and Democracy in Brazil," *Latin American Politics and Society* 43:2, Summer 2001, pp. 27–48.

10. For a paper that has underlined the significance of an approach from the perspective of the parties, see Humberto de la Calle, "La perspectiva desde los partidos políticos," unpublished paper presented at the conference "Dinero y contienda político-electoral: retos para la democracia," Mexico City, June 6, 2001. Of course, the significance of political finances to parties is acknowledged by most scholars. See, for example, the observations made by Luis Alberto Cordero, "Sistemas electorales y financiamiento de partidos políticos," in *El financiamiento de las campañas electorales* (Washington, DC, 1998), p. 36; and Daniel Zovatto, "Una visión preliminar comparada" in del Castillo and Zovatto, eds., *La financiación de la política en Iberoamérica*, p. liii.

11. See Margaret Weir, "Ideas and the Politics of Bounded Innovation," in Sven Steinmo, Kathleen Thelen, and Frank Longstreth, eds., *Structuring Politics: Historical Institutionalism in Comparative Analysis* (Cambridge: Cambridge University Press, 1992), pp. 188–216.

12. See John Dunn, ed., *Democracy: The Unfinished Journey, 508 BC to AD 1993* (Oxford: Oxford University Press, 1994), and John Dunn, *Setting the People Free: The Story of Democracy*

(London: Atlantic, 2005). See also the various relevant papers in the collection edited by Larry Diamond and Marc F. Plattner, *The Global Resurgence of Democracy* (Baltimore and London: Johns Hopkins University Press, 1993). For other recent discussions, see Ian Shapiro, *The State of Democratic Theory* (Princeton, NJ, and Oxford: Princeton University Press, 2003), and Guillermo O'Donnell, "Democracy, Law and Comparative Politics," Institute of Development Studies, IDS Working Paper 118 (June 2000).

13. Scott Mainwaring, "Transitions to Democracy and Democratic Consolidation: Theoretical and Comparative Issues," in Mainwaring, O'Donnell, and Valenzuela, eds., *Issues in Democratic Consolidation*, pp. 294, 296–97, 326–27. See Joseph A. Schumpeter, *Capitalism, Socialism and Democracy* (London and New York: Routledge, 1992; first UK edition in 1943).

14. The notion of "illiberal democracy" was popularized by Fareed Zakaria, "The Rise of Illiberal Democracy," *Foreign Affairs*, November–December 1997, pp. 22–43. See also his book *The Future of Freedom: Illiberal Democracy at Home and Abroad* (New York and London: W. W. Norton, 2003).

15. Guillermo O'Donnell, "Delegative Democracy," *Journal of Democracy* 5:1, January 1994.

16. Ibid., pp. 56, 60, and 62.

17. Laurence Whitehead, "The Alternatives to 'Liberal Democracy': A Latin American Perspective," in D. Held, ed., *Prospects for Democracy: North, South, East, West* (Cambridge and Stanford, CA: Polity Press and Stanford University Press, 1993), p. 313.

18. L. Vallenilla Lanz, *Cesarismo democrático: Estudios sobre las bases sociológicas de la constitución efectiva de Venezuela* (Caracas: Empresa El Cojo, 1919), p. 303.

19. Ibid., p. 236. On Vallenilla Lanz see Elena Plaza, *La tragedia de una amarga convicción. Historia y política en el pensamiento de Laureano Vallenilla Lanz, 1870–1936* (Caracas: Universidad Central de Venezuela, 1996).

20. For a critical, contemporary view of the dictatorial character of these populist tendencies from a liberal democratic perspective see Germán Arciniegas, *The State of Latin America* (London: Cassell, 1953).

21. Kingsley Davis, "Political Ambivalence in Latin America," *Journal of Legal and Political Sociology* 1:1–2, 1942, pp. 127–50.

22. For another similar observation at that time, see Robin A. Humphreys, *The Evolution of Modern Latin America* (Oxford: Oxford University Press, 1946), pp. 91, 94.

23. Russell H. Fitzgibbon, "How Democratic Is Latin America?" *Inter-American Economic Affairs* 9:4, 1956, pp. 65–77.

24. R. Fitzgibbon and K. H. Johnson, "Measurement of Latin American Political Change," *The American Political Science Review* 55:3, September 1961, p. 516.

25. John A. Peeler, *Latin American Democracies: Colombia, Costa Rica, Venezuela* (Chapel Hill and London: University of North Carolina Press, 1985), p. 24.

26. Quoted in Peeler, *Latin American Democracies*, p. 134.

27. Ibid, pp. 164–67. For this concept, Peeler found inspiration in C. B. Macpherson, *The Life and Times of Liberal Democracy* (Oxford: Oxford University Press, 1977).

28. Jorge Castañeda, *Utopia Unarmed: The Latin American Left after the Cold War* (New York: Vintage, 1993), especially chapters 11 and 12. On the general changing attitudes among progressive intellectuals toward democracy in the region see Scott P. Mainwaring and Aníbal Pérez-Liñán, "Latin American Democratization since 1978: Democratic Transitions, Breakdowns, and Erosions," in Frances Hagopian and Scott P. Mainwaring, eds., *The Third Wave of Democratization: Advances and Setbacks* (Cambridge University Press, 2005), pp. 44–47.

29. A similar conclusion can be reached after examining the concepts used by the Chilean sociologist Manuel A. Garretón in his *Reconstruir la política. Transición y consolidación democrática en Chile* (Santiago: Andante, 1986), pp. 25–35.

30. Dieter Nohlen, "Introducción," in Nohlen, ed., *Democracia y neocrítica en América Latina* (Madrid: Iberoamericana, 1995), p. 11. Of course this is not a homogeneous trend. For a forceful defense of a minimalist conception of democracy in Latin America see Valenzuela, "Democratic Consolidation on Post-Transitional Settings." A draft resolution presented to the General Assembly of the Organization of American States for an Inter-American Democratic Chart emphasized the notion of "representative democracy," although it also contained references to participation and developmental issues. See OAS, "Proyecto de resolución Carta Democrática Interamericana," June 3, 2001 (mimeo). I thank Michael Beaulieu for calling my attention to this document. For recent work that emphasizes "the possibilities of democratic or semi-democratic survival despite poor economic performance" see Hagopian and Mainwaring, eds., *Third Wave of Democratization*, "Introduction," p. 7.

31. See Abraham Lowenthal, "Latin America at the Century's Turn," *Journal of Democracy* 11:2, April 2000, p. 53; Patricio Aylwin, "Democracy in the Americas," *Journal of Democracy* 9:3, July 1998, pp. 4–6; and Fuentes, "Democracia latinoamericana." See also Kurt Weyland, "Latin America's Four Political Models," *Journal of Democracy* 6:4, October 1995, pp. 125–30. More recently, in attempting an answer for "what really went wrong" in Latin America, Peter Hakim stressed the deterioration of political parties and mediocre political leadership, among other factors, but concluded that the "greatest threat" for democracy in Latin America was the "inability of democratic governments to meet the most important needs and demands of their citizens." See his "Dispirited Politics," in *Journal of Democracy* 14:2, April 2003, p. 122.

32. See Geraldine Lievesley, *Democracy in Latin America: Mobilization, Power and the Search for New Politics* (Manchester and New York: Manchester University Press, 1999), p. 25. For recent critique of a "Latin American democratic tradition" that has "failed to build a democratic public sphere," which then offers an alternative democratic theory for the region based on the formation of "participatory publics," see Leonardo Avritzer, *Democracy and the Public Space in Latin America* (Princeton, NJ, and Oxford: Princeton University Press, 2002), especially chapters 3 and 7.

33. United Nations Development Program, "Ideas and Contributions: Democracy in Latin America: Towards a Citizens' Democracy" (New York and Bogotá: UNDP, 2004), pp. 27, 30, 68. In a forum to discuss the UNDP report organized by the Inter-American Dialogue in Washington, Carl Gershman suggested that the report risked undervaluing the importance of elections, while Arturo Valenzuela criticized the notion common in Latin America that democracy fails when it does not solve the problem of poverty. In response to these comments, the report directors noted that "delinking the discussion of democracy from social conditions invites a critique of democracy as 'merely formal,' a critique that has been gaining ground in Latin America and that the report sought to counter," in Inter-American Dialogue, *Scrutinizing Democracy in Latin America: A Discussion of the UNDP's Report on Democracy in Latin America* (Washington, June 2005), pp. 10–12. Available at http://www.thedialogue.org/page.cfm?pageID=32&pubID=1254.

34. UNDP, *Ideas and Contributions*, p. 69.

35. Hugo Chávez and Marta Harnecker, *Understanding the Venezuelan Revolution: Hugo Chávez Talks to Marta Harnecker* (New York: Monthly Review Press, 2005). Daniel H. Levine and Catalina Romero have observed that "the very word 'representative' barely appears in the Bolivarian constitution of 1999. Instead, Venezuelan democracy is 'and always will be democratic, participative, elective, decentralized, alternative, responsible, pluralist, and with revocable mandates.'" See Levine and Romero, "Urban Citizen Movement and Disempowerment in Peru and Venezuela," in Scott Mainwaring, Ana María Bejarano, and Eduardo Pizarro Leongómez, eds., *The Crisis of Democratic Representation in the Andes* (Stanford, CA: Stanford University Press, 2006), p. 251.

36. René Antonio Mayorga, "Outsiders and Neopopulism: The Road to Plebiscitary Democracy," in Mainwaring, Bejarano, and Pizarro, eds., *Crisis of Democratic Representation*, pp. 133 and 160.

37. See George Klosko, *Democratic Procedures and Liberal Consensus* (Oxford: Oxford University

Press, 2000). According to Klosko, "in modern liberal societies there is greater agreement on principles that deal with procedures than on matters of substance" (p. 231).

38. Miriam Kornblith, "Elections versus Democracy," *Journal of Democracy* 16:1, January 2005, p. 136.

39. See Richard Hofstadter, *The Idea of a Party System: The Rise of Legitimate Opposition in the United States, 1780–1840* (Berkeley, Los Angeles, and London: University of California Press, 1969). For a discussion on the problematic nature of parties see Marc F. Plattner, "The Trouble with Parties," *Public Interest*, Spring 2001.

40. Seymour Martin Lipset, "The Indispensability of Political Parties," *Journal of Democracy* 11:1, January 2000, p. 49.

41. On the crisis of parties and party systems in the Andes, see Mainwaring, Bejarano, and Pizarro, eds., *Crisis of Democratic Representation*, particularly chapter 1. On Chile see Alan Angell, "Party Change in Chile in Comparative Perspective," *Revista de Ciencia Política* 23:2, 2003, pp. 88–108, *Democracy after Pinochet: Politics, Parties and Elections in Chile* (London: Institute for the Study of the Americas, 2007), and J. Samuel Valenzuela, "Orígenes y transformaciones del sistema de partidos en Chile," *Estudios Públicos* 58, Autumn 1995.

42. See Eduardo Posada-Carbó, "La crisis política como crisis intelectual" in various authors, *¿Qué está pasando en Colombia? Anatomía de un país en crisis* (Bogotá: El Ancora Editores, 2000).

43. "Una charla con Eduardo Pizarro Leongómez," *Carta Financiera* 122, August 2002, pp. 71–72. Regarding the change in attitudes toward democracy among "leftist political actors throughout the region" see Ana María Bejarano and Eduardo Pizarro Leongómez, "From 'Restricted' to 'Besieged': The Changing Nature of the Limits to Democracy in Colombia," in Hagopian and Mainwaring, eds., *Third Wave of Democratization*, p. 243.

44. For Carlos Gaviria's views see "Uribe no es invencible," *El Espectador*, November 21, 2004, and "El candidato de la izquierda: ¿usted o Navarro?" *Semana*, June 12, 2005. For López Michelsen's comments see "El concepto de democracia" and "Una sociedad desgarrada," *El Tiempo*, April 17 and July 31, 2005.

45. See Andrés Hernández Quiñones, "Modelos de democracia liberal representativa: limitaciones y promesas incumplidas," *Co-Herencia* (Revista de Humanidades, Universidad EAFIT, Medellín) 4:3, January–June 2006, pp. 47, 59, 66, and 68; Oscar Mejía and Jacqueline Blanco, *Democracia y filosofía de la historia en América Latina* (Bogotá: Ediciones Jurídicas Gustavo Ibáñez, 2005), pp. 131–33.

46. For a brief outline of these measures in comparative perspective see Monica Barczak, "Representation by Consultation? The Rise of Direct Democracy in Latin America," *Latin American Politics and Society* 43:3, Fall 2001, pp. 51–52.

47. See, for example, Informe de la Comisión Ciudadana de Seguimiento, *Poder, Justicia e indignidad. El juicio al Presidente de la República Ernesto Samper Pizano* (Bogotá: Utópica Ediciones, 1996), and Mauricio Vargas, Jorge Lesmes, and Edgar Telléz, *El presidente que se iba a caer. Diario secreto de tres periodistas sobre el 8000* (Bogotá: Planeta, 1996). See also the account by former president Ernesto Samper, *Aquí estoy y aquí me quedo. Testimonio de un gobierno* (Bogotá: El Áncora, 2000). For the most comprehensive academic discussion on the subject of the financing of politics in Colombia see Fernando Cepeda Ulloa, *Financiación de campañas políticas* (Bogotá: Ariel, 1997) and his chapter in Malamud and Posada-Carbó, eds., *Financing of Politics*. See also Humberto de la Calle, "Financiación de partidos y campañas electorales" in *Revista de Derecho Público*, September 9, 1998, and his chapter in Del Castillo and Zovatto, eds., *La financiación de la política en Iberoamérica*.

48. Colombia, Ministerio del Interior, *Comisión para el estudio de la reforma de los partidos políticos: Memoria de Trabajo* (Bogotá: Ministerio del Interior, 1995). Also see Eduardo Pizarro Leongómez, "La Comisión para la reforma de los partidos," *Análisis Político*, September 1995.

49. Colombia, Ministerio del Interior, *Reforma política: Un propósito de nación. Memorias* (Bogotá: Ministerio del Interior, 1999). This project also included instruments to negotiate with the guerrillas in a newly established peace process.

50. "Reforma entró con pie izquierdo," *El Tiempo*, October 8, 1998. See the criticisms, along similar lines, by Noemí Sanín, a political leader in the opposition: "Acuerdo para una reforma integral," *El Tiempo*, October 2, 1998.

51. "Valencia, escudo del gobierno lo crítica," *El Tiempo*, December 2, 1998.

52. Colombia, Ministerio del Interior, "Exposición de motivos por la cual se convoca al pueblo soberano de Colombia a un referendo constitucional," unpublished photocopy, n.d. (probably 2000).

53. D'Artagnan, "Dejémonos de pomarricadas," *El Tiempo*, photocopy (2001).

54. Rudolf Hommes, "¿Pan o circo?" and Guillermo Perry, "Banana republic," *El Tiempo*, May 12 and July 9, 2000, respectively.

55. For the impact of these elections on the Colombian party system see Eduardo Posada-Carbó, "Colombia Hews to the Path of Change," *Journal of Democracy* 17:4, October 2006.

56. More than 120 such meetings took place between August 2002 and December 2005, when they were suspended as a result of the reelection campaign. See www.presidencia.gov.co.

57. See his speech at the third inter-American forum on political parties convened by the Organization of American States in Cartagena on November 23, 2003: www.upd.oas.org/lab/executive_coo/events/2003/cartagena_uribe_spa.htm. See also Cristina de la Torre, "Álvaro Uribe, neopopulista," *Revista Número* 44, 2006, in www.revistanumero.com/44/uribe.htm. For an argument rejecting Uribe's "neopopulism" see John C. Dugas, "The Emergence of Neopopulism in Colombia? The Case of Alvaro Uribe," *Third World Quarterly* 24:6, 2003. pp. 1117–36.

58. Former president and general secretary of the OAS César Gaviria has been a major figure behind the rallying cry to strengthen the parties. See his speech at the OAS 2003 forum at www.upd.oas.org. Gaviria is currently the leader of the Liberal party.

59. See Giovanni Sartori, "En defensa de la representación política," *Claves de Razón Práctica*, Madrid, 91, 1999, and Eduardo Posada-Carbó, *La nación soñada. Violencia, liberalismo y democracia en Colombia* (Bogotá: Editorial Norma/Vitral/Fundación Ideas para La Paz, 2006).

60. See "Ponencia para segundo debate en segunda vuelta al proyecto de acto legislativo," No. 06/00, April 27, 2001, unpublished document.

61. Bejarano and Pizarro Leongómez, "From 'Restricted' to 'Besieged,'" p. 247.

62. René Mayorga, "El financiamiento de los partidos políticos en Bolivia," in Del Castillo and Zovatto, eds., *La financiación de la política en Iberoamérica*, p. 33.

63. Zovatto, "Legal and Practical Characteristics," pp. 96, 98.

64. See Walter Little and Eduardo Posada-Carbó, "Introduction," in *Political Corruption in Europe and Latin America* (London and Basingstoke: Palgrave Macmillan, 1998).

65. Whether or not electoral costs have been steadily growing in the last decades is open to debate; see Zovatto, "Legal and Practical Characteristics," p. 97, and Casas Zamora, "State Funding and Campaign Finance Practices," p. 226.

66. For a detailed electoral agenda between the late 1970s and 1996 see Juan Rial and Daniel Zovatto, eds., *Urnas y desencanto político* (San José: IIDH/CAPEL, 1998), pp. 807–19.

67. Payne and Perusia, "Reforming the Rules of the Game," p. 77; and Josep M. Colomer, "Las elecciones primarias en América Latina," *Claves de Razón Práctica*, Madrid, 102, May 2000, pp. 14–21.

68. Maria D'Alva Kinzo, "Funding Parties and Elections in Brazil," in Peter Burnell and Alan Ware, eds., *Funding Democratization* (Manchester: Manchester University Press, 1998), p. 116, and *El Tiempo*, December 14, 2006. Brazilian elections have been described as "expensive across the board"; see David Samuels, "Informal Institutions When Formal Contracting Is Prohibited," in Gretchen Helmke and Steven Levitsky, eds., *Informal Institutions and*

Democracy: Lessons from Latin America (Baltimore: Johns Hopkins University Press, 2006), p. 95; and Samuels, "Money, Elections, and Democracy in Brazil."

69. This is a maximum estimated figure.

70. Poder Ciuadadano, "Cavallo, Duhalde y de la Rua informan sobre sus gastos electorales"; accessible at www.poderciudadano.org.ar.

71. Zovatto, "Legal and Practical Characteristics," p. 97, and Casas Zamora, "State Funding and Campaign Finance," p. 197.

72. Istoé Senhor, August 1, 1990, quoted in Mainwaring, Rethinking Party Systems in the Third Wave of Democratization, p. 151. Candidates for Congress "spent an average of about US$120,000 in 1994"; see David Samuels, "When Does Every Penny Count? Intraparty Competition and Campaign Finance in Brazil," Party Politics 7:1, 2011, p. 92.

73. On Venezuela see Carlos Subero, "La transparencia del financiamiento electoral y el papel de los medios de comunicación," in El financiamiento de las campañas electorales. Memorias, p. 138, and Diego Bautista Urbaneja and Angel Alvárez's "Financing Politics in Venezuela," in Malamud and Posada-Carbó, eds., Financing of Politics. On Chile see Manual Garretón's "Coping with Opacity: The Financing of Politics in Chile," in Malamud and Posada-Carbó, eds., Financing of Politics.

74. Ferreira Rubio, ed., Financiamiento de partidos políticos, p. 17; Mayne and Perusia, "Reforming the Rules of the Game," p. 78.

75. See Casas Zamora, Paying for Democracy, chapter 1. For Europe see Karl-Heinz Nassmacher, "Structure and Impact of Public Subsidies to Political Parties in Europe: The Examples of Austria, Italy, Sweden and West Germany," in Herbert Alexander, ed., Comparative Political Finance in the 1980s (Cambridge: Cambridge University Press, 1989), p. 238.

76. Nassmacher, "Structure and Impact of Public Subsidies to Political Parties in Europe," p. 238.

77. Michael Pinto-Duschinsky, "The Funding of Political Parties and Election Campaigns: The Experience from Western Europe," in Malamud and Posada-Carbó, eds., Financing of Politics.

78. See Michael Pinto-Duschinsky, "Notes on Political Financing in Britain," unpublished paper presented at the Seminario Internacional Financiación de Partidos Políticos y Campañas Electorales," Bogotá, April 14–17, 1999.

79. Pilar del Castillo, "Un encuentro necesario," El País, Madrid, January 6, 1994.

80. One significant exception is Great Britain; see "Blair eyeing state funding to put an end to donation row," Financial Times, April 7, 2002; and the report of the committee chaired by Lord Neill, Standards in Public Life: The Funding of Political Parties in the United Kingdom (London: Committee on Standards in Public Life 1998). On Britain see Justin Fisher's chapter in Malamud and Posada-Carbó, eds., Financing of Politics.

81. Daniel Zovatto, "La financiación política en Iberoamérica: una visión preliminar comparada," in Del Castillo and Zovatto, eds., La financiación de la política en Iberoamérica, p. xxix. The tendency seems to be to give prevalence to public over private funding; see Gabriel Murillo, "La reglamentación de la financiación de partidos políticos y de campañas electorales en la agenda de gobernabilidad democrática," in El financiamiento de las campañas electorales. Memoria, p. 100.

82. See Rosario Espinal and Jacqueline Jiménez Polanco, "El financiamiento de los partidos políticos en la República Dominicana," in Del Castillo and Zovatto, eds., La financiación de la política en Iberoamérica, pp. 515–44.

83. See Mainwaring, Rethinking Party Systems in the Third Wave of Democratization.

84. Ibid., quoted on p. 150. See also Samuels, "When Does Every Penny Count?" p. 95, and Kinzo, "Funding Parties and Elections in Brazil," pp. 117, 118, 122, 126. A similar situation is described for the Philippines by Joel Rocamora: "Every candidate must raise his own funds." See his paper "Campaign Finance and the Future of Philippine Political Parties,"

presented at the conference "Political Finance and Democracy in East Asia," Seoul, June 28–30, 2001.

85. Samuels, "Money, Elections, and Democracy," p. 42

86. Giovanni Sartori, *Comparative Constitutional Engineering: An Inquiry into Structures, Incentives, and Outcomes* (New York and London: New York University Press, 1994), pp. 143–47.

87. Margaret Weir, "Ideas and the Politics of Bounded Innovation," pp. 192 and 207.

88. Michael Pinto-Duschinsky, "Financing Politics: A Global View," *Journal of Democracy* 13:4, October 2002, p. 70.

89. On the general question of what drives electoral reforms see the collection of essays edited by Pippa Norris and her "Introduction: The Politics of Electoral Reform," in *International Political Science Review* 16:1, 1995. See also Fabrice Edouard Lehoucq, "Institutionalizing Democracy: Constraint and Ambition in the Politics of Electoral Reform," *Comparative Politics*, July 2000, pp. 459–77.

90. J. W. Jenks, "Money in Practical Politics," *Century Magazine*, New York, October 1892, p. 940.

***Eduardo Posada-Carbó** is a departmental lecturer in Latin American politics and a research associate at the Latin American Centre, Oxford University.

DISCUSSION QUESTIONS

1. Why might public financing of campaigns be more successful in Latin America than it has been elsewhere?

2. How do the rationales for campaign finance reform in Latin America differ from those in other countries?

3. What does the Colombian case say about the ability of Latin American governments to enact major reforms in the financing of elections?

Big Business and Political Finance in Australia: Ideological Bias and Profit-Seeking Pragmatism

by Iain McMenamin*

Like their counterparts in many other countries, Australian political parties are hugely dependent on business for their funding. This raises the obvious and important question of why businesses contribute to political parties. If business contributions are motivated by self-interest, what does the political system provide in return? This article aims to address this question by exploiting data generated by the disclosure regime operated by the Australian Electoral Commission between 1999 and 2005. Australia in this period is well suited to the study of business motivation of financing of parties because the level of disclosure was high and the system permitted large contributions without any important restrictions. By systematically studying the relationship between the flow of cash from business to parties and political conditions and business characteristics, it is possible to gain an important insight into how and why businesses contribute to political parties. The organization of this chapter is straightforward. I begin with some necessary context and an overview of Australia's political system and regulation of political finance, as well as the general financial situation of the parties. The chapter then proceeds to a brief theoretical discussion, before presenting the data set and analyzing it.

POLITICS IN AUSTRALIA

Australia's political system is both parliamentary and federal. It is parliamentary because governments and prime ministers are elected by and responsible to the legislature. It is federal because the constitution divides power between the Commonwealth of Australia and its six constituent states and two territories. The legislature of the commonwealth has two houses, as do all states except Queensland. All the upper houses are popularly elected and play an important role in politics but are clearly subordinate to lower houses. The commonwealth manages foreign and defense policy, as well as the macroeconomy. It uses its dominance of taxation to provide grants to the states, which are responsible for the vast majority of public services and welfare programs. With the exception of

Tasmania, elections to lower houses in Australia are by the "alternative vote," under which voters rank their preferences for candidates in a single-seat constituency. This system tends to reward major parties. The two major parties have been the Australian Labor Party (ALP) and the "semi-permanent coalition" of the Liberal and National parties (Sharman and Moon 2003, 241). These parties exhibit great strength in their near-monopoly control of both legislative and executive politics at federal and state levels. They can do so without large memberships because Australia's compulsory voting system removes the need for voter mobilization (McAllister 2002, 387).

The ALP has a socialist past and still maintains close links with labor unions. In the 1980s and '90s it was the Labor Party that deregulated and globalized the Australian economy (McEachern 1992a; McMullin 1991, 418–32, 442–43). Nonetheless, the party maintains a clear left-of-center stance on issues such as the environment and industrial relations. The Liberal Party tends to represent the center-right in Australian cities, while the National Party is important in many rural regions. The Liberals were traditionally, and sometimes almost literally, the party of business. In recent decades they have distanced themselves from firms and their interest organizations (McEachern 1992b). The relationship between the last commonwealth government (led by John Howard) and business has often been tense and tetchy. Business has been irritated by the government's regulatory instincts, while the Liberals have doubted the loyalty of the business community.

THE REGULATION OF AUSTRALIAN POLITICAL FINANCE

The contemporary era of the regulation of Australian political finance began with the advent of Bob Hawke's Labor government in 1983. The Political Broadcasts and Political Disclosures Act of 1991 brought all payments to parties within the disclosure regime (Chaples 1994, 31). The act also provided for a severe restriction on political advertising, banning it during campaigns and requiring broadcasters to provide free time instead. Use of this broadcasting time was confined to a figure talking to camera, without any dramatic effects (Chaples 1994, 34). Like Canada's attempted ban on third-party advertising, the broadcasting provisions of the act were struck down as unconstitutional (Orr, Mercurio, and Williams 2003, 384–85; O'Keefe 1992). Disclosure applies not only to parties but to "associated entities," defined, until 2006, as entities that are "either controlled by one or more political parties or operate wholly or to a significant extent for the benefit of one or more political parties" (Young and Tham 2006, 10). Income from associated entities has accounted for between

40 and 90 percent of the revenue of the major parties (Young and Tham 2006, 18). All payments, or in-kind contributions, must be reported and identified as either a "donation" or an "other payment." In law, donations are gifts, for which no, or inadequate, consideration has been received (Orr 2006, 107). This distinction does not separate political contributions from payments received in the course of running the party as a business. An employee of the Australian Electoral Commission explained, "So if you think you got $2,000 worth of networking opportunities as well as your meal and the glossy brochure, you don't have to declare it" as a donation (Sexton 2006). Moreover, the Australian Electoral Commission does not have the resources to contest the parties' classification of payments.

The $1,500 limit [all amounts in Australian dollars] for disclosure was introduced in 1984 and remained unchanged until 2006, when the limit was raised to $10,000, to be indexed annually (Coorey 2008). This meant that 1,000 fewer donations were reported than in the previous federal election year. Also, the percentage of receipts that had to be itemized dropped from 75 percent to 64 percent (Birnbauer 2007; Schubert and Rood 2008; Young and Tham 2006, 20). The drop in the percentage of revenue disclosed by associated entities was even greater (Grattan 2008). The limits are per donor, per jurisdiction. Therefore, a firm could have secretly but legally contributed almost $12,500 by splitting contributions of less than $1,500 among the nine jurisdictions. Since 2006, donations below $1,500 have been tax deductible.

Public funding has varied across the jurisdictions. In New South Wales, Queensland, and at the federal level, public subsidies for election campaigns were in place at the beginning of the period. Victoria introduced them in 2002. Western Australia brought in publicly funded elections in 2006, after the sample period. South Australia and Tasmania have not done so. In every case, the funds are limited by a threshold of 4 percent of the vote and distribute an amount of $1 to $2 per first-preference vote (Orr, Mercurio, and Williams 2003, 396; Young and Tham 2006, 39). Public funding provides about 20 percent of the income of the major parties (Young and Tham 2006, 13–14). New South Wales is the only jurisdiction to provide financial support for general party activities between elections (Young and Tham, 2006, 42), amounting to between 4 and 5 percent of the income of the major parties in 2004/2005. Australia does not have the large quasi-independent party foundations found in other countries. However, both Labor and the Liberal-National coalition have important organizations, which exist only to raise funds. The Greenfields Foundation collected contributions from businesses and passed them on to the Liberal Party, thereby avoiding the necessity to disclose the identity of the donors. Similarly, auctions or dinners organized outside the party could collect money without identifying the ultimate donors (Duffy 2000; Hannan and Carney 2005). A prominent example was the work of public relations company Markson Sparks on behalf of the ALP (Crabb and Rollins 2001). Both Labor and the Liberal-National coalition actively manage assets through companies, which their opponents suspect might also be conduits for undisclosed donations (*The Age* 2001; Gordon 2004).

The Finances of the Australian Parties

In common with many countries, the real cost of politics in Australia has risen steeply and consistently (McAllister 2002, 394). The main driver behind this rise has been the parties' increasing reliance on television and radio advertising. The most obvious reason advertising is important is that, in contrast to many other countries, it is allowed. However, the parties' small organizational bases and the epic scale of some constituencies restrict possibilities for public meetings and door-to-door canvassing. Especially in the last decade, both the ALP and the coalition have begun to cultivate their relations with business as part of the fundraising race. The relative dependence of the parties on corporate funding is quite similar. In 2001–2, 23 percent of the ALP's income came from itemized corporate receipts, with the Liberals and Nationals receiving 26 percent. Itemized trade union funding accounted for 9 percent of the ALP's income in that year (Young and Tham, 2006, 29).

Neither Labor nor the Liberal-National coalition was able to gain a substantial financial advantage over the other in the period 1999 to 2005. Even within jurisdictions, the two rivals do not usually exhibit markedly different financial situations. However, it can be noted that, at the federal level, the Liberal-National coalition managed two large surpluses, which the ALP did not, and in Victoria the ALP never ran a deficit, while the coalition twice endured substantial deficits.

More money is contributed to the parties in the states of Victoria and New South Wales than at the federal level. Victoria contains the traditional business capital of Melbourne. In recent decades, many firms have transferred their headquarters to Sydney in New South Wales. The small federal capital of Canberra is not a substantial center of private business and is dominated by government and universities. Perhaps more important, the states are responsible too for two highly politicized issues: property development and gambling (Horan 1997). Developers have been prominent political contributors in both Victoria and New South Wales (Clennell, Smith. and Robins 2008; Millar 2008a 2009; Skelton 2008; Smith 2008; Tham 2006; Dubeki and Baker 2004). One fundraiser said, "You get a lot of funding being in government at state level. If you're a property developer, what can the feds do for you? Getting development approvals or a planning policy change is not something the feds can do. Much of the relevant regulation is conducted at state level" (Elliott 2003). Sydney and New South Wales have become notorious for poker machines, on which clubs, pubs, and hotels often depend to survive (Verrender 2001; Skelsey 2003). This dependence has been reflected in political finance (Wainwright 2003).

THEORY

In this section, I briefly introduce the theoretical language with which I will analyze business financing of Australian parties. Business contributions to political parties are made as a result of two decisions. First, a business must decide to make a political contribution; second, it must decide how to distribute a certain amount of money. It can give all of its money to a political party; it can decide to split it equally between competing parties; or it can decide to bias its payments toward one party, without completely abandoning the competition. Most studies of political finance use one of these decisions as their dependent variable. In this article, I look first at the decision to contribute, and I then look at how biased that contribution is.

I take business to refer to a profit-seeking privately owned organization, including both companies and partnerships. Businesses, in this sense, form only a part of the overall business community, which is active in both politics generally and in the funding of political parties. Thus, I exclude state-owned firms, wealthy individuals, and business-interest organizations. While these other types of "business" actors are important, they are subject to quite different sets of incentives (McMenamin 2009, 212–14). The motivations of businesses contributing financially to political parties can be thought of broadly as either pragmatic or ideological (Clawson and Neustadtl 1989, 751). Ideological decisions do not survive a cost-benefit analysis and are instead motivated by a long-term commitment to a class interest or even the wider public good. Pragmatic contributions are business decisions motivated by the relatively short-term profit motive of a particular organization.

Political contributions in Australia, as in several other rich democracies, are widely acknowledged to be made with the intent of purchasing political access for businesses. Large contributors can demand one-to-one meetings with ministers at relatively short notice. Smaller contributions often grant business representatives the chance to mingle with politicians at dinners or receptions or attend a privileged advanced presentation of upcoming policy initiatives. Businesses and politicians deny that contributors receive decisions or influence in return for cash. Instead, they merely receive an opportunity to state their case or clarify some misunderstanding. The standard riposte is that

> if access is indeed the goal of . . . contributions, will [contributors] settle merely for the "opportunity to persuade"? Won't they expect success in a certain number of instances? Will they be satisfied with an invitation to the gaming table if they lose every spin of the wheel? (Souraf 2003, 409)

Some businesses go further and deny that they gain any benefit from the sale of access. Large companies are harassed by political parties and feel they must make some contribution to fundraising and send some representative to events, even if these activities make no difference to their ability to lobby successfully (Bachelard, Baker, and Millar 2007). While neither of these two "defenses" of the access system can be falsified by the pattern of contributions, both have an implication that should be observable in the Australian Electoral Commission data. If those who have purchased access have no greater policy success than those who have not, the partisan bias of contributions should not reflect changes in political competition. In other words, contributions should not follow political power because access does not grant influence over political power. Similarly, if contributions do not even buy access, they should not follow political power. Another implication might be that contributions are most likely to be made by the largest firms, which can afford to literally waste money on politicians.

I think of pragmatism as rooted in either the political system or the firm. Political pragmatism is a reaction to the supply of political benefits as reflected in the changing conditions of party competition. Economic pragmatism is a reaction to the demand for political benefits as reflected in the particular conditions of a firm's position in economic competition. The electoral commission data enable one to test the extent to which ideology, political pragmatism, and economic pragmatism can explain both the decision to make a political contribution and the decision regarding the distribution of that contribution among political parties.

If businesses react to political conditions, they essentially make calculations depending on which party is in power and which party they think will exercise power in the future. That is, they look at incumbency and at polls. These two variables interact with the electoral timetable. The farther away the next election, the more sense it makes to contribute to the governing party and not to the opposition. The closer an election, the more sense it makes to contribute to the party leading in the polls and not necessarily to the incumbent government.

The extensive American literature on political finance has tried to summarize the characteristics of individual firms using a wide variety of variables. Only three variables have consistently been found to be significant: size, regulation, and reliance on defense contracts (see, for example, Burris 2001, 371). Instead of trying to represent the diversity of the economy with one sector, in the following analysis I include dummy variables for the sector of the business. This variable enables me to state some clear general hypotheses for the effect of size on the dependent variables. The greater a firm's income, the proportionally smaller becomes the same cash contribution. The cost of political contributions may be so small relative to the income of the business that virtually any policy benefit would justify the expense. Therefore, large businesses are more likely to contribute to political parties. They are also more likely to distribute their contributions across the political spectrum: large firms may not have to choose between political actors because they have the resources to make substantial contributions to all relevant political players. In terms of the ideological logic, there seems to be no alternative to treating it as a residual category. I will infer ideological motivation from a political preference for the traditionally pro-business party that is not explained by measures of political and economic pragmatism.

DATA

The sample consists of 450 businesses, all of which were among the 1,000 largest enterprises in Australia in both 1998–99 and 2004–5.[1] The economic variables are income and indicators for 29 sectors. The political variables are an interaction of incumbency and the electoral timetable and an interaction of opinion polls and the electoral timetable. The incumbency variable ranges from 1 for a coalition government with four years to a mandatory election to 8 for a Labor government with four years to a mandatory election.[2] The poll variable is the difference between the Labor and coalition votes multiplied by a range beginning at 1 for an election year and 4 for four years until the next election.[3]

The Australian Electoral Commission reports disclosures of donations and "other payments" to both political parties and entities associated with those parties. Donations are defined narrowly as payments for which nothing was received in return. All analyses in this article are conducted twice, first for donations and second for all payments, which includes both donations and other payments. The basic measure of distribution is called bias, calculated as the Labor proportion of a given business's payments to Labor and to the coalition in a given year. Between 1998 and 2005, there were approximately 25,000 payments

Table 1: Decision to Contribute

	Federal Donations	Federal All Payments	State Donations	State All Payments
Electoral Timetable	-.348906 (.091085)**	-.198998 (.070773)**	-.27787 (.038373)**	-.133874 (.024941)**
Income	.1017 (.0159)**	.1955 (.0245)**	.07 (.000006)**	.1074 (.000006)**
Advices for Finance, Investment, Insurance	.186316 (.5909)	.445081 (.560821)	.52823 (.325294)	.639176 (.25991)*
Agriculture, Forestry and Fishing	-3.08837 (1.13643)**	-2.4713 (.846569)**	-3.07571 (1.0343)**	-2.61479 (.617027)**
Building Materials	-1.16392 (.546154)*	-1.24683 (.491006)*	-.65055 (.328904)*	-.586723 (.25402)*
Communication Services	-4.1528 (1.12365)**	-2.68731 (.641647)**	-2.67603 (.65059)**	-1.32488 (.288367)**
Construction	-1.6405 (.517865)**	-1.65425 (.467171)**	-.24329 (.28694)	-.262402 (.227196)
Cultural, Recreational Services	-2.1357 (.585397)**	-1.35715 (.496815)**	-.933282 (.312057)**	-.852473 (.252251)**
Electricity, Gas, Water	-3.7648 (.737462)**	-2.23557 (.489709)**	-2.1665 (.375122)**	-1.17759 (.242171)**
Finance, Investment	-2.04098 (.510323)**	-1.58653 (.439437)**	-.759382 (.28418)**	-.353752 (.21969)
Food, Beverages, Tobacco	-1.4681 (.491569)**	-1.35635 (.441111)**	-.78187 (.285238)**	-.915328 (.226458)**
Health, Community Services	-1.46674 (.60617)*	-1.08457 (.52131)*	-1.5623 (.464236)**	-1.03462 (.303174)**
Insurance	-2.42807 (.566272)**	-2.30904 (.502213)**	-1.58455 (.337726)**	-1.15089 (.243632)**
Machinery, Equipment	-3.70067 (.643411)**	-2.33009 (.470124)**	-1.7735 (.31278)**	-1.15676 (.22903)**
Metal Products	-1.63018 (.590241)**	-1.53631 (.529358)**	-1.47641 (.413283)**	-1.72772 (.332505)**
Mining	-3.6771 (.789797)**	-2.42107 (.591277)**	-2.20707 (.390842)**	-1.45126 (.260381)**
Other Manufacturing	Dropped	Dropped	-1.67418 (.761434)*	-1.6097 (.55311)**

Table 1: Decision to Contribute (continued)

	Federal Donations	Federal All Payments	State Donations	State All Payments
Personal, Other Services	Dropped	Dropped	.275222 (.515983)	.7246 (.384962)
Petroleum, Chemicals, Associated Products	-3.01864 (.566409)**	-2.0368 (.466956)**	-1.75578 (.318257)**	-1.5648 (.24088)**
Printing, Publishing	-3.53953 (1.10237)**	-1.7587 (.59411)**	-2.10535 (.567571)**	-1.03725 (.307177)**
Property, Business Services	-2.5396 (.512138)**	-2.02123 (.440171)**	-.660544 (.275179)*	-.256697 (.214796)
Retail, Food	-2.39046 (.658281)**	-2.5007 (.764184)**	-.553583 (.30289)	-1.11558 (.26305)**
Retail, Motor Vehicle Services	Dropped	Dropped	-3.63536 (.754231)**	-2.47457 (.353608)**
Retail, Personal, Household Goods	-3.92341 (.843821)**	-3.62647 (.713982)**	-2.27005 (.410647)**	-2.38122 (.320644)**
Services to Finance, Investment, Insurance	-1.22525 (.718522)	-.58748 (.628527)	-.29521 (.405188)	.280568 (.293921)
Textiles, Clothing	-.43777 (.649894)	-.54509 (.625858)	-1.35605 (.568474)*	-1.57643 (.466928)**
Transport, Storage	-1.84109 (.552503)**	-1.76881 (.493813)**	-1.69879 (.382062)**	-1.45262 (.273785)**
Wholesale, Basic Materials	-2.50101 (.560257)**	-2.70245 (.513236)**	-2.37723 (.399749)**	-2.17453 (.284148)**
Wholesale, Machinery, Motor Vehicles	-4.44877 (.739524)**	-4.28124 (.651659)**	-3.0168 (.389454)**	-2.30806 (.255424)**
Wholesale, Personal, Household Goods	-4.74532 (1.10084)**	-4.17645 (.822083)**	-3.31013 (.56495)**	-2.28706 (.30279)**
Constant	.35253 (.486865)	.16756 (.433338)	-1.43453 (.274926)**	-1.12466 (.216926)**
Chi2	227.40**	247.38**	602.52**	1169.41**
Observations	3031	3031	18900	18900

Notes: Coefficients from pooled logit with Newey-West standard errors in parentheses. *Significant at the 0.05 level. **Coefficient significant at the 0.01 level. No firms in Other Manufacturing; Personal, Other Services; and Retail, Motor Vehicle Services made payments at the commonwealth level. The dummies for these sectors have been dropped, along with 119 observations.

to Australian political parties, about 17,000 of which were from around 5,400 businesses. A mere 5 percent of firms in my sample made a donation every year, while 15 percent made a payment, whether donation or other payment, every year. Sixty-one percent did not make any donations in the relevant period, while 47 percent did not make any type of payment during the whole period.

These are significant limitations on the validity of the current analysis. However, it is important not to overemphasize them. While it is impossible to estimate the extent to which businesses channel money to parties outside the statutory framework, the sheer volume of payments disclosed and, in many instances, their size and potential for controversy convinces me that the official data provides a roughly accurate picture of overall business funding of parties. Crucially, even if a very large proportion of actual political contributions manage to evade or deceive the disclosure regime, the issue is whether these contributions are systematically different from the disclosed payments in terms of the models being tested in this article. There are no obvious ways in which this might be the case.

CONTRIBUTIONS

To investigate the decision to contribute, I employ a logit model. It is appropriate for a binary dependent variable like the decision to contribute to a political party. It calculates the logged odds of contribution as opposed to non-contribution. The Newey-West standard errors compensate for heteroskedasticity and also for autocorrelation, which are two serious statistical problems in data sets with data that track observations over time. I estimate four equations: federal donations, all payments at the federal level, state donations, and all payments at the state level. Three sector dummies and a number of observations have been dropped from the federal equations because of a lack of variation in the dependent variable.

If the coefficients in the table are positive, that means an increase in the value of the variable increases the probability of contribution. Negative values indicate that an increase in the value of the variable reduces the probability of contribution. Starred standard errors have reached the 0.05 or 0.01 levels of statistical significance. This means that had the samples of firms been repeatedly drawn, we would expect to reject the hypothesis of no relationship between the variable in question and the dependent variable 95 or 99 percent of the time. The four models suggest that business firm behavior is quite similar whether the federal or the state level is considered and whether contributions are defined by donations or all payments (see Table 1). For all four models, contributions are more likely to be made as elections approach; larger firms are more likely to contribute, and 22 to 23 of the 28 sectors are significantly different from the reference category of Wood and Paper, which is therefore not included in the tables. The probabilities of contribution for the different sectors are highly correlated across the four models. The different powers of the federal and state governments do not substantially change the frequency with which firms in different sectors contribute to political parties. This is reassuring, given the research design's assumption that the logic of political finance is essentially the same at different constitutional levels.

Holding income at the mean and the electoral timetable at an election year, it is difficult to confidently state which sectors are most likely to contribute to parties. The sectors that have a probability of making a contribution of half a standard deviation or more over the mean in each of the four models are Advices for Finance, Investment, Insurance; Services to Finance, Investment, Insurance; Wood and Paper. In addition, Textiles, Clothing has a high probability of making federal donations and all payments, while Construction, and Personal, Other Services, have a high probability of making state donations and all payments. These sectors tend to represent small numbers of firms, and their coefficients do not reach statistical significance. The sectors that have a probability of making a contribution half a standard deviation or more under the mean in each of the four models are Agriculture, Forestry, and Fishing; and Wholesale, Personal, and Household Goods. Both are statistically significant in every model. In addition, the following sectors had a low probability of contribution in three of the four models: Electricity, Gas, Water; Mining; Petroleum, Chemicals, Associated Products; and Retail, Personal, Household Goods. Again, all were statistically significant. These results suggest that political behavior varies across different sectors of the economy, but it is difficult to draw any firm theoretical conclusions from these figures.

Bias

The sample values indicate that, in the period under examination, Australian businesses have split their contributions between the two principal competitors but have tended to be biased toward the Liberal-National coalition. Labor received on average 43 percent of a given business's donation in a given year in a given jurisdiction, while it got 48 percent of all payments. It would be a mistake to interpret these values as indicating a lack of ideological preference among Australian businesses without controlling for the economic characteristics

Table 2: Distribution of Contribution

	Federal Donations	Federal All Payments	State Donations	State All Payments
Incumbency	.018529 (.014477)	.022344 (.009571)*	.028574 (.009554)**	.019151 (.006122)**
Poll	.000522 (.001015)	.003374 (.000702)**	.00013 (.000612)	.002639 (.00042)**
Income	.0075 (.0205)	-.00972 (.00973)	.0104 (.00708)	.0159 (.00547)**
Income2	-.000001 (.000001)	.000000 (.000000)	-.000000 (.000000)	-.000001 (.000000)**
Advices for Finance, Investment, Insurance	.238617 (.242445)	.076535 (.212573)	.074495 (.124184)	-.005616 (.09437)
Agriculture, Forestry and Fishing	Dropped	Dropped	-.08942 (.177811)	.009569 (.179046)
Building Materials	.083897 (.127889)	.028743 (.109194)	.107769 (.13412)	-.029556 (.107408)
Communication Services	Dropped	Dropped	.335666 (.241973)	-.027837 (.116722)
Construction	.037522 (.15239)	.176822 (.118464)	.081023 (.109565)	.069078 (.088281)
Cultural, Recreational Services	.197926 (.221772)	.269811 (.18248)	.102149 (.115133)	.032927 (.090913)
Electricity, Gas, Water	.050122 (.15019)	.17094 (.113318)	.348513 (.2005)	-.005679 (.136721)
Finance, Investment	.028757 (.13012)	.098274 (.104768)	.024145 (.11454)	-.101334 (.089766)
Food, Beverages, Tobacco	-.085301 (.140739)	-.02853 (.119727)	.008705 (.106912)	-.102891 (.08775)
Health, Community Services	Dropped	Dropped	-.052296 (.148467)	-.202955 (.11012)
Insurance	.173269 (.13311)	.080246 (.1119)	-.27978 (.16974)	-.215369 (.110592)
Machinery, Equipment	-.178 (.180172)	-.03806 (.1369)	-.006914 (.125533)	-.007953 (.098092)
Metal Products	Dropped	Dropped	.030429 (.14729)	-.058286 (.127304)
Mining	Dropped	-.154822 (.277072)	.1083 (.14239)	-.086378 (.099784)

Table 2: Distribution of Contribution (continued)

	Federal Donations	Federal All Payments	State Donations	State All Payments
Other Manufacturing	Dropped	Dropped	.588793 (.101739)**	.174404 (.169308)
Personal, Other Services	Dropped	Dropped	.192558 (.205487)	.115095 (.132284)
Petroleum, Chemicals, Associated Products	-.041443 (.189497)	-.023987 (.142054)	-.026181 (.13)	-.079169 (.099819)
Printing, Publishing	.232944 (.32047)	.415369 (.158195)**	-.435036 (.100011)**	.048314 (.117572)
Property, Business Services	-.028611 (.15605)	.009277 (.12105)	.007116 (.105584)	.01778 (.08456)
Retail, Food	Dropped	Dropped	.02668 (.133374)	.008676 (.105585)
Retail, Motor Vehicle Services	Dropped	.307388 (.149027)*	.100446 (.367271)	.071067 (.22376)
Retail, Personal, Household Goods	.035903 (.280859)	.100157 (.24353)	-.215535 (.172864)	-.102248 (.144154)
Services to Finance, Investment, Insurance	-.135193 (.171569)	.00449 (.135163)	Dropped	Dropped
Textiles, Clothing	Dropped	Dropped	-.14771 (.136345)	-.122507 (.143553)
Transport, Storage	Dropped	Dropped	.272016 (.134445)*	.043869 (.104678)
Wholesale, Basic Materials	Dropped	.547804 (.112078)**	-.02932 (.124154)	-.068665 (.108875)
Wholesale, Machinery, Motor Vehicles	-.296084 (.169903)	-.164448 (.137119)	-.084698 (.23381)	.078354 (.123675)
Wholesale, Personal, Household Goods	-.431077 (.141001)**	-.397318 (.126838)**	-.059123 (.27778)	-.050389 (.140797)
Constant	.316553 (.16253)	.208511 (.119571)	.23113 (.109417)*	.296642 (.089078)**
F	8.47**	50.33**	78.22**	3.88**
Observations	273	580	721	1582

Notes: Coefficients from pooled OLS with Newey-West standard errors in parentheses. *Significant at the 0.05 level. **Coefficient significant at the 0.01 level.

of firms and the political circumstances under which they have contributed to the parties.

Again, I present four models (see Table 2). This time they are estimated by ordinary least squares with Newey-West standard errors. Ordinary least squares is suitable for the continuous dependent variable of bias, which is a figure between 1 and zero. Its output is more straightforward than that of a logit model. The coefficients are the expected effect on the dependent variable of an increase of one unit in the independent variable. Income is expected to be associated with splitting between the two parties. Testing this hypothesis requires a quadratic specification. Hence the first income variable should have a positive sign, while the second (squared) income variable should have a negative sign. The incumbency and poll variables should have positive signs, as they are expected to increase the share of contributions going to Labor. While we expect the 29 sectors to be associated with differently biased contributions, there are no clear hypotheses in one direction or the other.

There are more differences in the four models of bias than there were in the models of contribution.[4] The economic logic is unable to provide an explanation for partisanship. The income variables are only significant in the model for all payments at the state level. Across the four models, between zero and four sectors are significantly different from the reference category. Only two sectors (Printing, Publishing; and Wholesale, Personal, Household Goods) are statistically significant in two of the models.

In contrast, the political variables perform better. Incumbency is significant in all equations except federal donations, which is, after all, suffering from a lack of observations. Take, for example, the model for State All Payments. It predicts a 0.019 percent increase in the share of a firm's political contributions going to Labor for every 1-point increase in the incumbency index. Using the full range of the index shows how big the effect can be. A shift from a coalition government with a full four-year term to run to an ALP government with a full term ahead of it produces a shift of over 15 percentage points to the ALP. Poll is significant in two equations, the exceptions being the two donations equations. Again looking at State All Payments, an increase of 1 percentage point in the ALP's opinion poll lead over the coalition is predicted to increase the ALP's share of a given firm's contribution by 0.0026 percent. If the ALP were to increase its opinion poll performance by 30 percent relative to the coalition, a given firm should shift toward the ALP by almost 8 percentage points. Therefore, I conclude that businesses react to political conditions. They concentrate their contributions on the party in government, reducing the bias as an election approaches. They also direct more money to the party that is ahead in the polls, increasing the bias as an election approaches.

In order to clarify the implications of these findings, I present graphs of predicted bias under a number of simulated political conditions (see Figure 1). This allows me to uncover the potentially ideological distribution of business contributions that underlies shifts from one party to another in reaction to political circumstances. First, I look at incumbency, contrasting positions of maximum advantage to the two major blocs in Australian politics. Under a Labor government, with four years to the next election, the model predicts that businesses will overwhelmingly opt to split their contributions, albeit with a minor overall bias toward Labor. Under a Liberal-National coalition government, with four years to an election, the majority of businesses will clearly bias their contributions toward the coalition. I undertook a similar procedure to uncover the effects of shifts in opinion poll popularity. In an election year, if there is no difference between the parties in the polls, over half of businesses will bias contributions toward the coalition. Heading into an election with a 10-point lead, the ALP can only expect to share business contributions equally. However, with the same 10-point lead in an election year, the coalition can expect that over 90 percent of businesses will bias their contributions toward the Liberals and the Nationals.

Essentially, political competition and ideological predilection interact as follows: If Labor has the political advantage, the dominant strategy of businesses will be to split their contributions between the ALP and the Liberal-National coalition. If the coalition has the political advantage, the dominant strategy will be to clearly bias payments toward the coalition. Australian business combines a pragmatic reaction to changing political circumstances with a massive ideological bias toward the more conservative parties. Without controlling for political competition, it is not possible to come up with a reasonable estimate of the importance of the ideological factor. The sample values indicate a relatively even split between the two adversaries (with a minor preference for the coalition). However, this is on the basis of a period where the coalition has had a mean poll advantage in only 1 out of 49 jurisdiction years (Victoria 1999) and has been in government for only 11 out of 49 jurisdiction years (7 years in the commonwealth, 3 in Victoria, and 1 in South Australia). The apparent "even-handedness" of Australian business has been a reaction to the political dominance of Labor.

Interestingly, newspaper reports on fundraising in anticipation of the last commonwealth election suggest that business behavior conforms very closely to my model. According to the model, a clear ALP advantage in the polls in

Figure 1: Simulated Partisanship of Business Contributions

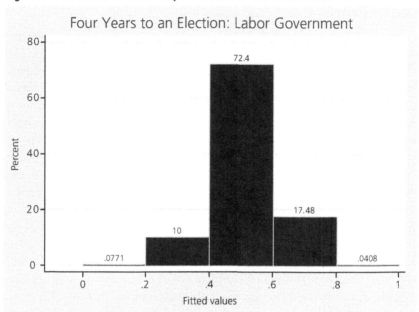

Four Years to an Election: Labor Government

Note: Fitted values from model for all payments at state level in Table 1 Incumbency = 8 for all observations.

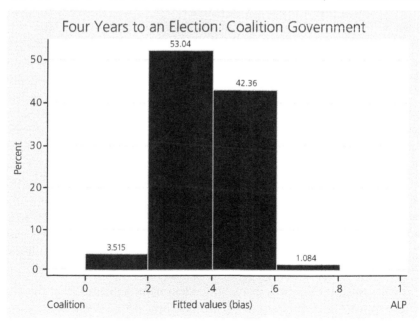

Four Years to an Election: Coalition Government

Note: Fitted values from model for all payments at state level in Table 1 Incumbency = 1 for all observations.

Figure 1: Simulated Partisanship of Business Contributions (continued)

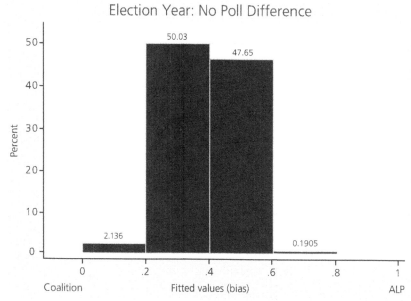

Note: Fitted values from model for all payments at state level in Table 1 Poll = 0 for all observations.

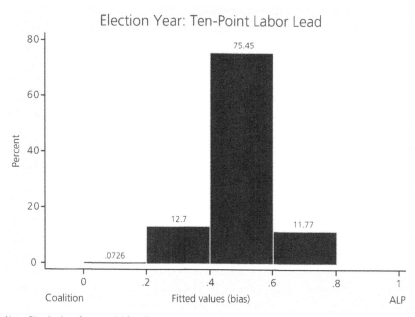

Note: Fitted values from model for all payments at state level in Table 1 Poll = 40 for all observations.

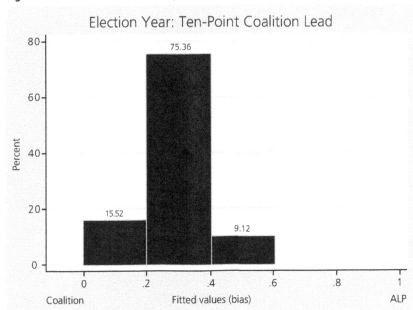

Note: Fitted values from model for all payments at state level in Table 1. Poll =-40 for all observations.

an election year should motivate business to split its contributions relatively equally between the government and the opposition. *The Australian* reports that "Conservative fundraiser . . . Brisbane-based Everald Compton said that donors who traditionally funded only the Coalition parties were now taking 'an each-way punt'" (Franklin and Karvelas 2007). Similarly, the *Canberra Times* reports that Liberal Party honorary secretary Mark Bethwaite said, "The even-handedness of some businesses in supporting both the Liberal Party and the ALP is not something that I applaud" (AAP 2007). It would be wrong to reify these comments and interpret them as a consistent business strategy. Instead, as I have shown, these comments probably represent a reaction to a particular ephemeral political situation.

CONCLUSIONS

The regulatory environment and democratic implications of Australian business funding of parties have been discussed here. However, this is the first systematic attempt to understand the calculations Australian businesses make when considering financial contributions to political parties. Contributions are made according to economic, political, and ideological logics. Businesses are more likely to contribute as an election approaches. The economic logic is important in explaining which businesses contribute. The larger the business, the more likely it is to contribute. The probability of contribution also varies from sector to sector. In contrast, the economic logic does little to explain the partisan distribution of contributions. This is best explained by an interaction of political and ideological logics. Australian business has a strong underlying ideological predilection toward the conservative coalition of the Liberals and Nationals. Nonetheless, businesses react strongly to changing political conditions. If the ALP has the political advantage, in terms of either control of government or a lead in the polls, business tends to be even-handed. By contrast, if the coalition has the political advantage, businesses target the vast majority of their money on the coalition.

ENDNOTES

1. Size is measured by income in billions of Australian dollars as reported in the *Business Review Weekly*. The sample excludes state-owned, nonprofit, New Zealand and Papua New Guinean enterprises. Partnerships have been included.

2. The range is narrower for Queensland and the commonwealth, both of which have three-year parliamentary terms.

3. For the commonwealth and five of the six states, which use the alternative vote, I use the two-party preferred voting intentions. Tasmanian elections are held under the "single transferable vote" (Farrell and McAllister 2006), so I used the first-preference voting intention. The source is the Roy Morgan Poll. In a study of the 2004 federal election, Jackman (2005) finds this to be one of the less accurate polls. The reason for using it is its greater coverage of all states, especially Tasmania. I would like to emphasize that the poll variable aims not to directly predict election results, but to measure attempts by business to predict which parties will control government.

4. These differences may reflect the effects of different numbers of observations as much as they reflect different behavior by businesses making financial contributions to political parties. The two models of bias at the federal level suffer from serious colinearity problems among the sector dummies. For this reason, 12 variables have been dropped from the donations equation and 9 from the equation for all payments. At the state level, one sector has been dropped from both equations for the same reason.

BIBLIOGRAPHY

Australian Associated Press 2007. "Top Lib slates businesses for equal party donations." *Canberra Times*, p. 7.

The Age. 2001. "A guide to the subtle art of giving but not revealing." Late edition, February 14, p. 13.

Bachelard, M., R. Baker, and R. Millar. 2007. "Taking their toll." *The Age*, Melbourne, 14 May.

Birnbauer, William. 2007. "How business muscles in on parties; Political Donations—Democracy at Work." *Sunday Age*, first edition, News, February 11, p. 5.

Burris, V. 2001. "The two faces of capital: Corporations and individual capitalists as political actors." *American Sociological Review* 66(3): 361–81.

Chaples, Ernest A. 1994. "Developments in Australian Political Finance." In *Comparative Political Finance among the Democracies*, ed. Herbert Alexander and Rei Shiratori, 29–40. Oxford: Westview.

Clawson, D., and A. Neustadtl. 1989. "Interlocks, PACs, and Corporate Conservatism." *American Journal of Sociology* 94: 749–73.

Clawson, D., A. Neustadtl, and M. Weller. 1998. *Dollars and Votes*. Philadelphia: Temple University Press.

Clennell, Andrew, Alexandra Smith, and Brian Robins. 2008. "MP took year to declare $65,000." *Sydney Morning Herald*, first edition, March 5, p. 2.

Coorey, Philip. 2008. "Disclosure level to be slashed; Party Donations—ALP in crisis." *Sydney Morning Herald*, first edition, February 26, p. 5.

Crabb, Annabel, and Adrian Rollins. 2001. "Party donation revelations spark claims of shady deals." *The Age*, February 2, p. 2.

Dubeki, Larissa, and Richard Baker. 2004. "Gaming, tobacco, developers fill party coffers; political donations." *The Age*, late edition, News, February 3, p. 2.

Duffy, Michael. 2000. "Arrogance struts the corridors of power." *Daily Telegraph*, November 11, p. 27.

Elliott, Geoff. 2003. "Coming to the party." *The Australian*, all-round country edition, Features, February 12, p. 11.

Farrell, D., and I. McAllister. 2006. *The Australian Electoral System: Origins, Variations and Consequences*. Sydney: University of New South Wales Press, p. 16.

Franklin, M., and P. Karvelas. 2007. "Corporations put money behind Labor." *The Australian*, Sydney.

Gordon, Josh. 2004. "Political party donors move to mask their identities." *The Age*, second edition, News, February 2, p. 3.

Grattan, Michelle. 2008. "We're going to find out more about who gives what to whom." *The Age*, first edition, p. 15.

Hannan, Ewin, and Shaun Carney. 2005. "Pressure on ALP for inquiry into fundraiser." *The Age*, first edition, p. 3.

Heinz, J., E. Laumann, R. Nelson, and R. Salisbury. 1993. *The Hollow Core: Private Interests in National Policy Making*. Cambridge, MA: Harvard University Press.

Horan, M. 1997. "Libs hypocrites on gifts from gaming, says ALP." *Courier Mail*, March 25.

Jackman, S. 2005. "Pooling the Polls over an Election Campaign." *Australian Journal of Political Science* 40: 499–517.

Kadushin, C. 1995. "Friendship among the French Financial Elite." *American Sociological Review* 60(2): 202–21.

McAllister, I. 2002. "Political Parties in Australia: Party Stability in a Utilitarian Culture." In *Political Parties in Advanced Industrial Democracies*, ed. P. Webb, D. Farrell, and I. Holliday. Oxford: Oxford University Press.

McEachern, D. 1992a. "Business Responses to Labor Governments." In *Business-Government Relations in Australia*, ed. S. Bell and J. Wanna, 92–100. Sydney: Harcourt Brace Jovanovich.

———. 1992b. "Political Parties of Business: Liberal and National." In *Business-Government Relations in Australia*, ed. S. Bell and J. Wanna, 80–91. Sydney: Harcourt Brace Jovanovich.

McMenamin, I. 2004. "Parties, promiscuity and politicisation: Business-political networks in Poland." *European Journal of Political Research* 43(4): 657–76.

———. 2009. "The Four Logics of Business, Money and Political Parties." In *Interest Groups and Lobbying in the United States and Comparative Perspectives*, ed. Conor McGrath, 207–24. Lampeter, NSW: Edwin Mellen Press.

McMullin, Ross. 1991. *The Light on the Hill: The Australian Labor Party, 1891–1991*. Melbourne: Oxford University Press.

Millar, Royce. 2008, "With strings attached? Politics." *The Age*, first edition, News, July 7, p. 11.

———. 2009. "Big property developers help line the pockets of ALP." *The Age*, first edition, February 3, p. 6.

O'Keefe, N. 1992. "When 'free speech' is costly." *Herald Sun*, September 7.

Orr, Graeme. 2006. "Political Finance Law in Australia." In *Party Funding and Campaign Financing in International Perspective*, ed. Kenneth D. Ewing and Samuel Issacharoff, 99–122. Oxford: Hart.

———. 2007. "Electoral Law in Australia: Lackadaisical Law." *Election Law Journal* 6: 72–88.

Orr, Graeme, Bryan Mercurio, and George Williams. 2003. "Australian Electoral Law: A Stocktake." *Election Law Journal* 2(3): 383–402.

Ramsay, I., G. Stapledon, and J. Vernon. 2002. "Political Donations by Australian Companies." *Federal Law Review* 29: 179–218.

Schubert, Misha, and David Rood. 2008. "MP bought seat for $280,000; Lib; Political parties set record for donations as Labor pledges to tighten disclosure rules." *The Age*, first edition, February 2, p. 12.

Sexton, Elisabeth. 2006. "Greasing the wheels." *Sydney Morning Herald*, first edition, News Review, p. 32.

Sharman, C., and J. Moon. 2003. "One System or Nine?" In *Australian Politics and Government*, ed. C. Sharman and J. Moon, 239–62. Cambridge: Cambridge University Press.

Skelton, Russell. 2008. "Power and dirty, sexy money; Political donations." *The Age*, first edition, Insight, March 22, p. 21.

Skelsey, Mark. 2003. "Pubs' late shout for ALP election battle." *Daily Telegraph*, Local, August 1, p. 3.

Smith, Alexandra. 2008. "Iemma injects a little honesty into donations; Labor in disarray." *Sydney Morning Herald*, third edition, February 29, p. 4.

Souraf, F. J. 2003. "Inside Campaign Finance: Myths and Realities." In *The Democracy Sourcebook*, ed. R. A. Dahl, I. Shapiro, and J. A. Cheibub, 408–18. Cambridge, MA: MIT Press.

Tham, Joo-Cheong. 2003. "Campaign Finance Reform in Australia: Some Reasons for Reform." In *Realising Democracy: Electoral Law in Australia*, ed. G. Orr, B. Mercurio, and G. Williams, 114–29. Annandale, NSW: Federation Press.

———. 2005. "Donor threshold over the top." *Sydney Morning Herald*, first edition, News and Features, May 30, p. 21.

———. 2006, "Party funds threaten democracy", *The Age*, May 26, News, p. 15.

Useem, M. 1984. *The Inner Circle: Large Corporations and the Rise of Business Political Actors*. New York: Oxford University Press.

Verrender, Ian. 2001. "The tide of pokie money that threatens to engulf Joe Tripodi; Power of the Pokies: A Herald Investigation." *Sydney Morning Herald*, late edition, News and Features, April 11, p. 1.

Wainwright, Robert. 2003. "Labor leads with a $10m party punch; Decision '03: Where the money is coming from." *Sydney Morning Herald*, late edition, Supplement, March 1, p. 26.

Young, S., and J.-C. Tham, 2006. "Political finance in Australia: A skewed and secret system." *Democratic Audit of Australia*. Canberra: Australian National University.

*Iain McMenamin is a senior lecturer in politics at the School of Law and Government and a member of the Centre for International Studies, Dublin City University, Ireland.

DISCUSSION QUESTIONS

1. Do the differences between business sectors described by the author correspond to differences one might observe among corporations in other countries?

2. Does the lack of restrictions on corporate contributions appear to have effects on the relationship between Australian businesses and political parties?

3. Does the transparency of the Australian system support the contention of some campaign finance scholars that transparency is more important than restricting contributions?